INDUSTRIAL DESIGN
LAW

AUSTRALIA
The Law Book Company
Brisbane ● Sydney ● Melbourne ● Perth

CANADA
Carswell
Ottawa ● Toronto ● Calgary ● Montreal ● Vancouver

AGENTS
Steimatzky's Agency Ltd., Tel Aviv;
N.M. Tripathi (Private) Ltd., Bombay;
Eastern Law House (Private) Ltd., Calcutta;
M.P.P. House, Bangalore;
Universal Book Traders, Delhi;
Aditya Books, Delhi;
MacMillan Shuppan KK, Tokyo;
Pakistan Law House, Karachi, Lahore

INDUSTRIAL DESIGN LAW

By

CHRISTINE FELLNER

LONDON • SWEET & MAXWELL • 1995

Published in 1995 by
Sweet & Maxwell Limited
of South Quay Plaza
183 Marsh Wall, London E14 9FT
Typeset by Mendip Communications Ltd.,
Frome, Somerset
Printed and bound in Great Britain
by Hartnolls Ltd., Bodmin

No natural forests were destroyed
to make this product only farmed
timber was used and re-planted.

A CIP catalogue record for this book
is available from The British Library

ISBN 0 421 451904

Preface

The U.K. Experiment in Industrial Design Protection

Although this book has taken an unconscionably long time to write, it is not put forward as the authoritative text on all aspects of U.K. industrial designs law but as a commentary on the radical reforms embodied in the 1988 Copyright, Designs and Patents Act six years after they were brought into effect. I was invited to speculate on the meaning of the Act's complex threefold scheme of protection, and have had little difficulty in doing so, since decided cases have been slow to accumulate. As is only to be expected in an imperfect world, since the manuscript was handed in several more have been reported, and comment has had to be incorporated during the proof stages.

It is hoped the book wil be of some value to industry as well as to lawyers, and to overseas observers as well as to those in the U.K. who have to operate the system. Many developing countries which are signatories to the GATT Uruguay Round with its attendant TRIPS Agreement are having to face the problems of industrial design protection for the first time, and they are difficult ones. Unlike most areas of intellectual property, there is little consensus even about *what* should be protected, let alone how. U.K. legislators and industry may groan at the characterisation of the reforms delivered in 1989, after 15 years' travail, as only an "experiment"; but that is what they are, and others may learn from them accordingly.

For the same reason, a short commentary on the proposed European Union Community Design has been included.

Statutory and other materials have been deliberately omitted to keep both size and price within reasonable bounds, and because they are readily available elsewhere, but there is liberal reference to the text to the Parliamentary debates. I can heartily recommend these as holiday literature, having first read them by hurricane lamp in a tent in France.

I should like to thank the various staff of the Patent Office in London and Newport who have helped me with background information, Professor W. R. Cornish of Magdalene College, Cambridge who read some of the early drafts, and my colleagues in chambers, particularly Michael Hicks who discussed a variety of difficult points with his customary philosophical cheerfulness. Also my clerk Barbara Harris and my publishers, who by a judicious combination of forbearance and scarcely-veiled menace finally forced me to finish the book, and my partner, Brian, who fed and cherished me throughout.

It goes without saying that all infelicities whether of content or of style are entirely my responsibility.

Christine Fellner
August 1995

Parturiunt montes, nascitur ridiculus mus.

Contents

UPDATE

Paras. 2.226 and 2.230: Since the last proof stage of the book was finalised, a further design right case has gone to trial. See *Hourahine v. Everdell* 1995 I.P.D. 18050, about pop-up greetings cards.

ERRATA

Para. 5.043, line 5: "lawful means" should read "unlawful means".
Para. 5.052, n.58: Add "But see 5.137 below".

Tables: The citations for the following entries in the tables contained inaccuracies or omissions which may be misleading; they are reprinted below as they should have read:

Baltimore Aircoil Co. Inc. *v.* Evapco (U.K.) Ltd 1991 I.P.D. 14157
Dean's Rag Book Co. *v.* Pomerantz (1930) 47 R.P.C. 485
Duriron Co. Inc., The *v.* Jennings (Hugh) [1984] F.S.R. 1
Ferrero (P) and C.SpA's Design Application [1978] R.P.C. 473
Guilford Kapwood Ltd *v.* Embsay Fabrics Ltd [1983] F.S.R. 506
Hanfstaengl *v.* W.H. Smith & Sons [1905] 1 Ch. 519
Hella K.G. *v.* ARIC SNC, January 18, 1993; [1994] 7 E.I.P.R. 309
Manners *v.* The Reject Shop Plc. [1995] E.I.P.R. 46; [1995] F.S.R. 870
Mayceys Confectionery Ltd *v.* Beckmann [1995] 4 E.I.P.R. D–101
P.S.M. International Plc. *v.* Specialised Fastener Products (Southern) Ltd [1993] F.S.R. 113, Patents County Court
Roberts (Patricia) *v.* Candiware Ltd [1980] F.S.R. 352
Shelley Films Ltd *v.* Rex Features Ltd 1994 I.P.D. 17001; [1994] E.M.L.R. 134
Stenor Ltd *v.* Whitesides (Clitheroe) Ltd [1948] A.C. 107; (1946) 63 R.P.C. 81
Tomy Kogyo Co. Inc.'s Design Application [1983] R.P.C. 207
Valeo Vision S.A. *v.* Flexible Lamps Ltd 1994 I.P.D. 17103; SRIS/C/47/94; [1995] R.P.C. 205
WHAM-O Manufacturing Co. *v.* Lincoln Industries Ltd [1985] R.P.C. 281 (Court of Appeal of New Zealand)
Wilden Pump Engineering Co. *v.* Fusfeld [1985–87] 8 I.P.R. 250

Table of Cases

Table of Statutes

1. Background to the Copyright, Designs and Patents Act 1988

INTRODUCTION

"Let other pens dwell on guilt and misery. I quit such odious subjects as soon **1.001**
as I can, impatient to restore everybody, not greatly in fault themselves, to
tolerable comfort, and to have done with all the rest". In conformity with
Jane Austen's plan,[1] this book will not dwell on the unhappy inconsistencies
of the old U.K. industrial designs law, which might protect bedpans[2] but not
furniture,[3] washers[4] but not babies' garments,[5] simply because in the
favoured cases the objects were made from recognisable drawings while in
the others they were three-dimensional prototypes. Rather, after a brief
account of the design protection systems previously adopted and canvassed in
the U.K., to show what Parliament faced when enacting the 1988 reforms, it
will describe the solutions chosen, so that readers can assess for themselves
how well or badly these serve industry.

What do lawyers mean by an industrial design?

When lawyers talk about industrial designs, they are referring to elements **1.002**
which influence what a commercial product *looks like*. They are not
interested in how it works or what it is made of, unless either of these
questions has some effect on its appearance. Take a car—some modern cars
have bodies made of fibreglass rather than steel, but so long as both are
painted, what they are made of does not matter. But the amount of
chrome-plated trim they have does matter, because it affects what they look
like—older cars tend to have much more than new ones. And the presence or
absence of a spoiler makes a difference to the look of a car, as well as affecting
its aerodynamic efficiency.

Cinderella's glass slipper would not have excited designs lawyers in their **1.003**
professional capacity except in relation to its shape—whether it had stiletto,
Cuban or wedge heels, pointed or squared-off toes—or to any decoration
such as rosettes or engraving. The mere fact that it was made of glass, thereby

---

[1] *Mansfield Park*, Chap. 48.
[2] *Vernon (Pulp Products) Ltd v. Universal Pulp Containers Ltd* [1980] F.S.R. 179.
[3] *Hensher (George) Ltd v. Restawile Upholstery (Lancs) Ltd* [1975] R.P.C. 31.
[4] *British Northrop Ltd v. Texteam Blackburn Ltd* [1974] R.P.C. 57.
[5] *Merlet v. Mothercare plc* [1986] R.P.C. 115.

1

no doubt disclosing disagreeably bunched-up toes and bunions, could have been dismissed as adding nothing significant to the store of human knowledge in the packaging art.[6]

1.004   Any product you can think of that has had a shape or pattern given to it by human intervention has a design—a lump of flint chipped into an arrowhead, a blouse, a flight of china ducks, refrigerators, Christmas cards, a mould for making plastic buckets, a tea service, a turbine, an exhaust pipe. The shape or pattern may be there because of what the product is going to do (a lump of flint is a lump of flint, but an arrowhead is for killing people), or simply to make a product look nicer than competing products (to make you choose this Christmas card rather than that one), or a mixture of both (you want a tea service with deep rather than shallow cups because in your experience tea gets a disgusting skin on it quicker in shallow cups, but within your price range you prefer the appearance of this one to that one). Many products have several design elements—a dress made of patterned fabric will be chosen for both the fabric design and the style elements—pleated, straight or flared skirt, long or short sleeves or hemline, round, draped or V-neckline.

1.005   Works of art like paintings and sculptures also have designs in the sense that the artists have decided what they will look like and have used paint and brushes or a hammer and chisel to express their artistic intent. But what distinguishes industrial designs from art for art's sake is that they are for products which have a job to do.[7] You buy a painting because you want to hang it on the wall and look at it (or lock it in a vault and pay insurance on it). But you buy a tea service so that you can consume tea and cream cakes, a refrigerator so you don't get poisoned by the cream cakes, an exhaust pipe because your existing one has fallen off, and a turbine because you want to generate electricity to sell to people. So manufacturers design their products with a view to making you buy theirs to do the job you want done, rather than someone else's. And, among many other things, anything about the *look* of a product which gives it a competitive edge will be of value to the manufacturer, and he will want to stop competitors adopting it and enjoying a free ride on his creative effort or investment.

1.006   The law recognises this, and offers ways of protecting "deserving" designs against copying or, in some cases, even inadvertent similarity. But it must beware of allowing a manufacturer to monopolise features of the appearance of his product which enable him to stifle competition based on quality, price, service, etc., and prevent others giving the customer a choice. As Lord Peston said in Parliament during the debates on the Copyright, Designs and Patents Bill,[8] "Competition ... is essentially about the ability of other producers to

[6] See *Aspro-Nicholas Ltd's Design Application* [1974] R.P.C. 645. This is a slight exaggeration, but the fact that a product is made of glass might well be treated as an "idea" which should not be monopolised.

[7] "The article must have some independent existence, not merely be the vehicle for expressing an artistic conception": Lloyd-Jacob J. in *Pytram Ltd v. Models (Leicester) Ltd* [1930] 1 Ch. 639, at 642—Boy Scouts' totem.

[8] 2nd Reading, November 12, 1987, *Hansard* col. 1530.

produce something similar to what is currently being produced. That is the whole point of it." Decorative features need not be copied, but others may be a result of the job a product has to do or the way it does it—an aircraft's wing may be the optimum shape for aerodynamic efficiency, the configuration of a mattress or VDU operator's chair may be the last word in ergonomic suitability for preventing bedsores or backache. And spare parts for things like cars present a particular problem, because allowing motor manufacturers to monopolise the aftermarket in spares by means of industrial design protection means that car owners "sell their souls to the company store"[9] and have to pay the manufacturer's asking price for replacement exhausts or body panels. The law has to steer a course between protecting design input and allowing others the freedom to compete, and this is done in the U.K. either by building safeguards into the statutes governing design protection or, at times, piecemeal by the courts in interpreting those statutes.

This pragmatic approach accounts for the lack of much profound philosophical speculation on the nature of design among U.K. commentators. It also explains, if it may not entirely justify, the apparent illogicality and unfairness of drawing a distinction between different "kinds" of creativity so as to give greater protection to the creator of decorative designs than to one whose task is to achieve optimum functional efficiency while constrained by a tight manufacturing budget and the technical requirements of customers.   **1.007**

EVOLUTION OF U.K. DESIGNS LAW

Although earlier practice was sometimes different, it seems to have been felt since the 1880s that some distinction should be drawn between works of pure art, intended to be valued for their own sake, and designs affecting the appearance of articles made to fulfil a particular function, whether those designs were meant to make the articles better fitted for their purpose, cheaper, or simply more visually attractive than competing articles.[10]   **1.008**

This distinction was recognised in the differing systems of legal protection provided. Works of art were protected by copyright—the right to prevent copying. There was no excuse for copying someone else's work; even if the subject-matter was the same, it could be treated in a different way. And artists primarily needed protecting against those who commercially pirated their work by producing illicit copies over which the artist had no control and from which he derived no benefit. Because of this, nothing outstanding in the way of novelty or originality of subject-matter was required to give a work   **1.009**

---

[9] Lord Templeman in *British Leyland Motor Corporation v. Armstrong Patents Co. Ltd* [1986] A.C. 577.

[10] The class of "functional" articles is by no means coterminous with "works of applied art", an expression more familiar to civil law systems and used in the international conventions governing copyright law. Although this covers many functional articles with appeal to the aesthetic sensibilities, artefacts bought purely to do a job, such as washers, sparking plugs, and indeed many internal components not visible in the finished object would not be included.

copyright: all that was needed was that it should not itself have been copied from another work and that some skill and labour should have gone into its making. Nor was it necessary to register or otherwise publicise the claim to copyright; anyone who knowingly copied someone else's work would justifiably be at risk. The period of protection could be long because it did not interfere with anyone else's freedom to produce his own work.

1.010   Functional articles, on the other hand, were bound to have a family likeness, dictated by the purpose they were made to fulfil. All that differentiated various shoes, for example, from the point of view of appearance was whatever gave them their individuality, the competitive edge which made people buy one pair of shoes rather than another. To protect that competitive edge, industrial designs legislation gave to a manufacturer who had contrived such individuality of appearance the right, if he wished, to claim, by registration, a short-lived monopoly of the features constituting that individuality, as applied to the basic form of a shoe. That basic form, the features which make a shoe a shoe and are therefore "dictated by function", would not be protected, because that would interfere with other manufacturers' freedom to make any shoes at all. And because a monopoly of the design was granted, so that nobody else could use it, even if he had arrived at it independently, the applicant for registration was required to demonstrate that the design was novel—that it had not been used or published before, because if it had, it would be wrong to give a latecomer the exclusive right to use it. Once registration had been secured, a representation of the article registered would be open to inspection by competitors, so that they would be able to see what they could and could not safely do. If a manufacturer did not bother or think it worthwhile to register a design, anyone else was free to adopt it, and of course once the monopoly expired, anyone could use the design, even by making a slavish copy.

1.011   This neat distinction was not always easy to apply in practice, because industrial designs are often based on drawings, which are themselves copyright works; and making a competing product could mean indirectly copying the drawing. Copyright has no "functionality" exclusion, it does not need one; nor does the subject-matter have to be novel. A publisher of pirate prints of a drawing cannot be heard to say that the drawing is of a boring old steam engine and so does not deserve protecting. But if industrial designs can be protected through the copyright in their drawings, the carefully-thought-out checks and balances in the registered design system are bypassed.

1.012   So the first consolidating copyright statute, the Copyright Act 1911, maintained a deliberate separation between works of art and industrial designs, the latter being then protectable by registration under the Patents and Designs Act 1907. That Act did not expressly exclude from the monopoly those features of a design which were "dictated by function", but case law had arrived at this result, and it was adopted in subsequent legislation (Patents and Designs Act 1919 and Registered Designs Act 1949). Under the

1911 Act,[11] copyright would only apply to a design capable of registration under the 1907 Act (even if not actually registered) if it could be shown that it was not used or intended to be used as a model or pattern for a mass-produced industrial design. Registrable designs required some "eye-appeal", but purely functional industrial designs were kept out of copyright in practice by continuing to classify "plans" (such as engineering drawings) as literary rather than artistic works, probably because it was recognised that their value lay in the information they conveyed on how to manufacture a product, rather than in any purely incidental skills of draughtsmanship involved in their making. Literary works were not infringed by making the article they described, only by copying the way they described it.

Thus the U.K. system set its face against protection of purely functional elements of industrial design and also against cumulative protection of non-functional elements by both copyright and industrial designs law. This meant that many designs went completely unprotected, either because they were too functional or because they had not been registered. However, a loophole for non-functional designs was revealed by the "Popeye" case in 1941.[12] Some years after the earliest drawings were made, the owners of copyright in the Popeye the Sailor Man cartoons had, without securing design registrations, licensed the manufacture of dolls in the likeness of the cartoon characters. The defendants, unlicensed manufacturers of dolls copied from the licensees', on being sued for infringement of copyright, argued that the plaintiffs had used the drawings, through their licensees, as models or patterns for mass-production; these designs would have been "capable of registration", having undoubted eye-appeal; and therefore under section 22 of the 1911 Act the plaintiffs had lost the right to assert infringement of copyright. The House of Lords disagreed. What mattered under section 22 was the artist's intention when the original drawings had been made. These cartoons had not then been intended as anything other than parts of a comic strip; the merchandising exercise had taken place much later, and copyright had therefore not been lost. The defendants by making their dolls had without consent reproduced the drawings in a "material form", even though in a different dimension, and this was infringement under the 1911 Act.

This latter finding was very important, because it established beyond doubt that making an article depicted in a drawing would infringe the copyright in the drawing, unless for some reason copyright relief was barred. By copying not just cartoon-character dolls, but most industrial artefacts, you reproduced the drawing, even if, as would usually be the case, you had never seen it, and it was no defence that what you had copied had no novelty about it.

The Popeye decision did not, however, affect the non-cumulation principle, nor did it concern purely functional designs, which were not caught by section 22 because they were not registrable. The Gregory Committee, on

1.013

1.014

1.015

---

[11] s.22.
[12] *King Features Syndicate Inc. v. O. M. Kleeman* [1941] A.C. 417.

whose 1952 report the Copyright Act 1956 was based,[13] also wished to maintain the separation between works of art and industrial designs, and to continue to exclude purely functional designs from protection.[14] The principle of separation was achieved by section 10 of the Act. The first step of the test was again whether the work of art was also a registrable design, but if it was, then copyright relief was denied (the section operated as a defence) if the design had been either registered or actually used in mass-production.[15] (Oddly, although you were protected by Schedule 1 to the Act against loss of your copyright where someone else registered a design for your product without your consent, you were not protected if, having yourself mass-produced your products, someone else got hold of even one of them and sold it without your consent, even if that person was a rival who thereby deprived you of the ability to prevent him selling his own copies.[16]) If you registered, you got a design monopoly but no copyright. If you mass-produced but did not register, you got no protection for your industrial applications, and this time you could not argue that you had only decided to use your copyright drawing for mass-production at a later stage, because the section contained no reference to anybody's intentions.

1.016   But in a way fatal to their intentions for purely functional designs, the members of the Gregory Committee were seduced by logic into abandoning common sense. They recommended that maps, charts and plans (and diagrams), because they expressed ideas in lines and shapes, would more rationally be protected as artistic than as literary works and, since they did not want judges refusing copyright because these works were not, in the layman's sense, "artistic", that they should be made protectable "irrespective of artistic quality". This was duly enacted; but copyright in these dubiously artistic works could now be infringed by indirectly reproducing them in three dimensions—by copying articles made from them.[17] Gregory realised that this could lead to copyright being given to industrial designs which would be unregistrable because entirely dictated by function, but they relied on the average person's inability to understand engineering drawings by recommending that no copyright action should succeed if a non-expert would not recognise the infringing article from the plaintiff's drawing. This recommendation became section 9(8) of the Act, and seldom fulfilled the purpose for which it was intended.

1.017   Six years after the 1956 Act came into effect came the case of *Dorling v. Honnor.*[18] The plaintiff sold kits of parts for self-assembly by sailing

---

[13] Report of the Copyright Committee, Cmd. 8662, HMSO London, 1952.

[14] Paras. 256, 258.

[15] Mass-production (applying a design industrially) meant applying it to more than 50 articles, or to goods manufactured in lengths or pieces like wallpaper or textiles: Copyright (Industrial Designs) Rules 1957, S.I. 1957 No. 867.

[16] Grateful acknowledgments for this point to the draftsman of the guidance Notes on section 52 of the 1988 Bill.

[17] ss.3(1)(a), 48(1).

[18] [1963] R.P.C. 205, [1964] R.P.C. 160 C.A.

enthusiasts into small dinghies, with the aid of plans also provided. Neither the plans, nor the individual parts, nor (by majority) the shape of the dinghy as assembled were registrable under the 1949 Act, for a variety of reasons including being "dictated solely by function",[19] so section 10 did not apply; but under the new definitions the plans of both the parts and the whole were artistic works, and the defendant had reproduced them in three dimensions by making the parts. The judges constituted themselves non-experts for the purpose of comparing the defendant's parts with the plaintiff's plans, and decided they could recognise them. Copyright for some industrial designs had unmistakeably arrived.

Disturbing anomalies

Only it was for the "wrong" type of design. In 1962, a departmental committee specifically considering industrial designs and section 10 had recommended[20] that in principle copyright as well as design registration should be available for industrial designs with eye-appeal (*i.e.* there should be cumulative protection), but it rejected the idea that either type of protection should be available for designs "dictated solely by function". Indeed, by the Design Copyright Act 1968, copyright was introduced for registrable designs to improve the remedies available against infringers—but it lasted for only 15 years from first marketing, and the Act said nothing about purely functional designs. Industry was left with the anomalous situation that registrable designs with eye-appeal were protected from copying for only 15 years, while purely functional designs (which were deliberately excluded from registration because they would impinge on the freedom of competitors) received copyright lasting for the author's life and 50 years thereafter.   **1.018**

The position was exacerbated by the House of Lords decision in *Amp v. Utilux*,[21] which narrowed what had previously been thought to be the scope of registrability by declaring that only designs intended by the designer to have eye-appeal could be registered. The exclusion of designs whose shape or configuration was "solely dictated by function" meant that if the designer had been guided solely by functional and economic considerations, then even though the finished design might have novelty and eye-appeal in the eyes of customers, and might not be the only technical solution to a particular design problem, it would not qualify. This was hard on designers who sought a monopoly, but they (or more usually their employers) were amply compensated by a lengthy copyright term without the bother of applying and paying for a registration.   **1.019**

This was not the only anomaly: copyright was fine for both eye-appealing and functional articles based on drawings, and might also serve designs   **1.020**

[19] Wording in section 1(3) of Registered Designs Act 1949.
[20] Johnston Report of Departmental Committee on Industrial Designs, Cmnd. 1808, HMSO London, 1962.
[21] [1972] R.P.C. 103.

stemming from prototypes classifiable as "sculptures",[22] which also got copyright irrespective of artistic quality. But any article based on a prototype which was not a sculpture could only be protected by copyright if the prototype was a "work of artistic craftsmanship"; such works, unlike drawings or sculptures, were required to possess artistic merit.[23] This split produced a result different from that in most European jurisdictions, where two-dimensional "dessins" and three-dimensional "modèles" were not distinguished.

Reform proposals

1.021 The governmental machine slowly scratched its head, and two years later appointed a committee under Whitford J. to consider the whole field of industrial design protection. The resulting Report in 1977[24] recommended abolishing registered designs altogether, because the system was relatively little used, and opted for copyright as the appropriate protection. However, because the minority balked at protecting purely functional designs by copyright, the Report divided designs into two classes, designating those bought for eye-appeal Category A and those bought solely to do a job Category B. While all the members would have given copyright to the former (but only for 25 years), a minority would have excluded the latter, leaving them without protection.

1.022 The crucial division had by now shifted from the original one between works of "pure" art, catered for by copyright, and industrial designs serving some functional purpose, catered for by specially-drafted legislation, to one situated wholly within the field of industrial design. The Whitford Category A/Category B distinction between designs with eye appeal to a purchaser and those without was not precisely the same as the registrable/non-registrable test of designer's intention, but no doubt that intention is market-led. A similar distinction between aesthetic and non-aesthetic designs is found in many other systems, and is of course somewhat arbitrary. It is not only "aesthetic" considerations which influence purchasers, and a designer may invest just as much creative effort, and a manufacturer just as much time and money, in achieving a successful design (and thus one more likely to be copied) for something which does not have eye-appeal as for something that does. The "solely dictated by function" test was thought before *Amp v. Utilux* to exclude a monopoly only where it would prevent a competitor from competing at all. The Whitford split should perhaps have come at the point

---

[22] The leading case was the decision of the New Zealand Court of Appeal in *WHAM-O Manufacturing Co. v. Lincoln Industries Ltd* [1985] R.P.C. 127—carved wooden model for frisbee. Other examples might be carved wooden templates, plaster models for new car bodies, moulds and the like. These were frequently pleaded as copyright works, but no prominent U.K. case seems to have gone successfully to trial.

[23] See cases cited at notes 3 and 5 above.

[24] Report of Committee to consider the Law of Copyright and Industrial Designs, Cmnd. 6732, HMSO London, 1977.

where design protection really does become undesirable—because there is no alternative solution or, as perhaps in the case of spare parts, if it is thought that consumers should not be tied to a monopoly supplier, or because protecting very simple and cheaply-designed components leads to wasteful duplication of effort and resources, or for some other properly-thought-out reason. It will be seen that the 1988 Act at least attempts to restore a "reasoned" division between "fine arts" copyright, albeit recognising that some artistic works do get industrially-exploited, and run-of-the-mill industrial designs.

Both during and after Whitford's deliberations the courts, up to and including the House of Lords,[25] took copyright for purely functional designs to their hearts, and while, say, jewellery and furniture designers received protection for only 15 years, makers of basic engineering components, devoid of novelty and possessing originality only in the sense that a routinely-trained draughtsman had put in an hour or so's work drawing them, were enjoying protection for the full copyright term. Sometimes the drawings thus protected were little more than updates of an earlier drawing or depictions of an existing prototype. Often this work, on which the whole edifice of copyright was erected, was actually duplicated by the infringer in making his own drawings—he would rarely have had access to the plaintiff's drawings, and would have to work out his own tolerances and the like by trial and error, just as the plaintiff had done.
1.023

Understandably, copyright was very popular with plaintiffs, for registrable as well as unregistrable designs: it arose automatically, without the need to apply and pay for registration and wait to sue until the application was processed; the test of infringement was less strict[26]; there was no "functional" exclusion or other monopoly safeguards; and the damages were incomparably higher, "conversion" damages enabling a successful plaintiff to expropriate virtually the whole of the infringer's turnover in the infringing goods.[27] Any defendant, even one with a strong case, had to think very carefully before running the risk of fighting rather than settling by getting off the market, faced with the possibility of such a penal remedy.
1.024

Four years after the Whitford Committee's inconclusive report, further governmental head-scratching resulted in the publication in 1981 of a
1.025

---

[25] *L. B. (Plastics) Ltd v. Swish Products Ltd* [1979] R.P.C. 551. Interestingly, the Court of Appeal in this case, which concerned a way of assembling chests of drawers, had held that the defendants had adopted only the idea or concept of the plaintiff's locking mechanism, not copied the design. Whitford J. and the House of Lords were more impressed by what the defendants' internal documents disclosed about their activities and motives.

[26] See Chap. 5 below.

[27] Conversion damages were based on the fiction that as soon as an infringing product was made, it belonged to the plaintiff. So he was entitled to claim as damages its full value to the defendant, usually the sale price, and not merely the profit he himself would have made if he had made and sold the product, or the profit the defendant has made, or a royalty, which are the bases of assessing financial compensation for other intellectual property infringements.

Consultative Document[28] adopting the Whitford minority view that copyright should be the means for protecting industrial designs but should not be available for purely functional designs, as protecting these would lead to industrial stagnation and waste of resources. In the intervening period, the spare parts controversy which has bedevilled U.K. industrial designs law had blown up, and the *British Leyland* exhaust pipe case was making its way through the legal system, pitting the original equipment manufacturer against the "pattern spares" manufacturer.[29] Industry groups responded passionately but diversely to the Consultative Document, and in 1983 a Green Paper[30] took a different line, suggesting the denial of copyright to "functional articles manufactured in quantity" but the extension of the Registered Designs Act to articles having "functional" as well as "aesthetic" novelty.

1.026   The first instance and Court of Appeal decisions in *British Leyland*[31] followed the orthodox copyright line in finding that by copying a BL Marina exhaust pipe to provide competing spares, Armstrong had infringed BL's copyright in its exhaust pipe drawings. The House of Lords[32] by a majority accepted the application of copyright to purely functional designs as too entrenched for them to change. But they were so struck by its anti-competitive effects in the field of spare parts that they invented a brand-new defence to deal with it.[33] BL was not to be allowed to interfere with a purchaser's right to repair his car with any spares he chose by preventing competitors from making these. This ruling effectively deprived original equipment manufacturers of the exercise of their copyright to control the aftermarket. It solved the immediate spare parts problem (though leaving many obscurities); but their Lordships called stridently for the law on functional design copyright to be changed, saying that its development had never been intended by Parliament. Embarrassment had already been caused by the Monopolies and Mergers Commission's finding[34] that the Ford Motor Company was acting anti-competitively by refusing to license other manufacturers to make replacement car body panels (for which it also had registered designs) and was charging inflated prices for its own spares. This practice was castigated from the consumer's point of view, but under copyright law as it stood before *British Leyland* the Monopolies Commission felt nothing could be done about it.[35] In both these cases, the competitors were not "pirates" in the sense of counterfeiters passing off their often inferior and sometimes dangerous products on an unsuspecting market, but highly respectable manufacturers,

---

[28] Reform of the Law relating to Copyright, Designs and Performers' Protection, Cmnd. 8302, HMSO London, 1981.

[29] "Pattern spares" is a term used for spares which are copied but not passed off as coming from the original manufacturer.

[30] Intellectual Property Rights and Innovation, Cmnd. 9117, HMSO London, 1983.

[31] *British Leyland Motor Corporation v. Armstrong Patents Co. Ltd* [1986] R.P.C. 279.

[32] [1986] A.C. 577.

[33] See 2.181 below.

[34] A Report on the policy and practice of the Ford Motor Company Limited in not granting licences to manufacture or sell in the United Kingdom certain replacement body panels for Ford vehicles, Cmnd. 9437, HMSO London, 1985.

[35] The Commission recommended a 5-year protection period for original spare parts.

often making original equipment themselves, who were perfectly open about what they were doing. Indeed, the complaining manufacturers themselves operated their own parts services through which they provided licensed spares for their competitors' vehicles.[36] This led to a good deal of schizophrenia within the industry and its trade association, the Society of Motor Manufacturers and Traders.

Finally, the government took the opportunity of a general reform of copyright law to try and take care of industrial designs by means of a specially-tailored scheme which should give some protection to design effort and investment while guarding against anti-competitive abuses. Its views were laid out in a 1986 White Paper,[37] in which it opted for three alternative systems of protection. Copyright would be retained for "articles which are themselves artistic works". Design registration (extended to 25 years) would be available for "genuinely" aesthetic designs: this "genuineness" would be secured by excluding the design of any article whose "aesthetic" appearance is not a material factor in its purchase, acquisition or use, or which is "an integral or working part of a further article, unless the appearances of the two articles are substantially independent". A new 10-year "unregistered design right" would be provided for "original" designs, including spare parts but excluding articles still to be protected by copyright, *i.e.* "articles which are themselves artistic works", and articles covered by a subsisting registered design. No other exclusions from the new right were proposed, but licences of right were to become available during the last five years of the term. However, this right was to be available to designs originating outside the European Community only on a basis of reciprocity—if equivalent protection were given to U.K. designs in the country of origin. 1.027

It seemed the White Paper's ideal solution would have been to banish copyright from the field of industrial design, and to substitute the new and comparatively short-lived unregistered design right as "the right generally applicable to the design of articles".[38] But it was recognised[39] that international Berne Convention obligations would prevent this where "articles ... qualify as artistic works in their own right". It was thus conceded that there are some industrial designs that are also artistic works, and copyright for these would have to be retained. The retention and strengthening of registered designs as an option was allegedly motivated by "the increased importance of aesthetic design in present day industry", but also apparently by the recognition of a class of "aesthetic" but not "artistic" industrial designs caught by the Paris Industrial Property Convention if not the Berne Convention, so that the affording of the unregistered right to foreign "aesthetic" designs only in cases of reciprocity would conflict with inter- 1.028

---

[36] One of the leading component makers, Lucas, apparently complained that component manufacturers were excluded from this cosy arrangement: *Hansard* debates on the 1988 Bill, H.L. Vol. 491, col. 1109.

[37] Intellectual Property and Innovation, Cmnd. 9712, HMSO London, 1986.

[38] Para. 3.32.

[39] Para. 3.32.

national obligations. The new registrable/unregistrable dividing line was placed more or less where the Whitford Committee had placed it, the test being whether purchasers buy something for its aesthetic appearance.

The 1988 Act

1.029 What was finally enacted as the Copyright, Designs and Patents Act 1988 was not quite what had been proposed in the White Paper. Some dual protection is permitted: a design may have both registered and unregistered protection, and in some cases a registered design may co-exist with copyright. Most importantly, the unregistered design right, which in any event has a higher protection threshold than copyright in that "commonplace" designs will not be covered, is now subject to the controversial "must-fit" and "must-match" exclusions, leaving some designs devoid of all protection, since the Registered Designs Act, as foreshadowed in the White Paper, has been amended to introduce a "must-match" exclusion and to filter out designs which normally have no aesthetic content.

1.030 Certain sections of the Act are unfortunately rather obscure. Until recently the only *travaux préparatoires* U.K. courts could consult to aid interpretation were departmental committee reports (like the Gregory Committee) whose recommendations had been adopted in the legislation concerned. In particular, they did not look at the verbatim records of Parliamentary debates published in *Hansard,* or other statements of government intent, because it was apparently thought this might make confusion worse confounded and anyway what mattered was what Parliament had said, not what the government might have meant. Happily or not, the House of Lords in a 1992 tax case, *Pepper v. Hart,*[40] held that where a statute was ambiguous or obscure or led to absurdity the courts could look at *Hansard* in the hope of finding a clear ministerial statement as to its intended purport. If the court can be persuaded that any parts of the 1988 Act are similarly ambiguous or obscure or lead to absurdity, *Hansard* may therefore be scoured in the hope of finding elucidation.[41] This may be a mixed blessing to litigants where the exercise may only compound obscurities and lead to prolonged argument, and it increases the work of lawyers and consequently the costs.[42]

[40] [1993] A.C. 593.
[41] It was by the Registered Designs Appeal Tribunal in the *Ford/Fiat* registered design case [1993] R.P.C. 399, discussed in Chapter 2 below, but the higher courts felt they did not need to.
[42] That the courts are not minded to encourage the habit may be deduced from recent Practice Directions containing onerous requirements as to advance provision of notes of argument and multiple copies of everything to be relied on, all conveniently and expensively put together.

OTHER PROTECTION FOR INDUSTRIAL DESIGNS?

In many overseas jurisdictions, the law of "unfair competition" is often **1.031** invoked to protect an unfairly appropriated industrial design, in addition to, or instead of, protection by copyright or designs law. This can operate more flexibly in relation to both right and remedy, and in practice may give rise to little more uncertainty than the convolutions of U.K. statutory interpretation. No such general jurisdiction exists in the U.K. and the White Paper[43] set its face against an "unfair copying" solution to the design problem. All that U.K. law at that time had to offer was protection of the shape of an article as a trade mark—unlikely to be available after the *Coca Cola* decision[44]—or by an action in passing off. This would require the plaintiff to prove that the actual shape or pattern, as opposed to the packaging or get-up, of his product had become so identified with him that the public would be confused as to the origin of competing goods of the same shape or pattern.

There have been a few cases where plaintiffs have succeeded in proving all **1.032** this, most recently the JIF lemon case,[45] demonstrating by extensive market research that the public is too idle to read labels and is readily conditioned into thinking of lemon juice packaged in a lemon-shaped container as "a JIF lemon" instead of lemon juice packaged in a lemon-shaped container. This finding is, however, of limited application, since Reckitt & Colman had contrived to be the only supplier packaging lemon juice in this way for over 25 years before the evidence was gathered.

An alternative to lengthy marketing may be intensive promotion: in *Mirage* **1.033** *Studios v. Counter-Feat Clothing Co. Ltd*[46] it was held that anyone seeing a Teenage Mutant Ninja Turtle adorning a T-shirt (and, presumably, appearing in its own right as a toy) would automatically assume it emanated only from some "licensed" character merchandiser. This is, however, a long way from warranting the supposition that the shape or pattern of a particular product would normally become so indissolubly associated with a particular manufacturer that even if a competitor's product is fairly and properly labelled and packaged, confusion will still occur. The industrial design protection dilemma as experienced in the U.K. is not primarily one of counterfeiting, for which passing off is often an effective remedy, but of balancing protection for innovation and investment against competitive freedom to make similar goods and to safeguard consumers against

---

[43] Para. 3.25.
[44] *In re Coca Cola Co.* [1986] 1 W.L.R. 695 (H.L.). Shape trade marks are now in principle registrable under the Trade Marks Act 1994, but may not be registered if they consist exclusively of the shape which results from the nature of the goods themselves, or is necessary to obtain a technical result, or which gives substantial value to the goods (section 3(2)). It does not look too promising, and there is not even a proviso permitting registration on evidence of acquired distinctiveness stemming from use.
[45] *Reckitt & Colman Products Ltd v. Borden Inc* [1990] R.P.C. 341.
[46] [1991] F.S.R. 145.

anti-competitive abuses. It is with this problem that the Copyright, Designs and Patents Act 1988, like its predecessors, set out to deal.

Recent international developments

1.034   After many tribulations the GATT Uruguay Round of international free trade negotiations came to a conclusion in 1994. It includes an Agreement on Trade-Related Aspects of Intellectual Property Rights (TRIPs), which binds the members to give protection in prescribed ways to the standard types of intellectual property including, in Part II, Section 4, industrial designs. It seems that in terms of both rights and remedies the U.K. will not have to make alterations to the system set up by the 1988 Act in order to comply.

1.035   More unsettling was the publication at the end of 1993 of a draft E.U. Regulation and Harmonisation Directive on industrial design. The Regulation, which would have direct effect, provides for a Community Design, along the lines of the Community Trade Mark, which would supplement national laws and have a mixture of registered and unregistered protection. The registered right would be administered centrally by a Community Design Office, and both rights could be invoked anywhere in the Union. The content of the proposed rights is similar to, but certainly not identical with, existing U.K. law. The Harmonisation Directive would have to be implemented by national legislation and its aim is to align member states' laws to meet certain minimum standards. It would involve quite extensive alteration to the Registered Designs Act 1949, and some changes will also have to be made to the 1988 Act.

1.036   The draft Regulation and Directive are being considered by the European Parliament and will be further considered by the Council of Ministers. Their passage has been considerably delayed by industry disagreements on the spare parts issue, which are by no means settled. A short account of the proposals appears in Chapter 6 of this book.

2. Scope and Content of Protection

REGISTERED DESIGNS

The 1988 Act in dealing with industrial designs adopts a number of crucial **2.001** expressions (like "shape and configuration", "article", and indeed "design"), which are familiar to lawyers from their use in the Registered Designs Act 1949. A knowledge of their meaning, as interpreted by the courts, may help to understand their meaning as used in the new legislation. Moreover, an entirely new provision, the "must-match" exclusion, which is common to both registered designs and the new unregistered design right, has recently received judicial interpretation[1] in the registered design context. So the first type of design right considered in this chapter is a "registered design": a monopoly for a limited term, granted to a *novel* "design" as defined in the 1949 Act, following examination by the Designs Registry (part of the Patent Office). Registered designs are part of the international "industrial property" régime established by the Paris Convention and as such are subject to "national treatment" under Article 2, so that applicants from other Convention countries are entitled to seek and enjoy U.K. protection on the same terms as U.K. applicants.

The 1949 Act was amended by the 1988 Act,[2] but (with a few exceptions) **2.002** only in relation to designs applied for on or after the date the 1988 Act came into effect—August 1, 1989. The term of a registered design runs from the date of application (or the date of an earlier eligible application in a Paris Convention country), not from the date of grant, so registered designs granted on or after August 1, 1989, but which stem from earlier applications, are not covered by the amendments. The effect is that *both validity and infringement* of a registered design granted on a pre-August 1, 1989 application are still judged by the law prevailing at the date of application. Certain additional transitional provisions cover designs applied for on any date after January 12, 1988 and before August 1, 1989.[3]

---

[1] *Ford Motor Company Ltd and Iveco Fiat's Design Application* [1993] R.P.C. 599; [1994] R.P.C. 545.

[2] See ss.265–273 and Schedule 3; the text of the Act as amended is printed as Schedule 4.

[3] See 3.130 below.

Definitions

"Design"

2.003 Not every novel design, in the sense of a collection of characteristics deliberately imparted to a product, qualifies for registration. The interpretation section of the amended 1949 Act (s.44), provides that "design" in the Act, except where the context otherwise requires, has the meaning assigned to it by section 1(1),[4] which in turn provides that "design" means (and therefore according to the normal rules of statutory interpretation means *only*)

> "features of shape, configuration, pattern or ornament applied to an article by any industrial process, being features which in the finished article appeal to and are judged by the eye ..."

The subsection immediately goes on to exclude from the definition three types of *feature* of a design which would or might otherwise fall within it, while still permitting registration as a whole of a design having non-excluded features. The excluded features are:

(a) a method or principle of construction
(b) features of shape or configuration of an article which:
> (i) are dictated solely by the function which the article has to perform, or
> (ii) are dependent upon the appearance of another article of which the article is intended by the author of the design to form an integral part.

The third of these exclusions, section 1(1)(b)(ii), was introduced by the 1988 Act, and is popularly known as "must-match". Two other subsections of section 1 exclude altogether from registration designs for two types of *article*. They are:

Section 1(3)

> "A design shall not be registered in respect of any article if the appearance of the article is not material, that is, if aesthetic considerations are not normally taken into account to a material extent by persons acquiring or using articles of that description, and would not be so taken into account if the design were to be applied to the article."

(this is another 1988 Act introduction which might be termed "who-cares-what-it-looks-like?") and section 1(5):

> "The Secretary of State may by rules provide for excluding from registration under this Act designs for such articles of a primarily literary or artistic character as the Secretary of State[5] thinks fit."

---

[4] Under the 1949 Act before amendment, the definition of "design" appeared in section 1(3).
[5] The equivalent subsection under the 1949 Act before amendment was section 1(4).

All five exclusions, as will appear, are dictated by policy considerations as to the proper scope of an industrial design monopoly. The first four may be regarded as preventing the stifling of competition by allowing one manufacturer to monopolise elements which should be available for use by all. The fifth herds into the copyright pen designs for articles which, though more often than not commercially inspired, are "primarily" literary or artistic, and can also serve to protect the Register of Designs from becoming cluttered with seasonal ephemera.

The reference to a design "as applied to an article" immediately high-lights the conceptual difficulties in this area of the law, because it treats the "design" as something abstract, initially divorced from the concrete object to which it is to be applied—a spirit looking for a body to inhabit. Pattern designs are not a problem—the textile manufacturer takes a length of white cotton and screenprints it with bunches of viper's bugloss in a novel repeating pattern, devised by his designer. The pre-existing flower design has thus been applied to the pre-existing fabric. Shape designs are less simple. The pin manufacturer makes an ordinary pin but gives it a large bevelled dodecagonal head (capable of supporting a greater than usual number of dancing angels, though at enhanced risk of the outermost ones falling off). His designer has supplied him with a drawing of the pin having this feature, but this "design" has been applied, not to any pre-existing article, but to a piece of metal, which is not an "article" within the meaning of the Act. What the user of the Act has to do to make sense of it, and what the designer did when conceiving the design, is to envisage a paradigm pin, the Platonic essence of a pin which makes it apt to perform the function assigned to pins—a pointed fastener which can penetrate layers of fabric, with a head to prevent it slipping or being forced out once in place. This notional article is then modified by having applied to it the additional or alternative features devised by the designer, and it is against this notional article that the features of the design now embodied in the pin itself are judged in terms of eye appeal, functionality, novelty and so on.[6] Features which partake of the Platonic essence, such as the point of the pin, no matter how eye-appealing, are likely to be caught by one or other of the exclusions, because to permit monopolisation of them would prevent other people making pins at all. Only the head is left—but because this is not offered to the public as an independent object of contemplation but as part of an everyday useful artefact, its character as such must continue to be taken into account in asking the basic question whether someone might, because of its design as defined by the Act, buy this pin rather than another one.

2.004

[6] For a similar formulation, see Lord Avonside in the Scottish case of *G. A. Harvey & Co. (London) Ltd v. Secure Fittings Ltd* [1966] R.P.C. 515 at 517–518.

"Features of shape, configuration pattern or ornament"

2.005   None of these terms is further defined in the Act, but decided cases largely treat shape and configuration designs as three-dimensional and pattern or ornament designs as two-dimensional, although there is no reason why features of ornament should not be three-dimensional, since they may be embossed or engraved or take the form of filigree, appliqué, lace or *broderie anglaise*. Shape and configuration are not quite synonymous. In *Cow & Co. Ltd v. Cannon Rubber Manufacturers Ltd*[7] the design was for a rubber hot water bottle having diagonally-disposed ribs on front and back to distribute the heat over a greater surface area and avoid burning the user. It was held that these ribs were features of configuration, rather than shape, in that they concerned the contour of the surface rather than the outline of the product itself, and an analogy was drawn with ridged rolls of butter wherein the overall form of the roll is a feature of shape while the ridges or corrugations are features of configuration.

2.006   This classification of some ornamental surface features as configuration rather than pattern can have significant effects where, as is usual, a distinction is made in seeking registration between shape and configuration on the one hand and pattern and ornament on the other. The statement of novelty required by the Rules will, as discussed later, normally claim only one or the other. In *Sommer Allibert (U.K.) Ltd v. Flair Plastics Ltd*[8] the registered design was for moulded plastic garden chairs having, among other things, perpendicular grooves moulded into their backs and seats. The defendant's chairs had horizontal grooves, which presented quite a different appearance. The statement of novelty had claimed only features of shape and configuration as important, and in an attempt to diminish the significance of the different grooves in assessing infringement, the plaintiff's counsel argued that they were mere features of pattern or ornament which should be disregarded. Both Whitford J. and the Court of Appeal disagreed. Even though the grooves were admitted in evidence to have been disposed in the way they were for aesthetic reasons, they were features of configuration applied to the chairs in the course of manufacture, not added as "two-dimensional ornament or decoration". It is a little difficult to see how a manifestly three-dimensional groove could ever be a two-dimensional anything, but the observation shows how deeply-ingrained the shape/configuration and pattern/ornament dichotomy has become. The manufacturing process seems to determine which camp a feature falls into, since any relief surface feature of a moulded or cast object, however decorative, must necessarily be imparted in the moulding or casting process, and therefore be configuration rather than pattern. Whether a design feature is regarded as configuration or pattern is also important in

---

[7] [1959] R.P.C. 240, 347.
[8] [1987] R.P.C. 599.

18

considering the section 1(1)(b) exclusions from the definition of "design", which apply only to features of shape or configuration,

The *Sommer Allibert* decision is in line with hallowed registered design **2.007** authority, Luxmoore J. in *Kestos Ltd v. Kempat Ltd*[9] having said in a much-quoted passage:

> "Shape and configuration are for all practical purposes considered as synonymous. Each signifies something in three dimensions; the form in which the article itself is fashioned. 'Pattern' and 'ornament' can, I think, in the majority of cases be treated as practically synonymous. It is something which is placed on an article for its decoration. It is substantially in two as opposed to three dimensions. An article can exist without any pattern or ornament upon it, whereas it can have no existence at all apart from its shape or configuration. As Lindley J. said in *Re Clarke's Registered Design* (1896) 13 R.P.C. 351 at 358, 'a design applicable to a thing for its shape can only be applied to a thing by making it in that shape'."

However, the Registered Designs Appeal Tribunal in the recent *Ford/Fiat*[10] case suggested that one of the designs, for a vehicle rear lamp having an arrangement of coloured lens segments with a clearly visible "pattern formed by the configuration of the interior face of the segments" might have been registrable as a "pattern" design. This suggestion did not have to be dealt with by the higher courts through which the applications progressed, and the design was by consent remitted to the Designs Registry for further consideration. Similarly, "pillow-case" mouldings on lamp lenses were held by Aldous J. in *Valeo Vision S.A. v. Flexible Lamps Ltd*[11] to be features of pattern, likely to be perceived as lines rather than ribs, and therefore to be disregarded in considering a design for shape and configuration. Probably the categories are not mutually exclusive,[12] which leaves room for argument in any particular case about the applicability of the section 1(1)(b) exclusions.

"Shape" designs need not be immutable: if a product is foldable, or opens **2.008** up telescopically, then provided the representation of the design which is filed shows it at all stages so as clearly to indicate what it does, it will be acceptable. Similarly with designs for flexible or articulated products like teddy-bears, which can be shown in a number of characteristic attitudes. Presumably inflatable products like balloons in the shape of Mr Blobby[13] should be shown inflated.

---

[9] (1936) 53 R.P.C. 139 at 152.
[10] [1993] R.P.C. 399 at 424.
[11] 1994 I.P.D. 17103.
[12] As was indeed held in *Re Rollason's Design* (1898) 15 R.P.C. 441 and 446 (a case about coffins).
[13] Or inflatable playmates delivered under plain cover, unless the Registry refuses to register such products as being mere representations of naturally-occurring phenomena, or on grounds of public morality—see further 3.010 below.

2.009   "Pattern" designs are probably most common in the fields of textiles and wallpaper, where there is detailed internal Registry guidance on the classification of different types of pattern—geometric, free, regularly and irregularly dispersed and so forth. Designs Rule 23 requires that the representation or specimen of the design lodged with the application "shall show the complete pattern and a sufficient portion of the repeat in length and width". But of course there are pattern or ornament designs to be applied to other products for purposes of decoration, notably in the field of pottery and ceramics, and Registry practice recognises that "ornament" may be in the round or in relief as well as in the flat.

2.010   It is not usual for colour to play much part in registered designs, whether in assessing registrability or infringement, despite the different appearance which may be imparted to, *e.g.* a textile design by use of different colourways. Indeed, there is authority[14] that it cannot be the sole subject-matter of a registered design, although it can be an element to be taken into account, as in *Secretary of State for War v. Cope*,[15] a design for a war medal ribbon. The topic is dealt with more fully in connection with novelty.

"Applied to an article"

2.011   Unlike the position in some overseas jurisdictions such as Germany,[16] a U.K. design registration must be of the design as applied to a specific "article", and it will be infringed only by use on that article (although in assessing novelty, any article to which the design has been applied can be invoked as an anticipation). This applies to pattern or ornament designs as well as shape and configuration designs, where the essence of the design is in the form of the article. There is no provision for registering a pattern design, for example a cartoon character or a device, or the type of pattern that is applied to a range of stationery, for application to a variety of articles, Each article on which it is intended to use the design[17] must be the subject of a separate application. The article must be named on the application form, and the Registry is alert to attempts to avoid the rule by defining the article too widely—"writing instrument", for example, is too wide, the applicant must specify ball-point pen, propelling pencil or fountain pen as the case may be.

2.012   "Article", according to section 44(1), means "any article of manufacture, and includes any part of an article if that part is made and sold separately". Article "of manufacture" does not cause many problems in practice, any more than does the requirement that the design be applied to the article "by any industrial process" (neither expression carries any implication that the design must be applied by machinery rather than by hand, only that it be

---

[14] *Grafton v. Watson* (1884) 50 L.T. 420.
[15] (1919) 36 R.P.C. 273.
[16] See *Deyhle's Design Application* [1982] R.P.C. 526.
[17] Save in the case of a "set" as explained below.

suitable for some kind of mass-production rather than being a one-off or limited edition), except in the field of construction. Conventional buildings have not been regarded as articles of manufacture to which a design is applied by an industrial process,[18] even if the building in the same form is intended to be erected in a number of different locations. But designs for portable buildings such as sheds may be registered, provided there is not too much "construction" work such as foundation-digging or piling or concreting involved in their erection on-site.[19] And "buildings" remain as possible candidates for registration according to the Registry's internal guidance, as indeed do dams and irrigation structures. The dearth of recent case law on the topic, despite the growth of prefabricated building methods, may reflect only a feeling among builders and architects that a registered design for an entire building is not commercially worthwhile. They have become used to relying on copyright in their buildings or, more usually, the plans for these. Construction materials are readily registrable, a couple of recent random examples being architectural panels simulating brickwork and interlocking concrete paving blocks having cut-outs through which grass can grow.[20]

Other articles normally sold in collapsed form for self-assembly, like much **2.013** modern furniture, can qualify for registration of their design when assembled, and this is reinforced by the new section 7(4) in the amended 1949 Act providing that the design for the whole of an article can be infringed by anything done in relation to a "kit" that would be an infringement if done in relation to "the assembled article". "Kit" is defined as "a complete or substantially complete set of components intended to be assembled into an article". This provision relates only to designs for articles registered pursuant to applications made on or after August 1, 1989; but since articles of this kind are only made collapsible for ease of transport and delivery, and are both advertised and displayed at point of sale, and usually on the packaging, in their assembled form, it would be unduly nitpicking (not that this deters a lawyer) to argue that self-assembly should deny registrability to an article as a whole just because it is put into its finished form at risk to the buyer's own nails, knuckles and temper rather than those of a workman or machinist.

Sets of articles

It is possible to register a design for a set of articles, but a kit of parts would **2.014** not normally constitute a set, which is defined in section 44(1) as "a number of articles of the same general character normally on sale or intended to be used together, to each of which the same design, or the same design with

---

[18] *Re Collier & Co.'s Application* (1937) 54 R.P.C. 253, a design for a petrol filling-station.
[19] *Re Concrete Ltd's Application* (1940) 57 R.P.C. 121, a reinforced-concrete air-raid shelter erected on site: registration refused, but judge expressly did not rule out building or structures altogether.
[20] *Ward Bros (Sherburn) Ltd's Application* 1981 I.P.D. 4036 and *K. K. Low & H. K. Tan, Application for Cancellation by G. & W. Ready-Mix Pte Ltd* 1993 I.P.D. 16102.

modifications or variations not sufficient to alter the character or substantially to affect the identity thereof, is applied". Although a kit of parts when fitted together makes a whole article, each part is differently-shaped, and even where the design is for pattern or ornament, each piece will normally bear only part of a larger pattern. The classic case of a set is a dinner or tea service bearing a pattern design, when each piece will have the same motifs, varying only in size or number of repeats depending on the size of each article. Even such services may not be registrable as a set if the pattern is for shape, because although the handles on cups, coffee or teapots, milk jugs, vegetable dishes and so on may be similar, the plates and saucers have no handles, and the various vessels are otherwise substantially different.

2.015   However, it is believed the Registry is not normally too difficult about such articles, nor about cutlery having a common handle design, or sets of glasses. Panelled or louvred doors in varying sizes for cupboards, kitchen units with common handles or knobs, nests of tables and probably sets of shelves of varying sizes for storing audio and video cassettes and CDs would be acceptable. A pen, pencil and ballpoint set registration might get round the refusal to accept "writing instrument" as a single article. On the other hand, what the layman would regard as a set, such as a collection of chessmen carved in the same style, would not fall within the definition, because the traditional shape of each piece differentiates it from the others, except for the pawns *inter se*. And in *Re Jury Borisovich Kotlyar's Application*[21] it was held that the definition of a set was not apt to cover a set of children's building blocks of which some were of novel shapes enabling the construction of pagodas and the like but the rest were standard cubes.

2.016   By section 44(2), any reference in the Act to an article in respect of which a design is registered is in the case of a set to be construed as a reference to any article of that set; and by section 44(3), there is no appeal from the Registrar's decision as to what constitutes a set.

"Any part of an article if that part is made and sold separately"

2.017   Designs for parts of articles are under section 44(1) only registrable if the parts are made and sold separately. Individual components of a "build-it-yourself" dinghy sold in kit form were held unregistrable partly on this ground in *Dorling v. Honnor Marine Ltd*,[22] and the front of an electric meter and the bezel of a valve were similarly held unregistrable in *Sifam Electrical Instrument Co. Ltd v. Sangamo Weston Ltd*[23] and *Drayton Controls (Engineering) Ltd v. Honeywell Control Systems Ltd*[24] respectively. The qualification has come to prominence as a result of the *Ford/Fiat*[25] design

[21] 1983 I.P.D. 6118.
[22] [1963] R.P.C. 205 at 214.
[23] [1973] R.P.C. 899.
[24] [1992] F.S.R. 225.
[25] [1993] R.P.C. 399; [1994] R.P.C. 545; [1995] R.P.C. 167.

applications relating to individual vehicle body panels, together with articles such as steering-wheels, lamps, seats, wheels and wheel covers, wing-mirrors and other accessories which, while not part of the vehicle body itself, form part of the overall design for a new vehicle. All such items, including body panels for sale as spare parts in the "aftermarket", were routinely registered before August 1, 1989, presumably because the articles *were* made and sold separately in the aftermarket. The "made and sold separately" objection was not initially raised by the Registry, which opposed the new applications on another ground.[26] But the objection was raised before the Registered Designs Appeal Tribunal, and that Tribunal, the Divisional Court (the Appeal Tribunal's decisions can only be attacked by judicial review) and the House of Lords (to whom the appeals went direct under a "leapfrogging" provision allowing this in suitable cases) held that the body panels were unregistrable because they were not sold separately. How was this decision reached, in the face of an active aftermarket, control of which was the applicants' reason for wanting separate registrations for the parts as well as a registration for the whole of the vehicle body shape?

Reliance was placed on Graham J.'s decision in *Sifam v. Sangamo Weston*, **2.018** although in that case there was no question of the meter fronts ever being sold separately, even by a component supplier to the meter assembler. Graham J. had rejected the argument that the definition meant "susceptible of being sold separately". Any part of an article, at least if physically detachable, which will generally be the case with machinery assembled from a variety of parts, could in theory be sold separately, but in that case any part could be registered, which would seem to defeat the intention of the Act. He said he thought "on the whole" that the legislative intention "must be" to grant registration "only for such articles as are intended by the proprietor of the design to be put on the market and sold separately, such as for example a hammer handle, or the bit of a bradawl". The proprietor's intention must, it seemed, be ascertained at the outset, possibly at the design stage, and the problem apparently presented by the present-tense wording of the definition ("if that part is made and sold separately"), which might seem to apply to a later stage but would thereby prejudice the novelty of a design application, would be solved by reading it as if it said "is to be sold separately". The Appeal Tribunal, supported by the Divisional Court, adopted this reasoning and held that the body panels had no "reality" or "independent life" as articles of commerce apart from forming part of, or an adjunct to, a composite vehicle.

The House of Lords agreed. They rejected the argument that the matter **2.019** should be looked at as at the date when a spare body panel, rather than the original vehicle, comes to be bought. This would mean that every spare panel would be an "article", and also that a design for a particular panel would be registrable when that panel is made for use as a spare but not when it is made for incorporation into a complete vehicle, and this would be unworkable. The

---

[26] The new "must-match" exclusion discussed below.

test must be applied at the stage of the application for registration, not in the light of what may become of some of the parts afterwards.

2.020 It remains to be seen what unintended effect this decision may have on subsisting registrations, since by constitutional theory the House of Lords does not make law, it merely declares that law as it has always been (even when it appears to be inventing a wholly new doctrine). Naturally, the present applicants' many existing registrations for body panels from their older models will be invalid.[27]

2.021 The other items (wing mirrors and the like) were not before either the Divisional Court or the House of Lords. The Appeal Tribunal had held them registrable in principle as they might be used with other vehicles as well as those for which they had been designed or selected, and had remitted them to the Registry for further consideration, and this finding was not disputed.

The design must "appeal to" and be "judged by" the eye

2.022 At this point the difficulties inherent in the way the section 1(1) definition of "design"[28] is structured begin to become apparent. This says quite plainly that "design" does *not* include three types of feature described in sections 1(1)(a) and (b). Therefore it would seem necessary to apply these exclusion tests at the outset to any design, in the layman's sense, which is tendered for consideration. Only those features which are left after applying the tests would then be considered, whether in determining eye-appeal, novelty (section 1(2) speaks of "a design which is new"), exclusion under sections 1(3) or (5), (both of which refer to "designs"), infringement (section 7 refers to exclusive rights in a "design"), or for any other purpose connected with the Act. This admittedly involves some terrible mental contortions, because having first envisaged, as suggested in 2.004 above, the paradigm article concerned, shorn of all additional or alternative features, one must then apply to it, not the whole of the features of the design under consideration, but only those which remain after performing the exclusion tests. The reality is that the sequential structure of section 1(1) tempts both the courts and commentators to consider the positive test of eye-appeal of the design as a whole (in the layman's sense) before the negative exclusions. This temptation is reinforced by the rules of procedure which have the applicant (or plaintiff in an infringement action) opening the case and claiming eye-appeal, and the Registry or defendant only later raising the exclusions by way of defence. Even the House of Lords,[29] therefore, has felt obliged to trudge through the

---

[27] Interestingly, the Court of Appeal of Turin in *Hella KG v. ARIC SNC*, January 18, 1993, see [1994] 7 E.I.P.R. 309, reached a similar but even further-reaching decision in declaring invalid design patents for head and tail lights, but the Court purported to look at the designs from the customer's viewpoint and found that he would perceive the vehicle as a whole and therefore no registration for any parts should be permitted.

[28] See 2.003 above.

[29] In the *Amp* case, see below.

subsection in strict sequence, solemnly considering (and differing about) the eye-appeal of a design for an electrical terminal ¾″ × ⅝″ × ¼″ buried inside a washing-machine, all the features of which they ultimately unanimously found to have been dictated solely by function and therefore not a "design" at all. Even Viscount Dilhorne, who did apply the exclusion first, went on to consider eye-appeal. Matters have been further confounded by the Privy Council in *Interlego AG v. Tyco Industries Inc.*,[30] who actually faced the problem head on but reached a result displeasing to many and one of whose consequences had to be corrected by the 1988 Act. All in all, it seems wise to take the usual course and stick to the order of key expressions in section 1.

The electrical terminal case was *Amp Inc. v. Utilux Pty Ltd*,[31] where the validity of the registered design, for a terminal used to join two wires together without welding, was challenged by the defendant in an infringement action. The case established the meaning of the exclusionary phrase "dictated solely" by function as described below (all features of the terminal were) but also contained observations on eye appeal. First, the eye-appealing features must be at least "visible" in the finished article (in this case the terminal, not the washing-machine) and more likely "noticeable", eye-catching or even "special, peculiar, distinctive, significant or striking". In *Stenor Ltd v. Whitesides (Chitheroe) Ltd*[32] it had been held at first instance, though deliberately left open on appeal, that a registered design had to be visible to the naked eye, but their Lordships in *Amp* did not mention this. Secondly, the eye which is appealed to and judges must be that of the customer, and not the court or (despite the occasional suggestion in the lower courts) a designer familiar with articles of the type in question. Thirdly, the design need not appeal in an artistic or aesthetic sense, though it may do so. Customers are drawn to one design rather than another for a variety of reasons. But if the appeal is solely on the basis of fitness for purpose, it will not be acceptable, because then it will not be judged "solely" by the eye (as required under the old section 1—this word has been deleted by the 1988 amendments, with what effect remains to be seen). Lord Reid gave the most sensible and commercial definition of eye appeal when he said he thought the policy of the Act was "to preserve to the owner of the design the commercial value resulting from customers preferring the appearance of articles which have the design to that of those which do not have it", and "Whatever the reason may be one article with a particular design may sell better than one without it: then it is profitable to use the design. And much thought, time and expense may have been incurred in finding a design which will increase sales". The only quibble with this is that a plaintiff may, but does not have to prove that his design sells better nor even, a registered design being a monopoly, that someone has thought it worth copying. Nor need he prove that it has cost him anything to design.

2.023

[30] [1988] R.P.C. 343.
[31] [1972] R.P.C. 103.
[32] (1946) 63 R.P.C. 81.

2.024   Since *Amp* there have been several cases which have illustrated the meaning of eye-appeal. *Ferrero's Design Application*[33] was about a chocolate egg having an inner layer in a different colour, the design consisting of the tonal contrast between the two layers. But this would only be seen when the egg was bitten or broken, and the Registry refused to accept the design because it was not visible until after the purchaser had bought it—and indeed begun to destroy it so that it was no longer a "finished article". Whitford J. disagreed. The design was at all times present in the finished article and there was nothing in *Amp* to require that it be visible at the point of sale.

2.025   *K. K. Kuwa Seikosha's Design Application*[34] was about a liquid-crystal display panel for a digital watch showing numerals (not forming part of the design) and symbols of a bell and a loudspeaker. It was rejected because the LCD would never show up in the panel (the "finished article") but only once it was connected to the watch circuitry and a battery installed. The panel would then have become part of another article altogether. Acceptance of this design would open the way to registering patterns written in invisible ink which only become visible when heated, or TV or radar screens which show a picture when connected to the picture signal circuitry. Falconer J. followed Whitford J. in *Ferrero* in holding that the design was immanent in the panel, even though not visible until after it was bought and connected up to do what it was intended to do. This does not answer the point about separate articles, or deal with the other interesting questions raised by the Registry, or the point that the precise nature of the display would vary from time to time, but is probably acceptable on a common sense basis. In both these cases, prospective customers were no doubt fully informed at point of sale or in promotional literature about what they would be getting. So they were in *Constable v. Clarkson*,[35] about registered designs for rubber moulds for making candles in the form of very lifelike fruit and vegetables. But the Court of Appeal, albeit on an appeal against refusal to grant an interlocutory injunction, where the merits are not much gone into, was persuaded that the moulds themselves had no eye appeal, and even though it might be inferred from their exteriors what their interiors would look like, these were functional—their function being to produce pear or tomato-shaped candles—and would be judged purely with this end in view.

2.026   *Lamson Industries Inc.'s Design*[36] was an interesting little case, turning on the meaning of "judged solely by the eye" in the context of a pattern design, where there is no statutory exclusion of features dictated solely by function. The subject-matter was computer printout paper on which the "staves" of fine lines, instead of being all one colour, were in alternating shades of green and orange. As well as looking attractive, this had the virtue of making the printout more legible and therefore allowing the staves to be printed closer

[33] [1978] R.P.C. 473.
[34] [1982] R.P.C. 166.
[35] [1980] F.S.R. 123.
[36] [1978] R.P.C. 1.

together, getting more material on one page and thus offsetting the higher price per page. Whitford J. held that this pattern was eye-appealing, and would readily be registrable for something like wallpaper, but could not be accepted for printout paper because the purchaser would choose that not for the pleasing pattern but only for reasons of economy. Given the 1988 deletion of the word "solely" in this context, the case might now be decided differently, particularly if suitable evidence were adduced to show that the attractiveness of the pattern, as well as its economic outcome, could influence buyers.

The *Lamson* conundrum of an attractive and eye-appealing "pattern" **2.027** which is also functional crops up in the field of graphic symbols such as "icons" used in computer programs, the little drawings on garment labels which tell you how to launder them, and road signs. All these are "patterns", some with a high artistic content, but their purpose is to be instantly and internationally recognisable as a means of conveying information. From the parochial point of view, they may be excluded from design registration under section 1(5) as "printed matter primarily of a literary or artistic character", as discussed below,[37] but they could also fall foul of *Lamson*, and there must be some doubt about the social desirability of any one person being allowed to monopolise them.[38] No objection was taken about the bell and loudspeaker symbols in *K. K. Kuwa Seikosha*—indeed it was only their presence which saved the design from failing for want of novelty once the eye-appeal point had been settled.

In *Kevi A/S v. Suspa-Verein U.K. Ltd*[39] Falconer J. said that the eye of every **2.028** customer in the distribution chain needed to be taken into account in assessing eye-appeal, so that a registered design for office furniture castors must be looked at successively or trifocally through the eyes of the furniture manufacturer, the shopkeeper selling the furniture and the ultimate purchaser, each of whom might notice different things about them. His Honour Judge Ford in a recent Patents County Court decision[40] about teardrop-shaped squash racquets reaffirmed that it is the customer/user's eye that counts, not that of a designer familiar with the engineering or manufacturing requirements, nor that of a tennis historian attracted by unconventional design features.

The Privy Council in *Interlego v. Tyco*[41] reached conclusions on the **2.029** meaning of eye appeal substantially in line with those set out above, but its findings on the features of a design to which the test was to be applied were less conventional, and will be dealt with later.[42]

---

[37] See 2.079 below.
[38] As will be seen in Chap. 6, the European Union's proposed Community-wide design would provide for them to be registered, and the accompanying Harmonisation Directive would require U.K. registered designs law to be amended accordingly.
[39] [1982] R.P.C. 173.
[40] *Prince Inc. v. Dunlop Slazenger International Ltd* SRIS/CC/29/94.
[41] [1988] R.P.C. 343.
[42] See 2.042 below.

Exclusions

"Method or principle of construction"

2.030   This is the first of the specific exclusions from the definition of "design", supposedly intended to prevent any monopolisation of manufacturing processes which should be protected, if at all, by a patent. There are a few cases under previous Acts containing similar wording, an early one being *Moody v. Tree.*[43] Here the design as registered was a picture of a basket, but it was supported by a claim to novelty in a pattern consisting of the osiers out of which the basket was made being woven in singly with all the butt ends outwards. This description could cover all sorts and shapes of baskets made in this way, not just the one in the representation, and it was held invalid accordingly. Another example was *Re Bayer's Design,*[44] which claimed novelty in a corset having gores or gussets cut horizontally and from front to back—again a principle of construction which could cover a variety of different appearances. Both these cases turned on the wording of the novelty claim filed with the design (which in those days more closely resembled a patent claim than do today's statements of novelty), which clearly covered more than the actual appearance of the particular article to which the design was applied. Nowadays a design for a paperweight made by fusing randomly-scattered coloured beads within a clear block might be refused on "method or principle of construction" grounds or, if allowed, would result in a virtually useless design because only an exact reproduction would infringe.

2.031   An attempt was made to argue that the hot water bottle ribs in *Cow & Co. Ltd v. Cannon Rubber Manufacturers Ltd*[45] represented a method of construction since they were there to distribute heat, but this was rejected, although the court observed that it might have been otherwise if the subject-matter of the design had been the grooved configuration of a mould used for applying the ribs. Possibly a modern example might have been an attempt by the first person to make a music centre by stacking the elements one above the other to claim a monopoly in this method of assembly. Pattern designs are not likely to be caught by the exclusion, even where the design is for something like a piece of fabric woven on a Jacquard loom, because modern statements of novelty tie down the claim to what is shown in the representation.

---

[43] (1892) 9 R.P.C. 233.
[44] (1907) 24 R.P.C. 65.
[45] [1959] R.P.C. 240, 347. See 2.005 above.

"Features of shape or configuration dictated solely by the function the article has to perform"

Method or principle of construction is not a common ground of challenge **2.032** nowadays, having been largely superseded by this second specific exclusion. Its limitation to features of shape or configuration is another reason why classifying a feature as configuration rather than pattern might at times be significant. *Amp v. Utilux*[46] is the leading case on the meaning of the exclusion, and it made a stir because it was believed to impose a new test for "dictated solely" which would dramatically reduce the registrability of designs for many utilitarian articles.

The predecessor phrase in earlier legislation had been "a mere mechanical **2.033** device", and it was obviously Luxmoore J.'s interpretation of this phrase in *Kestos Ltd v. Kempat Ltd*[47] as "a shape in which all the features are dictated solely by the function or functions which the article has to perform" which was imported almost verbatim into the 1949 Act, section 1(3) of which before amendment read:

> "In this Act the expression 'design' means features of shape, configuration, pattern or ornament applied to an article by any industrial process or means, being features which in the finished product appeal to and are judged solely by the eye, but does not include a method or principle of construction or features of shape or configuration which are dictated solely by the function which the article to be made in that shape or configuration has to perform."

Kestos was about a particular type of bra, and Luxmoore J. did not accept on the facts that all bras had to be made as shown in the design if they were to perform their function. In *Cow v. Cannon* the court rejected an argument that the hot water bottle ribs were solely dictated by the function of avoiding burning the user, on the ground that although they did this job, other arrangements of ribs, or indeed raised rubber rings or pimples, could have done it just as well. Both these formulations might suggest that the test was whether the arrangement under consideration was the only way in which the particular functional purpose could be achieved. If any other way could be envisaged, then the design was not dictated by function, and there was no need to fear granting a monopoly in it because other manufacturers would not be prevented from making something to do the same job. They would merely have to exercise a bit of ingenuity, and maybe forgo the advantage of using the proprietor's particularly effective design—an advantage properly to be preserved to him by a rational intellectual property system.

---

[46] [1972] R.P.C. 103.
[47] (1936) 53 R.P.C. 139.

2.034   But there were other pointers in the earlier cases to a different interpret-ation of "dictated solely" by function, notably in *Stenor v. Whitesides*.[48] Here the design was for a fuse to fit into a vulcanising machine to make it work. It was held that all its features were dictated by the job it had to do, it had none beyond those necessary for that purpose, and was therefore excluded under the "mere mechanical device" test as interpreted by Luxmoore J. in *Kestos*. However Lord Porter observed that "No doubt another shape of fuse and another type of machine could be invented to perform the same task. However, that may be, the only object of using the registered shape now under discussion is to perform the functional purpose of making the machine work." This clearly ruled out any totalitarian interpretation of "dictated", and it also incidentally illustrates the line which has usually been taken by U.K. courts that in a lock-and-key situation it does not matter which is designed first. This is now somewhat modified by the "must-match" exclusion, and by the "must-fit" exclusion which is the unregistered design right's version of "solely dictated by function".

2.035   In *Amp* the facts were that Hoover wanted an electrical terminal to be installed in a new model of washing-machine. Their requirements were very specific as to the type of device and the job they wanted it to do. There were space constraints and the terminal would need some special locking arrangements. Amp had nothing suitable in their catalogue, so they designed and made a new terminal to comply with Hoover's requirements, which was in due course approved by Hoover. The designer, the judge had found, "was not concerned at any time to devise some different appearance for the terminal or to do other than attempt to meet the practical requirements of the customer in the most efficient manner". Like other purchasers of electrical terminals, said Amp's chief engineer in evidence, Hoover did not buy "on appearance but on performance and delivery and price".

2.036   However, once the terminal had been made, the chief engineer thought it looked different from other types, and so a design registration was applied for and granted. The Court of Appeal had accepted on the evidence that differently-shaped terminals could have done the same job, and were persuaded that the design was not therefore "dictated solely" by function. But the House of Lords held that this was not the correct test: what mattered was the evidence that every single feature of the shape of the terminal shown in the design, as described in detail in the speech of Lord Pearson, was " 'dictated by' in the sense of being attributable to or caused or prompted by" the terminal's function of forming an electrical connection between other components. That was enough to bring it within the exclusion. Lord Morris of Borth-y-Gest conceded it was perfectly possible that a designer prompted mainly by functional considerations might add or apply some feature of shape supplementary to what was functionally required and so produce an eye-appealing feature which would make the design registrable by satisfying

[48] (1948) 65 R.P.C. 1.

the "positive" part of the test; but nothing that has not been included for the purpose of eye appeal can so satisfy it. Lord Morris offered no examples, but one might think of using more than the necessary amount of metal in making spot welds, so as to produce a visually-significant effect, or holding a wooden construction together with dowels having extended fluted ends, or indeed the pin described in 2.004 above with an unusually-large, unusually-shaped head.

Lord Reid, having said "If the shape is not there to appeal to the eye but solely to make the article work then this provision excludes it from the statutory protection", then appeared to perform a U-turn by saying that if a designer "who only thought of practical efficiency" in fact produced a design which did appeal to the eye, he would not be deprived of protection because that was not his object when he composed the design. This remark may have been made because Lord Reid's speech as a whole (with which Lord Donovan agreed) is put together on rather different lines from those of the other three, emphasising more strongly the place of the customer (to whose eye appeal must be made), and he felt the evidence had not fully explored this aspect. And when he referred to a design dictated solely by function (and he too expressly rejected the suggestion that this meant one which could not assume any other form, because he could not envisage a situation where this test could be satisfied) he spoke of one where the designer had added nothing to the prior art because every feature was functional.   2.037

Be that as it may, the majority held that, on the wording of the "solely dictated" exclusion, the designer's motivation is what counts. This is more convenient for applicants than having in every case to ask or guess at what customers would find eye-appealing, or to come up with alternative shapes to prove that the design is not "solely dictated" by function in the narrow sense—and thus no doubt to attract novelty objections from the Registry. At the application stage, the designer is likely to be around to give evidence of his motivation if called upon to do so. It may be more difficult where validity is challenged in a later infringement action, and inferring the designer's motivation from the likely realities of the situation in the absence of evidence from him may lead to false results. In *Gardex Ltd v. Sorata Ltd*[49] the designer convinced the judge that in designing the underside of a plastic shower tray he really did give some attention to eye-appeal (using, in doing so, arguments more apt to meet the narrower "functional" objection of "no other alternative shape"), and evidence from the defendants that the plumbers who bought it did not give a toss what the underside of a shower tray looked like did not displace the designer's evidence.[50]   2.038

But the convenience of the *Amp* test does not mean that it is right, or that their Lordships might not have done better to follow the suggestions in earlier   2.039

---

[49] [1986] R.P.C. 623.
[50] In *Valeo Vision S.A. v. Flexible Lamps Ltd* [1995] R.P.C. 205, Aldous J. seems to have applied the unreconstructed "dictated solely by function" test of whether the functional purpose *could*

cases such as *Kestos v. Kempat* and *Cow v. Cannon*[51] of whether the particular functional purpose *could* be achieved by alternative means. This is the view taken of similarly-worded exclusions in many European design protection systems,[52] although it can be difficult to find concrete examples when the question is considered *in vacuo*. Keys to fit particular locks are often cited, but burglars and security guards might find this example less than persuasive. Concorde's wings used to be invoked as an example of optimum shape, but this disregards the engineering reality that once you have found a shape that does the job you want done you will not bother to look further, though if you did so you might find something even better. The practical question in each particular case should not be "Could the proprietor have made the article in a different shape which would still have worked?" nor "Was it only functional reasons which prompted the proprietor to make the article in this shape?", but "Could a competitor make it in a different shape which would still work—is he prevented from competing at all in articles of this type, in which case no registration should in the public interest be allowed, or is he merely put to some extra trouble by the registration?" It is the competitor's design freedom which matters, not the proprietor's—but of course when considering registrability of the design the activities of competitors, except in the form of prior art, are not accessible for consideration. This may be an argument against a pre-grant registrability and novelty examination rather than a mere deposit system for registered designs, particularly when there is no provision for pre-grant opposition. In practice, a U.K. registered design may be no more secure against a later finding of invalidity than a design which is merely deposited. The alternative shape test may be resolved by evidence under the pressure of an infringement action, including evidence of what other competitors have actually done given the existence of the proprietor's registration. Also by then, evidence may be available of whether customers actually have had their eyes appealed to by the proprietor's design and have preferred it to others'. If they have, and if competitors have not been unduly inconvenienced, why should the proprietor not have the benefit of this (as Lord Reid suggested), simply because the designer was not motivated consciously to impart eye-appeal?[53]

Interlego v. Tyco

2.040 Commentators feared that *Amp* would markedly reduce the number of designs capable of registration, but given the type of designs which still get registered, it is not clear that it has done so. The case was probably most

---

have been achieved by different shapes—he observed that other shapes could have been used and had been used by others.
[51] (1936) 53 R.P.C. 139 and [1959] R.P.C. 240, 347; see 2.033 above.
[52] See *e.g.* Fellner, *The Future of Legal Protection for Industrial Design*, ESC Publishing Ltd, 1985, Chap. 6, *passim*.
[53] When the Community Design Regulation and Directive come into force, the test for the equivalent exclusion, with which the 1949 Act will have to comply, is likely to be that of alternative shapes rather than designer's intention—see Chap. 6 below.

commonly cited in copyright actions where defendants would argue that the articles concerned could have been the subject of registered designs and thus that the period of enforceable copyright was limited to 15 years from first marketing,[54] while plaintiffs sought strenuously to show that the articles were so purely functional that their designs could never have been (and if they actually had been, should not have been) registered, so that they would enjoy the full life + 50 years copyright term. One such case (the precise provisions involved were slightly different but the principles were the same) was *Interlego v. Tyco*[55] which came to the Privy Council from Hong Kong. The defendants were selling competing bricks compatible with and copied from the Lego system, and the plaintiffs sought to stop this by relying on copyright in their production drawings; but under the Copyright Act 1956 as extended to Hong Kong in 1972, there would be no copyright in these drawings if the subject-matter constituted designs capable of registration under the 1949 Act. Awkwardly, the plaintiffs had actually had U.K. registered designs for these bricks, but if they should show these had been invalidly registered, they would be free to rely on copyright. They accordingly argued that all the features of the brick designs were solely dictated by their function of interlocking, and also that they were not novel at the date of application.

Their Lordships refused on the evidence to find that the shape of all the **2.041** features of the bricks was solely dictated by function. In overcoming the Registry's initial reluctance to accept the designs for registration because of the functionality objection, Lego had stressed their intention of making "a good-looking brick", and that the knobs and tubes which admittedly served the function of interlocking had nonetheless been designed with appearance as well as function in mind—indeed the design had been changed at one time purely to make it look nicer. On this finding alone, the designs would have been registrable under the *Amp* test, with particular reference to the views of Lord Morris,[56] provided they did have eye-appeal to the customer. As to this, even without the evidence of the designer's intention, which was held to be relevant though not conclusive, it was difficult to believe that anything intended for use as a toy, even a "functional" toy like a Lego brick, would not have eye-appeal.

The Privy Council was, however, also concerned to decide which features **2.042** actually constituted the design to which the eye-appeal test had to be applied. It held that there were three possible interpretations of section 1(3) of the unamended 1949 Act[57]:

(a) that all that is registrable or is to be considered on an application for registration is that part of the shape or configuration which has eye-appeal, any purely functional feature being excluded from registration;

---

[54] See 1.017 above.
[55] [1988] R.P.C. 343.
[56] See 2.036 above.
[57] See 2.033 above.

(b) that any design which includes any feature dictated solely by function is to be excluded from registration; or

(c) that a design which, *ex hypothesi*, has eye-appeal will be excluded from registration only if every feature of it is one which is dictated solely by function.

Interpretation (b) is manifestly wrong, and was correctly dismissed. It is not features, but designs as defined, which are registrable. Interpretation (a) is closest to what the definition of "design" seems to require, although it would be more accurately formulated as "all that makes the design of an article registrable" rather than "all that is registrable". Almost any article in common use is going to contain some conventional features, but as will be seen, this does not preclude registration of its design so long as there are some features which are not conventional or the *arrangement* of features, all of which are in themselves conventional, is novel. It is just that in assessing infringement, at least, and probably novelty, the merely conventional features, or those caught by one of the specific exclusions, are disregarded—or that was the procedure normally followed before *Interlego*.[58] The same, it is submitted, should apply when considering registrability and eye-appeal, despite the mental contortions this entails, as pointed out in 2.024 above.

2.043   However, their Lordships dismissed this interpretation as making very little sense, since it is the design of the article as a whole (they said) in which there will be a commercial monopoly.[59] The correct way to approach section 1(3) was by way of interpretation (c). A design must have eye-appeal: unless it does, there is nothing for the exclusions to bite on. "There can be no purpose in an exclusion that applies only to a subject-matter already excluded. To give the exclusion any operation one has to postulate at least a situation in which the need for the exclusion arises. Thus the necessary condition for the exclusion to operate at all is the existence of a shape which has eye-appeal but which, because of features falling within the latter part of the definition, is nevertheless not to be treated as a design." Arguing in this way, they were able to accommodate Lord Reid's awkward deviation in *Amp* in favour of the fortuitously eye-appealing designer by suggesting his Lordship must have had in mind as saving a design some extra feature, even unintended, which imparted eye-appeal and could not be nipped off by the exclusion.

---

[58] See *Sommer Allibert S.A. v. Flair Plastics Ltd* [1987] R.P.C. 599 at 622.

[59] They also said no-one had contended for interpretation (a). This is hardly surprising, since it was in neither party's interest to do so. Tyco's counsel was afraid of a finding, as at first instance, that *every* feature was functional and therefore Lego could rely on copyright, when they would win. He therefore wanted to rely on Lord Reid's maverick view in *Amp*—see 2.037 above—that even a design in which every feature was dictated solely by function could be registrable if it had even accidental eye-appeal. Lego's counsel was afraid of his client's evidence of deliberate eye-appeal and wanted to show that if the features of shape were dictated solely by function, even deliberate eye-appeal would not save the design. This is one of the casualties of judge-made law: the arguments the judge considers may be only those the parties choose to put to him.

There may be some legalistic force in the contention that the overall design **2.044** needs eye-appeal in order for the exclusion to have something to bite on, but it has its practical inconveniences. Time may be wasted and additional costs incurred by lengthy arguments about eye-appeal. Parties may feel obliged to adduce evidence from customers (to whose eye the appeal must, as everyone agrees, be made), and there must be minute inquiry to ensure that the appeal is not the inadmissible one of pure fitness for purpose. What actually prompted the designer, function or appearance (the majority *Amp* test), may be a rough-and-ready guide, and open to abuse one way or the other by a well-briefed designer. But at least it may save time and expense.

Perhaps more tiresome is the Privy Council's assertion that it is the design **2.045** of the article as a whole in which there is a commercial monopoly. This upset the previous practice of disregarding excluded features in considering novelty and infringement. The 1988 Act felt it necessary specifically to exclude, by adding a new subsection (6) to section 7 of the 1949 Act, both "must-match" and "dictated-solely-by-function" features from consideration in infringe-ment actions, describing them as "feature[s] ... left out of account in determing whether the design is registrable". This is clearly intended to override the Privy Council's interpretation, both as to infringement and registrability. The precise wording of old section 1(3) was also altered in transposing it into section 1(1), "... does not include ... features of shape or configuration which are dictated solely by the function which the article to be made in that shape or configuration has to perform" being replaced by "... does not include ... features of shape or configuration of an article which ... are dictated solely by the function which the article has to perform". The new formulation appears to shift the emphasis from the shape or configuration of the article as a whole to the shape or configuration of the particular features to be excluded.

But these changes affect only designs applied for on or after August 1, **2.046** 1989, and as already observed, it is the old tests of both validity and infringement which still have to be applied to designs granted on pre-August 1, 1989 applications. In *Prince Manufacturing Inc. v. Dunlop Slazenger International Ltd*[60] the question was raised whether purely functional features were to be taken into account in assessing novelty and infringement and the plaintiffs argued that *Sommer Allibert* required them to be ignored on infringement, *Interlego* left the question open on novelty, and it would be inconsistent to treat them differently for these two purposes. Happily for the Patents Country Court, in that case it was able to find that no features were excluded by the functionality test.

Lego had further contended that quite apart from section 1(3) its registered **2.047** designs had been invalid for want of novelty because of earlier bricks. The Privy Council rejected this argument on legislative-historical grounds not

---

[60] SRIS/CC/29/94. Cf. *Valeo v. Flexible*, n. 50 above at 215, 11.16–18.

dealt with in detail because they will shortly be of historical interest only.[61] The result is that designs "capable of registration" under the 1956 Act means only designs so capable by virtue of complying with the definition of "design" in section 1(3). They will not be invalid because not novel as required by section 1(2).

The new "must-match" exclusion

2.048   The *British Leyland*[62] decision provided a defence to what would otherwise be copyright infringement where wholly functional spare parts for mass-produced articles like cars are concerned, in the interests of securing competition in the aftermarket. But the House of Lords expressly excluded cases where a plaintiff could rely on a registered design. This left unsolved the "anti-competitive" aspects of registered designs for parts having some "appearance" content under the *Amp* test, such as vehicle body panels, for which registrations were freely granted, although the problems they raised were the same. The U.K. Monopolies and Mergers Commission[63] had already criticised the Ford Motor Company's refusal to license competitors to produce replacement body panels, and pressure was growing from consumer and insurance lobbies to ensure free availability of competing spares.

2.049   The 1986 White Paper[64] therefore proposed to limit protection for all spare parts, functional or having some "aesthetic" content, to the new "unregistered design right", giving only ten years protection, with licences of right available for a royalty after five years. (This was *not* the scheme actually implemented.[65]) To avoid protection for "aesthetic" spares by the back door of registered design protection, the White Paper proposed amending the 1949 Act to deny registration to the design of any article where "the article is an integral or working part of a further article, unless the appearances of the two articles are substantially independent". In other words to cases "where there is no absolute necessity for a particular design to be used".[66]

2.050   The result as enacted was section 1(1)(b)(ii) of the amended 1949 Act, which excludes from the definition of "design".

---

[61] See [1988] R.P.C. 343 at 359–364. They depend on the link under the 1911 and 1956 Acts between registrability and copyright, not perpetuated in the 1988 Act. This link may still be significant in terms of the *copyright* in pre-August 1, 1989 designs whose date of expiry will vary depending on whether they were unregistrable, in which case their copyright will, unless the full normal term runs out earlier, expire on July 31, 1999, or registrable, in which case it may expire earlier than that date, on that date, or on some date between August 1, 1999 and July 31, 2004. See further Chap. 3 below.
[62] [1986] A.C. 577. See 1.025 above and 2.181 below.
[63] Cmnd. 9437, HMSO London, 1985. See 1.025 above.
[64] Intellectual Property and Innovation, Cmnd. 9712. See 1.026 above.
[65] See 2.235 below.
[66] Para. 3.037.

"features of shape or configuration of an article which . . . are dependent upon the appearance of another article of which the article is intended by the author of the design to form an integral part."

This wording is identical to that used for the similar exclusion from unregistered design right under section 213(3)(b)(ii) of the 1988 Act (except that there the word "designer" replaces "author of the design"), and it was in the unregistered design right context that the Parliamentary debates on the Bill took place. Lord Beaverbrook said the exception was intended to allow copying where "compelled by design constraints",[67] and made it absolutely plain that the government had body panels in mind when he denied the oft-repeated complaint that the exception was "a pirates' charter" and said "The fact of the matter is that in this kind of case competitors have absolutely no choice but to copy the entire article. Where the circumstances compel copying, we believe that the need for competition in the aftermarket must prevail."

He later[68] stressed that the test of the designer's intention is to be applied as at the stage when the "other article" upon whose appearance the article in question is "dependent" is being designed, and that the exclusion was not to apply where an independently-designed article is subsequently used by someone else with other identical articles as part of a larger article. As an example, he cited a free-standing strut,[69] later copied and assembled with others to form a grille. The later grille designer could not invoke "must-match" against an accusation of copying the strut, because the designer of the strut did not intend it to be an integral part of a grille, but an article in itself. The reference to the designer's intention was brought at Report stage into the exclusion clause as originally drafted in order to clarify this. **2.051**

A further introduction was the reference to the article in question being an "integral" part of "another article". This was to soothe the fears of people who commonly obtain "set" registrations[70] by preventing would-be providers of replacement teapot lids, or knives from a matching canteen of cutlery, raising "must-match" to legitimise their activities.[71] It may be doubted whether this effect has been achieved. Commercially and functionally, it is obvious that a teapot lid is, and is intended by its designer to be, an integral part of the teapot. It is "essential to the whole", to quote one dictionary definition. To save the lid from the exclusion, it is necessary to read into "integral" some suggestion that the part must in normal use be physically secured to the whole. This would save the cutlery maker as well, but the **2.052**

---

[67] *Hansard*, Vol. 491, col. 1111.
[68] Vol. 494, col. 699.
[69] For registered design purposes it would have to be a strut with some "aesthetic" content.
[70] See 2.014 above.
[71] The registration would have to be for a shape or configuration design, or "must-match" will not apply. The exception need not trouble the proprietor of a design for the viper's bugloss painted on the teapot and lid or the radishes painted on the salad servers' handles.

question in his case may be something of a red herring, because a "set" registration still operates as a registration for each individual article (section 44(2)), so each knife would be a separate "article", not a part of another article, the canteen. The teapot likewise is not part of the tea-service in this sense. But is the relevant article in the case of a teapot the teapot + lid, or would the teapot and lid be separate articles? They are certainly not usually "made and sold separately" except in the aftermarket for replacement teapot lids, so it cannot be argued that the lid would be regarded as having its own registration. Either way it seems to lose out under registered designs law, though the "made and sold separately" requirement does not apply to unregistered design right, where a part of an article may be a protectable "design" in its own right.

2.053   Thanks to Lord Beaverbrook, we know what the government had in mind for "must-match", but before we can apply this knowledge we must first show that the exclusion as it appears in the Act is ambiguous, obscure or absurd.[72] Is it? In considering this, it is probably simplest to conduct the discussion in terms of motor vehicles, since that is where the excitement has arisen, and we have the benefit of a decided case.[73] The first and third "articles" referred to in the exclusion clearly mean the article for which design registration is sought. Equally, in the context of a definition of the "design" sought to be registered, the "author" (or, for unregistered design right, the "designer") must be the author of the design for *this* article. He may, but will by no means necessarily, also be the designer of the "other article" of which he "intended" the relevant article to form an integral part. If the article in question is a body panel and the other article is a vehicle body, he probably will be; but if the article in question is a steering-wheel or a wing mirror or a wheel or wheel cover ("hubcap" to use old-fashioned terminology), he quite likely will not. His intention must then depend on whether his mission was simply to design a wheel or whatever for use on any car, when he would not have the necessary intention for his work to be caught by the exclusion, or to design a wheel specifically for use on a new model—when, subject to the meaning of "integral part", he would. It should be re-emphasised that the intention of the designer of the "other article" is *not* relevant to the exclusion, even though he is the one with the overall conception of what that article should look like.[74] Nor is the intention of the designer of a competing spare part relevant, although he knows best of all what "must-match" from the consumer's point of view. Perhaps if he is merely slavishly copying to meet his market, he is not meant to be dignified with the title of "designer" at all, even though he may invest a good deal of effort and skill in producing the article he slavishly copies—making his own

---

[72] See *Pepper v. Hart* [1993] A.C. 593 permitting recourse to clear ministerial statements in such cases—1.029 above.
[73] *Ford/Fiat* [1993] R.P.C. 399 and [1994] R.P.C. 545.
[74] In this instance, it looks as if the courts are meant to recognise that locks generally come before keys—see 2.034 above—even though the locksmith's intention is irrelevant.

manufacturing drawing, ascertaining tolerances, testing for safety and the like.

Does the "appearance" of the other article comprehend all its visible features, functional as well as aesthetic? In the *Ford* case, one of the parts whose design was sought to be registered was a bonnet. On one side of the centre line, this required a raised portion to accommodate the overhead rocker box used in some high-performance models. To this extent the raised portion was an outward and visible sign of an inward and functional requirement, and as such would not form part of the registered "design" at all[75]—although it seems that there was some design freedom in selecting the exact shape of the raised portion. But in order to preserve the visual symmetry of the bonnet's appearance a matching raised portion was moulded on the opposite side of the centre line, even though there was no functional need for it to be there. These twin protruberances, known as "power domes", are apparently prized by those motorists who care about such things as indicating that they are able to master a high-performance vehicle.[76] How should such features be treated?

2.054

This links in with another query based on the meaning of "dependent". In deciding whether a particular feature of shape or configuration of the article in question is "dependent" upon the appearance of the other article, must the comparison be made with the other article with the article in question fitted to it, or with the other article excluded? It will be appreciated that this is highly significant if the article in question has some features which it shares with other parts, such as a moulding extending all along the side of the vehicle, where clearly there must be matching and is "dependency" (this would also be the case with the outline of a panel, which enables it to mate with its neighbours, although this might be regarded as securing a fit and therefore functional), but others which are specific to it and not shared with any other parts, such as the power domes on the Ford bonnet. This became known in the *Ford* litigation as the "$n - 1$" question: where the other article has n parts, do you make the comparison with n, or with $n - 1$? If the former, you are effectively comparing, *e.g.* the bonnet with *itself* as fitted, and arguably regarding it therefore as "dependent" on its own appearance, not that of the rest of the "other article", except where there are shared features. This argument was extended to "$n - 2$" (where the doors of a two-door car are to be compared) and "$n - 4$" in the case of wheels. These questions are crucial, because if a body panel has any novel and eye-appealing features which can escape the depredations of functionality and must-match, they can form the subject-matter of a registered design (or, if not commonplace,[77] unregistered

2.055

---

[75] And could therefore freely be copied, because under the new infringement test it would have to be excluded from consideration under section 7(6), although under the old test as apparently imposed by *Interlego v. Tyco* on designs applied for before August 1, 1989, it might have to be taken into account if it had eye-appeal.

[76] Does this constitute acceptable eye-appeal, or only indicate fitness for purpose?

[77] See 2.256 below.

design right can subsist in them) which can give the motor manufacturer a competitive edge over suppliers of competing spares who can copy some but not all of the deliberate styling features.[78, 79]

2.056　　Is "dependency" in any case a subjective or an objective test, and if the former, whose subjectivity is to be regarded? Although it might be thought the designer's intention would be relevant, the exclusion does not invoke it in this context, but only in determining whether the article in question is meant to form an integral part of the other article. In commercial reality, it is the customer's view that counts: if he will only buy a spare panel where it looks exactly like the original, its design is indeed dependent on the appearance of the car as a whole.

2.057　　Does "dependent" on appearance mean wholly dependent, or will partial dependence be enough—and again, who is to judge? The integral part test does not help. Something may be intended by its designer to form an integral part of something else in the sense of being an essential part of it, even where appearance did not matter to the designer of either article. An obvious, if fanciful, example would be an aircraft's wing. Clearly its designer intended it to form an integral part of the aircraft, at least in use, and if a visual comparison is made it "must-match" at least the other wing, unless "$n - 2$" is adopted, in the sense that a carrier (and its passengers) would not much fancy an aircraft with non-matching wings, even if assured they were aerodynamically equivalent. But it is unrealistic to say that the shape of the wings is "dependent" on the *appearance* of the whole aircraft, at least if the test is wholly rather than partly dependent, whatever carriers may feel on behalf of their passengers.

Ford/Fiat

2.058　　With so many fascinating questions unanswered, it was felt that "must-match" was a prime candidate for judicial consideration, with liberal recourse to statements of government intention under *Pepper v. Hart*. This wish was partly gratified by a series of registered design applications filed by the Ford Motor Company and Iveco Fiat for a selection of "articles" chosen as test cases—body panels, bumpers, spoilers, grilles, seats, instrument panels, steering wheels, lamps, wing mirrors, wheels and wheel covers. By

---

[78] It must always be remembered that two-dimensional "pattern" features are not caught by "must-match" though they might perhaps be on the *Lamson* test—2.027 above—if they have a functional content. Thus "go-faster" stripes affixed by transfer all along the sides might be protected (since they do not make the car go faster). Likewise if a habit caught on among manufacturers of affixing transfers to the boot lid designed to indicate the target market for a vehicle and tell the world something about the driver—lager lout, executive woman, bishop or one of Her Majesty's counsel.

[79] The teapot designer is also going to be concerned with how the comparison is to be made, since while his lid must fit round the edges into the space left for it in the top of the pot, it may not, unless the knob echoes the shape of the handle, have other relevantly "dependent" features on an "$n - 1$" construction.

each application, registration was initially sought for the shape and configuration of the article. The evidence showed that even though in most cases the designers had, apart from attachment points and fitting constraints, had considerable design freedom, all the articles were designed for particular vehicles, or at least for a particular range of vehicles.

The Registry's view,[80] maintained following an oral hearing in *Fiat* and written representations in *Ford*, was that all the designs were excluded under section 1(1)(b)(ii). In each case their designer intended them to form an integral part of "another article", namely the particular vehicle or one of a particular range of vehicles. "Integral" did not mean, as had been argued, *essential* to the completeness of the other article in any specially intimate sense—an integrated part of the body contour, as opposed to "bolt-on" accessories like steering wheels, spoilers or mirrors. It simply served to exclude "parts not essential to the integrity or 'completeness' of another article" such as, in the case of a motor vehicle, a tool kit or a jack. Having regard to the section 44(1) definition of "article", the "$n - 1$" (or any other figure) approach was wrong, because the comparison had to be made with the other article as an article of manufacture in its (finished) form as made and sold, hence with the article in question fitted to it, and thus the dependency criterion was satisfied because the appearance of the spare part was indeed being compared with its appearance in its original incarnation. Nor did the "must-match" context require a different meaning to be given to "article" (as permitted by the introductory words to section 44). The superintending examiner did not appear to be impressed by Ford's argument that the dependency criterion could not reasonably be interpreted by having regard only to the preference of consumers for replacement panels having an identical appearance to the originals. And he did not accept[81] that the appearance of certain features of lamp lenses, wheels and wheel covers could be saved by being claimed as features of pattern and ornament rather than configuration where these were produced by moulding the material of which the articles were made. Running through the applications on the assumption that he was wrong on these points, he nonetheless found on the evidence that the features saved from "must-match" were mostly condemned either under the functionality exclusion or for lack of novelty. The one objection he did not take, however, and the one which was solely relied on by the House of Lords in rejecting the body panel applications,[82] was that the parts were not made and sold separately.

2.059

Between the *Fiat* and *Ford* decisions, *Pepper v. Hart* was decided, so the superintending examiner availed himself of the new freedom to peek at what the government had said. Not surprisingly, on the basis both of the observations of Lord Beaverbrook quoted above and others to the same effect

2.060

[80] [1993] R.P.C. 399.
[81] Following Slade L.J. in *Sommer Allibert v. Flair Plastics* [1987] R.P.C. 599—see 2.006 above.
[82] [1995] R.P.C. 167 see 2.019 above.

by Lord Young of Graffham on introducing the Bill and Mr John Butcher, the Minister of State, on second reading in the Commons,[83] he felt reinforced in his views.

2.061   On appeal to the Registered Designs Appeal Tribunal, the Registry did take the "not made and sold separately" objection, which succeeded. But the Deputy Judge, Julian Jeffs Q.C., also dealt with "must-match". He looked to "practical commonsense" and commercial reality. Although "visible" on the vehicle as sold (the "other article"), accessories like seats, wheels, wheel covers, steering wheels and wing mirrors are not caught by "must-match" because they can be fitted to other vehicles as well, and alternatives can be and indeed are fitted to the original vehicle, for a sportier appearance, greater comfort or a variety of other reasons. At most, the owner of that vehicle may wish the accessory to "blend in the general style of the vehicle". Such items are not "dependent upon the appearance" of that vehicle. Where they come in pairs or sets, like wing mirrors and wheels, they are only dependent on each other's appearance. Moreover, the designer of the original vehicle has "an open choice" of details like this. Many of these items would have functional parts like fixing points which would be excluded from any design registration; but they are all articles which are made and sold separately. These designs were remitted to the Registry for further consideration, as was one for a lamp. Although this fitted into a specific space on the original vehicle, it could be mounted on a different one, and although not so clearcut as the other accessory designs, there was enough doubt for the applicant to be given the benefit of it.

2.062   The body panels, along with instrument panels, grilles and bumpers, were a different matter. The Deputy Judge rejected the "$n - 1$" construction. Their designers had meant them to form integral (in the sense of "essential") parts of the vehicles with which the comparison was to be made, and this meant those vehicles with the parts in place. "The designer of the door did not intend it to form an integral part of a vehicle with a door missing. From its first conception, the door was intended to form an integral part of a complete vehicle". And even where pairs of articles like doors differ slightly from each other, "the general shape and configuration of one door is decided by the other. It must match", and "$n - 2$" was even more artificial than "$n - 1$". Moreover "as a matter of practical commonsense, if a door panel is to be replaced, it must be replaced by one which, for all practical purposes, is the same as the original". On this approach, the Deputy Judge was not prepared to decide fine details about power domes whose shape might not be dictated solely by function. They were out under "must-match".

2.063   The Deputy Judge agreed that the subsection was "ambiguous and obscure" and looked at *Hansard*, which he too found to fortify his view, although he lamented that many of the ministerial statements to which he was referred were as obscure as the Act.

[83] *Hansard*, November 12, 1987, col. 1479 and April 28, 1988, col. 597.

On judicial review, the Divisional Court agreed with the Tribunal's **2.064** decision. They were unimpressed by the argument that if the decision on "made and sold separately" was right, and all "integral" spare parts were excluded by it, there was nothing left for "must-match" to bite on. They did not accept that the degree of freedom left to the designer of the original part was significant; in any case, the person with design freedom was the designer of the vehicle. What mattered was the freedom of the designer of the competing spare part, and he did not have any because a part which did not look exactly like the original would be unsaleable. The Court felt able to reach these conclusions without recourse to the Parliamentary materials, although they looked at them *de bene esse* and found them insufficiently clear to be helpful.

On these findings, "must-match" is a wide exclusion, once it has been **2.065** established that a part is an "essential", rather than just a "visible" part of the whole on a commonsense test, the commonsense being that of the court. The same test is likely to decide the "made and sold separately" point. Where both these tests are decided against the designer of the original part, his design freedom, if any, seems irrelevant. If anyone's design freedom matters (according to the Divisional Court) it is that of the competing spares designer. This is not because the Act provides for it to be taken into account—it does not—but because his freedom is market-limited by the demand of his customer for an identical replacement part. The question of dependency is therefore left to the customer, whenever the other conditions are fulfilled. The "dictated solely by function" test need not arise if "must-match" is satisfied. The only exception is pattern or ornament features which are not caught by "must-match" at all, so the customer must do without them. Conceivably the original manufacturer might succeed in claiming a three-dimensional "configuration" design as pattern or ornament—one such, for a lamp lens, was remitted to the Registry for further consideration.[84]

The House of Lords disappointingly refused to consider "must-match". **2.066** The Registry had raised a new argument for the first time, namely whether it should have asked itself, in a case such as the bonnet with power domes, not whether the bonnet as a whole had to match the vehicle, but whether particular design features like the power domes had to match the correspond-

---

[84] See *Valeo Vision S.A. v. Flexible Lamps Ltd* [1995] R.P.C. 205 for a post-Divisional Court consideration of "must-match", also in relation to vehicle lamps. The registered designs were applied for between January 12, 1988 and July 31, 1989, and were therefore subject to "must-match" under transitional provisions in section 266 of the 1988 Act, the effect being that although the registrations would not be invalidated by this exclusion the designs would immediately be subject to licences of right and would expire on July 31, 1999. They were in fact held invalid on other grounds, but the court said that only the outside perimeter had to match the base, which was the only "other article" with which comparison could be made, and that *all* features of an article had to "match" before the exclusion could operate, an application of the *Interlego* principle. Under the new argument sought to be raised by the Registry before the House of Lords in *Ford/Fiat*—see 2.066—this decision might have been overturned, with consideration being given to individual design features, not the design as a whole. The case also dealt with the pattern/configuration problem in relation to lamp lenses, see 2.007 above.

ing ones. This might well have produced a different outcome, but would have involved considering whether the *Interlego* decision on the meaning of "design" (see 2.042 above) was wrong, and the evidence and findings of fact on which their Lordships would have had to operate were not fully adequate to do this, nor were there any expressions of opinion by the lower courts on which they could pronounce. In any case, the decision on "made and sold separately" would seem to have made the question academic. To attempt to provide a comprehensive disquisition (or, as Lord Mustill put it, to go on "a ramble through the statute, with a pause for your Lordships to express an opinion on every point of interest") would involve the decision of largely abstract questions, which was not their Lordships' function.

2.067   *Ford/Fiat* probably applied the law much as the government intended. It is idle to pretend that people do not want their replacement body panels to match the original in every particular, so if a free aftermarket is to have any reality, "must-match" must have a wide meaning and the customer must be the judge. It remains to be seen what other parts may be caught by it, though the inclusion of instrument control panels is worth noting. The CBI was quoted during Parliamentary debates as suggesting panels for kitchen furniture, wrought-iron panels for fencing, garage doors, casings and storage containers as candidates. Teapot lids do seem rather exposed. Much depends on whether there is, or should be, a viable aftermarket: where there is not, no one is going to be wanting to compete. Computers are likely to become technologically obsolete long before bits of their casings need replacing—and if they do get dented, they are not really "vanity" items like cars. It is understood that the Designs Registry is not taking many "must-match" objections, having been concentrating all its energy in this area on *Ford/Fiat*.

"Who-cares-what-it-looks-like?"

2.068   That is apparently not the case with the second new provision introduced into registered designs law by the 1988 Act, where the Registry is regularly raising objections. Unlike the earlier exclusions discussed, which take certain features out of the definition of "design", section 1(3) excludes designs for particular types of *article* from registration altogether, unless they are proved at the outset to have, or be likely to have, eye-appeal.

2.069   The Whitford Committee[85] in 1977 had recommended scrapping the registered designs system and protecting industrial designs by copyright, but split on whether this should apply to all or only some designs. A minority would not have protected "shapes of three-dimensional articles where the appearance of the article does not influence the purchaser, who buys the article only in the expectation that it will do the job for which it is intended."[86] Examples offered were propellers, aerofoils and spare parts for cars and other

[85] Copyright and Designs Law, Cmnd. 6732, HMSO, London, 1977—see 1.020 above.
[86] Para. 168.

machinery to which no decorative additions have been made. This class of designs (termed Category B) was said to correspond closely with the category of designs excluded under *Amp v. Utilux*—although the *Amp* test looks only at the designer's intention, while the Whitford test must be customer-led.

Nothing was done to implement the Whitford proposals, but its test was resurrected in the White Paper[87] as an avowed means, with "must-match", of preventing spare parts from securing design registration. The subsection as drafted provides that a design shall not be registered in respect of an article if the appearance of the article is not "material". This means that aesthetic considerations are not normally taken into account to a material extent by acquirers or users of such articles, and would not be so taken into account if the design were to be applied to the particular article in respect of which registration is sought. **2.070**

At Report stage of the Bill in the House of Lords, Lord Beaverbrook explained[88] the government's concerns in putting forward the clause, which go wider than those mentioned in the White Paper. It was felt that the Registered Designs Act was appropriate "only for articles which are chosen for their aesthetic appearance. That is to say, the Act applies only to articles whose aesthetic appearance matters—in other words, whose aesthetic appearance is taken into account to a material extent". The outward aesthetic appearance of articles like telephones and tractors probably did matter to potential purchasers, so here aesthetic considerations would be taken into account to a material extent, and would permit registration. "Indeed, wherever it could be said that aesthetic appearance matters" registration would not be excluded. "The only things which would definitely be excluded are things like structural girders and ordinary nails, screws and other essentially functional items where it *could not be shown*[89] that the aesthetic appearance matters." A little further on, he said that the words "to a material extent" in the clause were necessary because, without them, "it would be possible to argue that the shape of part of a wholly functional article such as an exhaust pipe or carburettor was aesthetically pleasing to someone ... What is needed is evidence that users would generally be influenced by the eye appeal of design features when acquiring that kind of article." These remarks were all made in the context of maintaining a distinction between the registered designs system, for articles with genuine eye appeal, and unregistered design right, which "embraces designs which are purely functional". **2.071**

It is scarcely to be recommended that anyone should look to this ministerial statement for clear guidance as to what section 1(3) means, because it may be taken to introduce into what could be a perfectly intelligible and sensible test, albeit one not always easy to apply, and open to manipulation, an additional and unnecessary requirement. **2.072**

---

[87] Cmnd. 9712, para. 3.37.
[88] March 1, 1988, col. 149.
[89] Emphasis added.

2.073   In this writer's view, what section 1(3) means is that there are many articles whose appearance does not normally influence purchasers when making their selection, because they are bought only to do a job. Designs for these will no longer normally be registrable. The Registry will use its own commonsense, and no doubt evolve guidelines in deciding what kinds of articles might be concerned. However, if in any particular case an applicant can show that if *his* design were to be applied to such an article, it *would* have a competitive edge because it would look nicer, then he should be able to get a registration. But he will have to produce some evidence to the Registry at an early stage to demonstrate this, and that evidence, under section 22(1)(b), will be open to public inspection once the design is registered, so that competitors who wish to challenge the registration will have some guidance as to what sort of evidence they themselves should provide.

2.074   This interpretation does not resolve all the infelicities of the subsection. It speaks of a "design", so *ex hypothesi* there must under section 1(1) be eye-appeal, unless this is a situation in which "the context otherwise requires", which it probably should be. The designer also risks letting competitors know of his proposed new product when canvassing opinion about its marketability. But the interpretation provides a practical solution where a designer takes the trouble to give added attraction to an otherwise purely functional article. It also covers the situation envisaged by Lord Reid in *Amp*,[90] where a designer who did not think of anything but function has nonetheless produced something with eye appeal. Indeed it is a direct test of eye-appeal, but with some evidence to go upon. Why ever should a more marketable design be excluded from protection? An example would be the pin with the unusual head described in 2.004 above. People do not normally buy pins because of the way they look, but they might buy *this* one, and if so, why should I not get a registered design for it?

2.075   The alternative interpretation of section 1(3), for which there is, alas, some support in Lord Beaverbrook's remarks, is that it is a two-stage test: first, the applicant must prove that, contrary to what might be supposed from the nature of the article, people *do* normally care to a material extent what it looks like when they are choosing one. He must then go on to show that they would still do so if his design were applied to one. However, this is such a silly approach that it is to be hoped the courts will not adopt it. Once an applicant has proved that people do take appearance into account when buying tractors, to use one of Lord Beaverbrook's examples, why should he then have to prove they will still do so when considering whether to buy his? And how much evidence will he have to produce at the first stage to show that people do buy (and use, given the reference to users as well as acquirers) nails because of their looks—if indeed he can do so at all, which Lord Beaverbrook suggests he could not?[90A] No such question could usefully be asked except

---

[90] See 2.037 above.
[90A] Hecan, from designers and major customers. The writer was wrong. The test is 2-stage and alternative: *Goodyear Tire & Rubber Co.* 1995 I.P.D. 18052; SRIS/0/93/94.

with reference to his proposed design, and market research or widespread inquiries in the trade would give competitors the chance to copy his design when he can neither sue them nor later recover damages, since he cannot do either until his registration is granted.

Of course, it may be that the government did intend as far-reaching a change as this. Lord Beaverbrook started from the position that too many purely functional designs were being registered; he did say that evidence would be needed that users would "generally" be influenced by eye appeal when acquiring particular kinds of article, and he did say that structural girders, ordinary nails and screws would "definitely be excluded"—although he went on to say that with such articles it "could not" be shown that appearance matters, and this must be wrong, because modern architecture increasingly makes a parade of its structural features, and nails and screws may be made with decorated heads because the designer wants them to be a design feature when in place. But if such a radical change was intended, it might have been expected to attract much more debate than it in fact did—and also that it would have appeared as section 1(1) of the Act and the definition of "design" been expressly made subject to it.   **2.076**

The Registry is regularly raising section 1(3) objections, particularly in the field of tools (both hand tools and machine tools), heating, lighting, refrigeration, cooking, lifting and conveying equipment, medical, surgical and veterinary devices, radio, electrical and optical equipment, pipes, tubes and holloware and ingots, girders, scaffolding and the like. Assessing the worth of evidence filed in response to these objections must place rather a heavy burden on Registry staff. How much should they call for, and of what type? If applicants need only show that people would care what the article looked like if their design were applied to it, then evidence from prospective customers would suffice, and it is understood that this is what is happening in practice. Obviously the system can be manipulated, but however much Registry eyebrows may be raised by some of the claims made in such evidence, there is not much they can do in the face of it but register and leave it to the courts to sort out. No challenges to evidence laid open to inspection seem so far to have been raised.[91]   **2.077**

It should be remembered that designs applied for after January 12, 1988 and before August 1, 1989 which would, if made after that date, have been excluded from registration under either section 1(3) or "must-match", will expire on July 31, 1999 and are already subject to licences of right.   **2.078**

---

[91] I am grateful to various members of staff at the Designs Registry for this information and for their help generally.

Designs excluded under section 1(5) and Designs Rule 26

2.079　The second exclusion from registration of designs for a type of *article* is for articles of a primarily literary or artistic character, as set out in Registered Designs rule 26. They are:

> "works of sculpture, other than casts or models used or intended to be used as models or patterns to be multiplied by any industrial process;
> wall plaques, medals and medallions;
> printed matter primarily of a literary or artistic character, including book jackets, calendars, certificates, coupons, dress-making patterns, greetings cards, labels, leaflets, maps, plans, playing cards, postcards, stamps, trade advertisements, trade forms and cards, transfers and similar articles".

This exclusion was first introduced by the 1949 Act, and it approximated to previous Registry practice. Medallions, labels and playing cards were added to the list in 1984.

2.080　Its effect is, as a matter of policy, to force the owners of these types of design to look to copyright for their protection.[92] So long as the registrability of a design determined either the availability or the term of copyright (as it did between 1912 and 1989 and still does in respect of designs which came into being before the latter date),[93] its effect was very important, and it still marks a difference between up to 25 years monopoly protection and life + 50 (soon to be 70) years protection against copying and denies the availability of both.

2.081　The Registry has always been unwilling to register this type of design, partly because many, at least in the third category, are ephemeral; and before the 1949 reform it habitually did so on the basis that the items mentioned were not "articles of manufacture" but were merely pieces of paper (or lumps of metal or clay) acting solely as carriers of the designs they bore. In *Re Littlewoods Pools Ltd's Application*,[94] a Registry decision refusing registration to a design for a football pools coupon on this ground was upheld by the court.[95] With respect, that distinction was a foolish one. It depends through whose eyes you are looking. For the artist, writer or designer, a piece of paper (or canvas or lump of bronze) is clearly an article of manufacture and of commerce, bought for use not adornment, but not registrable because no design has yet been applied to it. Equally clearly, for the national lottery proprietor or punter, dressmaker, supermarket proprietor or orienteer, an

---

[92] Where they are all likely to find it. Even a calendar, which displays information of a banal and predetermined character, will normally have some protectable features, whether by virtue of the photograph or drawing with which it is beautified or the particular layout or typographical arrangement which it adopts, or as a literary compilation, on which effort has been expended, of the banal with additional information.

[93] See further below and Chaps. 1, 3 and 5.

[94] (1949) 66 R.P.C. 309.

[95] On the other hand, designs for labels were regularly registered before their 1984 inclusion in rule 26.

entry coupon, paper pattern, sticky label or map is an article of manufacture and commerce, bought for use not adornment. Other items have a heavier adornment content: the publisher uses a book jacket to enhance the attraction of his product, the friendly or dutiful communicator chooses a greetings card or postcard for its visual appeal as well as its purpose. But this is not a difference of principle (although one does occur with something like a mass-produced picture to hang on your wall, if only the purchaser's view is taken into account). On the other hand the decision in *Masson Seeley & Co. Ltd v. Embosotype Manufacturing Co.*[96] against registering a design for a catalogue of typefaces (not the typefaces themselves) was clearly sensible because there was not going to be a trade in catalogues as such.

There were decisions the other way. In a copyright infringement action, **2.082** *Con Planck v. Kolynos Inc.,*[97] it was held that advertising showcards originally made by sticking lifesize photographs of faces and drawings of diminutive bodies onto wood could have been registered and therefore did not have copyright. A showcard design had already been accepted for registration in *Gunton v. Winox Ltd.*[98] Designs for boards for playing board games are also registered, as were designs for playing cards before 1984.

To resolve these difficulties, section 1(4)—as it then was—and rule 26 were **2.083** enacted. But it is still necessary to interpret its meaning in particular cases, and also to consider whether items not expressly included within it are "similar" to those which are. The use of the word "articles" in both the subsection and the rule suggests that the Registry's old argument that these things are not articles of manufacture at all can no longer apply, since the definition of "article" in section 44 means article of manufacture.[99]

Works of sculpture are excluded, except where they are prototypes for **2.084** mass-production, like the first version of a new garden gnome, ornament or toy—or dentures for sheep. Although there are no provisions laying down any prescribed number of products intended to be made, it is usual to use the criterion of more than 50 which crops up elsewhere in designs law. Wall plaques, medals and medallions, on the other hand, are excluded from registration altogether. Flights of china or plaster ducks are therefore out, although they would be perfectly acceptable if they were made in the round as ornaments, or marketed for use as door handles, or indeed were turned into wall-lights by having bulb fittings screwed into their beaks.

The list of remaining items is illustrative but not exhaustive, and a few cases **2.085** have reached the courts. The plans showing how to assemble a kit of parts into a sailing dinghy were conceded in *Dorling v. Honnor Marine*[1] to be unregistrable. In *Klarmann Ltd v. Henshaw Linen Supplies,*[2] a copyright

---

[96] (1924) 41 R.P.C. 160.
[97] [1925] 2 K.B. 804.
[98] (1921) 38 R.P.C. 40.
[99] Unless the context otherwise requires, and why should it?
[1] [1963] R.P.C. 205; [1964] R.P.C. 160.
[2] [1960] R.P.C. 150.

infringement action, the product was a plastic container for packaging cushions, with a drawing and some advertising literature printed on it. It was accepted that the product as a container alone would in principle have been registrable, but held that the literary and artistic matter which appeared on it turned it into a "trade advertisement" and made it unregistrable under rule 26. "Primarily of a literary or artistic character" referred to the article rather than the printed matter itself, but did not mean that the article had to be intended "primarily for a literary or artistic purpose"—most rule 26 articles are not. The design being unregistrable, the plaintiff had not lost its copyright, which it would otherwise at this date have done. This case suggests that packaging designs in general are probably not registrable, unless the Registry and the courts would normally equate them with wallpaper and textile designs, which are. The absence of any element of advertising might persuade them in this direction.

2.086   A rule 26 objection was raised in the *Lamson*[3] case, discussed above in relation to functionality. This was the design for computer printout paper, which does not expressly figure in the rule 26 list. The Registry declined to accept that the "article" in question under rule 26 was the paper before application of the design, when it would lack any literary or artistic significance, or that if the paper with the design applied to it was the "article", there was nothing on it to subordinate it to the status of a mere carrier, like the football pool coupon. The assistant registrar thought that the article had to be the article with the design applied to it, and this would have a literary significance to the user because the coloured "staves" were there to have literary matter (words or figures) printed on them. Whitford J., although he refused registration on the "functionality" ground, would not have done so under rule 26. He thought in this context that the ultimate use of the article to bear literary matter was insufficiently relevant, and that if anything the design as it appeared on the printout paper was artistic. On this basis, he equated it with wallpaper[4] and would have let it proceed to registration.

2.087   All the items mentioned in rule 26(3) would normally be printed on paper or card. Certainly textile designs have never been excluded, even when they are printed rather than woven. A teacloth with a calendar on it would probably be regarded as a teacloth rather than a calendar. "Transfers" are only excluded as such, *i.e.* where it is sought to register designs for transfers which can then be used for a variety of articles. The fact that a pattern is applied to an article such as a T-shirt or a child's dish[5] by means of transfers is irrelevant. Nor is it under rule 26 that letters and numerals are normally excluded from registration, but on grounds of novelty. "Printed matter" seems a rather archaic definition now, but it was not updated by the 1988 Act. It is not therefore clear whether icons and graphics used in computer

[3] [1978] R.P.C. 1. See 2.027 above.
[4] Rather than, say, a trade form.
[5] See *Ornamin (U.K.) Ltd v. Bacsa Ltd* [1964] R.P.C. 293.

programs or figures in computer games would be excluded by rule 26, although in practice this might not matter, since they usually also appear in printed form in manuals and instruction leaflets. Pictorial devices showing how to wash and iron clothes would be excluded under "labels", since these are the articles to which they are applied—they cannot be registered simply as devices. It is a nice question whether road signs are "similar articles" to the rest of the rule 26(3) list.

NOVELTY

This is the final but crucial requirement which a registrable design must under section 1(2) of the amended 1949 Act fulfil. The unamended Act also had an originality requirement, which is briefly considered later, since designs applied for before August 1, 1989 must still satisfy it. **2.088**

Novelty is defined in section 1(4), and sections 4, 6 and 16 provide a list of situations where a design which has on the face of it lost its novelty may still be saved. A design, under section 1(4), shall not be regarded as new if it is the same as a design: **2.089**

(a) registered in respect of the same or any other article in pursuance of a prior application, or
(b) published in the United Kingdom in respect of the same or any other article before the date of the application

or if it differs from such a design only in immaterial details or in features which are variants commonly used in the trade.

Novelty is judged as at the date of application, unless an earlier date based on an application in a Paris Convention country within the previous six months is relied on. It will be noticed that novelty is not limited in time (a very old design could anticipate a new one), but is limited in territory to the U.K. U.K. novelty would not be destroyed by publication of a photograph of the product in a U.S. magazine, unless shown to be in circulation here, nor by display of the product at an exhibition in Germany, nor even taking orders for it there, although it is obviously unwise to run such risks.

An earlier design under section 1(4)(a) must actually be registered in order to act as an anticipation, so applications which are abandoned before registration (and therefore before publication) do not count. However, an earlier application which does proceed to registration, even though not until after the date of the second application, will still anticipate, because its registration will be dated as of the date of its own application.[6] A design which turns out to be invalidly registered will not necessarily destroy novelty **2.090**

[6] *Re Shallwin's Application* [1961] R.P.C. 203.

(for example if it was obtained in breach of confidence), but even if it is not an anticipation as a prior registration it can still destroy novelty if it has been otherwise published or used under section 1(4)(b).

2.091   "Publication" in that subsection means making available to the public, and this may be by featuring in trade catalogues, by advertisements or editorial matter in periodicals circulating in this country,[7] by mention in patent specifications or other written descriptions (provided the design can be readily visualised[8]), or in any other manner including, obviously, by marketing of the article in question, if this can be proved—often surprisingly difficult if marketing took place a long time previously. In principle, the alleged anticipation should be a "direct hit" and it is not permissible to "mosaic" two or more documents to piece together an anticipation (though this can be done with prior registered designs), but in practice this is frequently done under the guise of demonstrating use of "common trade variants".

Novelty-saving provisions

2.092   Before discussing novelty in greater detail, mention should be made of the several situations in which, despite prior registration or publication, it need not be lost. The first is under section 4, which provides a mechanism for "associating" a later registered design with an earlier one which would otherwise anticipate it, and is dealt with further in Chapter 3. The second, under section 16, provides for the protection of designs communicated to an overseas government pursuant to an international agreement between it and the U.K. government. Thirdly, section 6 provides a relatively generous list of exemptions, the first being disclosure of a design by the proprietor to any other person in such circumstances as would make it contrary to good faith for that other person to use or publish it. So a proprietor looking for someone to exploit his design, or disclosing it to a manufacturer to investigate costing or make a prototype, or even demonstrating it to prospective customers, will not lose novelty so long as he obtains either an express confidentiality undertaking or it would manifestly be a breach of confidence for the disclosee to use or publish it.

2.093   There is also exemption where the design is disclosed in breach of good faith by anyone other than the proprietor. This would cover industrial espionage, and also disclosure by one of the disclosees suggested above—for example an overseas manufacturer who deliberately offers the design in breach of confidence to another U.K. company. But it is not clear that a

---

[7] But see *Bissell A.G.'s Application* [1964] R.P.C. 125, discussed below in connection with section 6(4).
[8] *Rosedale Associated Manufacturers Ltd v. Airfix Products Ltd* [1957] R.P.C. 239.

merely careless or accidental disclosure by such a person would count, though it is difficult to see any reason of principle why it should not, since the effect on the proprietor is the same. Nor is it clear whether an innocent acquirer from such a manufacturer would be affected. If a competing U.K. importer obtained the design from the overseas manufacturer knowing the proprietor had rights in it, he could scarcely complain if he later found himself prejudiced by the proprietor's registration, nor rely on his own prior sales to invalidate it. But what if he acted in good faith throughout? The wording of section 6(1)(b) provides that the proprietor's registration is not to be invalidated by reason *only* that there has been bad faith disclosure by someone; in this case its invalidity would stem in part from his competitor's innocent prior sales—but these would not have occurred but for the bad faith of the overseas manufacturer. Who is to be prejudiced—the innocent proprietor by being deprived of his registration or the innocent acquirer whose sales can be brought to an end by injunction once a design is granted?[9] Unfortunately there is no provision such as has now been introduced by section 8B(4) protecting the rights of those who start selling in good faith after a proprietor has failed to renew his registration in due time and before he has successfully applied to restore it.[10] This would allow an extended meaning to be given to section 6(1)(b) so as to save the registration, while protecting the innocent acquirer. If the facts fall out right, the proprietor may be able to take advantage of section 6(4), discussed below.

There are three other limited exemptions concerning the taking of a first **2.094** and confidential order for a textile design, communication to a government department, and display with the consent of the proprietor at an international exhibition (certified by the Registry) and subsequent publication or display by another person without the proprietor's consent; but the final exemption is rather in the nature of a "coach and horses" driven through section 1(4), because in some cases it can permit a "grace period" during which limited test marketing may be carried out without losing novelty. It was originally introduced into the 1949 Act by the Copyright Act 1956, and has under the 1988 amendments been split into two subsections, 6(4) and 6(5). Where the design is based on a copyright artistic work (which will normally be so if it is based on a drawing), the copyright owner will not be prevented from obtaining a registered design "corresponding" to the copyright work (which reproduces the copyright work whether in two- or three-dimensional form—section 44(1)) by reason only of any use he (or anyone else) has previously made of the copyright work, so long (section 6(5)) as that use did not involve marketing articles reproducing the design of which more than 50 have been made before date of the application to register. The limitation to 50 permissible articles is found in Registered Designs rule 35, which also

---

[9] He could not be penalised for his pre-grant sales because a proprietor cannot sue on his registered design before it is granted, nor can he then recover damages for any earlier date—section 7(5), formerly proviso to section 3(5).
[10] See 3.129 below.

provides that the 50 articles must not together constitute a "set" and that the exemption also applies to goods manufactured in lengths or pieces, other than hand-made goods. The situation originally envisaged was probably where an artist who initially had no intention of commercialising his drawing or sculpture later decided to do so; but there is no reason why the exemption should not apply equally to a drawing of a piston or a coathanger which was always intended for industrial use; so as long as he confines his initial production run to 50 or fewer, the manufacturer can test market to his heart's content and apply to register later.

2.095   Two cases illustrate the working of this provision. In *Bissell AG's Design*[11] the applicant had freely commercialised its domestic appliance by selling it in the U.S., and magazines containing advertisements for it had appeared in the U.K. However, it had not before the date of application for the U.K. design made or sold any appliances here which would have corresponded to its copyright drawings, and it could rely on the exemption—despite the prior publication in the magazines. *Bampal Materials Handling Co. Ltd's Design*[12] shows that the exemption can be subject to technical hitches. The proprietors had sold at least 36 trolleys before the date of their application to register, and were alleged to have sold far more. The appliance had appeared in their catalogue with no indication that there had been only a limited production run, and the proprietors had been encouraging their distributors to make sales, with the consent of one of their staff who was alleged to have owned the copyright in the drawings to which the design corresponded. This employee could not now be found, and there was no evidence that the design had been applied for with his consent. He had purported to assign the copyright to the proprietors several months after the design application was made. In these circumstances, since the burden of establishing the exemption is on the proprietor, the assistant registrar was not satisfied it had been made out. Anyone hoping to rely on the exemption must therefore be sure that both the prior use and the design application are made with the copyright owner's consent and that there is adequate evidence of this—or preferably get in the copyright beforehand. On the other hand, the exemption could be most useful to someone who has designed an article and done a little small-scale production and selling, and then finds someone who is willing to exploit the design industrially—provided he can prove that he did not make more than 50 articles before the design application is made.

2.096   In the case of novelty-destruction by the innocent acquirer of a design from a wrongdoer who has disclosed it in bad faith, the proprietor may be able to invoke section 6(4), provided his design is based on an artistic work in which he owns or effectively controls the copyright. If the innocent acquirer has sold articles made to a design "corresponding to" that work,[13] he may be argued

---

[11] [1964] R.P.C. 125.
[12] [1981] R.P.C. 44.
[13] See 2.094 above.

indirectly to have made use of that work, but this would not prejudice a later application to register by the copyright owner or with the copyright owner's consent. The intervening use would not have been made by the copyright owner or with his consent, so would not be implicated under section 6(5).

However, since section 51 now ensures that most "shape" designs will be   **2.097**
protected only by unregistered design right, not by copyright,[14] against the making of articles to the design, the fact that they are based on copyright artistic works may no longer have the same effect. The application of a "corresponding design" to the article sold by the innocent acquirer would no longer result in something which would be treated as a copy of the artistic work—or at least not as an infringing copy. But perhaps this would not matter. The article would still on normal copyright principles reproduce the work and so use it, and it does not need to be an infringing copy to come within section 6(4).

Novelty destroyed by design applied to any article

Subject to the exemptions set out above, section 1(4) says that a design can be   **2.098**
anticipated by another which has been applied to *any* article, so theoretically the scope for nasty surprises is wide. In practice, this does not happen very often. The Registry limits its searches for earlier designs by reference to an informal classification system, and probably limits its publication searches in the same way, and since people are often lamentably careless about keeping even their own old catalogues and cannot prove, in an infringement-and-validity action, their hunch that something similar was around about 20 years ago, the discovery of an anticipation in a completely different field must be largely a matter of luck. In *Stenor v. Whitesides (Clitheroe) Ltd*[15] a design for a fuse was anticipated by one for a bicycle crank axle, but at that time designs, like trade marks, were registered (and searched) in formal classes and these products were in the same class. Where the products were in different classes, the earlier one would destroy novelty only where the products were used for similar purposes. Thus in *Re Clarke's Design*[16] an electric lamp mimicked the form of, and was anticipated by, an old oil lamp, and in *Re Bach's Application*[17] a rose-shaped lampshade in china was anticipated by a similarly-shaped one in linen.[18]

There is doubtless more scope for anticipation with pattern designs, for   **2.099**
example where a textile or wallpaper design turns up later applied to the

---

[14] See below, *passim*.
[15] (1948) 65 R.P.C. 1.
[16] [1896] 2 Ch.D. 38.
[17] (1889) 6 R.P.C. 376.
[18] The Johnston Committee (Report of the Johnston Committee on Industrial Designs, Cmnd. 1808, HMSO London, 1962) thought the 1949 extension to anticipation by *any* other article was too wide, and would have recommended that the test should be whether the new article was an "obvious adaptation" of the design of the earlier one—a test familiar from patent law.

covers of a range of notebooks. And it was pointed out in *Dymo Design Industries Inc.'s Application*[19] that known shapes can be taken into consideration when determining the novelty of a pattern design.

2.100   But to destroy novelty there has to have been a "design" applied to an "article", meaning an article of manufacture (section 44), and so the first person (so far as is known) to apply the shape of Westminster Abbey to the handle of a teaspoon was entitled to a registration for the spoon so adorned.[20] Westminster Abbey was not an article of manufacture but a building, it was, like an Apostle, "a source common to all mankind". If this was not an acceptably novel design, you could never take a building or a naturally-occurring phenomenon like a tree or an elephant and use it to decorate an article unless you made it look quite different from the original. Applying the same reasoning, a design for a toy Mickey Mouse was accepted in *Dean's Rag Book Co. v. Pomerantz*,[21] even though the Mickey Mouse cartoons and films were widely-known. It is not clear whether the post-1949 law, with its wider trawl for anticipations, would now mean that once the gatehouse of Pentonville Prison has been applied to the handle of a cosh or the form of Lord Tebbit (with his permission—Designs rule 25) to a bicycle pump, these features can never registrably be applied to any other article. It may be that a sufficiently different view or treatment of the same subject would differ in more than immaterial details.[22] In practice, any character like Mickey Mouse will now be so tightly tied up by licensing arrangements that whatever the design law position be, any attempt to apply it to anything will be preventable under the law of passing off.[23]

2.101   Mere changes of scale do not, however, impart novelty. This is illustrated by two textile design cases, *Re Calder Vale Manufacturing Co. Ltd's Design*[24] and *Vlisco BV's Application*,[25] in which the later design differed through being woven on a different size loom and printed using a different size roller respectively. Similar considerations would seem to apply to exact or nearly exact replicas of Concorde—or indeed Westminster Abbey if merely a miniaturised model—though if there is a degree of stylisation, perhaps this need not apply. There used to be a feeling in the Registry against registering models of human beings, animals or existing objects,[26] which affected toys, artificial flowers, shop-window dummies and figures made of china, plastic and so on, unless they had some particularly striking feature, which would

---

[19] [1982] R.P.C. 437.
[20] *Saunders v. Wiel* (1893) 10 R.P.C. 29.
[21] (1930) 47 R.P.C. 485.
[22] In *Carr's Application* [1973] R.P.C. 689 a threepenny bit applied to a known shank for use as a cufflink was held unregistrable for want of novelty. There is not much to be done to alter the treatment of a threepenny bit.
[23] See the Ninja Turtle case, *Mirage Studios v. Counter-Feat Clothing Ltd* [1991] F.S.R. 145, 1.032 above.
[24] (1936) 52 R.P.C. 117.
[25] [1980] R.P.C. 509.
[26] See Report of the Johnston Committee on Industrial Designs, Cmnd. 1808, HMSO London, 1962.

largely lie in the eye of the examiner. But this seems to have been more on the grounds of lack of originality than want of novelty, and may no longer be so prevalent—although in the candle-mould case of *Constable v. Clarkson*[27] the reason why the moulds rather than the extraordinarily lifelike fruit and vegetable candles made from them were registered was that the Registry would probably not have accepted the candles as such.

Novelty judged by eye

Novelty is judged by the eye alone, and recourse may be had to the doctrine of **2.102** imperfect recollection used in trade mark law—the designs must be considered not only side-by-side but separately and assuming some time to have elapsed, to simulate ordinary conditions of commerce.[28] While with both eye appeal and infringement it is the customer's eye which must be looked through, there are various dicta[29] which suggest that in assessing novelty the rather more instructed eye of a designer concerned with the aesthetic appearance of his products may be applied. And expert evidence from designers was adduced by both sides in the Patents County Court in *Sony K.K. v. Win-Technic Electronics Pty Ltd*[30] as to the relative importance of design similarities and differences, on the basis that the whole function of designers is to be conscious of features likely to affect the minds of the interested purchasing public. Similarly, in *Prince v. Dunlop Slazenger*[31] a designer and an advertising consultant gave evidence that even quite small changes in the design of squash racquets can affect eye appeal. But the court is not, or is only marginally,[32] concerned with the amount of effort, labour or ingenuity expended by the designer, if the visual effect is negligible. If there is doubt, commercial success may be taken as an indicator that the public has found something eye-appealing about the design,[33] as may proof in an infringement action of actual copying by the defendant.[34] The quantum of novelty is supposed to be "substantial",[35] but as a matter of reality a glance at many designs registered over others shows that this is just not so. This question must then be how many of these would stand up in court—but also how many are really inconvenient to competitors, who can presumably get around them by the alteration of equally small details.

[27] [1980] F.S.R. 123; see 2.025 above.
[28] For a recent example, see *Gaskell & Chambers Ltd v. Measure Master Ltd* 1992 I.P.D. 15144 about "optics"—devices for dispensing a measured quantity of spirits.
[29] See, *e.g. Phillips v. Harbro' Rubber Co.* (1920) 37 R.P.C. 233, followed in *Goodyear Tire & Rubber Co. Application for Cancellation by Michelin et Cie* 1981 I.P.D. 4037.
[30] SRIS/CC/84/92—toy walkie-talkie mounted on watchstrap.
[31] SRIS/CC/29/94—squash racquets.
[32] In order to distinguish a design contribution from mere workshop alterations.
[33] *G. A. Harvey & Co. (London) v. Secure Fittings Ltd* [1966] R.P.C. 515 at 520.
[34] *C. H. Nevill v. J. Bennett & Sons* (1898) 15 R.P.C. 412. But see now *Gaskell & Chambers Ltd v. Measure Master Ltd*, n. 28 above, where the question of copying was dismissed out of hand.

[35] See, *e.g. Le May v. Welch* (1885) 28 Ch.D. 24.

2.103   It is not necessary that every part of a design should be novel. This can only rarely be so, and the addition of even one striking new feature may be enough.[36] Plenty of designs have *no* individual new features, but the new arrangement of old materials is sufficient to impart overall novelty. It is in relation to these designs that defendants in infringement actions or applicants for cancellation are most likely to argue that, in the closing words of section 1(4) they differ from earlier designs "only in immaterial details or in features which are variants commonly used in the trade".

2.104   To adopt a recent judicial utterance,[37] an "immaterial detail" is a detailed difference which has no effect on the identity of the design. Examples from the same case were the presence and position of an additional switch on a toy watchstrap-mounted walkie-talkie and the orientation of the strap at right-angles to the appliance rather than longitudinally. In the *Cow v. Cannon*[38] hot water bottle case, minor differences in the hanging-tab and filling-mouth were "immaterial details", and the presence on the defendant's product of a medallion with the word COSY moulded on one side was not a variation of the plaintiff's design but an addition leaving the identity of that design unaffected. In the days of workshops and hand-made goods, immaterial details were characterised as the kind of changes a competent workman might make in carrying out his daily activities. It will not escape the discerning reader that these definitions, like much else in this field, are of little use divorced from concrete examples.

2.105   It is in assessing whether design differences are the product of "variants commonly used in the trade" that evidence from designers versed in the particular art or trade can be useful. In *Phillips v. Harbro' Rubber Co.*[39] the subject of the design was the surface pattern of india-rubber pads or plates for the heels of boots and shoes. It featured a pattern of crossed lines, to avoid slipping. This was dismissed as a common trade variant, as being merely a particular way of securing a roughened surface. Although a new combination of known features could impart novelty, the position here was analogous to simply putting known spikes into the sole of a known design of running shoe. In *Ashelwood Products Pty Ltd's Design Application*[40] the addition of a hinge to a known shape of table to impart foldability was a common trade variant.

2.106   A case which neatly illustrates, albeit only at Registry level, both the limits of the common trade variants doctrine and how a combination of known features can nevertheless possess novelty is *M. & F. Jinks Ltd's Registered Design, Application for cancellation by Dunlop Ltd.*[41] The designs were for children's slippers having attachments to their uppers which gave the

---

[36] See *Gaskell & Chambers Ltd v. Measure Master Ltd*, n. 28 above.
[37] In *Sony v. Win-Technic* SRIS/CC/84/92.
[38] [1959] R.P.C. 240, 347.
[39] (1920) 37 R.P.C. 233.
[40] 1983 I.P.D. 5122.
[41] 1986 I.P.D. 8106.

appearance of a mouse, a rabbit and a panda. There was detailed evidence of the proprietor's use of felt cut-out noses, mouths, ears, eyes and so forth, all of which were known in the trade but which gave to the registered designs, according to the proprietor's expert, a retired children's footwear buyer, a novel appearance demonstrating artistic skill because of the way they were arranged. Dunlop's witness complained that they had used similar ears, etc., for years, and that allowing a monopoly of such common trade variants as their particular positioning would force every competitor to check the whole of the competition each time he wished to use them in a slightly different way.

The assistant registrar was satisfied that the registered designs were the result of the designer's artistic skill in using known embellishments to produce novel designs and condescended to particularities about the disposition of fluffy ears. He reminded himself of the observation in W. *Lusty & Sons Ltd v. Morris Wilkinson & Co. (Nottingham) Ltd*[42] that one should not pick a design to pieces feature by feature and kill its novelty by deciding that each one is a trade variant, or very few designs would ever get registered. Finally, as Graham J. had suggested at first instance in *Amp v. Utilux*,[43] to be relevant a variant had to be used and not merely published, and it must be shown by evidence to have been available in the U.K. from more than one source.

2.107

Colour

One example of a common trade variant is colour, because it it usually unlikely to make a significant difference to a design (and would result in a very narrow and easily-avoided registration). But it is not impossible for colour to play a part in novelty. Usually the precise colours used do not matter, the feature of pattern or ornament being the tonal contrast imparted by the use of different colours (as in the *Ferrero* chocolate egg case[44]). In July 1973 the Registry issued a statement of its normal practice in relation to colour, of which the foregoing is a summary, in response to a request from the judge in *Smith Kline & French Laboratories Ltd's Design Application*.[45] This was an application to register designs for a transparent pharmaceutical capsule with one end blue, the other yellow or orange, and a green band round the middle, through which tiny red or white pellets could be seen. The novelty claimed was for the ornamental combination of the pellet colours as seen through the variously-coloured portions of the capsule. Graham J. having looked at the statement of its practice, upheld the Registry in finding that although as a matter of law colour might sometimes make a material

2.108

[42] (1954) 71 R.P.C. 174 at 181.
[43] [1970] R.P.C. 397 at 429.
[44] [1978] R.P.C. 473—see 2.024 above.
[45] [1974] R.P.C. 253.

difference and impart novelty, in this case its impact on the eye, over other similar capsules got up in different colour combinations, was insufficiently striking. This is a notably uncommercial finding in view of the mass of evidence in passing off cases which shows that the public sets great store by having its medicines the same colour every time. One example suggested by the judge of a case where colour could be decisive was a fabric design illustrating the Ishihara colour-blindness test. Persons with normal vision can pick out an image from a pattern of differently-coloured spots, while a colour-blind person cannot. This is an interesting possibility in the light of illustrations now frequently appearing in periodicals in which some persons can, while others cannot, discern some image or another.[46]

2.109   One case in which colour was decisive, though subject to stringent conditions, was *Cook & Hurst's Design Application*.[47] This was for a design for the current England football shirt, being a white shirt of conventional shape having red and blue bands running around the collar, two similar but broader bands running from the collar over the shoulder down the arm to the cuff, and three alternating red and blue bands around the cuff. The prior art showed that variations in striping had become commonly used on sports garments. The Registry found that the colours were trade variants. However, Whitford J. held that in the particular circumstances the colour combination gave novelty, but directed that the registration be limited to stripes in these locations, in these colours, and only on football shirts—no doubt quite adequate for the applicant's purposes.

Letters and numerals

2.110   Letters and numerals are not normally regarded as forming part of a design, unless displayed in a particular novel or decorative fashion so as to form a design or part of one. Examples might be monograms or letter logos, or particularly significant dates, where the style but not the letters or numbers themselves would be protectable. The Registrar may by rule 22 require a disclaimer of any right to exclusive use of letters or numerals shown. Can a registration be obtained for or incorporating a word or slogan—applied, of course, to particular articles? Could the concessionaire of memorabilia from a theme park or football team register a particular decorative version of its name? There seems no reason why not, so long as the letters or numerals are treatable as pattern or ornament and there is no risk of their use as such being monopolised. Whitford J. implicitly recognised the commercial significance of such articles in the *Cook & Hurst* decision, and gave directions to ensure

---

[46] Ability to do so in these cases seems to depend on whether the viewer is able adequately to cross his or her eyes.
[47] [1979] R.P.C. 197.

the protection granted did not go too wide. This results in a very narrow registration, but if the particular appearance of the name, etc., is widely-enough promoted, so that people will instinctively look for it, rather than any other version, narrow protection may be enough.

Whole design to be assessed in judging novelty?

All authorities concur that a design is to be judged "as a whole" in assessing novelty. The question is what is meant by "design"—does it include or exclude purely functional (and now "must-match") features? As pointed out at 2.045 above, they used to be excluded, and were certainly also excluded in testing infringement: in *Sommer Allibert v. Flair*[48] it was remarked by Slade L.J. that "the overall proportions of both chairs were dictated by the function of providing a comfortable chair on which to sit, both parties in their design following recognised ergonomic standards in the industry ... in considering infringement, we must ignore the fact that [both chairs] possess these common characteristics". But this was upset, so far as pre-August 1, 1989 designs are concerned, by the *Interlego*[49] case, which held that unless all its features are dictated solely by function, an eye-appealing design is registered as a whole, and its novelty may fall to be assessed accordingly. Truly functional features probably will rarely possess novelty or will be common trade variants so the question may be largely academic. For post-July 31, 1989 designs, however, "must-match" features will have to be considered, and these may be bursting with novelty and eye-appeal. It is suggested that it would be undesirable to take them into account in considering novelty, and that the slight differences in the drafting of section 1(1) mentioned in 2.045 above, coupled with the direction in the new section 7(6)[50] to take no account on infringement of functional or "must-match" features "left out of account in determining whether the design is registrable", imply that they should also be ignored in relation to novelty, since novelty is part of registrability. On the other hand, it would have been easy enough for Parliament to say this in section 1(4), if that was what it meant.[50A]

2.111

Statement of novelty

Registered Designs rule 15 (though not the Act) requires except in the case of textile, wallpaper, wall-covering and lace designs a statement of the features of the design for which novelty is claimed to appear on each representation or specimen of the design. It is an aid to construction and an indication of what

2.112

---

[48] [1987] R.P.C. 599 at 622.
[49] [1988] R.P.C. 343.
[50] Which we know was inserted to take account of *Interlego*, because the government said so—see *Hansard*, November 3, 1988, col. 328.
[50A] See *Valeo Vision SA v. Flexible Lamps Ltd* [1995] R.P.C. 205 at 214, 1.16 and 215, 11.16–18.

features an applicant wishes to emphasise as his novel contribution[51] or, in so far as he does not mention them, to disclaim. The statement can expressly include or exclude particular parts of the representation of the design by circling or shading or otherwise indicating them. If no particular part is to be claimed or disclaimed, the statement will usually merely refer to the shape or configuration (or pattern and ornament) applied to the article as shown in the representations, and in that case the design will be looked at as a whole (in the sense discussed above).

2.113   Emphasising particular features means that if they are found in an alleged infringement the claim will probably succeed, but if they are not, it will probably fail. This is problematic where a design has more than one novel feature because an infringer who takes only one may escape. An attempt was made to deal with this in *Evered's Application*[52] by making two applications for different designs covering different features of the same window stay. The assistant registrar refused these as being applications in respect of parts of articles which were not made and sold separately, and suggested one design showing the two parts in different colours, with two separate suitably-worded statements of novelty, but it seems unlikely this would work. The judge agreed that two separate designs would not work, because by claiming novelty in only one feature in each design, the applicant would be impliedly disclaiming novelty in the other. However, similar problems arise with an article such as a vase, which has novel features of both shape/configuration and pattern/ornament. If all are claimed in the same registration, a competitor who takes *only* the pattern or *only* the shape may not infringe. But in such cases the Registry will readily accept two separate registrations, although it is wise to show the pattern as applied to a conventional shape, claiming only the pattern, and to show the shape unadorned. The article should in this case be described as widely as can be got away with, perhaps as a "container". A rather different case where features of both pattern and configuration are involved would be a knitted garment having both features of pattern in the form of tonal contrasts and configuration in the form of cable and rosette protruberances knitted into it. To add challenge, it could be of novel shape (if such can be conceived of in the fashion industry) and have the name and date of birth of a popular fictional character worked into it in a special decorative style. How many statements of novelty would be required to ensure protection for all these features?

2.114   A general claim normally requires all the features to appear in the alleged infringement. In *Best Products Ltd v. F. W. Woolworth & Co. Ltd*[53] the presence in a kettle of a markedly different spout was held to avoid infringement of a general statement of novelty, although this would not necessarily always apply.

---

[51] *Kent and Thanet Casinos Ltd v. Bailey's School of Dancing Ltd* [1974] R.P.C. 429.
[52] [1961] R.P.C. 105.
[53] [1964] R.P.C. 215.

Originality

Under the unamended 1949 Act, a design was required to be "novel or **2.115**
original". Although apparently expressed in the alternative, they tended to be
regarded as separate requirements both of which had to be fulfilled, and it will
be recalled that this old definition still applies to designs based on a
pre-August 1, 1989 application. There was lack of agreement as to exactly
what "originality" meant. Some indication can be obtained from two rather
similar cases involving ways of packaging goods. The first is *Aspro-Nicholas
Ltd's Design Application.*[54] This was an application to register a design for a
stack of tiny tablets contained within and visible through a transparent
two-part capsule, the whole thing being intended to be swallowed as a single
dose. Both the tablets and the capsule were of conventional shape, and such
capsules containing pellets (as in the *Smith Kline & French* case[55]) were also
widely-known. But this seemed to be the first time it had occurred to anyone
to make up the dose into miniature tablets rather than pellets.

The hearing officer had recourse to the notion of patent-style "obvious- **2.116**
ness" in rejecting the application. She accepted it was not for her to assess the
degree of mental activity which had gone into producing this "combination"
design. But she felt it simply was too obvious a combination to protect by a
monopoly—although she expressed her decision in terms of "common trade
variants" and thereby perhaps came too close to picking the design to pieces
and striking down each piece rather than looking at it as a whole.[56] Graham
J., however, agreed with her in rejecting the application. He confirmed that
the phrase "new or original" indicated something more than pure novelty; it
directed the mind and eye to seek "a difference of form or character which is a
departure from previous designs and which is therefore of some significance
or substance". He concluded more picturesquely that "nothing of real
significance has been added by these designs to the store of human knowledge
and experience in the packaging art", which is the language of "obviousness"
and inventive step.

The second case is *Caron International's Design Application.*[57] This was **2.117**
for a package of wool for making hand-hooked rugs, the short lengths of
wool being arranged roughly horizontally to form a vertical stack, the whole
enclosed in a rectangular transparent sealed envelope with a slot at the top for
hanging on a display stand. It was thus a very similar case to *Aspro-Nicholas*,
except that no one had previously thought of arranging rug wool other than
in cylindrical bundles from which you would fish each piece out by its end
rather than by its middle as in the present arrangement. The hearing officer
based his rejection on *Aspro-Nicholas*, but Whitford J. upheld the decision on

---

[54] [1974] R.P.C. 645.
[55] See 2.108 above.
[56] See 2.107 above.
[57] [1981] R.P.C. 179.

what might be regarded as a "method or principle of construction"[58] objection: anyone wanting to package rug wool in a long envelope rather than a cylinder would inevitably come up with a package looking much like this one. But while he did not whole-heartedly endorse Graham J.'s "obviousness" approach, he did decide to follow the *Aspro-Nicholas* decision, and he agreed that at least in some cases, of which packaging was one, something more than strict novelty might be needed.

2.118   Another kind of originality affects designs based on naturally-occurring objects, where too exact a resemblance to the real thing may lead to rejection.[59] This can also be regarded as a sort of obviousness objection, or it may recognise that mere care and skill in depicting a known object, imparting nothing of added visual significance over and above that possessed by the object, is not fit matter for industrial design protection.

2.119   Whatever "originality" may have added to "novelty", the need for it has now disappeared—with what result remains to be discovered. But it will be seen in Chapter 6 that the proposed E.U. harmonisation Directive will require U.K. registered designs law at some time over the next few years to begin applying a twofold test of both novelty and individual appearance as prerequisites to registration.

COPYRIGHT

THE 1988 ACT SCHEME

"The function of this clause is to take industrial designs out of copyright"

2.120   With these unequivocal words,[60] Lord Beaverbrook, introducing the clause which became section 51 of the 1988 Act, made plain the government's intentions. "We do not want copyright to apply to the manufacture of industrial design" reiterated John Butcher, the minister in charge of the Bill in the House of Commons.[61]

2.121   Of course, things could not be that simple. As both spokesmen immediately recognised, industrial designs are nearly always based on artistic works (usually drawings), which the Berne Convention requires us to protect by copyright for the full period of the author's life + 50 years (soon to be 70 years). In the case of works of applied art, Berne demands a protection period of 25 years from their making, unless they are protected by special designs legislation.[62] No solution which simply denied copyright to works forming the basis of industrial designs would be permissible. Nor could a practicable

---

[58] See 2.030 above.
[59] See 2.025 and 2.101 above.
[60] *Hansard*, Vol. 491, col. 185.
[61] *Hansard*, Standing Committee E, 8th Sitting, May 24, 1988, col. 244.
[62] Articles 2(1) and (7) and 7(4).

distinction be drawn between "artistic" and "functional" designs by reference to "useful" articles, as suggested by Lord Lucas of Chilworth.[63] Lord Beaverbrook pointed out that an artistically-crafted vase is a "useful" article because it is used to hold flowers, but ought not to be deprived of copyright protection for this reason.

But how to escape from the inexorable logic of artistic copyright, which **2.122** decrees, under the new Act as under the old, that a variety of artistic works including drawings and sculptures shall have copyright "irrespective of artistic quality", and that unauthorised copying of them, whether in the same or in a different dimension, and whether directly or indirectly, constitutes infringement?[64]

The device adopted, as with section 10 of the Copyright Act 1956, is to set **2.123** up a *defence* to an action for copyright infringement. The section is one of a clutch listing a variety of "acts permitted in relation to copyright works", ranging from printing poems in school anthologies to reproducing paintings in an auction catalogue to recording TV programmes for later viewing, all of which would be infringing acts if not permitted by the law for some overriding policy reason. Thus section 51 provides that it is not an infringement of any copyright in a design document or model recording or embodying a design for anything other than an artistic work[65] to make an article to the design or to copy an article made to the design—or thereafter to deal with articles or copies so made. The key word is "for": if the design is "for" an article which is not itself an artistic work—if it is a production drawing "for" a piston rather than a preliminary sketch "for" a portrait bust of a leading politician then copyright in the drawing will not be infringed by making or selling the piston. We are talking about an industrial design, and copyright is not to have any place here. This need not leave the piston-maker unprotected: if the piston fulfils the requirements of the unregistered design right, copying it will be an infringement of that right. And if he can show that elements of the piston are novel and have deliberately been given some eye-appeal, and that even if pistons are not normally bought for their looks, this one might be, then he can also get a registered design. Copyright in the drawing *as such* is unimpaired. If someone illicitly photocopies it and makes prints to hang on the wall, this is an infringement. But using it to make pistons is not.

There is a catch: the definition of "design" in section 51 (and in relation to **2.124** the unregistered design right) means that "surface decoration", even on an article which is not an artistic work, is still to be protected, if at all, by copyright. An ordinary milkjug to be sold in hundreds or thousands is not an "artistic work", and its shape can only be protected by unregistered design

---

[63] *Hansard*, Vol. 491, col. 183.
[64] See 1.013 above.
[65] Or a typeface, but typefaces are treated separately below so as not to distract attention from the basic principle of section 51.

right (and a registered design if appropriate), but if it has a flower glazed or embossed on it, this will be "surface decoration" and will still have to look to copyright for protection. This underlines the fact that section 51 and the unregistered design right (like the bulk of registered designs) are primarily concerned with industrial designs for the *shape* of manufactured articles.

2.125　Returning to the main theme of section 51, if the design *is* for an artistic work, then copyright operates in the usual way. If the drawing is a sketch for a portrait bust, then it *will* be an infringement of copyright to make the bust without the sculptor's consent, whether once or many times. We are dealing with the fine arts, and copyright belongs here. But what is to happen if the sculptor *himself* decides to step into the industrial arena? Suppose, following a change in the political climate, he licenses a manufacturer to produce the bust in sets of 10 for use instead of ducks in a shooting gallery? He has forsworn the fine arts—should he not at some stage be subject to the blasts of competition? The government's answer to this is section 52, which provides that where an artistic work is industrially-exploited by or with the licence of the copyright owner, that industrial exploitation operates (again) as a *defence* to an action for copyright infringement against an unlicensed competitor based on making or selling articles which are copies of the work—but not for 25 years. The sculptor thus has a period during which he can continue to protect his work by copyright, but the fact of industrial exploitation is recognised by abridging the full copyright term. After it has expired, anyone may compete, not only by exploiting the work in the same way, but also in different ways—the politician as paperweight or doorstop as well as duck.

2.126　Here no question of unregistered design right arises. The original design was "for" an artistic work, so copyright has always been the means of protection—section 51 has never "bitten". If the sculptor pleases, provided he applies before industrial exploitation on any scale begins so as to preserve his novelty,[66] he may apply to register a design for the politician as applied to a target. A registered design may co-exist with copyright, except where the design is applied to an article excluded from registration under section 1(5) of the 1949 Act and Designs rule 26,[67] and that would not be the case here because the politician's bust would have become a cast or model intended to be used as a model or pattern to be reproduced by an industrial process. But where this would be so, for example where a portrait of one of Her Majesty's judges is marketed as a transfer,[68] rules made under section 52(4)(b)[69] in the same terms as Designs rule 26 themselves exclude the application of section 52, so that a competitor will not, even after 25 years, be able to apply the judge without the copyright owner's consent, whether to transfers or to doors

---

[66] See sections 6(4) and (5) of the amended Registered Designs Act 1949—2.094 above.
[67] See 2.079 above.
[68] Application of such an image to a T-shirt was a fashion statement foreshadowed by Templeman J. (as he then was) in *Universal City Studios v. Mukhtar & Sons Ltd* [1976] F.S.R. 252.
[69] Copyright (Industrial Process and Excluded Articles) (No. 2) Order 1989, S.I. 1989 No. 1070.

for use in police stations. However, although there is this deliberate coincidence, intended to secure uniformity of untrammelled copyright protection for articles primarily of a literary or artistic character, there is no other connection between either section 51 or section 52 and the registered designs system. Unlike the position under section 10 of the 1956 Act, registrability or non-registrability is not the test of whether a design falls within section 52, still less is section 51 confined to unregistrable designs— the vast majority of registrable designs will be excluded from copyright by the much more stringent test of section 51.

"Hangover" copyright

That is the scheme for new designs under the 1988 Act. It is by no means free of difficulties, and it will be covered in greater detail later in this chapter. But since section 51 drastically cut down the wide copyright protection previously enjoyed, it was thought proper to allow rights acquired under the old system to continue for a time. So Schedule 1, paragraph 19 of the Act's transitional provisions postpones the application of section 51 to *designs already existing on August 1, 1989* until August 1, 1999, while subjecting them to licences of right from August 1, 1994. There is thus "hangover" copyright for these designs (unless it expires earlier through natural causes), and the subsistence and first ownership of this copyright is also still governed by the law in force when the designs were made,[70] although infringements taking place on and since August 1, 1989 are judged under the new infringement provisions (Schedule 1, paragraph 14). Further, Schedule 1, paragraph 20 modifies the effect of section 52 of the new Act in relation to certain existing designs.[71]

2.127

The result is that for the next few years there are two non-registered protection systems in force for the general run of industrial designs. Copyright will be available for "old" designs, as well as for new ones with a high artistic content, for "surface decoration" on new designs, and also in related areas such as packaging and promotional materials. Unregistered design right will be the protection for the bulk of three-dimensional industrial designs coming into being on or after August 1, 1989. Care must be taken to invoke the right one, though the utility of copyright in "old" designs for removing competitors from the market has been drastically reduced by the

2.128

---

[70] See Chap. 3. The Copyright Act 1956 came into effect on June 1, 1957. Naturally, given the normal length of the copyright term, many earlier works will still be in copyright, but by Schedule 7, paragraph 45 of the 1956 Act new provisions were applied retrospectively to existing works. Rather different transitional provisions had been applied under the Copyright Act 1911 to works existing before July 1, 1912, but the result is that even very old works have their character as copyright works judged by the 1956 Act tests.

[71] See Chap. 3.

availability of licences of right since August 1, 1994, competitors now being able to escape an interlocutory injunction by undertaking, without admission of liability, to take a licence of right and pay a royalty. The task of a commentator too is complicated by the need to describe both systems. However, despite section 51 copyright will continue even after the end of the hangover period to play a significant part in industrial affairs, and section 172(3) of the new Act provides that decisions under the previous law may be referred to in construing the new law, so these are still relevant. This section will therefore describe the scope of copyright in relation to both old and new designs, mention being made of the few changes in the definitions of artistic works made by the 1988 Act, which apply only to works made on or after August 1, 1989. The 1956 Act tests apply to works existing at midnight on July 31, 1989.[72]

Originality

2.129 "Works" are the building blocks of copyright: literary, dramatic, musical or artistic works, sound recordings, films, broadcasts (including satellite broadcasts), cable programmes and typographical arrangements of published editions of literary, dramatic or musical works. These are the tangible expressions of their creators' ideas, and without a work of one or other of these kinds, there can be no copyright. The works with which industrial designs relating to appearance are most closely involved are, of course, artistic works, although literary works also play some part. Artistic works express their creators' ideas in the form of lines or shapes, and may be two- or three-dimensional. Literary works express ideas in letters or figures.

2.130 These terms are deliberately neutral, because in neither case, with one or two exceptions,[73] is the law concerned with laymen's ideas of what is "artistic" or "literary". No aesthetic standard need be reached. The test of a work's entitlement to copyright is—is it "original"? This means, is it the product of independent effort, or has it been copied from another work? A and B may sit side-by-side making sketches of Westminster Abbey. If A looks only at Westminister Abbey (apart from his sketchbook), his drawing will be original, even if, as is likely, it closely resembles B's. But if he looks only at B's sketchbook, so that he is copying B's sketch, then his drawing will not be original.

2.131 There is no need for a work which is "original" in this sense to manifest "personal intellectual creation" or "the stamp of the designer's personality" as in some European systems.[74] The question is the more mundane one of

---

[72] See n. 70 above and 1988 Act, Sched. 1, paras. 1(3), (5) and (6).
[73] See 2.161 and 2.162 below.
[74] *Baumann v. Fussell* [1978] R.P.C. 485 might seem to contradict both this and the proposition in the previous paragraph. The defendant artist, without the plaintiff's consent, had used the plaintiff's published colour photograph of two cocks fighting as the inspiration for a painting.

whether skill and labour has been expended on producing the work, and this is often no more than the routine skill and labour of the trained draughtsman who has actually put pen to paper—although the efforts of the actual designer whose ideas the draughtsman reduces to material form, and the investment of their common employer, may be more or less overtly recognised.[75]

Nor is there any question of novelty or originality in the registered design sense[76] being required. The existence of "prior art" in the form of similar designs is of no significance unless the plaintiff copied them in producing its own (or the defendant did). Moreover, where a defendant has in fact copied the plaintiff's work, so that there is no real defence of independent design put forward, a court may be tempted to fall back on the maxim "what is worth copying is worth protecting" and not examine the originality of the plaintiff's work too jealously.　2.132

Nor is mere simplicity of subject-matter usually enough to negate originality. In *British Northrop Ltd v. Texteam Blackburn Ltd*[77] it was suggested that drawings of spare parts for weaving machinery including a rivet, a screw, a bolt, a metal bar, a block of leather and a washer might be too simple to attract copyright. Megarry J. disagreed. He observed that a straight line drawn with a ruler "would not seem to me a very promising subject for copyright", and a drawing traced directly from another would not be original because it would not "originate" with its maker. But there was no limitation to be found in the Copyright Act on what could constitute a "drawing".　2.133

Nonetheless there can be problems for a plaintiff where products have evolved over time and there is a long series of drawings recording modifications, some major, some minor. He will want to rely on the drawing or drawings used to make the article actually (or allegedly) copied, because otherwise he may fail to show an adequate causal connection between the drawing and the defendant's product; but that drawing may to a large extent be merely a redrawing of earlier drawings, updated to depict the current production version. As Megarry J. recognised, a mere tracing of an existing drawing would not be "original", and even where copying has taken place, it　2.134

He had adopted the attitude of the birds and to a certain extent the colours, but these were "heightened" and the majority of the Court of Appeal found that the defendant had imparted enough of his own "feeling and artistic nature" to the subject-matter to impart originality and take the painting out of infringement. This was probably the wrong test of infringement—the dissenting member held the defendant, in adopting the same attitude for the birds, had taken a substantial part of the photograph—although an infringing work like an unauthorised translation can still be original. The test of "feeling and artistic nature" can demonstrate originality, but is not a pre-requisite, and "inspiration" or copying is a matter of fact and degree.

[75] See, *e.g. L. B. (Plastics) Ltd v. Swish Products Ltd* [1979] R.P.C. 551, where Lord Wilberforce referred to "a great deal of effort and ingenuity" which had gone into *designing* the drawer components, Lord Hailsham spoke of "two years' travail consumed in design and development" and "much skill, labour and investment" expended during those years, and Lord Salmon said the plaintiffs had spent "a great deal of money in experimental work".

[76] See 2.115 above.

[77] [1974] R.P.C. 57.

would be improper to protect a work which does not fulfil even the rudimentary requirements for the subsistence of copyright.

2.135   This is particularly the case where earlier drawings may be out of copyright, as can sometimes happen where the design would have been registrable under the designs legislation and the copyright period is therefore much shorter than usual.[78] Too casual an attitude to the amount of old work copied into the more recent drawings can then effectively renew the copyright in the old ones.

2.136   This point was another one confronted by the Judicial Committee of the Privy Council in *Interlego v. Tyco*.[79] Lego sought to rely on their drawings as copyright works to prevent Tyco marketing its own system which was designed by reverse engineering (copying the actual LEGO bricks) so as to be compatible with Lego's system, and therefore indirectly reproduced Lego's drawings in three dimensions. The LEGO products had evolved over the years and those copied incorporated a number of design changes and improvements. Copyright in the earlier drawings had expired, but new ones had been made to reflect the design changes, and it was on these that Lego now sued. The new drawings had been made by copying the earlier ones but altering them where necessary to indicate dimensional and tolerance changes (shown by figures and arrows), altered radii, sharpened edges and the addition or removal of certain features occasioned by different manufacturing techniques. The drawings *looked* very little different from the earlier ones, but the exercise had involved quite substantial skill and labour in the sense that it had taken skilled draughtsmen several hours to redraw the drawings; and it was accepted that they reflected technically significant design changes which were the product of research effort and investment by Lego. On this basis Lego argued that the new drawings possessed sufficient originality to give them a new copyright. They were fortified in this argument by earlier authorities, such as Whitford J. in *L. B. (Plastics) v. Swish*,[80] where the originality of updated drawings (and also of drawings of existing three-dimensional prototypes) had been attacked. Whitford J. had held that sufficient skill and labour had been expended in both these exercises for the resulting drawings to be original.

2.137   The Privy Council rejected Lego's argument. The new drawings as visual images showed scarcely any differences from the earlier ones. The expenditure of skill and labour was a perfectly proper test of originality, but the court must take care, as Whitford J. had not, to identify the skill and labour expended, and to examine its purpose. Skill and labour, however extensive, expended merely in copying an existing drawing could not confer originality—because the images in the copied drawing would not "originate"

---

[78] See below.
[79] [1988] R.P.C. 343.
[80] n. 75 above.

with the later draughtsman, any more than the content of a laboriously and skilfully copied painting would originate with the copier. Nor could skill and labour expended in incorporating literary matter such as dimensions and tolerances expressed in figures, however technically significant and hard-won such information might be, confer *artistic* originality. Copyright was, after all, claimed in these drawings as artistic works, and unless the skill and labour resulted in some *visually significant* changes to the artistic images depicted, it was irrelevant—as was the research and investment involved in making technical improvements resulting in little or no visible alteration. There must be "some element of material alteration or embellishment" before a new drawing could be original. However, a quantitatively small alteration or embellishment, if qualitatively significant, might suffice; each case must still turn on its own facts. And on one point the Committee agreed with Whitford J.: it could well be that a drawing depicting an earlier prototype, itself not made or copied from a drawing, would be original, "for there is no more reason for denying originality to the depiction of a three-dimensional prototype than there is for denying originality to the depiction in two-dimensional form of any other physical object".[81] Presumably the same could be said of three-dimensional works based on sketches, and indeed wherever a production process involves different versions of a work produced by different people with different skills.[82]

The case was a valuable reminder of the nature of artistic copyright, and has been treated with suitable respect. It scotched any suggestion that the skill and labour involved in merely tracing or copying could be relevant; and the test of visual significance (already hit on independently by Whitford J. in *Rose Plastics GmbH v. Beckett*[83] which was cited in *Interlego*) has been regularly applied. Nonetheless, it turned to a substantial extent on its own facts, including the fact that the earlier drawings were out of copyright. Where designs have evolved over a period, or there have been several versions of the same basic design, but all the drawings are still in copyright, the court is disinclined to accept arguments based on originality from a defendant who has clearly copied one or another (or several) of them. Indeed two recent decisions have given summary judgment in favour of the plaintiff in such circumstances, where the evidence of copying was beyond dispute[84]—the more recent involving "chartlets" of ports and areas of coastline based largely on Admiralty charts also available to the defendants, whose only problem was that they had clearly copied the plaintiffs' version rather than the Admiralty's. **2.138**

The originality requirement for literary works likely to be encountered in the field of industrial designs is no more demanding—tables of dimensions or **2.139**

---

[81] At p. 371.
[82] *e.g. James Arnold & Co. Ltd v. Miafern Ltd* [1980] R.P.C. 397, see 3.060 below.
[83] [1989] F.S.R. 13.
[84] *L. A. Gear Inc. v. Hi-Tec Sports plc* [1992] F.S.R. 121 (shoes); *Macmillan Publishers Ltd v. Thomas Reed Publications Ltd* [1993] F.S.R. 455.

design modifications such as appear on engineering drawings, lists of components and knitting patterns are all fit subjects for copyright, based on what Americans call the "sweat of the brow" test: someone has gone to some trouble to compile them, even if everything tabled or listed is a piece of publicly-available information, and there is no reason why a competitor should be able to take the benefit of this effort while maintaining his own brow undelved.

Artistic works

2.140 Most copyright works directly involved with making articles to industrial designs will be artistic works. The provision[85] that reproducing a two-dimensional work in three dimensions and vice versa infringes copyright is expressly limited to artistic works. Case law has hitherto accepted that copyright in a literary work is not infringed by making an article described in it, even where the literary work consists of instructions to do just that—a recipe for a rabbit pie, a knitting pattern,[86] tables and notes of dimensions,[87] possibly a DNA nucleotide sequence for making a cell line.[88]

2.141 "Artistic works" under section 3(1)(a) of the 1956 Act were drawings, sculptures, paintings, engravings and photographs, all irrespective of artistic quality; under section 3(1)(b) works of architecture (either buildings or models for buildings); and under section 3(1)(c) "works of artistic craftsman-ship". "Irrespective of artistic quality" means that no test of artistic merit or achievement may be applied in determining whether a work so qualified is artistic. The test is purely whether the underlying idea is expressed in lines or shapes rather than words or figures. Nor is the artist's intention relevant. A sketch of a bedpan, made as the first step in designing the product, is just as much an artistic work as a preliminary sketch of a portrait or sculpture. Under section 4 of the 1988 Act, the same categories of artistic works are protected, though with some altered definitions and rather differently-organised, and with the addition of a "collage" as a newly-recognised form of artistic work.

Drawings

2.142 Drawings have been of critical significance to the development of copyright in industrial designs. By section 48(1) of the 1956 Act, "drawing" was defined, in accordance with the Gregory Committee recommendation,[89] as including

---

[85] Now section 17(3) of the 1988 Act.
[86] *Brigid Foley Ltd v. Elliott* [1982] R.P.C. 433.
[87] *Duriron Ltd v. Hugh Jennings* [1984] F.S.R. 1. This may now be changing, see 2.170 below.
[88] See "Could copyright safeguard the secrets of the genome?"—article in *New Scientist*, October 10, 1992 and letter in correspondence column, November 14, 1992.
[89] See Chap. 1.

"any diagram, map, chart or plan"—irrespective, of course, of artistic quality. "Diagram" and "plan" are apt to describe all kinds of engineering drawings of machinery and components, which had previously been classed as literary works because their prime function was to convey instructions about how the articles depicted were to be made. As literary works they were not infringed by making the articles, but as artistic works they were, because to reproduce without leave was to infringe (section 3(5)(a)), and by section 48(1) reproduction of a two-dimensional artistic work included making it in three-dimensional form. This is still the case under section 17(3) of the 1988 Act, which governs infringements taking place on and after August 1, 1989. It was not a defence that in most cases the drawings were not copied directly but by copying the plaintiff's own products made in accordance with them—reproduction could be indirect as well as direct, and again this is spelt out in section 16(3)(b) of the 1988 Act. Moreover under section 49(1) of the 1956 Act and section 16(3)(a) of the 1988 Act, copyright was and is infringed by copying not only the whole of a work but also a substantial part of it; and the courts in deciding what is a substantial part have applied a test which is as much qualitative as quantitative—copying a small part of a drawing which is crucial to the working of the part or machine depicted has been held to be infringement.[90]

The commercial importance of copyright to manufacturing industry, as well as the pure functionality of many of the designs litigated, can be judged by a random list of the subject-matter of reported cases: screws, bolts and washers, being spare parts for looms,[91] pulley wheels,[92] plastic knock-down drawers,[93] spare parts for vacuum cleaners,[94] traffic safety cones,[95] septic tanks.[1] Of course, copyright has also been widely-used in fields such as textiles, and in clothing design, where actions have been commonly based on design sketches[2]; and arguably cutting patterns, which are drawn and then cut out, are "drawings" for the purposes of the 1956 Act.[3] In *Ornstin Ltd v. Quality Plastics*[4] labels were made by cutting out pieces of coloured paper and sticking them on card. The judge decided that these were drawings, observing that "the word 'drawing' does not mean that the author must produce his work by means of pen or pencil, but denotes that the work is the product of an artist who represents his ideas by line or delineation or colour". Works of this kind might now more properly be characterised as "collages". A further area where drawings have proved useful is architecture, where the use in litigation of plans which are produced in three dimensions by erecting

2.143

---

[90] *Hoover plc v. George Hulme (Sto) Ltd* [1982] F.S.R. 565. For further discussion, see Chap. 5.
[91] *British Northrop Ltd v. Texteam Blackburn Ltd* [1974] R.P.C. 57.
[92] *Solar Thomson Engineering Ltd v. Barton* [1977] R.P.C. 537.
[93] *L. B. (Plastics) Ltd v. Swish Products Ltd* [1979] R.P.C. 551.
[94] *Hoover v. Hulme*, n. 90 above.
[95] *Johnstone Safety Ltd v. Peter Cook (International) plc* [1990] F.S.R. 161.
[1] *Entec (Pollution Control) Ltd v. Abacus Mouldings* [1992] F.S.R. 332.
[2] *J. Bernstein Ltd v. Sydney Murray Ltd* [1981] R.P.C. 303.
[3] *Radley Gowns Ltd v. Costas Spyrou* [1975] F.S.R. 455.
[4] 1990 I.P.D. 13027.

buildings in accordance with them has superseded reliance on copyright in buildings as such.

2.144   The fact that a drawing has been produced with the aid of a computer (as with many architects' plans, layout drawings for offices, kitchens and the like, motor car body designs and, increasingly, textile and knitwear designs) is not thought to prevent it being a "drawing". There is authority (*Express Newspapers plc v. Liverpool Daily Post and Echo plc*[5]) that a "literary" work (a sequence of numbers for a newspaper bingo competition) did not lack copyright because it was generated by the author's specially-written computer program rather than as a result of innumerable calculations made by him with pencil and paper. Whitford J. remarked that the contrary argument would suggest that the works of Charles Dickens emanated from his pen—a colourful way of recognising that the computer had been used merely as a tool, to take the sweat out of a lengthy and mechanical task. The same reasoning would apply to a drawing, provided that a hard copy or screen display is available to "prove" what the drawing looked like, the actual information stored in the computer being in numerical (literary) rather than artistic form. The computer can save time by generating views and elevations, or stitch displays, which would otherwise have to be laboriously drawn out on squared paper, but the inspiration remains the designer's. This is so even where the software contains a "library" of standard images representing trees or desks or gas hobs, because it is in the selection and arrangement of these rather than their individual depiction that the essence of a design will usually be found.

2.145   A potential though rarely successful defence in drawing cases which is no longer with us was section 9(8) of the 1956 Act, which sought to minimise the use of copyright for purely functional articles based on engineering drawings by providing that if a layman would not recognise the defendant's article from the plaintiff's drawing there would be no infringement. This was repealed along with the rest of the 1956 Act and was not replaced with any corresponding provision. It could still be pleaded as a defence to "secondary" infringement (infringement by knowingly dealing in, rather than making, infringing copies) where the copies were made before August 1, 1989 in circumstances where the defence might have been available, and have been dealt in since,[6] but with the passage of time this is decreasingly likely.

2.146   Drawings continue to be protected as artistic works under the 1988 Act. (In considering any new definitions, it should be noted that section 172(2) says, helpfully or unhelpfully, that a provision which corresponds to a provision of the previous law shall not be construed as departing from that law "merely because of a change of expression".) Drawings under section 4 of the new Act form part of a newly-coined class of "graphic works", again protected "irrespective of artistic quality". A "graphic work" is not exhaustively

[5] [1985] F.S.R. 306.
[6] Sched. 1, para. 14(3)(a).

defined: the expression merely "includes" drawings, paintings, diagrams, maps, charts and plans, and engravings, etchings, lithographs, woodcuts or "similar works", so there is room for other, presumably substantially two-dimensional, works. The use of "graphic" may resolve lingering doubts as to whether the products of computer "graphics" programs such as bar and pie charts and little men and women doing the world's work, or indeed "simulated" paintings, of increasing importance in, *e.g.* textile and clothing design, advertising, packaging and display, animation and broadcasting, are artistic rather than literary works. An animated cartoon produced on a computer, if it is not a painting or drawing, might be a graphic work; so arguably might be a version of an existing black-and-white film "colourised" by computer (as well as being a film with its own copyright). "Virtual reality" creations, whereby the solitary can view on helmet-mounted screens landscapes or people generated by a computer working on drawings to produce an illusion of depth and perspective, could also be comprehended in the definition.

Paintings

"Painting" is not further defined in either Act, but normal dictionary **2.147** definitions, supplemented by recognition of computer painting techniques as mentioned in the preceding paragraph, provide an adequate guide.

Sculpture

Sculpture was not under the 1956 Act and is not now defined, other than as **2.148** including a cast or model made for the purposes of sculpture. Most people will have a fairly clear idea of what they mean by sculpture—Chantrey busts, bronze statesmen, marble worthies on staircases, carved wooden statuettes. Certainly for copyright purposes all of these are covered, along with humbler artefacts like toy soldiers,[7] tombstones[8] and wolf cubs' heads for totem poles.[9] But the *Shorter Oxford English Dictionary* defines sculpture as:

> "Originally the process or art of carving or engraving a hard material so as to produce designs or figures in relief, in intaglio, or in the round. In modern use, that branch of fine art which is concerned with producing figures in the round or in relief, either by carving, by fashioning some plastic substance, or by making a mould for casting in metal."

[7] *Britain v. Hanks Bros & Co.* (1902) 86 L.T. 764.
[8] *Swinstead v. R. Underwood & Sons* [1923–28] M.C.C. 39.
[9] *Pytram Ltd v. Models (Leicester) Ltd* [1930] 1 Ch. 639.

Webster's Third New International Dictionary prefers:

> "1. The act, process or art of carving, cutting, hewing, moulding, welding or constructing materials into statues, ornaments or figures
>
> 2. The act, process or art of producing figures or groups in plastic or hard materials."

The *New Encyclopaedia Britannica*,[10] observes that the definition of sculpture is constantly changing, but that the abiding concern of sculptors is with "the branch of the visual arts that is especially concerned with the creation of expressive form in three dimensions".[11] Not all these definitions labour the "fine arts" and although they no doubt primarily envisage the doing of the various acts mentioned by hand, there seems no reason why the "act" or "process" of "moulding" or "constructing" materials into statues, ornaments or figures or "producing" figures or groups in plastic or hard materials, with due regard for "the creation of expressive form in three dimensions" should not cover turning out thousands of plastic garden gnomes or plaster herons or reconstituted stone gatepost lions from moulds. Or myriads of "souvenir" trinkets—Eiffel Towers, Statues of Liberty, London buses and horrid little figurines of birds, beasts and humanoids— made from metal or plastic. This is the more so because both the 1956 and 1988 Acts protect sculptures as artistic works "irrespective of artistic quality", so preclude any aesthetic judgments. Included within the statutory definition are casts or models made for purposes of sculpture, so if the various end products mentioned do qualify as sculptures, the original casts or models from which they are made will be "made for purposes of sculpture". This may be highly significant for the new régime under section 51.

2.149   Moreover, not all production processes for articles which are not sculptures are based on or include drawings. At least while "hangover" copyright lasts, if there is anything in the production process of an industrial artefact which might fit the dictionary definitions of "sculpture" (such as a carved template or a clay model of a new car body) it may be possible to plead it as the "founding" copyright work which is indirectly infringed. In the famous New Zealand case of *WHAM-O Manufacturing Co. v. Lincoln Industries*,[12] decided under an Act almost identical to the 1956 Act, the plaintiffs persuaded the Court of Appeal that a hand-carved wooden model which was the second stage in the design of their FRISBEE flying discs was a sculpture whose copyright was indirectly infringed by the defendant's moulded plastic discs copied from the plaintiff's discs. In a U.K. case at about the same time, though only recently reported, *Breville Europe plc v. Thorn EMI Domestic Appliances Ltd*,[13] Falconer J. accepted that plaster models of sandwiches used in shaping the die-casting moulds for making the heating

---

[10] Vol. 16, p. 421.

[11] These definitions are taken from the report of the New Zealand Court of Appeal decision in *WHAM-O Manufacturing Co. v. Lincoln Industries Ltd* [1985] R.P.C. 127, discussed below.

[12] [1985] R.P.C. 127.

[13] [1995] F.S.R. 77.

plates of a toasted sandwich maker could be sculptures. He was saved, on the facts, from deciding whether toasted sandwiches could be infringing copies of these sculptures.

However, in the later U.K. case of *Davis (Holdings) Ltd v. Wright Health Group Ltd*,[14] the court was more sceptical. The articles allegedly copied were dental impression trays produced by a process of modelling a number of "standard" mouths in plasticine modelling material, from which casts in dental stone were made; these were used to produce plastic prototypes from which in turn tooling was made for the production of trays. There were also drawings traced from sections cut from casts. The models and casts were relied on as "sculptures". Whitford J. had no hesitation in dismissing this suggestion. The models and casts were merely steps in the production process, never intended to have any continuing existence—indeed, the models had not been kept and the designer had laboriously to reconstruct them to demonstrate what they had looked like. A hand-carved wooden model might be a sculpture, but these things were not, nor were they made "for purposes of sculpture", this expression being taken apparently—and sensibly—to import some regard to the designer's intention. The drawings failed the section 9(8) lay recognition test, and were in any event mere tracings.[15]   **2.150**

Engraving

Reliance on dubious "sculptures" was thus discouraged, and Whitford J. made a mildly disparaging reference to judicial extension of words in the Copyright Act to a point where their meaning bore very little relation to the meaning non-lawyers would give them. He was not called upon to comment on the other *WHAM-O* finding that the dies and moulds (based on the wooden model) used to make the flying discs, and the plastic discs themselves, were "engravings"—defined in section 48(1) as including "any etching, lithograph, woodcut, print or similar work"—because the moulds were "similar to" woodcuts and the discs could be regarded as "prints". However, there the finding is, and the earlier U.K. decision in *James Arnold & Co. Ltd v. Miafern Ltd*[16] had already treated rubber stereos fitted on to rollers for printing a pattern on scarves as "engravings" within the 1956 Act. The stereos were another example of steps in a production process, lighted on because nothing else seemed suitable and saved by the section 3(1)(a) exemption from any scrutiny of their artistic quality.   **2.151**

"Engravings" are part of the new class of "graphic works" under section 4 of the 1988 Act, still protected irrespective of artistic quality. The definition   **2.152**

---

[14] [1988] R.P.C. 403.
[15] The New Zealand courts are unrepentant. In *Mayceys Confectionery Ltd v. Beckmann* [1995] 4 EIPR D-101 the Auckland High Court held that plaster of Paris models of jelly crocodiles were sculptures, and the rubber moulds made from them were engravings.
[16] [1980] R.P.C. 397.

of graphic work no longer includes the expression "print", so the FRISBEE discs at least would not now qualify as engravings; but the *Shorter Oxford Dictionary* still offers us "to sculpture, to cut into, to mark by incisions, to carve upon a surface, to represent by incisions upon wood, metal, stone, etc., with the view of reproducing by printing" and "an impression from an engraved plate", and section 4 itself gives us "etching" and "lithograph". These expressions are apt to cover various kinds of jewellery, coins, medals, but possibly also CDs, vinyl records and tyre treads.

Collage

2.153 There is no definition of "collage" in the 1988 Act, where it is introduced for the first time as a type of artistic work. It would cover a collection of photographs, drawings, cuttings and so on stuck to some kind of backing,[17] and there seems no reason why it should not also cover pieces of fabric so stuck. But it is not clear that it would cover patchwork which is not mounted on anything.[18] Collages are interesting in that they are works which will incorporate parts, substantial or otherwise, of other works which are likely to have their own copyright. It may be acceptable to cut out photographs, etc., from magazines to make a collage,[19] but if the collage is then itself photographed or shown on television or incorporated in a film, the photographer would have grounds for complaint.[20] In this respect, collages have a lot in common with "megamixes" and sampling in the music industry, where snippets are taken from a variety of other recordings and incorporated in complex medleys.[21] Or with "deconstructionism" in literature, which seems to involve a similar process of "quotation" in relation to literary works.

Photograph

2.154 "Photograph" was defined in section 48(1) of the 1956 Act as "any product of photography or of any process akin to photography, other than part of a film". Photography utilises the operation of light on a suitable medium, so photolithography and photogravure processes, photographic typesetting and the like and "mask works" for semiconductor chips were covered. So was the

---

[17] Like the labels in *Ornstin Ltd v. Quality Plastics* 1990 I.P.D. 13027—see 2.143 above.

[18] The omission of a definition was deliberate. Lord Beaverbrook said magisterially "The courts ought to be able to recognise one if they have one before them": *Hansard*, Vol. 493, col. 1067.

[19] Though a photographer who retains copyright may argue that the licence he gave to the magazine to publish it does not extend to permitting readers to incorporate it into another work.

[20] See, for an old example, *Hanfstaengl v. W. H. Smith & Sons* [1905] 1 Ch. 519—collage of advertisements.

[21] See, *e.g. Morrison Leahy Music Ltd v. Lightbond Ltd* [1993] E.M.L.R. 144.

humble photocopy, but since copyright photographs must be "original", making a photocopy seemed unlikely to qualify. For the same reason, photographs have not played much part as "founding" works in industrial design cases, since they merely record the appearance of a product or are a step in the production process. But in a recent criminal prosecution, *Manners v. The Reject Shop plc*,[22] a photocopy (which no longer existed) was accepted as an original work in which copyright subsisted.

The complainant is a tilemaker to the rich and famous. His tiles are handmade and the patterns are formed by inlaying different coloured clay into suitably-shaped recesses stamped onto the tile before firing. Templates for forming the recesses are made by taking a photocopy of a working drawing, reducing or enlarging the photocopy by further photocopying (to allow for shrinkage of the clay and hence the image on firing), and gluing the "final image" so obtained to formica which is then cut out with a saw. The Bow Street magistrate accepted that "final image" as the copyright work. He considered the *Interlego* requirement[23] for some "visually significant" alteration or embellishment to give a copied drawing originality, but decided that as a matter of degree the distorted photocopy possessed it.[24] The Reject Shop and one of its then directors was convicted of selling copies of the tile pattern on a range of tinware and notebooks. The case is under appeal, not least because the requisite knowledge that the design infringed was arguably not proved even to the civil standard of balance of probabilities, let alone the criminal standard of beyond reasonable doubt. **2.155**

The new definition of "photograph" under section 4 of the 1988 Act speaks of a recording of light or other radiation on any medium on or from which an image is or can be produced. This was meant[25] to make clear that other forms of radiation than light alone, *e.g.* electron rather than photon beams, are covered. Holograms, three-dimensional images produced from the recording of information about both amplitude and phase of incident light on a very thin film of emulsion, already came within the old definition. **2.156**

Semiconductor chip topographies

As well as being protected as "photographs", *sui generis* protection for these was contained in the Semiconductor Products (Protection of Topography) Regulations 1987,[26] made in compliance with E.C. Directive 87/54, the E.C.'s response to the U.S. Semiconductor Chip Protection Act 1984, which gave protection only to countries adequately protecting U.S. chips. The U.S. had by Presidential decree already granted interim protection to U.K. chips on the **2.157**

---

[22] See Case Comment at [1995] 1 E.I.P.R. 46.
[23] See 2.137 above.
[24] The government would be most distressed by this, see *Hansard*, Vol. 493, col. 1072.
[25] *Hansard*, Vol. 493, col. 1065.
[26] S.I. 1987 No. 1497.

basis of their falling within the 1956 Act. Topographies created before November 7, 1987 are still a matter for copyright and their infringement would be treated accordingly. The only difference is that licences of right will not automatically be available during the last five years of the "hangover" copyright term.[27]

2.158   The *sui generis* right under the 1987 Regulations related to a "topography". This was the design, however expressed, of the pattern fixed or intended to be fixed in or upon a layer of a semiconductor product, or a layer of material in the course of, and for the purpose of, the manufacture of a semiconductor product, or the arrangement of such layers in relation to one another. A "semiconductor product" was an article whose purpose, or one of whose purposes, was the performance of an electronic function and which consisted of two or more layers at least one of which was made of semiconducting material and in or upon one of which was fixed a pattern appertaining to that or another function. The topography had to be original, in the sense of resulting from the creator's own intellectual effort (or the combined intellectual efforts of more than one creator),[28] and it must not be "commonplace" among creators of topographies or manufacturers of semiconductor products—although a topography might be original by virtue of its combination of elements in themselves non-original or commonplace (paragraph 3(3)). The 1987 Regulations were superseded after less than two years by a fresh Regulation when topographies were largely absorbed into the unregistered design right régime, and are further considered below, but it should be noted that in the interim copying them in two dimensions (*i.e.* other than by making the chip) was, by a combination of paragraphs 4(2)(d) and 9(1) of the Regulations, treated as an infringement of the copyright in the topography.

Works of architecture

2.159   These are, under both the 1956 and 1988 Acts, buildings or models for buildings. The 1956 Act defined a building as including "any structure"; the current definition changes this to any "fixed" structure and also includes a part of a building or fixed structure. Much of the Parliamentary debate centred on the desirability of protecting the works of engineers as well as architects, so that bridges would benefit. There seems no reason why they would not have done so under the old definition, which was as wide as it could be, and apparently apt to cover moveable structures such as helter-skelter towers in fairgrounds and stage sets. The bridge point (and a Blackpool Tower point) were conceded in debate, but "fixed" was introduced to make it plain that ships were not to be covered,[29] so no-one seems

---

[27] Para. 10(3) of the Design Right (Semiconductor Topographies) Regulations 1989, S.I. 1989 No. 1100.

[28] This requirement reflects European thinking.

[29] *Hansard*, Vol. 493, col. 1071.

much better off. Designers of moveable structures may still argue that "building" "includes" but does not "mean" a fixed structure and therefore does not "exclude" a moveable one, but their position seems somewhat weakened.[30] They may now have to look to registered or unregistered designs for their protection.

The reference to "parts" of buildings was meant[31] to make it plain that the   **2.160**
Meikle v. Maufe[32] decision prohibiting unlicensed extensions repeating the design of a building should continue to apply. It would also cover features like canopies, gables, window details and so on. But the expression is very wide indeed and may also cover wholly structural members like joists and beams (if original).

Whether it does depends on whether works of architecture have to be   **2.161**
"artistic", on which opinion is divided. Under the 1911 Act, they expressly did, but the 1956 Act dropped this requirement. On the other hand, it did not include works of architecture within the "irrespective of artistic quality" exemption. The question has been of little significance because buildings have been protected as three-dimensional reproductions of their plans, but now that section 51 requires a three-dimensional end-product of any design process to be itself an "artistic work" if it is to enjoy copyright, it becomes important again.

Works of artistic craftsmanship

This was the most vexing of the categories of artistic work under the 1956   **2.162**
Act, and the expression is unchanged in the 1988 Act. These works are not further defined, and they are not subject to the "irrespective of artistic quality" exemption. They are the last recourse of the would-be plaintiff who can rely on neither drawing, sculpture nor engraving, and consequently have been little litigated in the field of industrial design and never (at least in reported cases) successfully taken to trial. There are only a few major cases to consider. In Burke v. Spicers Dress Designs Ltd,[33] decided under the 1911 Act, the judge found a dress not to be a work of artistic craftsmanship because the artistry had been contributed by the designer but the craftsmanship by the dressmakers. In any event, he felt the word "artistic" required the work to be that of an artist who "cultivated one of the fine arts in which the object is mainly to gratify the aesthetic emotions by perfection of execution, whether in creation or representation". Hensher Ltd v. Restawile Upholstery (Lancs) Ltd[34] is the leading case, having gone to the House of Lords. It was about a suite of furniture, designed and made for the mass market. The original

---

[30] And will be weakened still further if the court reads col. 1071.
[31] Hansard, Vol. 493, col. 1069.
[32] [1941] 3 All E.R. 144, see 3.059 below.
[33] [1936] 1 Ch. 400.
[34] [1975] R.P.C. 31.

sketches were so rudimentary that the section 9(8) lay recognition defence actually succeeded—the judge could not recognise the defendant's suite as a reproduction of them. The plaintiff was forced to rely on a prototype which was no more than a wooden frame with upholstery tacked to it. The trial judge did not think it necessary to consider artistic merit, but applied what is in effect the test for design registration—did people buy the furniture at least in part for the way it looked? He found that they did, and that the test of artistic craftsmanship was thereby satisfied.

2.163 The Court of Appeal used a different test to find against the plaintiff. People, it felt, buy furniture, at least furniture of this kind, for its functional utility rather than any appeal to aesthetic taste—to sit on rather than to contemplate. The judge's test might be apt to decide whether there was an "original design" whose appearance was one of its commercial selling points, but this was not good enough for copyright. The Gregory Committee would have agreed; they felt that works of artistic craftsmanship should not be mass-produced goods, for which registered design protection would be suitable, but the works of silversmiths, potters, hand-embroiderers and the like.

2.164 The House of Lords also found that copyright could not subsist in the prototype, even taking into account the character of the finished goods, but reached no unanimity as to why this was. Lord Reid accepted it was right to look at what the public thought, but found no evidence that they thought the furniture was "artistic"; they merely liked the look of it. Lord Kilbrandon thought the designer's intention was the only sure guide—had he thought he was producing a work of art? Clearly not. Lord Simon of Glaisdale believed the test was whether the design was the work of artist/craftsmen in the William Morris tradition—equally clearly not. Viscount Dilhorne and Lord Morris of Borth-y-Gest came closest to a coincidence of view, both feeling that the question was one of evidence. Lord Morris conceded some weight to the purchaser's view and some to the designer's intention, but one of the witnesses had denied that the furniture was aesthetically good, and on the whole his Lordship felt unable to find it "artistic". Viscount Dilhorne said "works of artistic craftsmanship" was a phrase made up of ordinary English words to be given their ordinary and natural meaning in the light of all the evidence, including expert evidence, and since both expert and non-expert witnesses had said variously and frankly that the furniture was "horrible", "flashy" and "vulgar", even though commercially successful, there was no basis for finding it "artistic".

2.165 The third major case is *Merlet v. Mothercare plc*[35]. The plaintiff, who happened to be a professional fashion designer, while experiencing inclement weather in Scotland, cut out of waterproof fabric and stitched a mackintosh cape, with hood and drawstring neck, so that she could keep her small baby warm and dry when she carried it outdoors. She made no preliminary

[35] [1986] R.P.C. 115.

sketches as she had no need to, but when she decided to commercialise the design she made cutting patterns for the fabric pieces. When her design was copied, she sued on the cutting patterns, and on the prototype garment as a work of artistic craftsmanship. The case on the cutting patterns failed (again) under section 9(8), and the judge refused to recognise the garment, which he termed "a basic commodity item", albeit useful and stylish, as a work of artistic craftsmanship. The Court of Appeal agreed. The plaintiff's counsel blandished the court with an advertisement showing a mother cradling her mackintosh-caped infant, suggesting that the whole ensemble could be taken into account in considering artistry; but the judges refused to permit their grandfatherly emotions to be ravished into error.

With the exception of *Burke v. Spicers*, these cases turned on their evidence, as indeed the House of Lords on balance felt they should, and it is not impossible that with suitable expert evidence and designers willing to emphasise the artistry of their intentions (and ideally the dexterity of their fingers),[36] items at the luxury ends of the fashion and furnishing trades might succeed in proving themselves works of artistic craftsmanship, or at least arguably so for the purposes of an interlocutory injunction. The fashion trade seems particularly promising and less likely to fall foul of the *Hensher* Court of Appeal's "primarily functional" objection: while most furniture, however attractive, is bought to sit on, eat off or store things in, one extra "artistic" woolly jumper or exclusive designer dress is more a matter of self-indulgence than the preserving of decency.   **2.166**

Despite pressure, the government declined to attempt a definition of a work of artistic craftsmanship when drafting the new Act. Lord Beaverbrook[37] regarded the category as a safety net to catch deserving works not falling within any of the other clauses—"works of genuine artistry such as pottery, embroidery and other forms of craftsmanship with an artistic element". This stress on craftsmanship could be unfortunate if it were taken to require that such items must be handmade. Many designers who might regard themselves as artist/craftsmen in the William Morris tradition (Lord Simon's test in *Hensher*), because their work involves a high degree of artistry and is not mass-produced, nowadays use computer-controlled machines to make up their designs, particularly for knitwear and embroidery. This saves time and sweat and allows them to experiment much more quickly with a variety of designs and variations, increasing the input of artistry even though diminishing the input of the relatively mundane skill of manipulating needles. Dictionary definitions are not very helpful, the *Shorter Oxford Dictionary*   **2.167**

---

[36] "Craftsmanship" is not an empty requirement. In the Australian case of *Komesaroff v. Mickle* [1988] R.P.C. 204 the plaintiff produced a device for making "sand pictures"—an arrangement of coloured sand, liquid and a layer of air bubbles sandwiched between two glass plates. Miniature sand landscapes evolved when the sands trickled through the bubbles under the influence of gravity. The plaintiff failed to prevent the defendant copying the device, for the sound reason that it was no more than an idea, since she did not arrange the landscapes herself, but also because no craftsmanship was involved.

[37] *Hansard*, Vol. 490, col. 847.

offering "craftsman: a man who practises a handicraft". "Craft" is a little more helpful, offering "craft: a calling requiring special skill and knowledge, *esp.* a manual art", which allows some room for updating.

2.168   Lord Beaverbrook's notion of "craftsmanship with an artistic element" was exemplified by the interlocutory decision in *Shelley Films Ltd v. Rex Features Ltd.*[38] This was a successful attempt to stop publication of photographs showing the sets, costumes and other details of the film *Mary Shelley's Frankenstein* during closed-set shooting. The plaintiff claimed that the costumes and sets were works of artistic craftsmanship, being the result of minute historical research, hundreds of drawings and sketches and careful selection and treatment of materials and fabrics, all infused with the artistic and imaginative values and concepts of the story and film. Further, the "body" of the "creature" and aspects of other characters' makeup consisted of latex prostheses taken from body casts, moulded and hand-painted and with individual hairs inserted one by one. The production team consisted of artists, designers, sculptors, carpenters, plasterers and technicians whose work was both original and artistic. The judge held it fully arguable that the costumes, prostheses and sets were works of artistic craftsmanship.

Typefaces

2.169   Original sets of type have long been protected by artistic copyright, based on the drawings depicting them, and therefore the Act does not treat them separately, except to make it clear in section 178 that "typeface" includes an ornamental motif used in printing, which seems apt to cover logos, monograms and the like. Individual letters and handmade type generally may be works of artistic craftsmanship. The "typographical arrangement" copyright under section 8 of the 1988 Act[39] can protect against facsimile copying of pages printed in a typeface, whether original or not, so long as they form part of a published edition of a literary, dramatic or musical work which is not simply a reprint. Any unlicensed reproduction of a typeface is still infringement[40] and this is specifically exempted from the operation of section 51, even where the reproduction consists of making the typeface. However, many new typefaces are produced by, or at least stored on, computer, and are protected, or treated for practical purposes as protected, by literary copyright in the software in which they are embodied. Their use, like other software, is tightly-controlled by licensing.[40A]

---

[38] 1994 I.P.D. 17001.
[39] s.15 of the 1956 Act.
[40] See Chap. 5 below.
[40A] For a fuller treatment, see "Protection of Software Fonts in UK Law" by Justin Watts & Fred Blakemore, [1995] 3 E.I.P.R. 133.

OTHER TYPES OF COPYRIGHT WORK

Given the complexity of modern production processes, not to speak of the **2.170** whole area of advertising and promotion, marketing and information technology, it will be appreciated that other types of copyright work such as films and videos, sound recordings and cable programmes can be relevant. These are beyond the scope of this book. But a recent decision on copyright in circuit diagrams, *Anacon Corporation Ltd v. Environmental Research Technology Ltd*,[41] opened up interesting possibilities of treating the *literary* content of drawings recording industrial designs as infringed by incorporating the information they contain in a different form which can then be used to make a competing three-dimensional product.

As mentioned in 2.140 above, it has been assumed that literary works **2.171** could not be infringed by following their directions so as to produce a three-dimensional object, on the ground that the law found it necessary to provide specifically[42] that reproducing a two-dimensional work (drawing) in three-dimensional form (article depicted in drawing) should be infringement. Without this provision, the change in dimension would take the case out of infringement. Still more so would a change in medium of expression. This ignored a number of factors. First, the 2-D/3-D provision did not appear in the Copyright Act 1911, but this did not prevent the House of Lords in *King Features Syndicate Inc. v. O. & M. Kleeman Ltd*[43] from holding that dolls and brooches of Popeye the Sailor Man were infringing three-dimensional reproductions of the two-dimensional comic strips. Second, both the 1956 and 1988 Acts prohibit the reproduction of a literary work "in any material form", which is a very wide provision. Third, all three courts in *British Leyland v. Armstrong*[44] held that Armstrong infringed BL's copyright in its exhaust pipe drawings, even though on the evidence all that mattered about the drawings was the co-ordinates (expressed in figures, and therefore a literary work) showing the location and radius of the bends in the pipe. The lines and shapes on the drawings were irrelevant in conveying the information, both to BL's own workmen, who used the co-ordinates in programming their pipe-bending machine, and to Armstrong, who measured the co-ordinates from the actual exhaust pipes and in turn used it to program their pipe-bending machine. Fourth, in *Patricia Roberts v. Candiware Ltd*[45] the defendant was making up and selling on a commercial scale the plaintiff's jumpers knitted from a pattern on sale to the public. The point about not reproducing a literary work by making the article was not taken, the defendant rather arguing that the sale of the pattern must carry with it an implied licence to make the garment. Millett J. agreed, but suggested the licence would be limited to making the garment for private purposes only.

[41] [1994] F.S.R. 359.
[42] 1956 Act, s.48(1); 1988 Act s.17(3).
[43] [1941] A.C. 417.
[44] [1986] R.P.C. 279; [1986] A.C. 577—see below.
[45] [1980] F.S.R. 352.

The approach would solve the practical problem of treating as an infringement the very thing the literary work instructs one to do.[46]

2.172   In *Anacon* the plaintiff had made a circuit diagram (long recognised as an artistic work) showing the components (resistors, transistors, capacitors), indicated by their conventional symbols, linked together in a schematic way. Against each component was written its rating, *e.g.* ohms for the resistor. The plaintiff's circuit board made from the diagram did not *look* like it, as they often do not. The appropriately-rated components were all present, but although linked to each other topologically in the same way, the linkages did not match the schematic way in which these were presented in the diagram.

2.173   The defendants were inferred to have made, from the plaintiff's circuit board to which they had access, a "net list" of all the components, with a *written* indication in the case of each one of what other components it had to be connected to and where, and from this they had made their own circuit board—probably by feeding the net list into a computer which would have produced its own circuit digram and possibly a scheme for making the board. Neither the net list nor the defendants' board resembled the plaintiff's circuit diagram in any *visually significant* way, and hence on *Interlego* principles, applied as a test of infringement rather than originality,[47] they could not be an infringement of its artistic copyright. But this was not the end of the story. The plaintiff's circuit diagram was a literary as well as an artistic work: "literary work" includes a written table or compilation (1988 Act, section 4), and "writing" includes "any form of notation or code, whether by hand or otherwise and regardless of the method by which, or the medium in or on which, it is recorded" (section 178). The conventional symbols for resistors, etc., were electrical engineers' notation which could be read, together with the rest of the written matter, to reveal the information also conveyed graphically by the diagram. The defendants' net list embodied, and so reproduced in material form, the skill and labour expended in compiling the information taken from the diagram, and was an infringement. This finding looks past the particular form in which the information is expressed in the original, grabs the information itself, and identifies it again in the copy, disregarding the particular form in which it is there expressed. Normally with infringement of literary copyright, a fairly close textual identity between the two versions is required, but this is a matter of degree, and the plot of a play can be infringed even though the dialogue may not be closely copied.

2.174   Having found infringement by the net list, Jacob J. did not have to decide whether the defendants' actual circuit board reproduced the literary elements of the plaintiff's diagram; but he felt it arguably did, "not because of the presence of the components in the circuit, but because in relation to each of the components there is also a written or coded indication of what it is. So

---

[46] For a fuller treatment of these arguments, see Case Comment on *Anacon* by John Reynolds and Peter Brownlow at [1994] 9 E.I.P.R. 399.
[47] See further Chap. 5 below.

that one can read the circuit as well as use it".[48] But the effect of *Anacon* even without any such finding is that if the literary element of a work having both literary and artistic elements is taken *and used* to make the article depicted by the artistic element, then infringement has taken place and the making of the articles can be restrained, even though they do not themselves infringe the artistic element because they do not recognisably reproduce it. So taking the literary information contained in a knitting pattern *and using it* to make a garment, in which the information is still identifiable by counting stitches[49] could also be infringement. The implications of *Anacon*, if any, will have to be worked out by experience. Unfortunately, as Jacob J. pointed out, for procedural reasons the defendants were no longer represented, so he did not have the benefit of alternative arguments.

REMAINING EFFECTS OF "HANGOVER" COPYRIGHT

Until July 31, 1999, copyright works made before August 1, 1989 which are **2.175** "design documents" as defined in section 51[50] but whose copyright would otherwise be unenforceable because of the new defence introduced by section 51, may still be sued on under the transitional provisions in Schedule 1, paragraph 19. This includes many designs which were registered or registrable under the 1949 Act in so far as their shorter 15-year copyright period under section 10 of the 1956 Act has not already expired. Additionally, some such registered or registrable designs with a high artistic content which would not be caught by section 51 may continue to be sued on in copyright until their 15-year periods expire, which at latest will be July 31, 2004. Before parting with this "hangover" copyright, we must briefly consider some distinctive features of the old system which it temporarily preserves—the availability of dual protection by both registration and copyright, the abridged 15-year copyright period for registrable designs, the ability of copyright to protect purely functional designs for the full normal copyright period, and the *British Leyland* "spare parts exception". Although in their different ways these features are mainly the product of particular *defences* to copyright actions in certain cases, their effect on the *scope* of rights is so marked that they are better dealt with here.

Registrable designs

The Design Copyright Act 1968 altered the long-standing practice[51] of **2.176** denying an enforceable copyright to registrable designs (whether registered or not) which had been "applied industrially" (to more than 50 articles or to

---

[48] This is not, of course, the case with a rabbit pie, where additionally some of the ingredients, such as the flour and butter used in making the pastry, are no longer identifiable once mixed, let alone cooked.
[49] See *Brigid Foley Ltd v. Elliott* [1982] R.P.C. 433—see 2.140 above.
[50] See 2.188 below.
[51] See Chap. 1.

goods manufactured in lengths or pieces[52] such as textiles and wallpaper).[53] However valid the principles behind their exclusion from copyright, it was accepted that registration did not adequately serve industries like the Birmingham costume jewellers, whose new collections could be copied as soon as they appeared, while they had to wait for registration applications to be processed and could not sue until they were granted, nor claim damages from any date earlier than the date of grant. Having copyright would allow them to seek intelocutory injunctions immediately. In its original form, section 10 of the 1956 Copyright Act had provided that once a registrable design "corresponding" to an artistic work (a design which when applied to an article resulted in a reproduction of the artistic work) was either registered or applied industrially with the licence of the copyright owner but without registration, copyright could not be used to restrain any subsequent industrial application of the design by another. The 1968 Act partially "reversed" section 10 by amending it so as to provide that where a corresponding registrable design was applied industrially (whether registered or not) by or with the licence of the copyright owner, copyright could be used to restrain industrial application by another, but only for 15 years after first marketing of the plaintiff's own products, whether in the U.K. or elsewhere. Thereafter (probably) no industrial application of a corresponding design would be actionable. The section as amended was, to put it politely, not free from obscurity as to exactly what would happen on the expiry of the 15-year period,[54] but this does not seem to have caused problems in practice.

2.177   The Design Copyright Act amendments have been of great benefit to designers and manufacturers of products with some "aesthetic" appeal, whether the foolish virgins who neglected or chose not to register or the wise ones who did both and gave themselves the dual protection which for the first time had become available. There would be a slight disharmony between the 15-year periods, because the registration period ran from the date of application whereas the copyright period ran from first marketing. The fate, under the 1988 transitional provisions, of 15-year periods already running as at August 1, 1989 is mentioned above and discussed in detail in Chapter 3, but except for those registrable designs which would escape the operation of section 51 if made on or after August 1, 1989, the benefit of this copyright is much diminished by the availability of licences of right since August 1, 1994. This allows defendants to avoid interlocutory injunctions[55] by undertaking, without admission of liability, to take a licence at a royalty to be agreed, or settled by the Designs Registry in default of agreement, and limits any damages after July 31, 1994 to double that royalty.[56] This may make it

---

[52] Copyright (Industrial Designs) Rules 1957, S.I. 1957 No. 867.
[53] Unless, for designs deriving copyright under the Copyright Act 1911, such industrial exploitation had not originally been intended.
[54] See the excellent discussion in Laddie, Prescott & Vitoria, *The Modern Law of Copyright*, 1st ed. 1980, 3.58–3.66.
[55] Temporary injunctions pending trial—see Chap. 5.
[56] See Chaps. 4 and 5.

uneconomic to take the action to full trial in the hope of getting a final injunction which will have only a short time to run. The provision does not, however, prevent full enforcement of any *registered* design still in force.[57]

"Registrable" artistic works made before June 1, 1957 and applied or intended when made to be applied industrially did not acquire copyright through the amended section 10 because it had already been ruled out by Schedule 7, paragraph 8 of 1956 Act; nor can they acquire it under the 1988 Act (Schedule 1, paragraph 6). **2.178**

The criteria for registrability applicable to "old" copyright works are those set out in the Registered Designs Act 1949 before its amendment by the 1988 Act. The *Interlego* case established that there is no need for such designs also to satisfy the novelty test.[58] Recourse may be had to the earlier part of this chapter in considering whether or not a particular "old" copyright work depicts a registrable design, bearing in mind that the 1949 Act in its unamended form contained fewer exclusions and therefore a more liberal test of registrability. **2.179**

Non-registrable designs

The untrammelled application of copyright to non-registrable designs based on drawings, or on anything in the production process which might be characterised as a sculpture or engraving, has already been described.[59] Its failure to protect designs based on prototypes which do not fall within any of the recognised categories of "artistic work" will also be recalled.[60] Some limited drawing-back based on the need for "visual significance" in assessing both originality[61] and infringement[62] has recently taken place. **2.180**

But the only major curb on copyright in industrial designs before the 1988 Act reforms was what Lord Scarman tactfully described as "the principle latent in our law but not fully discussed or expressed until the present case"—the "spare parts exception" disclosed in the *British Leyland* case.[63] BL made exhaust pipes from drawings in which they had copyright, and sold their cars with the pipes attached. In the nature of things, exhaust pipes need replacing several times during the life of a car. BL supplied their own spares, but a purchaser was not bound to buy them, since the owner of a complex piece of machinery which is likely to need repair has an "implied licence" to **2.181**

---

[57] Unless it was applied for after January 12, 1988 and before August 1, 1989 and would now be caught by the "must-match" or "who-cares-what-it-looks-like?" exceptions, when it will have been subject to licences of right since August 1, 1989—see 2.078 above.

[58] See 2.047 above.

[59] See 2.142 *et seq.* above. The "discovery" of the usefulness of copyright for purely functional designs in the important case of *Dorling v. Honnor Marine* [1963] R.P.C. 205, [1964] R.P.C. 160 is dealt with at 1.015 above.

[60] See 2.162.

[61] See 2.137.

[62] See 2.173.

[63] *British Leyland v. Armstrong Patents Co. Ltd* [1986] A.C. 577.

repair it and to sub-contract this repair to someone else.[64] However, this right is of limited value to car-owners, who want to have their exhausts replaced quickly and cheaply wherever they happen to be, not to go searching for a workshop which will make them a new one to order. The defendants, Armstrong, along with many other companies, therefore entered this aftermarket and supplied spares, which they made by copying a BL exhaust pipe to ensure that the spare would fit.[65]

2.182   BL successfully sued Armstrong for infringing the copyright in its drawings by making three-dimensional reproductions of them. The car-owner's implied licence could not be relied on because it was based on a contract between BL and the car-buyer, to which a competing spares manufacturer was not a party. But the House of Lords would not tolerate the effective monopoly on spares which this gave BL, so they devised a way round it. It would, they said, be a "derogation from the grant" of the car to the purchaser to use the copyright in the exhaust pipe drawings to prevent other manufacturers making replacement exhausts. Such a derogation could not be permitted. Further, the manufacturer "exhausted his copyright" by first sale of the vehicle with the exhaust pipe fitted to it; and outside component manufacturers did the same with the parts they made. These principles could not be excluded by contract. Only where a part is covered by a patent or registered design would the exception not apply.

2.183   The *British Leyland* decision was unashamedly one of policy, which trawled for the legal garments to cover its nakedness in the murky waters of real property and E.C. law; and it left many questions open. It is clear from the decision that it applies to mass-produced multi-component consumer goods which regularly need parts replacing, and thus covers household appliances and most vehicles.[66] Its seems capable of covering any part the car-owner may *need* to replace during the life of the car, and possibly, since the "exhaustion of rights" and "derogation from grant" formulations are wide, anything he might simply expect to be allowed to replace if the fancy takes him—like swapping the original for "sportier" wheel covers, or a basic for an upgraded or luxury part. On the other hand, as was seen earlier, these parts may be the subject of enforceable registered designs, in which case the copyright defence will not prevent the registered design from being enforced.

2.184   In principle there seems no reason why the spare parts exception should not also apply to producer goods used in agriculture or industry, such as combine

---

[64] *Solar Thomson Engineering Ltd v. Barton* [1977] R.P.C. 537, which extended to copyright a doctrine already established in patents and registered designs law. The "licence" is a term implied into the contract between the manufacturer and purchaser of a complex machine so as to give it "business efficacy", and it is also implied into any contract between the purchaser and a subsequent owner, and so on down the line.

[65] See 2.171 above for details of how they did so.

[66] As a matter of practicality there is unlikely to be an aftermarket in parts for Formula 1 racing cars, but in the lower formulas where money and sponsorship are tighter and cars more uniform, the problem of pattern spares is not unknown.

harvesters, or the looms in *British Northrop*,[67] or machine tools, although it is doubtful that their Lordships had such products in mind, and the aftermarket conditions may be very different. But what about atomic power-station machinery or pollution-control equipment which is very expensive to develop and of which relatively few examples are made? What about applications where quality-control is crucial, and cannot be ensured by simply reverse engineering? What about a government department which wants parts of its carpets replacing because they have worn out, and finds a manufacturer who can do this more cheaply than the original supplier?[68] And perhaps most important, does it only apply where the competing spares manufacturer *has* to copy in order to make a part which will fit and do the job it is intended to do, so that the original equipment manufacturer's copyright would otherwise give him, in fact if not in law, a monopoly on the spares? Or does it apply to any spares where it is economically desirable for the competing manufacturer (and hence probably for the consumer) to copy rather than develop his own alternative? What about a part which has to be a copy at one end in order to fit an existing machine, but could otherwise be different, like add-on ploughing and harrowing devices for tractors? If the consumer is sovereign, the answer would be yes, in the absence of registered design or patent protection. But this is, as will be seen, laxer than what was contemplated by the government when formulating the "must-fit" and "must-match" exceptions to unregistered design right. These questions are still unsettled, but they remain relevant because Schedule 1, paragraph 19(9) preserves the spare parts exception during the "hangover" copyright period.

This was confirmed in *Flogates Ltd v. Refco Ltd*,[69] where the court also **2.185** observed that section 171(3)[70] would have the same effect. This case was an attempt to apply the *British Leyland* defence to refractory parts for sliding-gate valves used in the molten metal industry. These needed frequent replacement, and were crucial to the operation of the equipment. The

---

[67] [1974] R.P.C. 57—see 2.133 above.

[68] It is thought likely that in cases such as this the manufacturer would be able, if he has enough bargaining muscle, to impose suitable terms in the original supply contract. Despite the fiction of the implied licence in the contract between a car manufacturer and the car-owner, there is in reality no such contract, since motorists buy from dealers not from manufacturers. Large-scale producer goods are different; there is more reality to the implied licence—see for example *Weir Pumps Ltd v. CML Pumps Ltd* [1984] F.S.R. 33—but also the chance to contract out of it.

[69] 1994 I.P.D. 17072.

[70] "Nothing in this Part affects any rule of law preventing or restricting the enforcement of copyright, on grounds of public interest or otherwise". Attempts have been made in other fields to invoke a *British Leyland* defence: in *Digital Equipment Corpn v. LCE Computer Maintenance Ltd* 1992 I.P.D. 15121 the defendant, a company offering independent maintenance of computer equipment, including the plaintiff's, was sued for software copyright infringement by using diagnostic software supplied by the plaintiff on the plaintiff's customers' computers. The plaintiff claimed that the defendant should obtain a separate licence to use the software on each such computer. The defendant pleaded that by analogy with spare parts, customers should be entitled to have their equipment maintained by whom they chose without further onerous conditions being applied to independent maintenance providers. The plaintiff tried to strike out this defence, but failed. But in another software case, *Total Information Processing Systems Ltd v. Daman Ltd* [1992] F.S.R. 171, it was held that the defence had no application as between two small companies competing with one another.

plaintiff argued that they were not spare parts but "consumables", like vacuum cleaner bags or coffee filter papers—replacements for which there would be a regular and predictable requirement. The commercial position was different too—there was a "club" of licensed suppliers, so that the customer would not be dependent on Flogates for his supplies. The defendant argued that anything that was vital to the working of a complex machine, however ephemeral, was a part of that machine. A true consumable would be something on which the machine operated, like staples in a staple gun. Jacob J. felt inclined to agree that the refractories were consumables rather than spare parts used for repairing a machine that had broken down, but accepted that some of Lord Templeman's observations in *British Leyland* went beyond mere repairing—for example his reference to the exercise of copyright rendering a machine unfit for the purpose for which it was held. However, the judge refused to decide the point without full evidence and argument, so the case is as yet only a straw in the wind.

2.186   To have commercial efficacy the *British Leyland* exception must extend to copying anything *necessary* to its exercise. The independent spares manufacturer should be able to make his own manufacturing drawings (otherwise another indirect infringement of copyright), produce a catalogue cross-referenced to the original manufacturer's part numbers (likewise capable of infringing the literary copyright in original catalogues of parts lists) and illustrate his catalogue and assembly instructions with drawings or photographs of parts. However, the independent will be well-advised to make such drawings or photographs from his own parts; and he should take care to produce his own catalogue copy and assembly instructions, because the exception has no need to extend to copying more than is absolutely necessary. In the recent case of *Baltimore Aircoil Co. Inc. v. Evapco (U.K.) Ltd*[71] the court held that a licence of right did not entitle the licensee to copy the plaintiff's bulletin. Care must also be taken not to infringe the manufacturer's trade marks,[72] nor to pass off the spares as his.

2.187   The original equipment manufacturer may be tempted to make the spare parts exception less damaging by, for example, trade marking visible parts and restraining independent suppliers from using the marks, so that purchasers will want to buy original spares that match or have the same cachet as the original. In *Saab-Scania A.B. v. Diesel Technic (U.K.) Ltd*[73] Millett J. refused an interlocutory injunction to restrain the defendant supplying spare wheel rims, mud flaps and front badges with the SCANIA trade mark stamped on them, on the ground that in these locations the mark

---

[71] SRIS/C/38/94.
[72] In *British Northrop v. Texteam Blackburn* [1974] R.P.C. 57 the defendant's catalogue referred to "manufacture of NORTHROP parts", an infringing reference—if the wording had been "parts suitable for use with looms made by British Northrop" the position would have been clear, and such wording would also have avoided any risk of passing off. See now s.11(2)(c) of the Trade Marks Act 1994.
[73] 1991 I.P.D. 14157.

was part of the design, showing that the vehicle was a SCANIA vehicle, and to restrain its use would circumvent the spare parts exception.

THE NEW COPYRIGHT PROVISIONS: NEW DEFENCES

Exclusion of articles in which design right may subsist: section 51

The purpose of section 51 is to exclude from copyright those articles in which   **2.188**
unregistered design right may subsist. So the definitions of "design" and
"design document" in section 51 mirror those to be found in Part III of the
Act which creates the new right. Unregistered design right is wider than
industrial design copyright for those articles which it covers, in that it does
not depend on the existence of a copyright artistic work, but requires only
that there be some record of the design from which it can be identified. So the
definition of "design document" embraces not only artistic but also literary
works and may, as discussed at the beginning of Chapter 3, also cover a sound
recording or a film. None of these[74] is a likely copyright work in connection
with an industrial design which is reproduced in three-dimensional form by
making articles to it.

Section 51(1) says: **2.189**

> "It is not an infringement of any copyright in a design document or
> model recording or embodying a design for anything other than an
> artistic work or a typeface to make an article to the design or to copy an
> article made to the design."

Subsection (3) has its own definition of "design":

> " 'design' means the design of any aspect of the shape or configuration
> (whether internal or external) of the whole or part of an article, other
> than surface decoration."

and of "design document":

> " 'design document' means any record of a design, whether in the form
> of a drawing, a written description, a photograph, data stored in a
> computer or otherwise."

"Model" is defined neither here nor elsewhere in the Act, but no doubt means
a three-dimensional prototype. It could be an artistic work like a model for a

---

[74] Unless the *Anacon* decision discussed at 2.172 above indicates a new trend which may not have
been in the draftsman's mind when the 1988 Act was formulated. On the other hand, it is
possible to argue that some support for *Anacon* may be found in the inclusion of non-artistic
copyright works in section 51 by importing the whole of the design right definition of "design
document" rather than saying "It shall not be an infringement of copyright in any artistic work
recording or embodying a design for anything other than something which is itself an artistic
work" or some such formulation.

building in section 4(1)(b) or a model for the purposes of sculpture in section 4(2), or a work of artistic craftsmanship; or it could be a prototype heart valve. "Artistic work" has no special definition within the section, so it must have the meaning given to it by section 4.[75] "Typeface" is not defined, but as we have seen, these are covered as types of artistic work without the need for further definition, and since they are in any event not caught by section 51 we need not consider them further. No attempt has been made, either here or in any other relevant Part of the Act, to define "article", but it is apparent from the definition of "design" that parts of articles can be covered, and there is no requirement, as there is in registered designs law, that such parts be made or sold separately.

2.190   "Design" as defined is clearly not the same as the "design" of which it is a sub-class, and of which no further definition appears in the Act. But it is clear from the context, and from subsection (1), which speaks of a design "for" something which may or may not be an artistic work, that this wider "design" refers to something which is merely a step in the process of producing some other article, to which the narrower definition of "design" refers. As John Butcher put it to the House of Commons Standing Committee,[76] "The first question to bear in mind is whether a [copyright] work ... is produced for its own purpose or for subsequent exploitation as ... another article". If the copyright work in question is a painting of a vase of flowers imagined by the artist, or an embroidered altar-cloth with an elaborately-scalloped edged for the parish church's tercentenary, or a carved wooden figurine for presentation to a visiting head of state, it is not a "design", nor does it "record" or "embody" a "design"—it is a thing in itself, a work of art for art's sake, and section 51 has no application.

2.191   So if someone makes unlicensed copies of the painting, the altar-cloth or the figurine, he will be infringing the copyright in each of these artistic works, and can be restrained in the usual way.[77] If a commercial potter were to presume to make and market the vase shown in the painting, this too would be an infringement—it would be a reproduction of a substantial part of the painting in three-dimensional form. The artist in painting the picture was not making a design for the vase, it was simply the subject-matter of his painting. Nor would it be any different if the artist had painted a piston merely to make an artistic statement and with no intention of making pistons or persuading anyone else to make them. No motor manufacturer could safely adopt the piston for his new engine.

2.192   But if the work is a preparatory sketch for the painting, or for the shape and stitch-pattern for the altar-cloth, or a model of the figurine submitted to the Foreign Office for approval—or an engineering drawing of a piston or a photograph of the prototype of a cast-iron lavatory cistern with embossed ivy

---

[75] See the earlier part of this section for discussion of the various types of artistic work.
[76] *Hansard*, May 24, 1988, col. 247.
[77] See Chap. 5.

leaves cast into it—then it *is* a design, because it is only a step in the production of something else. The drawings, stitch-pattern and photograph are all design documents recording a design, the model figure is a model embodying a design, in each case for their end-products. They must be submitted to the tests in section 51 to see if they survive them.

"Design"

The next stage is to look more closely at the narrower subsection (3) **2.193** definition of "design". It is directed only to aspects of the *shape* or *configuration* of the whole or any part of the article. "Article", as we have seen, is nowhere defined, and it is used in some places in the Act to refer to what are clearly substantially two-dimensional objects: section 52, for example, refers to making and marketing articles, and finds it necessary to exclude from its operation by the Copyright (Industrial Process and Excluded Articles) (No. 2) Order[78] a list of "articles" including labels, maps, plans and trade forms.[79] But it will be remembered from the discussion of registered design that the words "shape" and "configuration" are taken to refer to three-dimensional features,[80] and although they are not defined in the 1988 Act it is likely the draftsman selected them with a view to their bearing this familiar meaning. This is supported by the reference to external and internal parts of an article. It looks therefore as if only designs for three-dimensional articles are caught by section 51. If this is so, then everything else must remain in copyright.

In fact, we know from the Parliamentary proceedings that this is what was **2.194** intended. Lord Beaverbrook makes it plain[81] that *relief* surface decoration was regarded as "an aspect of shape or configuration" which had deliberately to be excluded from the definition of design for unregistered design right, because it was "properly a matter for copyright", and consequently also from the closely-similar definition in section 51 to make sure it did not escape protection altogether. "Thus", he said, "relief decoration will, like two-dimensional surface decoration, remain within copyright".

If only designs for three-dimensional articles are caught by section 51, then **2.195** the preliminary sketch for the painting cannot be affected at all. Even when it is mounted or framed for display it is still for all practical purposes a two-dimensional article, and any illicit copies made of it, whether by laborious copying by hand, or by photographing it or scanning it into a computer to make prints of it, or even to make transfers for applying to

---

[78] S.I. 1989 No. 1070.
[79] The same "articles" as feature in Designs rule 26.
[80] See, *e.g. Sommer Allibert v. Flair Plastics* [1987] R.P.C. 599 and *Cow v. Cannon* [1959] R.P.C. 240, 347, 2.005/2.006 above. But there is still room for argument about whether "configuration" is exclusively three-dimensional, and this is one of the problem areas with section 51, which is highlighted later.
[81] *Hansard*, Vol. 493, col. 1179.

three-dimensional articles, will also be two-dimensional. The altar-cloth is more problematical, since although normally spread flat, it does have the "feel" of an article. It can be folded up and carried around and put through the washing-machine. It is not "printed matter" and would probably rank as an "article" for registered design purposes. Moreover its scalloped edge gives it a shape, although its embroidery, even if it features French knots and cross-stitch as well as satin-stitch, is obviously "surface decoration". Its preliminary sketch will therefore have to join the piston drawing and the photograph as "design documents" to undergo the final test of whether there is anything about the articles they are designs "for" which can qualify those as "artistic works".

"A design for anything other than an artistic work"

2.196 Since there is no special definition of "artistic work", we have to apply the section 4 test. This is easy enough with the piston. There is no category of artistic work into which a piston can fall. The model figurine is also easy. It is a model for a sculpture, and a sculpture *is* an artistic work.[82] The lavatory cistern is not completely cut-and-dried. As such, it is of course not an artistic work. It is a cast or model, but not made for purposes of sculpture. However, it has in the embossed ivy leaves an element of surface decoration which is left to copyright. The altar-cloth is all right, so long as it is hand-embroidered. Even if it is an "article", it is a work of artistic craftsmanship. But if it is not hand-embroidered—if it has been designed with consummate artistry but the sketch has been used to program a computer-controlled machine to cut the fabric and do the embroidering—the designer may be in difficulty. The surface decoration will be protectable, but not the shape.

"Make an article to the design"

2.197 The result of applying these tests is that without infringing copyright a rival piston-maker may make[83] pistons to the design by copying the pistons themselves—copying an article made to the design—if they are on the market, or, it seems, by copying the drawing if he has access to it—making an article to the design. He should exercise caution about the drawing. If his access is legitimate, he may also be able to use any confidential information, such as dimensions and tolerances, which appear on it. But if he has it illegitimately, for example through theft, or by virtue of being a former sub-contractor who should have returned it when his sub-contract terminated, he would be unwise to make any use of it at all, and should make his own drawings *from the piston*—"copy an article made to the design", which is also permitted by section 51(1).[84] However, the section 51 defence does *not* affect the copyright

---

[82] The status of the model as an artistic work is actually in doubt. If it was "made for purposes of sculpture", as a dry-run for the sculptor, it will be an artistic work in its own right, but since it was made for the purpose of securing Foreign Office approval, it may not be.

[83] And sell or include in a film, broadcast or cable programme—s.51(2).

[84] It seems most unlikely that "article" would be construed to cover anything wider than the exact scope of "design" in section 51(3), even if an engineering drawing, as a "plan", is an

in the drawing as such, so that copying it directly (by tracing or photocopying) would still be infringement; and in the absence of some sort of permission or acquiescence, using the confidential information would also be prohibited.[85] He should also make up his own promotional material, whether artistic or literary.

Even if he has the drawing legitimately, the rival piston-maker must emphatically *not* use it as the basis for his next Christmas card or, in reduced form, as his logo should the copied piston form the basis of his firm's fortune and international success. This is not at all what section 51 permits. **2.198**

A rival lavatory-cistern maker is in the same position, except that he should take care with the embossed ivy leaves. Whether there is any enforceable copyright in this surface decoration depends on whether it is based on a drawing—the photograph is of an existing cistern, and may lack sufficient originality to be a copyright work in itself—but competitors should be aware of the risks. **2.199**

In all the above examples, the copyright works which functioned as design documents were artistic works. If they had been literary works (and the design sketch for the altar-cloth will also exist in the form of a computer program if that is how it was made) the normal questions about whether you can infringe a literary work by making the article described in it will arise. You can certainly infringe the copyright in an artistic work by scanning it into a computer (section 17(1)—"storing the work in any medium by electronic means"). If the program were copied as such, the copy would infringe, unless the designer's program were held to lack originality as a mere copy of the artistic work—unlikely, given the effort and skill involved in writing a program. Literary copyright has the virtue of expressly including compilations,[86] and adaptation is also an infringing act, which it is not with artistic copyright. "Adaptation" in relation to software appears to be defined more widely than for the general run of literary works, covering an "arrangement or altered version" as well as a translation.[87] **2.200**

Areas of obscurity

The examples already given are the really easy ones, where either the artistic work in which copyright subsists is not a "design" because it was the final form of its author's inspiration or, where the work is an intermediate "design", the end-product manifestly is or is not an artistic work within section 4. Other areas where problems have sometimes been suggested also **2.201**

---

article for the purposes of the Excluded Articles Order, see n. 43 above. If he has the drawing, he should check its date. If it turned out to have been made before August 1, 1989, even though the pistons were not marketed until afterwards, he could be liable for some unexpected royalties.

[85] See *Weir Pumps Ltd v. CML Pumps Ltd* [1984] F.S.R. 33.
[86] s.3(1)(a).
[87] s.21(3)(ab).

yield fairly readily to a commonsense approach to section 51, for example the argument that "back-of-a-fag-packet" sketches (which are undoubtedly artistic works and design documents) should be regarded as preparatory designs for worked-up production drawings (which may be "articles") rather than for the wheelbarrows or electric-oven entrails which they depict. The clay model of a car body shell is another of these regularly-occurring examples. It is certainly a sculpture, but the car body is not, and a preliminary sketch or model for the full-size clay model is only arguably a cast or model "made for purposes of sculpture". The WHAM-O[88] situation (carved wooden model of a FRISBEE = sculpture, dies and plastic injection moulds = engravings according to the dictionary) demands a stronger telescope to see the ultimate destiny of the design, but the plastic discs themselves would no longer constitute "engravings" under U.K. law because of the removal of "prints" from the definition of "engraving".

2.202 The same reasoning would apply to shadowmasks for silicon chips: These happen to fall within the definition of "photograph", because they are produced by a process of photoetching, but it would not work to argue that preparatory drawings of them should escape section 51 because they are designs "for" artistic works. Their ultimate destiny is to become a layer of a chip, which is not an artistic work (in any case, they are expressly covered by unregistered design right).

2.203 Where anomalies may arise is in the possibly discrepant treatment given to, say, garden gnomes and costume jewellery. A gnome prototype is probably a sculpture; the production gnomes, too, may well be sculptures, even though turned out from moulds, if the wider definitions of "sculpture" mentioned in 2.148 above are adopted[89]—bearing in mind that sculpture is protected by copyright "irrespective of artistic quality". It is not certain that the government fully understood this. John Butcher, addressing Commons Standing Committee E,[90] spoke in encouraging terms of "garden statuary" surviving section 51 (he may have been thinking of Aphrodite rather than gnomes), but in the same breath he mentioned art for art's sake and the designer's intention. This would suggest that the section 51 test was meant to be not whether a design is "for" an artistic work as defined by section 4, but for what the layman would recognise as a "work of art". If the designer thought he was creating a whimsical little humanoid with a fishing rod, with no thought of industrial multiplication, his creation would then survive section 51. If he thought he was making a prototype garden gnome, it would not. The Minister stressed that the most important task of section 51 was "to keep ordinary, truly industrial designs out of copyright and to keep truly artistic works in copyright", and spoke hopefully of allowing the courts "the freedom to reach sensible conclusions". If section 51 was intended to have

---

[88] [1985] R.P.C. 127—see 2.149 above.
[89] "The act [or] process ... of moulding ... materials into ... ornaments or figures" or "producing figures or groups in plastic or hard materials".
[90] Hansard, May 24, 1988, col. 247.

this effect, it seems not to have succeeded. There is a limit to what the word "for" can bear, and no other warrant in the section for such an interpretation, or for such a distortion of the meaning of "artistic work".

Costume jewellery, however, is not sculpture. If it is anything, it must be a **2.204** work of artistic craftsmanship; but even if the prototype can be so treated, it is difficult to see how the mass-production versions can be, unless "craftsmanship" is given a more extended definition than it has so far been; and it is they that must be looked at if the interpretation of "design for an artistic work" adopted above is correct.[91] They would not do any better if their designs were first recorded in drawings, since it is still the end-product test that must be applied—unlike the old law, which only required an artistic work somewhere in the production process. The same must be true of quality furniture. It may be of excellent design, just the kind of thing a rational design law should protect and encourage—but if it is mass-produced, will it survive section 51?[92]

Works like this are clearly meant to be caught by section 52[93] since its **2.205** 25-year copyright term is presumably meant to comply with the Berne Convention minimum requirement where "works of applied art" are protected by this means. The trouble is that section 52 can probably only operate on that which survives section 51. If section 51 has to be applied at the date the design document or model comes into being, then these things may not survive it.

Embroiderers and potters are also routinely consigned to the limbo of **2.206** works of artistic craftsmanship.[94] Mass-produced embroidery may do all right because it is "surface decoration". Potters, including commercial potters, had better quickly start calling themselves sculptors.

"Surface decoration"

As has been seen, "surface decoration", whether two- or three-dimensional, **2.207** is protected by copyright. The likelihood, from the choice of the word "decoration",[1] leaving aside Parliamentary pronouncements, is that deliberate embellishment is required, so that functional features like knurling or milling on a nut or knob to improve graspability would be left to unregistered design right as "configuration", as would features of dials, dashboards,

---

[91] Ironic, since it was the Birmingham costume jewellers who sponsored the Design Copyright Act 1968 and won themselves 15 years copyright because they found the registered designs system inadequate.

[92] The anomaly is the more startling when it is considered that parts of buildings are protected, on one argument, with no need to show artistry, and that joists, beams and other structural members will thus enjoy copyright as "artistic works" in their own right. See Laddie, Prescott & Vitoria, *The Modern Law of Copyright*, 2nd ed. 1994, 46.31.

[93] See below.

[94] See Lord Beaverbrook, *Hansard*, Vol. 493, col. 847.

[1] It may be wondered in passing why the draftsman did not choose a word hallowed by authority, like "ornament".

control panels and the like. So far it does not seem that designers have been electing to decorate their knobs with stars rather than knurling, to improve their competitive edge.

2.208   The cleavage of surface decoration from shape and configuration seems likely to cause inconvenience in practice, not least to the clothing industry. "Structural" and styling features of garments will be excluded, but surface decoration included, within copyright. When do pin-tucks (tiny gathers stitched part-way down to produce what is essentially a surface effect) turn into pleats, which form part of the shape of a garment? Should the visible stitching on the seams of jeans be treated as surface decoration, when it is integral to the formation of a particularly strong seam (and might be excluded from unregistered design right as a method or principle of construction[2]). Where do lace, *broderie anglaise* and crochet fit in? Lace, particularly, can be used to make entire garments, but also, when stitched to a blouse (or the neckbands of female counsel) purely as a surface addition. Frills may be inserted into or removed from bodice seams without altering anything other than the appearance of a garment, but a skirt may be composed entirely of layers of frills. Considerable care will need to be taken in pleading such cases.

2.209   Two final queries: Is a golf course an article? Is a ship? We know a ship is not a building,[3] because it is not a fixed structure. Will the designer of the non-immediately-capsizing ro-ro ferry get unregistered design right, or will he get no protection at all?

Reduced protection for artistic works industrially exploited: section 52

2.210   It is clear from the Parliamentary debates that this section was originally meant to cater for those artists for art's sake who, perhaps long after they had completed their triptych or erected their statue of a great warrior queen, decided to apply one of the panels to tin trays[4] or to sell miniature warrior queens to those with a taste for such things. In terms of some of the examples used in discussing section 51, the altar-cloth designer might decide to market suitably-scaled versions for use as bedlinen or sideboard runners, or the artist to market the vase out of his picture. In practice, it seems likely the section will deal mainly with people who are and always have been gnome-makers—people whose intentions have always been entirely commercial, but who have managed to get through section 51 unscathed.

2.211   The section bites, also by way of *defence* to an action for copyright infringement, by cutting down the period of copyright where the copyright owner has made and sold, or licensed someone else to make and sell, "articles"[5] which are copies of the artistic work—which reproduce it in any

---

[2] See 2.236 below.
[3] *Hansard*, Vol. 493, col. 1071.
[4] The example used in the debates—are there such things as tin trays any longer?
[5] Not including films (s.52(6)). This is intended to ensure that copyright in, *e.g.* cartoons is not cut down by their being made into films.

material form, including by storing it in a computer, and also by reproducing it in a three-dimensional form if it began life in two dimensions, and vice versa. The defence operates by cutting down the period of copyright to 25 years from the end of the calendar year in which copies were first marketed (sold, let for hire or offered or exposed for sale or hire) whether in the U.K. or elsewhere. This is the same period for which the Berne Convention requires "works of applied art" to be protected by copyright if a member country chooses so to protect these.[6] It is also approximately the same as the period for which a registered design could be obtained, except that that would run for a maximum of 25 years from the date of application (or a Convention priority date if there is one). There is no objection to such dual protection by both copyright and registration,[7] and the novelty of the design will not be prejudiced so long as the proprietor applies before he has made or licensed the making of more than 50 copies of the artistic work.[8]

This is effectively the same test as is applied to determine whether an **2.212** artistic work has been "exploited" for the purposes of section 52: have more than 50 articles which are copies of the artistic work (or part of it if part only is exploited) and which do not together form a "set" under the Registered Designs Act[9]) been made, and has at least one been marketed?[10] If the form of exploitation is as a machine-made textile or wallpaper design (goods manufactured in lengths or pieces) it seems that the sale of one length or piece will be enough. For some reason this making of 50 or more articles is called "making by an industrial process", which is as meaningless as the parallel provision in section 1(1) of the Registered Designs Act. It does *not* normally mean that the articles must be manufactured as opposed to hand-made. However, in the case of wallpaper and textiles it *does*, which seems to mean that hand-woven textiles or hand-painted wallpaper do not get their copyright period cut down.

Once the 25-year period is up, competitors are free to copy the work (or the **2.213** part which has been exploited) by "making articles of any description", and to do anything "for the purpose of making articles"—making production drawings, transfers, software and so forth—and to market them freely. This would obviously include taking photographs of them for use in catalogues; but as with section 51, competitors would be wise to photograph their own goods rather than the copyright owner's, because his copyright in the underlying artistic work as such *remains unimpaired*. It is only against industrial exploitation that the copyright becomes unenforceable, though this is not limited to the same kind of exploitation as the copyright owner undertook; even if he used his work only on tin trays, a competitor may use it for dishes, T-shirts or motor cars. This is similar to section 51, where the

---

[6] Art. 7(4).
[7] Except for Designs rule 26 articles, see further below.
[8] Registered Designs Act 1949, ss.6(4) and (5)—see para. 2.094 above.
[9] See Registered Designs Act s.44(1), 2.014 above.
[10] s.52(1) and the Copyright (Industrial Process and Excluded Articles) (No. 2) Order 1989, S.I. 1989 No. 1070.

copyright is only unenforceable against those who make and deal in "articles" made to the design, not against those who, say, take photographs of a drawing and sell them as picture postcards.

"Excluded articles"

2.214 This example leads on to the fairly major exception to section 52, which is also made by the Excluded Articles Order, and which is in the same terms as Designs rule 26.[11] It applies to:

> "works of sculpture, other than casts or models used or intended to be used for purposes of sculpture;
> wall plaques, medals and medallions;
> printed matter primarily of a literary or artistic character, including bookjackets, calendars, certificates, coupons, dress-making patterns, greeting cards, labels, leaflets, maps, plans, playing cards, postcards, stamps, trade advertisements, trade forms and cards, transfers and similar articles."[12]

The copyright owner may exploit his artistic work by applying it to any of these things without having his copyright cut down at all. Competitors will need to watch very carefully what he has actually done by way of industrial exploitation, because however wide his exploitation has been in relation to any of these articles, it will not free them to compete after 25 years. There may sometimes be genuine difficulties if, for example, the artistic work has appeared on a multitude of articles but it turns out all the copyright owner has done is license the work for making transfers. Would he then be taken to have licensed it for all uses to which it has actually been put, or only for transfers? Or licensees may have exceeded their rights—the copyright owner may have licensed his ducks only for use as wall plaques in the normal set of three different sizes, and therefore not lost his copyright, but an unscrupulous licensee may have turned the littlest ducks into door handles. The innocent competitor who starts to market them as door-knockers will then be caught out, unless some sort of estoppel or acquiescence can be pleaded against the copyright owner. Moreover, he may also be liable for breach of the copyright owner's moral rights if the latter considers his duck has been derogatorily treated.

2.215   One notable omission from the list is prints. It seems that exploiting a picture by licensing prints of it, or posters (as opposed to postcards) may escape the rule, unless they can be argued to be "similar articles"—but why not have included them and taken the opportunity of issuing new Registered Designs Rules to amend rule 26 to mention them expressly?[13]

[11] See 2.079 above.

[12] For the question whether unregistered design right might have a part to play where any of these articles have features of shape or configuration apart from their literary or artistic content, see below.

[13] Strangely, Mr Butcher expressly mentioned prints in Committee as things the government intended to be covered by the "printed matter" exclusion—*Hansard*, May 24, 1988, col. 249.

The result of all this is that many substantially two-dimensional exploitations will not trigger the abridged copyright period, but neither will the copyright owner be able to register designs for such articles, whereas in other cases (such as mass-produced sculptures) he will be able to have dual protection, although only for the shorter period. The reasoning behind this scheme is not very clear. It was originally intended that there should be no dual protection, and impassioned pleas to the contrary were rejected, but some sort of compromise seems to have been arrived at. **2.216**

Another related defence: section 53

The possibility of dual protection, and of the copyright and registered design being in different hands,[14] has led to the provision of a further defence, in section 53, which covers someone who has taken an assignment or licence from the registered proprietor of a "corresponding design".[15] So long as this assignee or licensee has acted in good faith in reliance on the registration, and without notice of any proceedings for its cancellation or rectification, he will have a defence in relation to anything which would otherwise be copyright infringement. This is so even if the person registered as the proprietor of the design was not the proper proprietor for the purposes of the 1949 Act. This immunity seems a little tenuous if it can be terminated by mere notification of an application to cancel or rectify, however ill-founded. A manufacturer in full flight might find himself faced with such a notification coupled with an application for an interlocutory injunction to restrain further production. His past acts cannot be the subject of complaint, but his future activities can. **2.217**

An obscurity

What happens if an artist who has painted a picture of a piston, which would have survived section 51 because it was not a "design" for anything and so not a design document, later decides to make and market the piston? Production drawings are prepared and thousands of pistons are made and marketed. Does the artist get unregistered design right, at least in the parts of the piston not shown in the painting? 11 years later (after any unregistered design right in the pistons has expired) a competitor, unaware that the piston originates from a painting, copies the pistons. Can the artist sue him for infringement of copyright in the painting, which still has 14 years to run in relation to industrial exploitations? Or has his picture, because of his **2.218**

---

[14] Which may easily happen: the copyright owner may license someone else to manufacture certain articles only, which would entitle him to register designs only for those articles, the copyright owner in the meantime retaining all his rights in relation to excluded articles, which may long outlast any registration as their copyright is unimpaired.

[15] A design within the meaning of the 1949 Act which if applied to an article would produce a copy of the artistic work.

subsequent exploitation of it, become a design document, so that section 51 can be applied to it? It is not clear that it has. The real design documents in relation to the artist's piston are the production drawings, but the artist is not suing on these. Unless there is to be some implied "exhaustion of rights" in relation to a part of an artistic work which has been exploited, it seems the artist may be able to extend in this way his protection period in what is, or has become, pre-eminently an industrial design.

2.219   The interrelationship between section 51 and section 52 is by no means as clear as might have been hoped, but practical problems do not yet seem to have arisen. Apparent obscurities may be clarified when the sections are used, as they will be, as defences in would-be copyright infringement actions where all the facts and the history of the use actually made of the designs can be looked at. However, section 52 is not approved of in Europe[16] and is menaced with compulsory harmonisation under a draft Directive which will require the abridged 25-year period to be abolished. This may present an opportunity for infelicities to be rectified.

UNREGISTERED DESIGN RIGHT

"The Government proposes to protect original designs of all articles (including spare parts) which are not artistic works by a new unregistered design right . . . [for] 10 years from first marketing but with licences available as of right during the final 5 years of that term"

2.220   This is the solution proposed in the 1986 White Paper[17] to the perennial problem[18] of how to protect deserving features of industrial designs while safeguarding competition. It was recognised[19] that there are "many innovative industrial products which are costly to design but which are not truly inventive and which therefore do not qualify for patent protection".[20] Some protection should be available for these. It was also recognised, in the light of *British Leyland*[21] and the Monopolies and Mergers Commission report on Ford body panels,[22] that spare parts posed problems of monopoly abuse once an aftermarket developed.[23] An "unfair copying" case-by-case approach along the lines of overseas unfair competition jurisdictions was rejected as being too uncertain.[24] But any uniform term of protection would necessarily

---

[16] See Chap. 6.
[17] Intellectual Property and Innovation, Cmnd. 9712, para. 3.39.
[18] See Chap. 1.
[19] White Paper, para. 3.21.
[20] Tony Blair observed that of all the parts in Concorde only 12 were patentable, Frank Doran that Ford spent £80m on the bodywork design for the Sierra: *Hansard*, H.C. Vol. 138, col. 41 and Standing Committee E, June 14, 1988, col. 543.
[21] [1986] A.C. 577.
[22] Cmnd. 9437. The MMC felt that a 5-year protection term for spare parts would be suitable.
[23] White Paper, para. 3.26. See 1.031 above.
[24] Para. 3.25.

be a compromise, because product lives and design costs vary so enormously. Nonetheless, some way forward had to be found, and this new custom-designed right for "original" designs was the chosen way. It was to resemble copyright in that the right would come into being automatically as soon as the design was made, and would be infringed only by copying, but it would last for a much shorter time and would be subject to compulsory licensing in its later years. It was to cover both aesthetic and functional designs, although it was primarily conceived for the benefit of the latter. With one major change, the introduction of the "must-fit" and "must-match" exceptions, this is the scheme as finally enacted.[25]

It borrows heavily, though without acknowledgment, from the tailor-made protection for semiconductor chips introduced by the E.U. in a harmonisation Directive[26] applicable to all Member States which was implemented in the U.K. by the Semiconductor Products (Protection of Topography) Regulations 1987.[27] These required topography designs to be original ("the result of the creator's own intellectual effort") and not "commonplace" among chip creators or manufacturers, whether in relation to particular elements of the design or to the design as a whole. They provided a 10-year term from first exploitation, or 15 years from creation if exploitation did not take place, though without compulsory licensing. This special protection for a very specific product has not always translated easily into a right intended to cover a multiplicity of products with the most diverse uses and antecedents.

2.221

Definitions

Unregistered design right, or "design right" as the 1988 Act calls it, is dealt with in Part III, and definitions are to be found in section 213. "Design" means:

2.222

> "the design of any aspect of the shape or configuration (whether internal or external) of the whole or part of an article."

The definition is the same as in section 51, except that the exclusion of surface decoration from design right is effected, along with the other exclusions, by section 213(3)(c). As foreshadowed in the White Paper, no distinction is drawn between articles which have aesthetic appeal and those which are purely functional. This is underlined by the reference to internal as well as external aspects; and there is no equivalent to the "who-cares-what-it-looks-like?"[28] exclusion for registered designs.

---

[25] The design right clauses were among those most extensively debated: see in particular *Hansard*, Vols. 491 and 494/5 (H.L.) and H.C. Committee June 14/16, 1988 and Vol. 138, July 25, 1988.

[26] 87/54/EEC (O.J. L25, 27.1.87) [1987] O.J. L24/36.

[27] S.I. 1987 No. 1497.

[28] See 2.068 above.

"Article"

2.223   Since the design, as with registered designs, is regarded purely in its application to "an article", we might have expected to find a definition of "article": but there is none, nor is any direct illumination to be found in the Parliamentary materials. The word is presumably to be widely-construed.[29] Some guidance by way of exclusion can be found elsewhere in the Act. We know from the discussion of section 51 that anything which is itself an "artistic work"[30] is unlikely to be a relevant article, because it will have copyright. It is clear both from the White Paper and from the Parliamentary debates that copyright and design right are not to co-exist.[31] This rules out anything which can be characterised as a sculpture,[32] work of artistic craftsmanship, collage, photograph or graphic work. But pottery, cutlery, clothing, common or garden ornaments and trinkets, lamps, furniture, bathroom and kitchen fittings, tools, domestic appliances, vehicles of all kinds including aircraft and oil tankers,[33] and all sorts of industrial products and equipment, including all the separate external and internal parts of any articles assembled from a congeries of other articles, to name but a few examples, will be articles. Buildings, it will be remembered, have copyright, so long as they are "fixed structures" (which is also meant to cover bridges and towers[34]). Conceivably-portable buildings like sheds, even though they may be fixed to concrete bases, are likely to be articles, but parts of buildings are problematic, as they also can have copyright on the wording of section 4—in the view of some, without regard to artistry. The courts may have to use their common sense and look at the ultimate destination of the thing in question to decide whether, say, a girder is in any particular case an article or part of a building.[35]

2.224   To answer the question posed in the last section—whether a golf-course (or show-jumping course or landscaped garden or kitchen design or anything else which is laid-out or arranged and for which people pay a designer) is an "article"—it is suggested that none of them should be so regarded, although some of the items used in their design, such as jumps and kitchen units, would be. It seems to fly in the face of reality to call such items of real property articles, and if they are not, they escape section 51 and section 52 and can readily be protected by copyright as three-dimensional reproductions of their design drawings.

---

[29] *Shorter Oxford Dictionary*: a distinct part or portion, a piece, a commodity, a piece of goods or property.
[30] See 2.196 above.
[31] See also s.236, dealt with in Chap. 5.
[32] Gnomes?
[33] See 2.159 above on ships.
[34] *Hansard*, Vol. 493, col. 1071.
[35] Or whether a general-purpose window is a part of a building or part of a kit for assembling a take-it-with-you-when-you-move bolt-on conservatory or extra-commodious garden shed.

Shape or configuration

As observed in connection with section 51, it is likely from the adoption of   **2.225**
terminology familiar in the registered design field (and is clear from the
Parliamentary materials) that design right subsists only in the three-
dimensional elements of an article. The meaning of "shape or configuration"
for registered designs is discussed in paragraphs 2.005–2.008. "Configuration" allows for surface features like knurling as an aid to graspability and
studs on paving stones to inform visually-impaired people when they are
approaching a light-controlled pedestrian crossing, to have design right.
Since surface *decoration* is expressly excluded from design right, "configuration" does not have the problems encountered with registered designs in
deciding whether it may additionally be a feature of pattern and so possibly
have to be treated differently. It does not matter whether configuration is
imparted at the same time as shape[36] or is added subsequently.

It should be noted that there is no express exclusion from design right (as   **2.226**
there is from design registration[37]) of articles constituting printed matter
primarily of a literary or artistic character, in so far as these may also have
features of shape or configuration. These are *ex hypothesi* "articles", because
they are excluded as such from the operation of section 52.[38] Because there is
this express exclusion, they are assumed to survive section 51, so that
copyright is their means of protection. But this need refer only to their literary
or artistic content, not to their shape or configuration. Many greetings cards
are folded in particular ways, or have pop-up features, as do children's books.
Playing-cards for the visually-impaired may have the suits embossed.[39] Labels
may be made in a particular shape, or with particular patterns of perfor-
ations.[40] Calendars have devices allowing the outdated pages to be flipped
over, or may be made free-standing. All these may be matters for design right
rather than copyright. Wallpaper and textiles, on the other hand, which *are*
registrable, are unlikely to have design right because even if they are textured,
the texture will probably be regarded as surface decoration.

Another difference from registered designs is that design right can subsist   **2.227**
even though the design (and maybe even the article) is not visible to the naked
eye. This follows from the lack of any need for eye-appeal (and the express
protection of semiconductor topographies), and it was made plain in the
debates that it was intended to be so.[41] It opens up fascinating fields of

---

[36] See *Sommer Allibert v. Flair Plastics* [1987] R.P.C. 599.

[37] s.1(5) and Designs rule 26—though see for example *Lamson's Design Application* [1978]
R.P.C. 1.

[38] See 2.214 above.

[39] An unfair advantage for the dealer?

[40] Nice questions arise where it is the user who supplies features of configuration hitherto only
latent, *e.g.* by pushing out the pop-up or by punching holes in parking tickets to show his time
of arrival. *cf. K. K. Kuwa Seikosha's Design Application* [1982] R.P.C. 166 discussed at 2.025
above.

[41] *Hansard*, H.C. Report, Vol. 138, col. 69.

speculation. It was suggested in debate that heat treatment can impart a particular visual arrangement to the crystalline structure of a metal or alloy, but this might be fortuitous, and thus perhaps outside the meaning of "design". It might also be outlawed as protecting a method or principle of construction.[42] However, micro- and nano-engineering techniques can result in designs which have configuration[43]; and "designer" molecules have elements of configuration ("shape or aspect as produced by relative position of parts"[44]) in the sequence of their constituent amino acids or nucleotides and the electrochemical forces which cause them to fold in particular ways.

Part of an article

2.228　Again unlike registered designs, it need not be the whole of the article with the design applied to it which is considered. Design right can reside in only *aspects* of an article's shape or configuration—and in only part of an article, internal or external. There is no requirement, as for registered designs, that that part be made and sold separately. Nor does "part of an article" only mean part of a complex article made up of many parts—like one single part within a car or washing-machine. It can also cover what in the registered design context would be a single "feature" of a single article, whether that article is large (the "power domes" on the bonnet of a Ford car[45] as part of the overall design of a car body) or small (one tube or stud on a LEGO brick). Several different design rights may therefore be claimed in a single article. In two recent unreported cases[46] it was conceded or held that separate design rights could arguably subsist respectively in the internal construction (frame) of a suite of furniture, the individual components of the suite and the external shape imparted by the upholstery,[47] and in the following elements of a remote control system for a crane:

— rubber switch mat on transmitter with raised and lowered nodules to achieve tactile "feel" for two-speed function
— transmitter buttons
— transmitter casing as to shape, width and depth, and with inset key switch
— sensor circuitry.[48]

At the other end of the scale, the electrical terminal in *Amp v. Utilux*[49] measured only ¾″ × ⅝″ × ¼″, but it was a distinctive T-shape, the upright

---

[42] See below.
[43] Like blasting the letters IBM in single atoms on a thin film visible only with a scanning-tunnelling electron microscope.
[44] *Pocket Oxford Dictionary*
[45] See 2.054 above.
[46] Both only at the interlocutory injunction stage, so the plaintiff needed to show only an arguable case.
[47] *Contour Mobel Ltd v. Cover Up Creations Ltd* SRIS/C/54/92.
[48] *Telemotive (U.K.) Ltd v. Davidson* SRIS/C/96/92.
[49] [1972] R.P.C. 103. See 2.023 above.

having twin channels formed by the metal being bent up and over into incomplete rolls, the crossbar having differently-shaped "ears" at each end. It possessed numerous other features of shape or configuration. Lord Pearson took five paragraphs to describe it. Subject to falling foul of any of the exclusions mentioned below, any of these features could be the subject of a separate design right.

If the section 213(2) definition of "design" alone is looked at, each part of an article in which design right is claimed would apparently have to be assessed independently of its position as part of that or any other article. If someone designed a teapot handle in the shape of a pterodactyl with bowed head and folded wings, he would be able to restrain its use as a handle for a walking-stick, or a plunger for clearing blocked pipes. Some small part of a purely functional article such as the heat-distributing ribs on a hot-water bottle (or one of the "ears" on the *Amp* connector) may turn up elsewhere doing the same job. This is not the case with registered designs, where although novelty can be destroyed by prior use or publication of a design applied to a different article (section 1(4) of the 1949 Act), a design is only infringed by its application to an article of the kind for which it is registered (section 7(1)). Nor is it the case with copyright, where infringement occurs only when the whole or a substantial part of a work is reproduced.[50]   **2.229**

In fact the test of design right infringement in section 226 is couched in terms of whole articles—reproducing the design by "making articles to" the design, further defined as "copying the design so as to produce articles exactly or substantially to that design". Since there is no definition of "article" to include parts, as there is in the Registered Designs Act, there is no warrant for supposing that parts are included unless, as in the section 213(2) definition of "design", they are expressly referred to. The only design right case so far known to have gone to trial illustrates how a design for only part of an article was treated. In *C. & H. Engineering v. F. Klucznik & Son Ltd*,[51] the "article" was a pig fender. This is a barrier placed around the front of a pig ark which is high enough to confine the piglets but low enough to permit the sow to step over it. However, a suckling sow is low-slung, and needs to be protected from the sharp metal top of the fender, so a roll-bar can be provided. The fender in suit used a 2″ metal pipe as a roll bar, and this was the sole feature of the fender in which design right was found to subsist. Nonetheless, when infringement came to be considered, Aldous J. compared the allegedly infringing fender as a whole with the design document (a drawing of the whole fender), and found there was no infringement because *other* features of the fender were noticeably different, even though the metal roll-bars were substantially the same.   **2.230**

This decision has been criticised, but on the wording of section 226, which does *not* refer to parts of articles, appears to be right. Admittedly in *Klucznik*   **2.231**

[50] See Chap. 5.
[51] [1992] F.S.R. 421.

the design document depicted the whole article; perhaps cunning designers will adopt the practice of depicting (or describing, since a design document can consist of a written description) each part, even of a single article, separately. But this would be exceedingly artificial, and would not be possible where a prototype of the article, rather than a drawing or description, is relied on as the design embodiment.

2.232   On the other hand, this interpretation does leave the pterodactyl-handle designer out in the cold when his design is applied to other articles. A registered design for the handle as applied to a teapot will do him no good when it is applied to anything else. He will be prevented by section 51 from relying on copyright in his drawing, even if it is of the handle alone, because handles are articles which are not themselves artistic works—unless he can argue that this handle is in fact a sculpture and his drawing a preparatory sketch for it (an unlikely proposition), or that the identifiably pterodactyloid features are properly to be regarded as surface decoration of the basic form of a handle.[52] *A fortiori* the rib designer. If a part of an article *has* been copied (which is a pre-requisite to design right infringement), why should the copier not be liable?

2.233   In practice the courts will probably adopt a "substantiality" test not unlike that used in copyright cases.[53] If what has been taken from one article is so significant in relation to the other article of which it also forms part as to be strikingly recognisable, whatever the purpose of the other article, then "articles ... substantially to that design" in section 226 may be interpreted accordingly. This seems to have been envisaged in the debates, when it was observed that a doll later applied to ornament a toothbrush-holder would be protectable as what was termed a "derivative" design.

2.234   Of course, design right may subsist in the whole of an article by virtue of the collocation of the individual parts, even if they would not themselves qualify for a separate design right. Conversely there is a "kit" provision, as with registered designs; section 260 applies the Act to "a complete or substantially complete set of components intended to be assembled into an article", and indicates that design right can subsist in any aspect of the design of the components of a kit as opposed to the design of the assembled article. This provision, according to Lord Beaverbrook,[54] was inserted to ensure that vegetable dishes with lids (and doubtless teapots) would not be left without protection by the "must-match" exclusion!

---

[52] This would be to apply something like the "separability" or "scindibilità" test of, respectively, U.S. and Italian copyright law, which requires artistic features of a utilitarian article to be conceptually separable from that article before copyright protection can be accorded.

[53] See Chap. 5.

[54] *Hansard*, Vol. 495, col. 704.

EXCLUSIONS

Under section 213(3), four aspects of a design are excluded from protection: **2.235**

    (a) a method or principle of construction

    (b) features of shape or configuration of an article which—

        (i) enable the article to be connected to, or placed in, around or against, another article so that either article may perform its function, or

       (ii) are dependent upon the appearance of another article of which the article is intended by the designer to form an integral part, or

    (c) surface decoration.

"Method or principle of construction"

This exclusion has the same wording as the one for registered designs,   **2.236**
considered at 2.030 above. Possibly it will need to be given a wider construction in the context of purely functional designs if undue monopolisation is to be avoided. As suggested in relation to crystalline changes brought about by heat treatment, any feature of shape or configuration which results from the way something is made or what it is made of should be jealously scrutinised. In the *Telemotive* case[55] on parts of a remote control system, it was suggested that there could be no design right in the "concept" of insetting a key into the transmitter casing. This is a reference to the "idea/expression dichotomy" invoked in copyright law (with varying success) where what has been copied is said to be an idea rather than the plaintiff's particular detailed elaboration of it—or indeed where the plaintiff's expression of an idea is said to be the only conceivable way of expressing it.[56] There is no warrant for the importation of this notion into the carefully-defined and circumscribed design right, but a similar safeguard against too covetous exercise of the right could be a wider use of the method or principle of construction exclusion, as was pointed out in *Telemotive*. An example from a different field would be the use of two rows of stitching on the seams of jeans and other denim garments, which stems from the nature of the seam adopted to impart extra strength and to discipline an intractable fabric.[57]

---

[55] SRIS/C/96/92, see 2.228 above.

[56] See, *e.g. Kenrick v. Lawrence* (1890) 25 Q.B.D. 99—drawing of hand holding pencil and making cross on ballot paper to show the illiterate how to vote—only more or less exact replica would infringe; Court of Appeal in *L. B. (Plastics) Ltd v. Swish Products Ltd* [1979] R.P.C. 551—fastening method for self-assembly drawers: only idea taken (reversed by House of Lords). The latter formulation of course resembles the narrower, rejected version of the registered designs "dictated solely by function" test, see 2.039 above.

[57] These examples might alternatively be denied design right as being "commonplace", as discussed below.

"Must-fit"

2.237   This exclusion denies design right to parts of articles which enable them to interconnect or interface with other articles so that either article may perform its function. Those parts of either article can therefore be freely copied by anyone wanting to compete in the making of either article. The general purport of the subsection is pretty clear. The prongs of an electrical plug must fit the socket into which they are to be inserted, or neither will be able to perform its function of conducting electricity from the mains to an appliance. Therefore they can be copied either from a competing plug or from the socket. A harrow must be capable of being linked to a tractor, or it will not be able to harrow up the soil. The function of the tractor as a vehicle would here be unaffected, but it is only necessary that one of the articles be made capable of performing its function. The door seal for a washing-machine must be able to be placed around the particular door aperture so as to fulfil its function of preventing leakage. The keypad of a telephone handset must be placed against the corresponding parts of the underlying circuit board, or nothing will happen when the keys are pressed.[58] Unusually-shaped tiles must fit together so that spilt liquids or condensation do not make their way between them to the detriment of floors and walls. And so on.[59]

2.238   However, the wording is not free from problems. Several questions spring to mind. Does the exclusion only operate where *no other* shape would enable the contemplated interconnection or interfacing to take place? Can every feature of the interacting areas be copied, or only those which are strictly necessary to the functioning of either article? Is it permissible, under the guise of "must-fit", to copy the whole of an interaction in relation to both articles, thereby perhaps taking the whole of an ingenious interconnecting device? And what about the rest of each article?

2.239   The exclusion speaks of "enabling" rather than "permitting" interconnection or interfacing, which perhaps suggests a construction more benign to the copier. So long as a particular shape "facilitates" interconnection, it can be copied without inquiring whether it is the only shape which would permit it. This is a tenuous indication, but so far as there is doubt, the Parliamentary material makes the government's intention clear. In introducing the Bill on Second Reading in the House of Lords,[60] Lord Young of Graffham spoke rather vaguely of "design freedom": where it exists, a competitor must utilise

---

[58] This point was made in *William Henney Electronics World Research Ltd v. K-Link Electronics Ltd* SRIS/C/01/93 in relation to a control panel which had to fit against a printed circuit board, certain items on which protruded through the panel. The court observed that it was not necessarily well-taken in that case—different panels could have been adopted, although copies of the original were no doubt the most convenient.

[59] Synthetic enzymes "must-fit" into the appropriate sites on their substrates, synthetic pharmaceutical compounds into the right receptors on their destination molecules. Acknowledgments to Laddie, Prescott & Vitoria, *Modern Law of Copyright*, 2nd ed., Butterworths, 1994.

[60] *Hansard*, November 12, 1987, col. 1479. See also 2nd Reading in the House of Commons, Vol. 132, col. 530.

it, but where there is a "need" to copy, then copying must be allowed. However, at Report stage[61] Lord Beaverbrook specifically rejected an amendment that would have limited "must-fit" to situations where copying was "absolutely unavoidable and essential". He said this would be "far too narrow", and a "recipe for litigation", and added "We do not want British industry to spend all its time arguing over whether minor design details are or are not covered by the must-fit exception."

The lock-and-key situation illustrates the second question. A key is designed to fit all the intricacies of a particular lock and to operate smoothly; but the lock may also be operated, though perhaps less easily, by a skeleton key. Or an octagonal nut might be tightened and loosened with a square-jawed spanner, but at the cost of unequal wear, greater slipping and diminished convenience and efficiency. Must the copier limit himself to the features absolutely essential to the functioning of either article, or is he entitled to copy every detail so that his competing version is just as satisfactory as the original? By parity of reasoning with the Parliamentary observations quoted above, it would seem he can take the lot.   **2.240**

The third question reflects the fact that "must-fit" was inspired, like so much else in the new legislation, by the spare parts problem. The paradigm competitor is providing an alternative *part* to fit a given, much more complex, article. But the wording of the exclusion is just as apt to cover, say, a new type of childproof cap for a medicine bottle having co-operating features on both the cap and the neck of the bottle. The cap and the bottle are prima facie separate articles, and the particular features enable each to be connected to or placed in, around or against the other so that each can perform its function of making it difficult for a child to separate them. A competitor could apparently proceed to make both, and raise "must-fit" in relation to both. The courts will probably look for ways round this result, perhaps by preferring to regard the bottle-and-cap assembly as a single article, or introducing some concept of "predominant" function. Both bottle and cap have functions other than that of childproofing—containing tablets and protecting them from loss and contamination respectively—and the safety function may be classified as subsidiary, whereas an exhaust pipe's only function is to conduct and disperse waste gases and particles. But the position is not very satisfactory for the deviser of the new arrangement, who will be well-advised to seek a patent—always supposing he thinks about it early enough, or can afford it, or that the design, while novel, is not obvious.[62]   **2.241**

The whole question of what function of either article has to be made possible by the interconnection or interface is not always adequately   **2.242**

---

[61] *Hansard*, Vol. 494, col. 109.
[62] If "must-fit" can operate in this way, then as well as other latching, coupling and otherwise co-operating articles, LEGO and other systems of mutually-compatible products could be caught. As will be seen in Chap. 6, a similar exclusion from the proposed Community Design Right has had to be provided with a special "exclusion from the exclusion" for products within what is termed a "modular system".

answered by the subsection. If all the pod-and-pylon engines are removed from a Boeing airliner, it will not fly, so clearly the fixing points "must-fit". It will fly without its lavatories being emptied through an interconnecting pipe, but without the interconnection the pump will not be able to fulfil its function. No problem. But suppose a maker of process equipment for mixing ice-cream thoughtfully provides interconnecting means so that each individual mixer, though operating perfectly satisfactorily on its own, can be coupled up to others to form as long a line as a manufacturer finds convenient, all controllable from a single panel. Is the function of each article just "mixing ice-cream", or is it "mixing ice-cream as part of a centrally-controllable line"? If the latter, the thoughtful machine-maker will be robbed of his competitive edge immediately, because anyone can copy his interconnecting means if not his machines. (Or, if you are advising the defendant, the maker will quite properly be balked of his anti-competitive desire to tie ice-cream manufacturers to his machines.)

2.243   The fourth question is easily answered: it is only the actual interconnecting or interfacing parts which are deprived of design right. The rest of the articles may not be copied. The body of the electrical plug cannot be copied, nor can the harrowing tines or their disposition, the holes or slots of the telephone earpiece or mouthpiece, the overall shape of the medicine bottle or cap or of the LEGO brick. An example used in the debates was the roller from a vacuum cleaner: the fixing points at each end were subject to "must-fit", but not the remainder of the roller. Lord Beaverbrook was at pains to make clear to the Carbon and Ribbon Manufacturers Association, who had wanted some sort of *de minimis* provision to allow them to copy the few small features of typewriter cassettes which are not fit-constrained, that even small non-constrained features could be protected.[63] This is all very right and proper in principle, but may prove difficult to operate. There are bound to be arguments about where design freedom begins and ends in relation to a part which interfaces in more than one way or place; and designers of competing spares will have to be briefed very carefully (but, alas, speculatively) about what they may and may not copy. Lord Beaverbrook's intentions here do not entirely chime with his desire, expressed a few columns earlier, to spare British industry the fret of arguing about whether minor design details are covered by "must-fit".

2.244   It will have become apparent that "must-fit" is *not* the same as "dictated solely by function", nor as the *British Leyland* spare parts exception. The test is more objective than "dictated solely", the designer's motivation being irrelevant except perhaps in cases of doubt. If a part does in fact interconnect or interface for functional reasons, that is that. But if it does not, then it does not matter how functional it is. If the article is a car bonnet, the fixing points obviously must fit, as must the outer shape, but other internal features such as

---

[63] *Hansard*, Vol. 494, col. 124. He instanced "the fins which are now starting to appear on the ends of aircraft wings. They are certainly very small in relation to the size of the wings. But I understand they have very significant effects in improving the performance of the aircraft".

stiffening ribs do not have to do so, and their shape and disposition can be protected. *British Leyland* took the view that copying an entire part, without over-nice discrimination about design freedom, was permissible so long as it was a replacement part, or possibly even a consumable, without which the vehicle would be "unfit or materially unfit"[64] for the purpose for which it had been sold. This at least had the virtue of simplicity, in comparison with "must-fit", and both original equipment manufacturer and spares manufacturer knew where they stood.

"Must-match"

This exclusion uses exactly the same wording as the amendment to section 1   **2.245**
of the Registered Designs Act,[65] but it cannot be assumed that it means exactly the same. For one very important thing, there is no requirement that parts of articles be made and sold separately if they are to enjoy protection. The ratio of the decision to refuse registration to body panels in *Ford/Fiat*,[66] cannot therefore be applied to unregistered design right, where parts of articles (whether parts of a complex article or parts of an article which may itself be part of another one) are explicitly protected, unless falling within one of the exclusions. In theory the court could not refuse to consider arguments in favour, say, of a body panel having only a single styling feature which does not have to match anything else on the car as a whole.

However, it seems likely that body panels are a lost cause for the present,   **2.246**
under design right as under registered designs. Although the findings of the Registered Designs Appeal Tribunal and the Divisional Court on the meaning of "must-match" are strictly *obiter*, since the applications were disposed of on another ground, it is difficult to believe that the lower courts would do other than adopt their views on the meaning of "integral" and "dependent", the identification of the "other article" and the designer whose intention is relevant, and, most significantly, how the comparison is to be made (with the "other article" having all the original parts in place so that they are being compared with themselves). Indeed the language of both the "must-fit" and "must-match" exclusions is unsuited to dealing with parts of articles other than in the sense of parts of a complex article which is the relevant "other article". This is not surprising, since it was presumably inserted at whatever point the decision was taken to abandon the White Paper scheme, which did not provide for these exclusions, and impose them also on unregistered design right.

Moreover, in so far as the court would be prepared to look at the   **2.247**
Parliamentary materials, it would find Parliament's dishonourable intentions

[64] Lord Templeman, [1986] A.C. 577.
[65] Discussed at 2.048–2.067 above.
[66] [1993] R.P.C. 399; [1994] R.P.C. 545; [1995] R.P.C. 167 (H.L.).

towards body panels clearly reflected since, as already pointed out, the debates on "must-match" took place almost entirely in the context of unregistered design right.

2.248   A further consideration is that the meaning of "must-match" for unregistered design right would have to be determined in the context of an expensive infringement action (or action for a declaration of non-infringement), or at best a contested dispute before the Comptroller under section 246[67] followed by appeals. Given the importance of the matter, and his views as already known from *Ford/Fiat*, the Comptroller would be eminently likely to refer such a dispute to the court himself under the power given to him by section 246(2)(a).

2.249   It is equally likely that the wing-mirrors, wheel covers and so on which secured registration would be treated the same way under unregistered design right, except that their fixing points would be excluded by "must-fit" instead of "dictated solely by function" and want of novelty as a further objection would be replaced by allegations that a design was "commonplace". The lamp lenses remitted to the Registry for further consideration as having three-dimensional "pattern or ornament" features produced by moulding the glass would possibly be excluded from design right as surface decoration, although they might be argued to serve the largely functional purpose of diffusing or concentrating the light.

2.250   Other articles mentioned in the registered designs discussion of "must-match"—matching storage containers and matching panels for kitchen furniture—may paradoxically escape the exclusion in the unregistered design right context, because although in the layman's sense they pre-eminently "must-match" each other, they do not form an integral part of each other (unless a kitchen is an article, which it is believed not to be). This interpretation is supported by Lord Beaverbrook, who denied that one piece of a three-piece suite of furniture would be caught,[68] because it is not an integral part of another article. Misgivings have been expressed about the status of teapots and lids,[69] but it seems that a tea service as a whole would not be an article of which the teapot as a whole would be an integral part, it would merely be a collection of articles. If this is so, the preferences of customers for matching crockery as well as body panels will have to go unsatisfied. Only time and legal precedent will confirm these guesses, and as with other aspects of design right, litigants seem to have been chary of making themselves test cases.

---

[67] Which allows disputes about, *inter alia*, the subsistence of design right to be referred to him.
[68] *Hansard*, Vol. 494, col. 110. Would one piece of a three-piece suit? Is there an aftermarket in waistcoats?
[69] See 2.052 and 2.067 above. Lord Beaverbrook would call them "kits".

"Surface decoration"

As explained in considering section 51, three-dimensional surface decoration is excluded from design right and is a matter for copyright, provided a copyright work can be identified. In deciding what constitutes decoration, it is likely that evidence both of the designer's intention and knowledge of the market, and of the views of customers, will be relevant—though the court will, it is imagined, be sceptical of claims that the configuration of the underside of a shower tray owed anything to decorative intentions.[70] The fate of functional surface features like knurling to make knobs less likely to slip in wet or oily fingers or raised patterns to help the visually-impaired will depend on whether they have any decorative content.[71] The knob with star-shaped protrusions mentioned elsewhere would very likely qualify for copyright— unless the star shapes were provided to allow a volume-control knob to be distinguished from a tuning knob adorned with pyramids?

2.251

Surface decoration could be a way round "must-match" for determined body panel designers, providing them with copyright in high- or low-relief decorative features. The customer who wants his replacement panels to be the same as the originals would then have to buy the originals; but the apparent survival of the *British Leyland* exception under section 171(3))[72] as a defence to copyright infringement may yet indulge him.

2.252

SEMICONDUCTOR TOPOGRAPHIES

These are regulated by the Design Right (Semiconductor Topographies) Regulations 1989[73] which, except where the context otherwise requires, are to be construed as one with unregistered design right. A "semiconductor product" means:

2.253

> "an article the purpose, or one of the purposes, of which is the performance of an electronic function and which consists of two or more layers, at least one of which is composed of semi-conducting material and in or upon one or more of which is fixed a pattern appertaining to that or another function."

and a "semiconductor topography" means a design within section 213(2) of the Act which is a design of either of the following:

(a) the pattern fixed, or intended to be fixed, in or upon
   (i) a layer of a semiconductor product, or
   (ii) a layer of material in the course of and for the purpose of the manufacture of a semiconductor product, or

---

[70] See *Gardex Ltd v. Sorata Ltd* [1986] R.P.C. 623.
[71] Would it matter if their intended customers cannot see them?
[72] See para. 2.185 above.
[73] S.I. 1989 No. 1100.

(b) the arrangement of the patterns fixed, or intended to be fixed, in or upon the layers of a semiconductor product in relation to one another.

Such designs, although referring to "patterns", are hardly likely to fall within the surface decoration exclusion, or "must-match". A chip mounted on a circuit board may be implicated in a "must-fit" situation, but "method or principle of construction" would seem to have little part to play. Topographies must, however, like other designs, be original.

"Original"

2.254 Under section 213(1), design right subsists only in an "original" design.[74] Under section 213(4), a design is not original if it is "commonplace in the design field in question at the time of its creation". This appears to be a two-stage test. First "originality" is assessed, on undefined criteria, then the design is scrutinised to see whether its originality by these criteria is to be discounted because it is commonplace. This was in fact the procedure applied in *C. & H. Engineering v. F. Klucznik & Son Ltd*,[75] the pig fender case. Aldous J. looked first at section 213(1) and held that "original" should be given the same meaning as in copyright law—"not copied but the independent work of the designer". He contrasted this with the novelty requirement for registered designs.

2.255 Pausing here, the adoption of the copyright test does not mean that it will necessarily be applied in exactly the same way. It will be recalled from the discussion of originality in copyright[76] that where there has been a series of design sketches or drawings reflecting the evolution of a product over a relatively short time, or slightly different versions of the same product with minor styling changes, then particularly where the defendant has clearly copied one or other of them, arguments based on lack of originality because the drawing copied reproduces much of the earlier work will not receive much sympathy. There may be a difference with design right, since each design recorded in a design document or embodied in an article made to the design has an entirely separate potential design right,[77] which must be separately assessed for originality (and commonplaceness). If the design document for the article actually copied is a drawing, or the design is exemplified in an article, and neither shows much difference of any visual significance from earlier versions, it may be easier on the *Interlego v. Tyco*[78] test to attack its originality. On the other hand, the *Interlego* attack was

---

[74] Lord Beaverbrook: "the creator's own work and not a copy", *Hansard*, Vol. 494, col. 112.
[75] [1992] F.S.R. 421.
[76] See 2.129–2.139 above, and particularly *L. A. Gear Inc. v. Hi-Tec Sports plc* [1992] F.S.R. 121 and *Macmillan Publishers Ltd v. Thomas Reed Publications Ltd* [1993] F.S.R. 455.
[77] "Design right does not subsist unless and until the design has been recorded in a design document or an article has been made to the design": s.213(6).
[78] [1988] R.P.C. 343.

inspired by the fact that it was *artistic* copyright that was being relied on, and therefore visual content had to have some importance. With design right, a design document can just as well be a written description. This suggests that although originality is still necessary, it can be imparted by technical and manufacturing changes which are functionally even if not visually significant.[79]

"COMMONPLACE IN THE DESIGN FIELD IN QUESTION AT THE TIME OF . . . CREATION"

"Commonplace" is not further defined, nor is "the design field in question". **2.256** As pointed out, this phraseology derives from the semiconductor topography Directive[80] via the 1987 Regulations,[81] and the design "field" was therefore limited to semiconductors. In the Act there is no such convenient factual background to provide a limitation on the design field, nor is there any indication whether comparison is to be made only with U.K. designs (as in the Registered Designs Act). Lord Beaverbrook unhelpfully admitted that "commonplace" does not have a precise meaning. But the government believed that "in the context of this Bill it will provide a perfectly comprehensible and workable threshold for design right. In our view the meaning which would be given to . . . 'original' if this were not qualified . . . is too generous a test for the acquisition of design right . . . It could allow someone to acquire a right for . . . re-designing the wheel. Our intention is to avoid giving design right to mundane, routine designs of the kind which are common currency in the particular field in question."[82]

One point that was made clear in the debates is that, as might be expected, **2.257** it is the design, and not the article to which it is applied, that must not be commonplace. Aldous J. in *Klucznik* found pig fenders as such to be commonplace, but not the particular metal roll-bar in issue. He thought that the "not commonplace" requirement appeared to introduce "a consideration akin to novelty",[83] although finding that a metal roll-bar was not commonplace over a wooden one suggests a pretty relaxed test. "Novelty", however, was *not* the word chosen for the Act, so it would not be right simply to import registered design concepts wholesale. On the other hand, since the starting-point for design right is originality, a less demanding standard than novelty,

---

[79] Though John Butcher told the Commons Committee that minor and incremental design changes would be defeated for want of originality on *Interlego* principles: *Hansard*, 15th Sitting, June 14, 1988, col. 577.

[80] 87/54/EEC.

[81] S.I. 1987 No. 1497.

[82] *Hansard*, Vol. 494, col. 112. Faced with quotations from the same ministerial brief in the Commons Committee, Frank Doran, by origin a Scottish lawyer, said tartly "I struggle to understand why we should expect the judiciary to define what is commonplace when we do not trust them to define an original design": *Hansard*, 15th Sitting, June 14, 1988, col. 575.

[83] Thereby underlining the risk referred to above of a designer anticipating his own design and making it commonplace through his earlier versions.

and since "novelty" is deliberately avoided, it might be fair to assume that the draftsman had in mind something between the two.

2.258   On this basis, a few guesses can be hazarded. There seems no reason, in the absence of a specific limitation, to confine the design field to the U.K. if there is a flourishing international trade in the articles concerned. "Commonplace" is a more objective test than "original", so there is room for the citation of prior art, even if the plaintiff's designer did not copy any of it so as to render his design non-original. But whereas with registered design novelty a design can be ruled out if it has been applied to *any* article before, it is suggested that "the design field in question" is limited to designs for articles of the same general kind as the ones involved. This is how the "common trade variants" test is applied in registered designs law[84] (since "the trade" must be an identifiable trade if it is to be scanned for common variants) where it serves the purpose of not allowing one particular manufacturer to monopolise a feature which should be open to all. If shoe soles are commonly treated, by grooving or being provided with a raised criss-cross pattern or whatever, to avoid slipping, then unless the pattern imparted is particularly striking or has a very specific functional advantage, it should be treated as commonplace. So should standard methods of setting in sleeves, or cutting tweed jackets with one or two back vents, or providing raincoats with epaulettes and little buckled straps on the cuffs. But a satin evening dress made with all the features of a raincoat, or a tweed jacket with vents all round, would not be commonplace, because known features would have been applied in an unfamiliar context.

2.259   The inclusion within design right of purely functional designs does pose additional problems, because a functional advantage may be conferred in a hitherto unfamiliar context by use of a feature perfectly well-known in a host of other areas. Aerosol dispensers are widely-known in the perfume and deodorant field, and also for spraying water on house-plants, surface cleaning fluids on surfaces, flea-killer on cats and so on. But as a means of dispensing Thousand Island dressing to secure a uniform and thorough coating for the prawns in a prawn cocktail, some protection might be deserved, at least until the constant clogging of the outlets proved it a device not worth copying.

2.260   Aesthetic designs may raise these questions too. Chocolate bunnies are well-known: should a soap bunny get design right? Are toiletries a sufficiently different design field from confectionery, even though both products may be designed to appeal to children? If frog-shaped soap tablets are known, should a frog-shaped sponge get design right? Here the fields are so close that it probably should not. Rubber ducks, and indeed beautiful carved wooden ducks with every feather in place and all the colours right, are well-known. But would they make a beautiful carved wooden duck with a telephone keypad set into its underside, whose eyes light up in use and which quacks instead of ringing, commonplace? This is more like applying Westminister

---

[84] See discussion at para. 2.105 above.

Abbey to a teaspoon. The courts are likely to be called upon to do some creative thinking about design fields, and it is possible that something rather like the "goods of the same description" test from trade mark law may evolve, examining not only who manufactureres the goods but also the trade channels through which they are distributed (with evidence about how supermarkets are laid out) and who are the target customers.

The quality of the evidence relied on will play an important part. In the *Telemotive* case about remote control equipment for cranes,[85] it was suggested that the plaintiff's rubber switch-mat was commonplace. The plaintiff claimed that it had been specially-developed for it and was unique in the market. The defendant said that it utilised well-known design principles and embodied no unique technology. This could only be decided at trial. Expert evidence might be required, the designer would need to be heard from, and customers might be consulted about their views. If customers testify that a particular feature is striking and important, can it really be dismissed as commonplace? Commercial success with a registered design can bolster a claim to novelty. If a designer has laboured long and hard, should it not be assumed he has done so to some effect? John Butcher, perhaps incautiously, told the Association of Manufacturers of Domestic Electrical Appliances that if a company had spent two years designing something the result would hardly be likely to be commonplace.[86] The trouble is that a defendant would no doubt be able to find someone to testify at length that the plaintiff's designer was just not very good at his job. **2.261**

The commonplace test may prove to be a useful if rough-and-ready way of weeding out undeserving claims or, like so much else in the 1988 Act, it may be a source of delight to lawyers, both in advising on proposed designs and in litigating those that have been copied. It must of course be borne in mind that particular features of a design or parts of an article may be commonplace without rendering the whole article unworthy of design right, which as usual adds an extra twist. While there is authority that the common trade variants test in registered designs law should not be used so as to pick a design to pieces and knock out each feature one by one, giving insufficient weight to the design as a collocation, the design right test, for good or ill, seems to invite doing just that. **2.262**

Overall, it seems likely that unregistered design right will in the long run prove less satisfactory for plaintiffs than copyright, which seems to be what was intended. To take a random example, clothing designs have hitherto been litigated by plaintiffs with reasonable success, provided there is an adequately detailed design sketch containing all the features. With design right, there is more scope for writing off the majority of the styling features as commonplace. But in the short run, unless the courts are prepared to listen more closely to evidence and argument on the merits and not pressure defendants **2.263**

---

[85] SRIS/C/96/92; see para. 2.228 above.
[86] *Hansard*, House of Commons Report stage, Vol. 138, col. 66.

into conceding that there is an arguable case, there is a risk that interlocutory injunctions will be granted where they should not be. Since very few cases go to trial, the purpose of the law may be thwarted.

Spare parts under the 1988 Act

2.264 Leaving aside the "hangover" copyright (subject to the *British Leyland* exception) in relation to designs made before August 1, 1989, how do spare parts made on or after that date fare under the new Act? The government repeatedly insisted during the Parliamentary debates that the Act would provide some protection for them, as the White Paper originally proposed it should. So it does: but it is quite heavily circumscribed by the exclusions from design right, by the apparent survival of the *British Leyland* exception as a defence to copyright infringement, and possibly by the doctrine of the owner's "implied licence" to repair the product he has bought.

2.265 To take the example of a car, essentially what the fuss was all about and what the exclusions were custom-designed for: the external appearance of its body panels, on *Ford/Fiat* principles, will largely be excluded from both registered designs and design right because of "must-match". Some protection could be available under copyright to both two- and three-dimensional surface decoration (subject to argument about the meaning of "decoration" where a three-dimensional feature like the rocker-clearing power dome is attributable partly to function), including trim and insignia; but this might be defeated on public interest (right to repair) principles by *British Leyland*, which seems to survive as a defence to copyright infringement under section 171(3).[87] The question would be whether the inability to have a completely matching panel would render the car "materially unfit" for its purpose. Both the Registered Designs Appeal Tribunal and the Divisional Court in *Ford/Fiat* accorded respect to customer preference by recognising that replacement panels would be unsaleable if they were not identical,[88] so interpretation may be quite liberal.

2.266 Dashboards seem to be treated like body panels, except for any purely decorative features. But mirrors, steering-wheels, seats, wheels, wheel covers and some aspects of lamps can enjoy both registered and unregistered design protection, except for those parts which "must-fit".

2.267 Internal parts do better than those with "appearance" content, because it is clear that except for the areas caught by "must-fit", design right can apply wherever it is not defeated by the commonplace test. Thus most internal parts struck down by *British Leyland* can now claim protection again, even if registered designs are ruled out because of "dictated solely by function" or

---

[87] "Nothing in this Part [*i.e.* the copyright Part of the Act] affects any rule of law preventing or restricting the enforcement of copyright, on grounds of public interest or otherwise."

[88] See 2.062 and 2.064 above.

"who-cares-what-it-looks-like?" It is not absolutely clear that *British Leyland* does not apply to design right, but there is no saving provision like section 171(3), and certainly it was not the government's intention that it should.[89] Lord Beaverbrook made it quite plain that the exception would be superseded by the new statutory code, and indeed it is difficult to make sense of the design right provisions otherwise. Unfortunately, perhaps, although urged to spell out its intentions, the government declined to do so.

The doctrine of the owner's "implied licence" to repair stems originally   **2.268**
from patent law. Without the patentee's licence, it is an infringement even to use a patented product, let alone sell it. But it was recognised that a person who had bought a patented article must be entitled to use it, and to sell it on if he chose, so a licence to do so had to be implied on a sale, unless expressly excluded by the original sale contact. The law also accepted that in order to get his full value, the owner of a patented article should be allowed to repair it, so long as this would not amount to replacement of the whole article. By parity of reasoning, this doctrine would apply to articles protected by a registered design; and in *Solar Thomson Engineering Co. v. Barton*,[90] the reasoning was applied to an article protected by copyright. Since repairs would often need to be carried out by sub-contractors, the implied licence, to make business sense, had also to cover the activities of these sub-contractors, when done in response to instructions from the product's owner. It was urged on the Court of Appeal in *British Leyland*[91] that to make business sense in the modern world the implied licence should be extended to cover third parties making infringing parts ahead of need and without specific instructions from individual vehicle owners. They refused to do this, and the House of Lords invented the non-derogation from grant exception instead. However, the implied licence as covering a vehicle owner and sub-contractors expressly authorised by him seems to be unaffected.

This is unlikely to have much practical significance for mass-market cars   **2.269**
and other domestic appliances, where most repairs are effected using mass-produced spares. But it could play a part where large-scale machinery is concerned and users may prefer to choose their own sub-contractors to do repairs using spares made by them, rather than go to the original supplier. The doctrine may, however, be eroded by the ability of design right to subsist in parts of articles as well as the whole of them, so that the repair/replacement distinction is less easy to draw.

---

[89] *Hansard*, Vol. 491, col. 1113.
[90] [1977] R.P.C. 537.
[91] [1986] R.P.C. 579.

3. Subsistence, First Ownership and Duration

3.001   Chapter 2 considered the scope and content of the three types of design right. This chapter deals with whether or not they subsist in any particular case, who is the first owner of them, and how long they last. Subsistence in the case of copyright and unregistered design right normally depends on whether the creator of the copyright work or unregistered design or, in the case of unregistered designs, sometimes its first owner, was a "qualifying person" or "qualifying individual" at the relevant time. Additionally, U.K. copyright may subsist in a work by virtue of its place of first publication, and unregistered design right may subsist in certain circumstances by virtue of the person by whom and the place where first marketing of articles made to the design took place. A registered design subsists by virtue of registration, but the applicant must have been a person who was entitled to apply.

3.002   First ownership ("proprietorship" in the case of a registered design) is important, because where someone who is not the first owner or proprietor seeks to assert the right, or to deal with it by assignment or licensing, he must be able to trace the devolution of his title back to the first owner or proprietor.

3.003   In this and the next two chapters on dealings with and infringements of the three design rights, they are treated in reverse order from that adopted in Chapter 2.[1] This is because only a minority of right owners trouble to obtain registered designs, whereas unregistered design right and copyright arise without the need for any active steps to be taken, and are likely to be the first ports of call for those looking for rights to enforce. And if the U.K. government's attempts at distancing copyright from the field of industrial design have been successful, it is with unregistered design right that most people will have to grapple. For brevity, the right will again be referred to simply as "design right", which is indeed the terminology adopted by the 1988 Act.

---

[1] For the reasons explained in that Chapter, see 2.001 and 2.120 above. Note also possible effects of E.U. "term" Directive, see 3.080 below.

UNREGISTERED DESIGN RIGHT

Limited Availability of Right

One of the criticisms directed against the U.K.'s generous protection of **3.004** industrial designs by copyright was that it could be invoked here by foreigners to protect their designs against U.K. competitors, even where those designs would enjoy no rights in their "home" countries and nor would similar U.K.-originated designs. This was because the "national treatment" requirement in the Berne Convention was regarded as obliging the U.K. to give the same protection to authors of works originating in another Convention country as it gave to its own nationals. In fact Article 2(7) of Berne would have entitled the U.K. to exclude from copyright designs which in their "home" countries were protected (or protectable) only by special industrial designs legislation. And Berne demands protection only for "works of applied art" (undefined, but eminently unlikely to extend to bits of machinery), so some discrimination could lawfully have been exercised on this ground too; but it was not. The result was that Japanese or American car manufacturers would be able to stop U.K. companies making replacement exhaust pipes, whether for the U.K. market or for export to Japan or the USA, although neither they nor any U.K. manufacturer would be able to prevent local manufacturers in those countries from doing the same.

When the unregistered design right was invented, the government took the **3.005** deliberate policy decision to make it available on a reciprocal basis to non-E.U. designs (E.U. designs could not be discriminated against because of the free movement of goods provisions in the Treaty of Rome) only where it was satisfied that adequate protection would in fact be given to British designs in the country of origin. Because it is a *sui generis* right, the government takes the view that it is not covered by either the Berne or the Paris Convention (which also requires "national treatment"). It was argued in the White Paper[2] that Paris covers only designs which are inventive or aesthetic, not those which are purely functional (because otherwise there would be no need for separate provision for semiconductor chips). Therefore purely functional designs are outside Paris and there is no need for "national treatment", which would be given only for designs capable of registration under the 1949 Act.

This may or may not be correct: Paris Article 5 *quinquies* demands the **3.006** protection of "industrial designs" in all Convention countries, and Article 1 requires that "industrial property", including industrial designs, "be understood in the broadest sense", so it may be argued that any right conferred on what are in fact industrial designs is caught by Paris. The 1988 Act (sections 217 and 256) makes no distinction between aesthetic and functional designs in dealing with the conditions under which reciprocity will be granted, but

---

[2] Intellectual Property and Innovation, Cmnd. 9712, para. 3.34.

section 211 provides for the making of Orders in Council conferring unregistered design right, subject to any specified requirements, on overseas designs to fulfil any U.K. international obligation, and different provision may be made for different descriptions of design or article. Lord Beaverbrook in Committee of the House of Lords during passage of the Bill[3] indicated that this section would be used for compliance with Paris; presumably, as interpreted by the government, so as to give design right to registrable (as judged by civil servants) but unregistered designs.

3.007   As for Berne, the government in paragraph 3.32 of the White Paper recognised that the Convention requires copyright still to apply to artistic works (in the section 51 rather than section 4 sense). Berne Article 2(7) gives freedom to Member States to provide special legislation for "works of applied art [whatever these may be] and industrial designs and models", requiring only that if there is no such special legislation, such works and designs originating in another Member State be protected as artistic works. Where works of applied art are protected as artistic works, Article 7(4) requires a minimum term of 25 years; it does not mention industrial designs and models. Since the U.K. *has* enacted special legislation for works of applied art and industrial designs, by way of unregistered and registered design rights, and since industrially-applied artistic works get 25 years copyright under section 52, we seem to have complied with Berne. Nonetheless, deep offence is felt in many non-E.U. countries at the overt exclusion of their designs from the new unregistered design right.

3.008   Semiconductor topographies receive more generous reciprocal treatment. Recent statutory instruments[4] extend reciprocal protection to chip designs from Australia, Austria, Finland, Japan, Sweden, Switzerland and the USA and, on slightly less favourable terms, to Iceland and Norway. This is in addition to the Isle of Man, the Channel Islands, Gibraltar and other U.K. colonies. Austria, Finland and Sweden are now of course members of the E.U.

Subsistence

3.009   Design right, under section 213(6) and (7), cannot subsist unless and until the design has been recorded in a design document, or an article has been made to the design, in either case on or after August 1, 1989. We met design documents in Chapter 2,[5] and the same definition is repeated in section 263(1): "design documents" means "any record of a design, whether in the form of a drawing, a written description, a photograph, data stored in a computer or otherwise". The "design" is not the same thing as the record of it, being capable of existing in the designer's mind before any such record is

---

[3] *Hansard*, H.L. Committee (7th Day), January 1, 1988, col. 1129.
[4] Design Right (Semiconductor Topographies) (Amendment) Regulations 1991 and 1992, S.I. 1991 No. 2237 and S.I. 1992 No. 400.
[5] See 2.189 above.

made; the significance of a design document is purely as a record from which the design can be identified and the term of its protection dated. Although in most cases it will be the designer himself who records the design, since only he knows what is in his head, there is no actual requirement for this to be so, or even for the record to be made with his consent, which may sometimes lead to difficulties in identifying who the true designer is, and cause the protection term to start running at an earlier date than the designer would have wished.

The definition of "design document" is wide, and the listed items are only examples. They are not given separate definitions in the design Part of the Act,[6] and the definitions of "drawing" and "photograph" (and "literary work") provided for copyright in Part I are limited to that Part. Nonetheless, they will doubtless be taken at least as guides. "Drawing" can be anything from a rough sketch to a fully-worked-up production drawing, so long as it shows all the features in which design right is claimed—bearing in mind that the right can subsist in parts of articles as well as articles as a whole. Although section 213(6) refers to "a" design document, it would seem unduly restrictive not to allow several drawings to be put together for this purpose,[7] although if they were made on different dates the protection terms of the different elements of the design will differ accordingly. Since a written description can also be a design document, written explanatory matter on a drawing can freely be taken into account, so long as it relates to features of *appearance* deriving from shape or configuration. Copies of original drawings would be acceptable as design documents, so long as their provenance is adequately shown. Those accustomed to dealing with copyright must remember that it is the *design*, not the design *document*, which has to be "original"; but defendants must be alert to attempts by plaintiffs to manipulate the design's date of birth or its parentage by putting forward inadequately-attested design documents.

3.010

A written description of a design must only be an acceptable design document if it conveys all the relevant features of shape and configuration with sufficient precision to identify one particular appearance. If what can be visualised or made from the written description can assume more than one shape, what is described would appear to be a "method or principle of construction" in which design right cannot subsist. Nor would the design be adequately identified. So it would not be enough for a dress designer to write merely "a pleated skirt", because the pleats could be concertina pleats or kilt-type pleats or box pleats as in a gymslip, each of which would give a different visual effect. On the other hand, an engineer who wrote down a series of co-ordinates from which a pipe of specified diameter and wall-thickness could be bent to one shape only would have produced a perfectly adequate design document. Subject to this, "written description" embraces a wide variety of documents, including patent specifications, assembly instructions, software for programming machine-tools to make articles to the

3.011

[6] Part III.
[7] This is permitted under copyright, see, *e.g. British Leyland v. Armstrong* [1986] R.P.C. 279.

design, and even (conceivably) chemical formulae for making "designer" molecules. More mundanely, a knitting pattern of the "k1p1wfdp1sl1k1psso" variety would be an acceptable record of the design of a jumper, since following the instructions would produce an article made to the design.[8]

3.012   In most cases a photograph, although useful for evidential purposes, is unlikely to be the first record of a design which starts the protection term running, because the object appearing in the photograph—prototype, VDU display—will have secured design right already. But for micro-engineering designs which are too small to be seen by the naked eye, a photograph will be a convenient first record (but may be one not made by the designer). Semiconductor topographies may take advantage of this, since they are themselves "photographs" produced by light-etching.

3.013   The inclusion of "data stored in a computer" among design documents means that a design comes into being without the need for any hard copy to have been made. The design can be worked on from time to time and when completed it can be sent, still in digital code, by modem to another computer which will program a machine to make an article to the design; but the clock will start running for the protection term once the final design is in memory,[9] not when the first article is made.

3.014   Other forms of design documents could be a punched card for programming a Jacquard loom (if such antiquated methods still persist), a film or video (though subject to the same caveat as photographs when it is a record of a pre-existing object) and, perhaps, a sound recording of someone describing a design.[10] Since it is suggested there is no need for the design document to have been made by the designer or with his consent, people would do well not to describe designs too fully in conversation (or in the hearing of a voice-activated computer), lest someone record the description and start the clock running.

3.015   The other way of giving birth to a design is by making an article "to" it, and this is how articles which are made from non-artistic prototypes will receive protection under design right which they did not enjoy under copyright. Some

---

[8] Copyright in the pattern as a literary work failed in *Brigid Foley Ltd v. Elliott* [1982] R.P.C. 281 as a means of preventing competitors copying the jumper, because you (probably) do not infringe copyright in a literary work consisting of instructions for making something by making it.

[9] Which can be checked from the computer's internal recording system showing when documents were last worked on.

[10] A sound recording, whether or not made by the speaker, adequately "records" a literary work for the purpose of conferring copyright under section 3 of the Act—although that is in Part I, not Part III. Further, data stored in a computer can be a design *document*, and there seems no very good reason why an analogue sound recording, and *a fortiori* when these become common, a digital sound recording should not also be a document, since it is a record from which an oral description can be transcribed. In *Dun & Bradstreet Ltd v. Typesetting Facilities Ltd* [1992] F.S.R. 320, Harman J. held that an application to inspect the contents of computer tapes and disks was to be made under R.S.C., Ord. 24, r. 10 (discovery of documents) rather than Ord. 29, r. 2 (inspection of property).

"articles" may still get copyright protection through being sculptures,[11] and if so, section 236[11A] will ensure that copyright prevails, but a prudent plaintiff will plead both in the alternative if his business is garden gnomes or the like. But the piston designer can now rely on his first prototype (or the production version if that is sufficiently different visually from the prototype not to have its originality compromised) as the record of the design. Indeed any design right owner may want to rely on the design as embodied in his production version, since it is that which will have been copied, but he must expect to be subjected to searching inquiries from the defendant about its originality, and if time has elapsed between design and production in fast-developing or fast-changing fields like aerospace or fashion, he must beware of accusations that his design has become commonplace in the meantime.

It will be apparent that careful record-keeping will be important in establishing design right, and designers should be briefed accordingly.   **3.016**

"FIRST OWNERSHIP"

There are several paths by which a particular design can "qualify" for design right. With one exception[12] (and slightly different treatment for semi-conductor chips), they depend on identifying the "first owner". Only then can it be determined whether that person "qualifies" the design for design right.   **3.017**

"Creator"

Under section 215(1), the first owner, unless the design was created in pursuance of a commission or in the course of employment, is the designer. This, according to section 214(1), is the "person who creates the design". A similar definition of "author" is introduced for the first time by the 1988 Act in relation to both copyright works (section 9(1)) and registered designs (section 267(3) and Schedule 4, section 2(3)). Decades of case law hold that the author of a copyright work is he who puts pen to paper,[13] even if this is to express the ideas of someone else—thus it is the engineering draughtsman whose skill and labour reduces the designer's ideas to visible form who is the "author" of the drawings, and the "ghost" writer tends to get copyright in the celebrity's memoirs. But as pointed out above, with design right the designer is the person who conceives the design, not necessarily the person who records it in a design document, still less makes the first article. In the first (and so far the only) design right case to go to trial, *C. & H. Engineering v. F.*   **3.018**

---

[11] See Chap. 2 above.
[11A] See Chap. 5 below.
[12] See 3.039 below.
[13] Or finger to keyboard or hand to mouse. Malcontents might observe that this has not been held to apply to the humble and usually female shorthand-typist who uses her skills and labour to reduce her boss's words to intelligible form; she is a mere amanuensis.

Klucznik & Son Ltd,[14] the question arose of who owned the design right in a pig fender of which the only non-commonplace feature was a roll-bar of 2″ tube. The design had been evolved by the counterclaiming defendant's salesman and other employees, together with the customer who first ordered the fender. All drawings had apparently been made by the employees; but the judge held that the "creator" of the design was the person who had the idea of using the 2″ tube. Since there was a dispute, which the judge felt unable, on the evidence given, to resolve, about whether this had been the customer or the salesman, he found that the defendant had failed to prove its case. This illustrates the difficulty of pinpointing the incidence of first ownership. It may be that greater use will have to be made of the concept of joint designs and co-ownership, but this can be inconvenient, although it may more accurately reflect the increasingly international nature of design, where creative input may come from a variety of people titivating the basic design which is flashed around the world from one to another by computer and modem.

3.019   For "computer-generated" designs, there is a special rule in section 214(2) that "the person by whom the arrangements necessary for the creation of the design are undertaken is to be taken to be the designer". A computer-generated design is defined in section 263 as one which is "generated by computer in circumstances such that there is no human designer". It would not cover the normal case of computer-assisted design or graphics, where the computer is used only as a sophisticated tool. A car body or office layout, or a page of a magazine, will still have a human design (or design team); all the computer does is save labour by displaying a design from several angles to save multiple sketches or resetting a page of text and pictures without lengthy cutting and pasting. Even if the designer uses a library of pre-programmed shapes or symbols, these will have been provided at some point by another human being. What the definition (the copyright section of the Act, and the Registered Designs Act as amended by the 1988 Act have a similar one) was intended to cover was the products of artificial intelligence, such as designs produced by "expert systems". These comprise a computer-usable "knowledge base" which distils the wisdom of one or more individual experts with the aid of a "knowledge engineer" and a systems designer, and can then be consulted to provide, by a series of questions-and-answers, a medical diagnosis, a legal opinion, or the solution to the complex design problem.[15] Under the Act, the "designer" of that solution may well be none of the human beings involved in this process, but rather the proprietor of the completed system—or the user, if the system is hired out to perform certain tasks. Similar, but worse, conundrums could occur with the development of "neural network" or "evolutionary" systems, where computers "learn" by trial and error which is the best way to approach a given task. The pragmatic choice of one person who sets up the arrangements for use of a system to be designated

---

[14] [1992] F.S.R. 421.

[15] For a fuller description, see *Wang Laboratories Inc.'s Application* [1991] R.P.C. 463, where (interestingly) an expert system was held to be unpatentable because it related to "a scheme, rule or method for performing a mental act" using a computer program.

as the "designer" is analogous to the copyright position with sound recordings and films where, for convenience and certainty, the "author" is the producer, "the person by whom the arrangements necessary for the making of the recording or film are undertaken".[16] He will clear for use, and remunerate the authors of, the various copyright works incorporated in the recording or film, and can then exploit the finished work.

One area where computer-generated designs are already being used is the layout of the connections on printed circuit boards, where the optimum positioning of the tracks to avoid mutual interference and facilitate manufacture can be worked out by a suitable program with little human intervention. The provision may also be important in the design of semiconductor chips, and increasingly in complex multi-component products.　　　**3.020**

Employed designer

Where a design is created by an employee in the course of his employment, it　　　**3.021** is under section 215(3) his employer who is "first owner" of any design right—in the case of a chip design, this is subject to any written agreement to the contrary.[17] "Employee" means a person employed under a contract of service or apprenticeship (section 263), and not an independent contractor employed under a contract for services. This is a distinction well-known in other areas of U.K. law (it is narrower than the U.S. "work made for hire" concept), and various tests have been used to pinpoint the difference.[18] A rough-and-ready test is whether the design has been made "in-house" or by an outside designer, whether a "creative" designer or merely a contract draughtsman. Clearly where a component is designed and manufactured by an outside firm, it will not fall within section 215(3). Another useful test, at least in the U.K., is whether the employee receives his remuneration from the employer in question subject to deduction of tax under Schedule E and Class 1 national insurance contributions, or whether he takes care of these matters himself or some other employer does so for him.[19] This is likely to be of

---

[16] 1988 Act, s.9(2)(a). That this definition cannot be relied on to produce easy answers may be seen from the recent cases of *Century Communications Ltd v. Mayfair Entertainment UK Ltd*, *Beggars Banquet Records Ltd v. Carlton Television Ltd* and *Adventure Film Productions S.A. [22]v. Tully* [1993] E.M.L.R. 335, 349 and 376 respectively.

[17] Design Right (Semiconductor Topographies) Regulations 1989, S.I. 1989 No. 1100, para. 5.

[18] See, *e.g. Beloff v. Pressdram* [1973] 1 All E.R. 241, where a journalist working for the *Observer* but having considerable independence as to what she wrote about and also broadcasting and writing for other periodicals was held to be an employee of the *Observer* because her job was full-time, she had paid holidays, an office and a secretary provided by the paper, she used its equipment, was a member of its pension scheme, her pay was not dependent on the paper's financial fortunes, and she paid PAYE tax.

[19] This is no longer such a clear test given the recent drive by Schedule E tax inspectors to bring the self-employed into their fold by increased use of the "control" test—can a university or college "control" how the occasional giver of a seminar course carries out his task (other than by not inviting him back)? But see *Hall v. Lorimer* [1994] 1 W.L.R. 209: failure to subject a freelance vision mixer using his temporary employers' equipment to Schedule E. And for a different perspective altogether based on the increase in self-employment, see *Lane v. Shire*

increasing importance with the growth of collaboration between universities and industry: an academic may be, loosely speaking, "on secondment" to an industrial firm and in receipt of consultancy fees, but the university continues to pay his salary and deduct his tax and hence still "employs" him under a contract of service. To whom will the rights in any design created during the course of his secondment belong? If he is expressly commissioned to produce a particular design, or to solve a particular problem, they are likely to belong to his industrial associate under the "commissioning" provision in section 215(2) (see below), from which again there is no express power to contract out, although since "commission" is not defined other than to say that it is a "commission for money or money's worth" (section 263), disputes may still arise—likewise difficult problems of commercial confidentiality versus academic enlightenment and the spread of knowledge. But he may simply be pursuing a line of research of interest both to the associate and to his employing institution, where the commissioning analysis may not fit. It is clearly important to settle these matters in advance, if necessary by the execution in favour of one party or the other of an assignment of future design right under section 223,[20] so that anything he does produce will be caught.

3.022   An employee must have been employed as a designer before the section 215(3) will apply: a cost accountant or company secretary who comes up with a bright idea may be able to assert his ownership of the design against his employer, because he did not make it "in the course of his employment". The employer by paying his salary buys his accountancy or legal and administrative skills, not any design skills he may possess (although if he puts his design at the disposal of his employer's competitor, or competitively exploits it himself while still employed, he will doubtless be in breach of his common law "duty of fidelity"). On the other hand, the designer who produces a design in his spare time and without using his employer's materials may well be caught, because he is employed in a design capacity, unless the design is in an area quite different from that in which his employer operates. "Moonlighting" employees and competitors for whom they moonlight are likely to find their designs scooped up under section 215(3).[21]

3.023   Company directors, and partners in a firm, will only fall within section 215(3) if they are employed under contracts of service. Managing and executive directors normally are, but non-executive directors are not, and the position of partners, especially in small firms, may not be entirely clear. Here, however, equity provides the useful concept of a "fiduciary duty" to the company or firm,[22] which may require the director or partner to hold any design he makes within its area of interest effectively on trust for the company or firm; he retains the legal title, and will be the "first owner", but the

Roofing Co. (Oxford) Ltd, The Times, February 22, 1995, on duties of care in relation to safety.
[20] See Chap. 4 below.
[21] *Missing Link Software v. Magee* [1989] F.S.R. 361.
[22] See *Antocks Lairn Ltd v. I. Bloohn Ltd* [1972] R.P.C. 219 at 222. But each case turns on its own facts, see *Coffey's Registered Designs* [1982] F.S.R. 227.

company or firm obtains an equitable interest and can demand an assignment of the legal title. The courts may also be very willing to find an implied contract between the parties that anything produced for the purposes of the company or firm should belong to it, because of the inconvenience and damage that would ensue if the designer left taking his design with him. A recent example of such judicial willingness in a copyright case is *Ibcos Computers Ltd v. Barclays Mercantile Highland Finance Ltd*,[23] where the principle was applied not only to modifications to the software in suit made by the second defendant during his association with the partnership, but to the program originally written by him and brought into the association.

It was argued strongly during passage of the Bill through Parliament that there should be provision, as in the Patents Act 1977, for employees to share in the benefit from particularly successful designs.[24] This was rejected by the government in principle, it being pointed out that no such provision has ever been available under the registered designs legislation (or indeed under copyright). There is, however, a provision in Schedule 5, paragraph 11, inserting a new subsection 39(3) into the Patents Act 1977, to ensure that where an employee (X) owns an invention *vis-à-vis* his employer (Y), Y should not be able to frustrate X by asserting copyright or design right in any related documents or models which may have been brought into being by Y's employees in connection with applying for a patent or working the invention.

3.024

Commissioned designs

Some of the problems outlined above in ascertaining first ownership are eased by section 215(2), which provides that where a design is created in pursuance of a commission, the person who commissions it is the first owner of any design right in it (in the case of a chip design, subject to any written agreement to the contrary). The work of outside designers brought in for a particular purpose will be caught by this subsection, which will also override any rights which an outside firm would otherwise have in the work done by its employees in the course of their employment. "Commission" is defined in section 263 as "a commission for money or money's worth". A mere casual request to a friend for help with a particular design problem will therefore not do, although nice questions could arise if as a *quid pro quo* you agree to mend his lawnmower or look after his cat while he goes on holiday. "Commission" also implies some sort of agreement in advance, so although this provision might give a company design right in work produced by the academic on secondment from a university, it would not solve the problem of the accountant, creative in an unexpected area, who produces the design solution you have long been looking for.

3.025

[23] [1994] F.S.R. 275.
[24] *Hansard*, H.L., November 12, 1987 (2nd Reading), col. 1485; March 1, 1988 (Report), col. 130.

3.026   Probably the designer need not actually have been paid the agreed fee for the commissioning provision to operate. The "money or money's worth" need be only a promise to pay which is enforceable by action, in line with the court's usual aversion of its gaze from the fact that debtors often go bust or evade satisfying judgment debts.

3.027   It was contended in Parliament[25] that both the "employee" and "commissioned design" provisions should be expressly subject to contrary agreement, as is the case with copyright in relation to employees (and with semiconductor chips in relation to both employee and commissioned designs); but the government again preferred the parallel with registered designs. There may be nothing legally to prevent a designer (if he has sufficient commercial clout) from insisting on more favourable arrangements, but this is clearly not envisaged by section 219 which confers design right by virtue of qualification by the employer or commissioner and which is disapplied in the case of a semiconductor topography where the parties have made, as they are specifically permitted to, alternative arrangements for first ownership.

3.028   Questions were also raised as to ownership where a designer creates a design unsolicited and offers it to a manufacturer who requires certain modifications to be made before he will accept it. Will it thus become a "commissioned" design and belong to the manufacturer? And any designer, it was said, will bring to a design he is commissioned to make a good deal of "background" skill and knowledge, and experience of particular solutions to design problems, before there is any "foreground" input from the commissioner about his special needs. Is it fair that the commissioner should own the whole design?

Co-ownership

3.029   These are questions that apply equally to registered designs and copyright, where they do not seem to have caused significant problems. Design right is in theory better adapted to deal with them because of the express provision in section 213(1) that design right can apply to only part of an article, and section 258(1) which envisages that different aspects of the same design may be in different ownership, which could be by partial assignment, inputs from different designers (or from the same designer partly independently and partly on commission or in the course of employment), commissioning of different parts by different people or otherwise. Each owner can look after his own aspect and deal with it separately, and if more than one aspect is infringed, each owner can sue or not as he chooses. But this is not in law a case of co-ownership at all, although in practice it will have similar inconveniences

[25] *e.g. Hansard*, H.L. Committee (7th Day), January 12, 1988, col. 1116; March 1, 1988 (Report), col. 130.

where a product as an article of commerce needs to be dealt with and sued on as a whole.

The Act also contains in section 259 a definition of "joint design" as one **3.030** produced by the collaboration of two or more designers in which the contribution of each is not distinct from that of the other or others, and where this is so, any references to "designer" are normally to be construed as references to all the designers. Who owns the rights in a joint design again depends on the capacity in which the designers operated—independently, on commission or in the course of their employment.

The practical effect of all this is that anyone planning to make and sell **3.031** articles in which design rights subsists will be well advised to gather in all the rights before he begins, and that the right owners will be well-advised to make the most of any bargaining position this gives them.

Relationship with copyright ownership

In so gathering in the outstanding rights, the would-be manufacturer must **3.032** also take account of the copyright position. It has already been pointed out that so far as design right is concerned, the design need not be recorded in a design document, nor the first article made, by the designer himself. Unless the recorder (or maker of the article if it can be classed as a sculpture) acts purely as an amanuensis, *he* will have copyright in the design document or sculpture. And if, as often happens, the designer produces only rough sketches, the full elements of the design may only be apparent once the sketches have been worked up by a professional draughtsman into production drawings. Even where the designer does produce the documents himself, ownership of design right will not necessarily correspond with ownership of copyright, notably because of the lack of any "commissioning" provision in copyright law. Where the designer is an employee, copyright as well as design right will normally vest in the employer (though with copyright there is provision for agreement to the contrary), but where the design is commissioned, copyright in the documents will remain with the designer unless the commissioner takes active steps to secure it, as described in the section on copyright ownership. In many cases, section 51 will ensure that this does not matter from a practical viewpoint because copyright cannot be enforced against articles "made to" the design document or model where it is for something which is not itself an artistic work (and many three-dimensional "models" will not have copyright at all). The designer's concurrence will not be needed to enforce the design right against third parties. Nor will he be able to enforce his copyright in the design document or model against the manufacturer, so long as the latter merely makes and sells the article; and, as a matter of business efficacy, the manufacturer will probably have an implied licence under the copyright to reproduce the design document itself in a catalogue or instruction leaflet. However, if he takes it into his head to reproduce the blueprint for a phenomenally successful design on the firm's Christmas card, he may get into trouble, because he is then not making the article but reproducing the copyright drawing. Similarly if, being a car manufacturer, he makes a giant reproduction of his outside designer's sculptured clay model for the beautiful AARDVARK limousine to adorn his forecourt (or miniature models for his friends' coffee tables) without taking the precaution of getting in the copyright, he may find himself called upon by the designer to deliver them up.

3.033 Apart from these fanciful flights, genuine difficulties will arise when a design, as with a dinner service, is partly for the shape and configuration of an article and partly for surface decoration, because the latter is protected only by copyright. The manufacturer must then take care to get this separately assigned, and to get a moral rights[26] waiver. The moral right of paternity in the original design documents or model is not a problem where copyright is not enforceable under section 51(1), because there is a specific exception in section 79(4)(f), but apart from this, moral rights remain liable to be asserted by an outside designer. Likewise, if what is commissioned is arguably, but not clearly, a design for an artistic work, the commissioner should demand the copyright and a moral rights waiver at the outset and not take a chance on there being only design right.

"QUALIFICATION"

Qualifying individuals and qualifying persons

3.034 Having fixed on the person, legal or natural, who will be entitled to design right for any particular design if such a right arises, it is then necessary, in order to see whether it will in fact arise, to decide whether this person is a "qualifying person" under sections 217–219. A qualifying person may be either an individual or a body corporate. A "qualifying individual" is a citizen or subject of, or habitually resident (probably according to Inland Revenue criteria) in, a "qualifying country". A "qualifying person", where not a qualifying individual, is a body corporate or other body having legal personality which is formed under the law of a part of the U.K. or another qualifying country and has in any qualifying country (*i.e.* not necessarily in the country of incorporation) a place of business in which substantial business activity is carried on. In determining whether substantial business activity is carried on at a place of business in any country, "no account shall be taken of dealings in goods which are at all material times outside that country" (section 217(5)). Thus there will be no point in setting up a mere administrative office, or even headquarters, in a qualifying country if the

---

[26] See 3.072 below.

goods manufactured or traded in never enter that country. Nor will it be enough for a U.S. company, for example, to move its design department to a qualifying country, unless the goods to which designs are applied are actually traded in that country.

For the semiconductor topography right, a "qualifying individual" in relation to the U.K. means a British citizen. A "qualifying person" is a qualifying individual, or a body corporate or other body having legal personality which has in any qualifying country or in Gibraltar a place of business at which substantial business activity (as defined in section 217(5)) is carried on, or a person who falls within one of the additional classes set out in Part I of the Schedule to the Design Right (Semiconductor Topographies) Regulations 1989—citizens or habitual residents or bodies corporate of various places to which reciprocal obligations are due, currently as set out in 3.008 above. Qualifying persons include the Crown and the government of any other qualifying country; but only the U.K. and the other E.U. Member States are qualifying countries, subsistence of the right being otherwise governed (except in the case of Gibraltar where specific provision is made), by inclusion of the first owner's country in the Schedule as amended from time to time.[27]

3.035

"Qualifying country" for design right means:

3.036

— the U.K.,[28] or
— any other E.U. Member State, or
— the Channel Islands, the Isle of Man or any U.K. colony if the Act has been duly extended to these territories under section 255 (so far it has not been), or
— a country designated by Order in Council under section 256 as enjoying reciprocal protection for its designs by virtue of affording "adequate" protection for British designs. "Adequate" is not defined, so the government retains a wide discretion to exclude foreign designs if the Secretary of State for Trade and Industry does not fancy what is on offer for British designs. He may also pick and choose and extend reciprocal protection only to certain classes of designs or articles if only these are correspondingly protected in the country concerned. At the time of writing, the only countries designated under section 256 are New Zealand and a collection of other territories and U.K. colonies, including the Isle of Man, the Channel Islands and Hong Kong and Gibraltar, to which the Act could have, but has not, been "extended" under section 255.[29] It is not known whether these provisions have yet encouraged significant numbers of foreign freelance designers not working

---

[27] S.I. 1989 No. 1100, para. 4.
[28] By section 257, the U.K. is taken to include territorial waters, and the Act also applies to things done "in the U.K. sector of the continental shelf on a structure or vessel which is there for purposes directly connected with the exploration of the sea bed or subsoil or the exploitation of their natural resources", *e.g.* oilrigs, support vessels and accommodation platforms, but presumably not helicopters.
[29] Design Right (Reciprocal Protection) (No. 2) Order 1989, S.I. 1989 No. 1294.

pursuant to commissions to settle on South Georgia, St Helena or the Pitcairn, Henderson, Ducie and Oeno Islands.

3.037   Under section 218, a design qualifies for design right where the first-owning designer is a qualifying individual or, where the design is a joint one, any of the designers is a qualifying individual or person (but only that designer gets the right). Under section 219, the design gets design right if the first-owning commissioner or employer (not the designer) is a qualifying person or, where the commission or employment is joint, any of the commissioners or employers is a qualifying person (but only that commissioner or employer gets the right). Where the design is an employee or commissioned design for a semiconductor topography but the parties have by written agreement contracted out of the normal first ownership provisions, it is by reference to the designer alone that subsistence of design right is ascertained.[30]

3.038   Interestingly,[31] it may be that none of the above persons need "qualify" at the date the design is made—at least, the Act does not say so, either in section 213(5) or in sections 217–219, and section 213(4) merely says that design right shall *not* subsist unless and until the design has been recorded in a design document or an article has been made to the design, not that it *shall* subsist once these conditions have been fulfilled provided there is then an available first owner. In this respect the design provisions differ from the copyright provisions in section 154, which require persons to "qualify" at the "material time" as defined in subsection (4)—making or first publication. It may therefore be possible for design right to come into being some time after the design is first taken to subsist, for example by a change of citizenship or residence by the designer, commissioner or employer. Perhaps this is why "residence" is required to be "habitual", which for copyright it is not. This must be very inconvenient both for the Comptroller-General of Patents, Designs and Trade Marks, to whose miserable lot it may fall under section 246 to decide such points, for the courts and for competitors, entailing minute inquiry into the history and intentions of the persons involved. At least it does not seem to affect the duration of a design.

Qualification by first marketing

3.039   There is one other way in which design right may arise, and this is by first marketing under section 220. If the design is a foreign one which does not qualify for protection under sections 217–219 because there is no qualifying person, the person who first markets articles made to the design in the U.K. or an E.U. Member State (but not in a country to which the Act has been reciprocally applied) becomes entitled to design right for it if he is a

[30] S.I. 1989 No. 1100, para. 4.
[31] See Copinger & Skone James on *Copyright*, 13th ed. Sweet & Maxwell, 1991.

"qualifying person" and is exclusively authorised (by the person who would be the design right owner if he or it were "qualified" or anyone lawfully claiming under him) to put such articles on the market in the U.K. "Marketing" under section 263(2) means selling, letting for hire or offering or exposing for sale or hire in the course of a business, but excludes any merely "colourable" marketing not intended to satisfy the public's reasonable requirements.[32] It appears from the structure of section 220 that the marketing within the territories mentioned must be the first marketing anywhere. The exclusive authorisation must be "capable of being enforced by legal proceedings in the U.K.", a caveat entered to take into account the fact that E.U. competition law (directly applicable in the U.K.) will not permit exclusivity to be enforced if its effects would be anti-competitive or interfere with the free movement of goods between Member States—for example, a U.K. exclusive licensee cannot keep out parallel imports where the goods have been marketed in France by the French exclusive licensee, and vice versa. It also means that the exclusive authorisation agreement (which apparently need not be in writing, since it would be enforceable as an ordinary contract) must not contain a provision giving exclusive jurisdiction to non-U.K. courts or arbitrators.

At first sight section 220 looks helpful for a U.K. importer as it allows him to protect his business here without the need for involving the foreign producer in any legal proceedings against infringers; but it may prove worthless because of the apparent requirement that he be the first marketer of the product anywhere. It will not help him if, like many importers, he merely selects his goods from those already on the market in India or the Far East, and negotiates exclusive distribution rights for the U.K. or E.U. And if he commissions his designs from the Far East because this is cheaper, he will get design right by virtue of section 219 and will not need to invoke section 220. **3.040**

It is not intended to, nor does it unless careful arrangements are made, provide a means whereby foreign designers or organisations can gain the benefit of design right by use of a U.K. distributor. On the contrary, a Japanese designer who exclusively licenses a U.K. company to be the first marketer of his product will find that the company can use the design right it gets to keep out the designer's own products should he try to market them, quite apart from its action for breach of the contract of exclusivity. Imports of the designer's own products from elsewhere could also be kept out. He cannot, other than by contract, enforce the policing of the right against infringers, nor benefit from any damages awarded for infringement. And if the distributor terminates the agreement, even improperly, he will only be liable for breach of contract, and will probably be free to exploit the design right himself. The only way to avoid these problems would seem to be by a contract binding the U.K. distributor to hand over the design right once he **3.041**

---

[32] For a copyright example of how little marketing there may need to be see *Francis Day & Hunter v. Feldman & Co.* [1914] 2 Ch. 728.

obtains it, and hope he fulfils it. There may be some doubt as to whether specific performance of such a contract (a discretionary remedy) would be ordered if it was seen as a blatant attempt to get round the Act.

3.042   An overseas multinational will only be able to take advantage of section 220 for designs which it is prepared to market first in the U.K. or E.U. through its U.K. subsidiary (if it has one), or through an E.U. subsidiary which can be given exclusive marketing rights in the U.K. Only such subsidiaries will be "qualifying persons". This may be suitable for a Japanese or U.S. company with a U.K./E.U. market big enough (and different enough) to justify its own designs, *e.g.* where General Motors wants to market a small car which would not sell in the U.S. It may not be inconvenient to limit first marketing to the E.U. countries and extend it to other European countries a few days later. It is less likely to help a non-E.U. European company such as Skoda, which might not want to have a new model available somewhere else even a few days before it goes on sale at home. If the home marketing department jumps the gun, U.K. design right will be lost. And because of the "genuine and not merely colourable" marketing proviso in section 263(2), it will not suffice to place just one new model in a U.K./E.U. distributor's main show-room if vehicles are not immediately available to the buyer.

3.043   Again, semiconductor topographies are treated differently: by paragraph 4(4) of the Design Right (Semiconductor Topographies) Regulations, a chip design which does not otherwise qualify for design right will do so if first marketing is by a qualifying person exclusively authorised to put the articles on the market in every E.U. Member State and takes place within the territory of any Member State. The requirement that the exclusivity be capable of enforcement by legal proceedings is not limited to legal proceedings in the U.K. By paragraph 5 the first marketer is the first owner of design right. However, by paragraph 7, the first marketing does not count if it was subject to an obligation of confidence unless the particular article in question had been marketed before (in which case it is difficult to see how there can be a "qualifying" first marketing within the E.U. in any event), or the obligation of confidence is imposed by the Crown or an overseas government in the interests of security connected with the production of arms, munitions or war material.

3.044   Where first marketing is relied on, there may be even more problems than usual with fragmented rights. Copyright in surface decoration elements of an article may be anywhere, and should clearly be got in if possible. The U.K. distributor will, on the other hand, be well-placed to apply for a registered design, since he is the one who owns the unregistered design right and the "design" has become vested in him rather than the original proprietor by operation of law (his exclusive contract), even if not by express assignment (1949 Act, section 2(2)). This is something which will need careful watching by an overseas designer hoping to use first marketing as a way of getting hold of design right.

Given that the overseas beneficiaries of design right are limited as described, efforts may be made to circumvent the limitations by finding suitable "qualifying individuals" to produce design documents who are not themselves the real designers, and defendants should be alert to this.   **3.045**

Duration

Basic period—10 years from first marketing

Under section 216, the basic design right period is 10 years from the end of the calendar year in which articles made "to the design" (*i.e.* presumably in accordance with the design as exemplified in the design document or model) are first made available for sale or hire by or with the licence of the design right owner anywhere in the world. Under this provision, it is not the marketing of the design itself which counts, but of articles made to it. It is therefore thought that a designer who merely offers his design to prospective manufacturers would not be "making it available" so as to start the 10-year period running, although arguments might arise where his portfolio comprises a prototype product as opposed to a mere paper design. But the alternative 15-year period discussed in 3.048 below seems intended to deal with such situations. Since articles must be "available for sale or hire", pre-marketing promotion, including exhibitions, would not be enough to set the period running; actual examples of the design must be in the shops, or at least capable of being ordered. It will not escape the astute salesman that putting a new product on the market early in the year will guarantee anything up to an extra 364 days' protection. Going for the Christmas trade will be a lot less favourable.   **3.046**

Much is sometimes made of the alleged dificulties for a prospective plaintiff in having a protection period run from first marketing, because of alleged uncertainty, but this is surely nonsense. The right owner is in the best possible position to know, from invoices, delivery notes and the like, when (and where) he first marketed. If he has a practice of destroying such documents after a limited period of time less than 10 years, he must simply set up proper procedures to preserve these records to the limited extent needed. Owners of a right which requires nothing from them by way of registration or other formal assertion should at least be prepared to take such minimal steps to safeguard themselves. They are in any event assisted by the rebuttable presumption in section 228(4) that where an article is shown to have been made to a design in which design right subsists or has subsisted at any time, it is presumed to have been made during the protection period unless the contrary is proved (by the defendant). Why a plaintiff should have the benefit of this presumption in the case of such a short-lived right whose genesis is easily provable by him is not clear. It is far more likely to cause problems to   **3.047**

141

competitors who need to know when a design has expired, or when they can apply for licences of right. These people cannot even be helped by section 246 (under which the Comptroller-General of Patents, Designs and Trade Marks can decide disputes relating to subsistence, term or first ownership of design right) because, despite representations made in the House of Lords during debate on the Bill, this jurisdiction only applies where a "dispute" has actually come into existence. Once it has, the defendant may force the plaintiff to disclose details of first marketing by discovery or interrogatories.[33]

Extended period—15 years from first recording/making

3.048   Ten years from first marketing was the duration for unregistered design right foreshadowed in the White Paper; but it was soon realised that this would be inappropriate for "articles" such as aircraft and weapons systems which, if they are ever to be made at all, have to be sold off the drawing board. Unless there are firm orders, manufacture simply will not be undertaken, so there would be no article whose first marketing could trigger design right. Nonetheless, the designers of these articles must be entitled to protection against copying at the design stage by those to whom they show the design or who might become aware of it by industrial espionage. To cover such cases, section 216(1)(a) provides additionally that design right can last for 15 years from the end of the calendar year in which the design was first recorded in a design document or a prototype was made ("an article was first made to the design"), whichever first occurred. Once, however, first marketing of an article made to the design takes place, provided this is within five years of first recording/prototype, the normal 10-year period starts to run. The provision, of course, also benefits the freelance designer who needs protection when attempting to find a manufacturer for his design and may find the law on breach of confidence inadequate because of the difficulties of proof or because large manufacturers with their own design departments often expressly refuse to recognise that any disclosure is confidential.

3.049   Some examples will illustrate the effect of these provisions:

— W on August 15, 1995 moulds a prototype set of plaster vultures which he immediately begins to market as free gifts to be given by barristers to solicitors who regularly instruct them. There is a great demand for these at the beginning of the Michaelmas Law Term when many barristers wish to remind solicitors of their existence. W's design right will expire on December 31, 2005, 10 years from the end of the calendar year when he first marketed the vultures—if it is design right he has and not copyright: the prototype vultures may be models embodying a design for sculptures as discussed in 2.203 above. Perhaps a satisfied customer will take a test case to the House of Lords without fee in the event of

---

[33] cf. *Valeo Vision S.A. v. Flexible Lamps Ltd*, October 22, 1993, SRIS C/64/93.

infringement. Alternatively, the vultures could be electronically-controlled models which flap and squawk;

— X designs a helicopter; he finishes the drawings or completes the prototype on July 31, 1995. If he does nothing further, or if he fails to interest anybody in ordering it, his design right expires on December 31, 2010, 15 years from first recording the design in a design document or completing the prototype. During that period, he can sue anyone making or selling a similar helicopter—provided, of course, he can prove they had an opportunity to copy the design documents or prototype which have stayed snugly in his filing cabinet or hangar;

— Y designs a better helicopter (or has better marketing contacts); his drawings or prototype, also completed on July 31, 1995, entice buyers to place orders, and his first production helicopter is delivered to the Erewhon Air Force on May 25, 1998. His design right expires on December 31, 2008;

— Z designs a far from commonplace artillery piece which fires live tarantulas. The rifling inside its barrel is of a peculiar configuration, and its loading mechanism embodies features imparting a most unusual appearance, both of which protect the ammunition from the g-forces imposed on firing. His prototype is completed on September 30, 1995. Initially there is market resistance, but after years of energetic promotion, Z on Christmas Eve 2010 sells his first production version to the Ruritanian army. Crack invading troops from neighbouring Utopia stampede back across the border after the first volley, and the world's armed forces flock to buy the weapon. Unfortunately, it is immediately copied by A, B and C, and Z can do nothing about it because his design right expired a week after his first sale. He does not get the usual 10 years from first marketing, because this did not take place within five years from the end of the calendar year in which he completed the prototype.

The examples of X, Y and Z of course ignore the reality that helicopters and weapons are not really "articles" in themselves (except for their overall silhouette), but are collections of components all of which will have reached design document or prototype stage on different dates, making it important to keep track of these. Some components may acquire design right well over five years before the first complete helicopter is marketed, and will therefore lose it earlier than the machine as a whole. **3.050**

Design right in semiconductor topographies lasts by paragraph 6 of the Regulations for 10 years from first marketing anywhere in the world by or with the licence of the design right owner (subject to the provisions as to marketing under an obligation of confidence mentioned in 3.043 above). If neither the topography nor articles made to it are marketed within 15 years of the first recording of the topography in a design document or the first making of an article to it, then the right expires 15 years from the earlier of those two events. **3.051**

Licences of right during final five years of term

3.052   One of the crucial components of the government's grand plan to balance the need for industrial design protection against the need for competition is the licensing of right arrangements. During the final five years of the design right, licences to copy the design are to be available as of right to would-be competitors, subject to settlement of terms by the parties or, in default of agreement, by the Comptroller-General of Patents, Designs and Trade Marks. And if the Monopolies and Mergers Commission on a reference from the Secretary of State should find at an earlier stage in the design right term that the right is being abused in certain specified ways, the Secretary of State may order that licences of right should be available forthwith. These provisions are discussed in Chapter 4. Under paragraphs 9 and 10 of the Regulations, licences of right are not available for semiconductor topographies, but abuses may be referred to the Monopolies Commission.

3.053   Understandably, there has been considerable discontent among those who produce high-technology, high-investment, low-volume functional goods about the selection of so short a term as 10 years for unregistered design right—particularly when ornamental designs of no great merit or commercial significance can get 25 years' monopoly protection by registration. More than one member of the House of Lords pointed to the lengthy development period required for complex and expensive machinery and systems and the corresponding need to recover development costs on spare parts (even to the extent that these get design right at all) over a long product lifetime. Lord Campbell of Alloway wondered whether his noble friend the Minister "could give some consideration to the very real disparity between perhaps millions of pounds spent on research and development over a long period of time in one place to produce a design and nothing or £10 spent in the other and regard the new right not as giving rise always to exactly the same measure of protection".[34] His noble friend the Minister and his government colleagues did consider the point, but felt unable to accede to it.

COPYRIGHT

SUBSISTENCE

3.054   Subsistence and first ownership of copyright are governed by the law in force when the work was made. By Schedule 1, paragraph 5 of the 1988 Act, copyright subsists in a work that existed at midnight on July 31, 1989 only if it subsisted immediately before that date, except where it only acquires copyright later by virtue of first publication[35] in a Berne Convention member

---

[34] *Hansard*, H.L. Committee (7th Day), January 12, 1988, col. 1121.
[35] "Publication" under section 175 of the 1988 Act means the issue of copies to the public, including making the work available by means of a publicly-accessible database. In relation to

country or first application of the 1988 Act to its territory of origin. Subsistence and first ownership of copyright in pre-August 1, 1989 works will therefore still fall to be judged by the provisions of the 1956 Act (including the transitional provisions in Schedule 7 relating to earlier works). It should be noted that, as under Schedule 7, paragraph 8 of that Act, Schedule 1, paragraph 6 of the new Act continues the exclusion from copyright of registrable industrial designs made before June 1, 1957 which were always used or initially intended for mass-production.

Copyright subsists in a 1956 Act unpublished literary or artistic work **3.055** (including a typeface) if the author was a qualified person at the time the work was made (for a photograph, the author may be a body corporate[36]). If the work has been published, copyright subsists if first publication took place in the U.K. or another country to which the Act extended or had been applied, or if the author was a qualified person at the date of first publication; or, if he was then already dead, was so immediately before his death (section 3(2) and (3)). The typographical arrangement copyright in a published edition subsists if the publisher (who is also the first owner) was a qualified person, natural or corporate, at the relevant date.

Under section 1(5), a natural "qualified person" was a British subject or **3.056** protected person, or a citizen of the Republic of Ireland, or domiciled or resident in the U.K. or in another country to which the Act extended or had been applied at the date the work came into being. A corporate "qualified person" was a body incorporated under the laws of any part of the U.K. or of another country to which the Act extended or had been applied at that date. The 1956 Act "extended" to the Isle of Man, the Channel Islands and various British colonies and dependencies, such as Hong Kong (section 31). It had been " applied" by Order in Council under section 32 at various dates[37] to the other Berne and Universal Copyright Convention member countries, but it should be noted that certain significant countries such as the USA, which were only in the 1952 UCC, did not come within the ambit of the Act until relatively recently—in the case of the USA, September 27, 1957. While for various reasons unpublished U.S. works had U.K. copyright before that date, as did U.S.-published works by persons who were "qualified" at the date of first publication, works made by non-qualified persons such as U.S. citizens, which were first published in the U.S. before that date and not published in a Berne country (such as Canada) within 30 days of first U.S. publication,[38] did

---

an artistic work it does *not* include exhibiting the work, including it in a film, broadcast or cable programme or, where it is a building or model for a building, a sculpture or a work of artistic craftsmanship, issuing to the public copies of a graphic work or a photograph of it. But issuing copies to the public *can* include marketing the work itself, or three-dimensional copies of it if it is a drawing. Thus marketing articles made to industrial designs is publication. The 1956 Act in section 49 had similar definitions of publication, except that constructing a building did not publish it and works of artistic craftsmanship were not mentioned.

[36] See definition of "photograph" in section 48(1).

[37] To check on places and dates of application of the 1956 Act, see Copyright (International Conventions) Order 1979, S.I. 1979 No. 1715.

[38] 1956 Act, s.49(2)(d).

not have U.K. copyright. The U.S. joined the Berne Convention with effect from March 1, 1989, and the effect of the Copyright (Application to Other Countries) Order 1989,[39] made under section 159 of the 1988 Act and applying it to Berne Convention countries, is that most U.S. works first published on or after June 1, 1957 have U.K. copyright.

3.057 Copyright under the Semiconductor Products (Protection of Topographies) Order 1987[40] subsisted where the topography's creator (or employer or commissioner or first exploiter within the E.C.) was a qualified person as defined in paragraph 3(4) of the Order (approximately similar to a 1956 Act qualified person but including residents of Gibraltar and citizens, etc., of other E.C. Member States).

3.058 Subsistence of copyright under the 1988 Act for works coming into being on or after August 1, 1989 is determined by section 154 (author a "qualifying person" when unpublished work first made or, where work published, on first publication or earlier death) or section 155 (first publication in U.K.[41] or another country to which Act then extended or applied,[42] or publication in such country within 30 days of first publication elsewhere). "Qualifying person" means a person who, at the date the work is made or first published (or at the date of his death if he died before first publication), is a British citizen, subject or protected person of various kinds, an individual domiciled or resident in the U.K. or another country to which the Act then extended or had been applied, or a body corporate then incorporated under the laws of the U.K. or such other country.

First ownership

3.059 Unlike the position with unregistered design right, first ownership of copyright does not determine subsistence, which is governed either by reference to the author or to the facts of first publication. However it is still highly significant, because of the need to show devolution of the copyright, or at least an equitable title to it, to the prospective plaintiff before an infringer can be sued, and because exploitation of a work may be limited by the extent of any licence from the copyright owner granted or implied by law. For example, under the general law and the RIBA terms of engagement, architects retain the copyright in their drawings or models and the person engaging

---

[39] S.I. 1989 No. 988, see now the Copyright (Application to Other Countries) Order 1993, S.I. 1993 No. 942. These provisions are too complex in their effects to deal with here. They bring into copyright some works which were previously in the public domain, and provide rights for persons who incurred expenditure or liability in connection with acts done or contemplated when the works were in the public domain to continue to do such acts unless compensated by the copyright owner or his exclusive licensee.

[40] S.I. 1987 No. 1497.

[41] By section 161 the U.K. is taken to extend to territorial waters and to things done on the Continental Shelf as set out in n. 28 above. In matters of copyright the Act also applies to things done on British-registered ships, aircraft or hovercraft (s.162).

[42] Under ss.157 or 159.

them is only entitled to reproduce these by constructing the building contracted for.[43] He may not extend the building by repetition of a recurring design feature,[44] nor use the plans to erect other buildings. Similar principles usually govern advertisements, in which advertising agencies or their sub-contractors will normally retain the copyright. And with the proliferation of brochures, catalogues, logos and trade marks as marketing tools designed by specialist firms rather than in-house, care must be taken by the commissioning organisation to get in the copyright, if it wishes, for example, to take advantage of cheaper printing rates elsewhere or to have the freedom to make alterations.

Under section 4 of the 1956 Act, copyright in an artistic (or literary) work, **3.060** belonged to the author—undefined, but essentially the person who put pen to paper. (Under section 48(1), the "author" of a photograph was the person who owned the film when it was taken.) There were three exceptions, all subject to contracting out if the author had sufficient bargaining power. One related to employed journalists and is of little significance to industrial design. The most important one gave first ownership of copyright in a work produced by an employee under a contract of service to his employer.[45] The third applied to portraits, engravings and photographs commissioned by another person who paid or agreed to pay for them in money or money's worth: the commissioner got the copyright. This was (and is) convenient in relation to photographs taken for publicity or promotional purposes.[46] It could (and can) also be useful where a 1956 Act industrial design is based on an "engraving", as was illustrated by the case of *James Arnold & Co. Ltd v. Miafern Ltd.*[47] Here, the plaintiff had been asked to produce a scarf printed with a particular pattern. It proposed to do this by means of heat transfer papers, and commissioned another company, Kentex, to make these. Kentex in turn commissioned Precision Printing Plates to make the rubber stereos which would be fitted over rollers to print the transfer papers. This was a complicated process involving the preparation first of detailed drawings of the pattern, then of photographic negatives for each colour component which were used for the photo-etching of zinc to produce "positive" plates. "Negative" Bakelite moulds were then made from these plates, and in turn produced the "positive" stereos. The judge found (with some hesitation) that the stereos were "engravings". He was then able to find that the copyright in

[43] Reconstruction of a building, *e.g.* after a fire, is permitted under section 65 provided the building was not originally erected in infringement of copyright.

[44] See *Meikle v. Maufe* [1941] 3 All E.R. 144, where the defendant's building (Heals in Tottenham Court Road) designed by the plaintiff architect having been bombed, the defendant was held to be licensed to use the original plans to rebuild it but not, without further fee, to extend it by several extra identical bays.

[45] For a recent example of a 1956 Act case where the employer and employee were found to have contracted out of this provision, see *Noah v. Shuba* [1991] F.S.R. 14. The plaintiff was a consultant epidemiologist who in his spare time and on his own initiative wrote a book about hygienic ear-piercing, quotations from which were made improper use of by the defendant.

[46] For interpretation of these provisions in relation to photographs, see *Apple Corps v. Cooper* [1993] F.S.R. 286.

[47] [1980] R.P.C. 397.

them belonged to the plaintiff as the person who had commissioned them. Kentex had merely sub-contracted a step in the process of executing the commission.

3.061   Under section 11 of the 1988 Act, the "author" of a work is again normally first owner of the copyright in it. Definitions of "author" are found in section 9: for artistic works (including photographs), it is the person who creates the work,[48] unless it is a "computer-generated" work, where the definition is in the same terms as for unregistered designs.[49] For sound recordings and films, the author is the person by whom the arrangements necessary for the making of the recording or film are undertaken (this is why advertising agencies retain the copyright in TV commercials, promotional videos and the like). The only exception is now where a literary, dramatic, musical or artistic work is made by an employee in the course of his employment when, as under the 1956 Act, the first owner of copyright is the employer, subject to any agreement to the contrary (which need not be in writing). As pointed out earlier, this rule may allow the regular employer to deprive a moonlighting employee and his clandestine master of the fruits of the former's extra-mural activities. Although the "commissioning" exceptions have now disappeared, Schedule 1, paragraph 11(2) provides that they should still govern first ownership where a work was made on or after August 1, 1989 but pursuant to a commission given before that date.

Co-ownership

3.062   Under both the 1956 Act (section 11(3)) and the 1988 Act (section 10(1)), a work is one of "joint authorship" where it is produced by the collaboration of two or more authors and the contribution of each author is not "separate" (1956) or "distinct" (1988) from that of the other author or authors. Neither of these words is further defined, but it does not seem that the contributions being separately *identifiable* alone causes them to be "separate" or "distinct". In *Stuart v. Barrett*[50] the court in a 1956 Act case found joint copyright where the plaintiff's contribution to a number of songs was the "significant" drum part. Joint first ownership may arise quite separately from joint authorship, for example where a 1956 Act photograph was jointly commissioned.[51] Joint

---

[48] A puzzling case arose in Lincolnshire. Someone utilised a duck to make a painting, laying down paint and encouraging the duck to paddle through it. It is believed the procurer of the duck's services was held to be the author. I am grateful to Alison Firth of counsel and Queen Mary and Westfield College for this information.

[49] See the feeding of the defendant's net list taken from the plaintiff's circuit diagram into a computer for production of a circuit diagram and a scheme for making a printed circuit board in *Anacon Corporation Ltd v. Environmental Research Technology Ltd* [1994] F.S.R. 359 discussed at 2.172 above. Other examples suggested in the Notes on the Bill provided to interested parties were programs for updating databases from many sources and for operating on databases to create statistical tables, weather maps and newspaper financial pages.

[50] [1994] E.M.L.R. 448.

[51] See *Mail Newspapers plc v. Express Newspapers plc* [1987] F.S.R. 90—jointly-commissioned wedding photographs.

works are regulated in detail by the Third Schedule to the 1956 Act. Under the new Act, section 10(3) merely provides that "author" is normally to be construed as referring to all authors of a work of joint authorship. The most significant effect is that the permission of all joint authors must be secured before a work can be exploited by any of them, and all must join in any assignment or licence.[52] In practice, joint authorship has not hitherto posed much of a problem in relation to industrial designs, because of the general principle that he who puts pen to paper is the author. But a tricky area in practice under the new provisions of the 1988 Act is where a commissioned design for an article which is not itself an artistic work (like a milkjug) also has features of surface decoration. This is *not* a case of joint copyright—either the copyright in both shape and decoration belong to the same designer, or if there were two designers, their contribution is probably to be treated as "distinct", and in either event the copyright in the shape is unenforceable under section 51 and the design right belongs to the commissioner. Nonetheless the problems resemble those with joint copyright and the outstanding copyright should be gathered in.[53]

Knowing who joint authors were will of course also be important in relation to the term of copyright, as discussed later.[54] **3.063**

Equitable title to copyright

Because of the inconvenience that could arise where copyright vested in an independent contractor and no assignment had originally been obtained, the courts developed the doctrine of "ownership in equity". This was particularly useful when, as is still the case with "hangover" copyright enforceable under the transitional provisions of the 1988 Act, industrial design cases depended on restraining three-dimensional copying of engineering drawings. Suppose a small engineering company wanted to produce a new component: the works manager sketched it out roughly, but production drawings were needed. However, the company had no drawing office, so an outside firm of draughtsmen was asked to make a set of drawings. One of its employees did so, the firm was paid its normal fee, and that was that. Nothing was said about copyright. The outside firm did not itself manufacture, and although it probably kept a set of copy drawings for its records, it would not have regarded it as proper to use these for the benefit of anyone other than the company who originally ordered them. However, since it was an independent firm, it undoubtedly retained the legal title to the copyright in those drawings, which were made by its employee. Several years later, the engineering company found its component being copied, and wanted to sue the copier. In circumstances like these, it was probable that the court would treat the outside firm as holding the legal title to the copyright "on trust" for the **3.064**

---

[52] s.173(2).
[53] As pointed out in 3.033 above.
[54] See 3.078 below.

engineering company who, as the only beneficiary, could call for an assignment of the legal title to perfect its beneficial interest. The advantage of this to the prospective plaintiff company was that it could commence proceedings, and even obtain an interlocutory injunction, without first getting a legal assignment or joining the outside firm as a party,[55] although it would have to "get in" the legal title before trial, or join the outside firm either as a plaintiff or as a non-participating defendant, before it could obtain a final order confirming subsistence and infringement and thus affecting the copyright owner's property rights. This analysis is naturally still applicable where inconveniently-outstanding copyrights are concerned.

3.065   Of course, if the outside firm disputes the "trust" analogy and asserts a contrary interest, it will have to be joined anyway and the question of title resolved. But the device is a convenient one, and has also been applied in cases where the draughtsman was a partner or director of the plaintiff company and thus under a fiduciary duty to hold work he produced for the company's benefit as a constructive trustee for it.[56] In *Cableship Ltd v. Williams*[57] the defendant was actually the legal owner of the software copyright concerned, and his rights were successfully overridden by the plaintiff who was the equitable owner.[58]

3.066   A further example is where it is a term (express or implied) of the initial contract between "commissioner" (in the layman's sense) and outside designer that the latter will assign the copyright to the former, but no assignment has actually been made. The commissioner will have a right to enforce the making of an assignment by an action for specific performance, and by analogy with other types of contract, such as one for the sale of land, this will give the commissioner an equitable interest in the subject-matter of the contract, here the copyright.

3.067   It must be stressed that this device is a creation of the courts, and it is for the court to decide, in the light of all the surrounding circumstances, whether an equitable interest arises or whether, for example, all the commissioner gets for his money is an implied licence to use the design for the purpose for which it was intended (which might include reproducing it for the purpose of catalogue illustrations or instructions manuals), but for no others. This is the position with architects' drawings and architectural copyright in buildings, and such a licence would not of itself give a right sue for infringement. *Ironside v. H.M. Attorney-General*[59] is a recent case instructive on these points: Mr Ironside was the man who designed the reverse sides of the coins for the U.K. decimal currency issued in 1971; he was paid an agreed fee, but nothing was said, either orally or in writing, about copyright. Mr Ironside

---

[55] *Performing Right Society Ltd v. London Theatre of Varieties* [1924] A.C. 1.
[56] *Antocks Lairn Ltd v. I. Bloohn Ltd* [1972] R.P.C. 219.
[57] 1991 I.P.D. 14205.
[58] See also *Ibcos Computers Ltd v. Barclays Mercantile Highland Finance Ltd* [1994] F.S.R. 275, mentioned at 3.023 above.
[59] [1988] R.P.C. 197.

accepted that the arrangement gave the Royal Mint a licence to use his designs on currency in normal circulation, but argued that the licence did not extend to using them on "proof" sets of coins produced for sale to museums and collectors, which were accordingly infringing copies of his designs. After considering all the facts, including his finding that the plaintiff would at all times have been aware that proof sets were likely to be issued, the judge concluded that the transaction constituted an outright sale of the designs to the Mint, giving them an equitable interest in the copyright, rather than merely a licence for a limited purpose. The equitable interest would have been perfectible by an assignment of the legal title, had the judge not also decided that because the designs were first published under the direction and control of a government department, they were Crown copyright under section 39(2) of the 1956 Act.

It is not wise, however, to rely on the facts falling out satisfactorily, and every well-regulated company should have proper procedures for locating the copyright in industrial designs. For one thing, some designers will not be prepared to part with their copyright for the commissioner's convenience. If this is so, it is as well to know it at the outset so that the manufacturer can find out exactly what the fee he pays allows him to do with the design and so that arrangements can be made for the designer to be joined as a party should infringement proceedings be necessary. For another, it must be remembered that although an equitable interest can come into being by operation of law, it can only be validly transferred in writing, under section 53(1)(c) of the Law of Property Act 1925. In an embarrassing case called *Roban Jig & Tool Co. Ltd v. Taylor*,[60] of the three sets of drawings in suit, two had been prepared by an outside firm for a partnership and the third by one of the partners. The partnership was later incorporated but, as too frequently happens, it was simply assumed that all the partnership assets passed to the company and there was no written instrument. The company then innocently sued a third party for infringement, but the proceedings were struck out because the company did not own the copyright: the partnership no doubt had an equitable interest in all three sets of drawings, given the circumstances in which they were made, but that interest had never been transferred to the company in writing, so when the writ was issued it had no title to sue. All company lawyers, and accountants advising on incorporation and takeovers, should have a knowledge of intellectual property rights and how they have to be transferred; lamentably often, they do not.   **3.068**

Crown and Parliamentary copyright

Brief mention should be made of these matters, though they are of decreasing significance in relation to industrial designs. Under section 39 of the 1956   **3.069**

---

[60] [1979] F.S.R. 130.

Act, copyright in any original artistic work made by or under the direction or control of Her Majesty or a government department, or first published by or under such direction or control, vested in the Crown unless otherwise agreed with the author. The "first publication" provision could have quite wide effect, covering such things as patent drawings, new coinage or banknote designs and possibly diagrams and specifications for the products of defence contractors. Under section 163 of the 1988 Act, first publication no longer suffices: only where a work is "made by Her Majesty or by an officer or servant of the Crown in the course of his duties" is the Crown first owner of the copyright, nor is it now enough that the work be made "under the direction or control of a government department". Because of this limitation, there is no longer provision for contracting-out.

3.070   Parliamentary copyright is a new creation of the 1988 Act, subsisting in works made by or under the direction or control of the House of Commons or the House of Lords. It covers any work made by an officer or employee of either House, but section 165(4) specifically provides that a work is not to be regarded as made by or under the direction or control of either House by reason only of its having been commissioned by or on behalf of that House. Parliamentary copyright will presumably cover Select Committee reports and the like, and apparently also Bills introduced in either House, since Crown copyright under section 164 subsists only in actual statutes.

3.071   Both the 1956 Act (section 33) and the 1988 Act (section 168) confer copyright on works made by officers or employees of, or first published by, designated international organisations (such as the United Nations and its specialised agencies) where copyright would not otherwise subsist because the author was not a qualified/qualifying person and first publication was not in a Convention country.

MORAL RIGHTS

3.072   These inventions of the devil (from the industrialist's point of view) were introduced by the 1988 Act, but they apply to works which came into being before August 1, 1989 unless the author was already dead by that date, or he had already assigned or licensed the copyright, or it never vested in him, *e.g.* because he was an employee (Schedule 1, paragraph 23). The right under section 77 to be identified as author (sexistly nicknamed the "right of paternity") entitles the author, provided he asserts the right in one of the ways specified in section 78,[61] to have his name on every copy of the work published commercially or publicly exhibited, unless he made the design as an employee (section 79(3)(a)). Thus the outside designer of the pattern on a milkjug or a set of jewellery (if a work of artistic craftsmanship) can demand that his name appear on each piece, or at least on the packaging (section 77(7)(a)). There is no exemption for industrial designs still having enforce-

---

[61] In an assignment of copyright or by written instrument signed by the author.

152

able copyright, as opposed to design right, where section 77(5)(f) excludes the right of paternity where section 51 precludes infringement of copyright.[62]

Possibly more troublesome is the section 80 right to object to derogatory   **3.073** treatment of a copyright work—"treatment" being any addition to, deletion from, alteration to or adaptation of the work, and "derogatory" treatment being distortion or mutilation of the work or something otherwise prejudicial to the honour or reputation of the author. There is also infringement where someone possesses or deals with copies of derogatorily treated works knowing or having reason to believe that they have been so treated (section 83). Where the author was an employee, the right still applies, but only where he has been identified at some point, and a suitable disclaimer of his involvement will then avoid infringement (section 82). But where he was not an employee but a partner or other person in a fiduciary relationship, or was "commissioned", so that the "equitable interest" device can be adopted, his moral right will remain intact.

This could pose awkward problems where an industrialist, who has   **3.074** acquired the copyright in a work and wants to make certain alterations to it, perhaps to accommodate changing tastes or cheaper manufacturing techniques, finds himself challenged because the author feels that such alterations spoil his original conception. A case where moral rights could have raised such difficulties if they had then existed was *Warner v. Gestetner Ltd and Newell & Sorrell Design Ltd.*[63] Gestetner wanted to develop a brand image for a desktop publishing package, and retained Newell & Sorrell to create a mark. They in turn approached the plaintiff to prepare the artwork for the "observant cat" silhouette they had decided to use, and he prepared four silhouettes at an agreed price. Newell & Sorrell assigned their rights in these drawings to Gestetner, who used the silhouettes, in some cases minus the tails. Disputes arose as to the terms of the oral agreement between Warner and Newell & Sorrell, Warner arguing that he had parted only with a licence of the copyright limited to use at a particular exhibition, the defendants that he had sold it outright. On the facts, the court found the defendants to be correct, and Gestetner could do what it liked with the drawings and its equitable interest in the copyright. Nowadays, however, Warner could claim that to deprive his cats of their tails amounts to mutilation by deletion, and Gestetner's acquisition of the copyright would be no defence, since moral rights are inalienable and do not pass with the copyright. Moreover the section 80 right applies not just to a substantial part but to any part of the work, so quite small alterations will suffice. The prudent industrialist will therefore do all he can to secure a written waiver of moral rights under section 87. The prudent designer will do all he can to to provide no such thing, with a view, if not to safeguarding the integrity of his creation, at least to securing a further fee if later alterations are contemplated.

---

[62] There is a similar exemption in section 77(5)(g) where an artistic work has been industrially-exploited under section 52.

[63] High Court, Whitford J., December 17, 1987; [1988] 4 E.I.P.R. D-89.

3.075 It remains to be seen how moral rights will now fit in with the loose doctrines of "equitable" copyright described above. The courts have leaned very far towards the interests of industrial exploiters of copyright works, whereas moral rights are deliberately skewed towards the interests of their creators. Mr Ironside does not, by virtue of the secondary finding that copyright in his coinage designs vested in the Crown, have any enforceable moral rights under sections 77 or 80 since August 1, 1989.[64] But Mr Warner may yet have some, since moral rights apply to works existing on August 1, 1989 copyright in which vested in the author (unless he was then dead). The only ways round this would be if he had already assigned his copyright before August 1, 1989 (which he may have been forced to do in the light of the findings in his case) or if he were held to have granted a licence (which would be inconsistent with the findings).[65] Or would the courts now readily deem him to have retrospectively "consented" under section 87(1) to any infringement of his moral rights, or to have "informally waived" them under section 87(4) by virtue of the general law of contract or estoppel?

3.076 Neither Mr Williams in *Cableship* nor the second defendant in *Ibcos*[66] had moral rights to exercise, since both were software cases, and under sections 79(2)(a) and 81(2) the authors of computer programs are not entitled to either the right of paternity or the right to object to derogatory treatment. The authors of typefaces are similarly excluded from claiming the paternity right (section 79(2)(b)).

3.077 Authors do have a moral right under section 84 not to have a work falsely attributed to them—under section 43 of the 1956 Act this was also civilly actionable as a breach of statutory duty.[67] The section is apt to catch cases where copies of a work are published or dealt with in an altered form without the author's consent, and not only those where there is a complete misattribution, provided there is an express or implied statement as to authorship. So the author of a "designer" garment or accessory or piece of furniture which has been modified for the mass market may have an action for false attribution (as well as passing off[68]) even where the modifications have been sufficient to take the mass-produced article out of copyright infringement, provided the attribution, albeit implied, is clear enough.

---

[64] 1988 Act, Sched. 1, para. 23(3)(b).

[65] Sched. 1, para. 23(3)(a).

[66] See 3.065 above.

[67] It was rarely used, but *Noah v. Shuba* [1991] F.S.R. 14 was a recent example, where the inclusion within the same set of inverted commas containing a quotation from the plaintiff's book of one extra (but important) sentence which he had *not* written was sufficient to constitute a breach of section 43.

[68] See Chap. 1.

DURATION

Up to now, the rules on duration of copyright have been no more tortuous   **3.078**
and fraught with traps than many other rules in this field. The "normal" term,
in accordance with the Berne Convention, has been the author's life + 50
years from the end of the calendar year in which he died. So if his death was
precipitated by an extended New Year's Eve carouse, the term is almost 51
years, but if it was brought on by fury and disgust at the 25th Boxing Day
television repeat of an Indiana Jones film, it is barely more than 50 years. This
"normal" term has been the one applicable to most artistic works, and hence
to copyright-protected industrial designs, except where artificially shortened
terms are imposed by way of defence.[69] There is an exception for computer-
generated works, where it is 50 years from the end of the calendar year in
which the work was made (section 12(3)). Typographical arrangement
copyright expires 50 years from the end of the year in which the edition was
first published (section 15). Care has needed to be taken in the cases of
pre-August 1, 1989 photographs and engravings, particularly those made
since May 31, 1957 which, if not published before August 1, 1989, continue
in copyright until the end of 2039.[70] The copyright term in works of joint
authorship is determined by the life of the last author to die: section 11 and
the Third Schedule to the 1956 Act and section 12 and Schedule 1, paragraph
12 of the 1988 Act. The latter provisions and the Second Schedule to the 1956
Act deal with anonymous and pseudonymous works (apart from photographs), which may be relevant to industrial designs where the identity of the
original draughtsman is not known. For those wishing to make industrial use
of an old artistic work, section 57 of the 1988 Act provides, with certain
exceptions, that copyright will not be infringed by an act done at a time when
it is not possible by reasonable inquiry to ascertain the identity of the author,
or any author if the work is of joint authorship, and it is reasonable to assume
either that copyright has expired or that the author, or last surviving author,
died 50 years or more before the beginning of the calendar year in which the
act is done.

Moral rights last under section 86 for the same period as copyright, except   **3.079**
for the right to restrain false attribution, which ends 20 years after the
author's death (apparently the actual date of death).

---

[69] It is not strictly correct to say that the term of copyright in these works is shortened, because
these provisions merely render it unenforceable in the situations concerned. It remains
enforceable for other purposes.

[70] See section 3 of the 1956 Act and the transitional provisions in Schedule 1, paragraph 2 of that
Act and Schedule 1, paragraph 12 of the 1988 Act.

The E.U. "term" Directive

3.080   As from July 1, 1995 E.U. Council Directive 93/98[71] will require changes in the law to harmonise the term of copyright for literary and artistic works originating in Member States to an E.U. standard of life + 70 years. This will not simply mean that works still in U.K. copyright get a longer term. Works which are still in copyright *anywhere* in the E.U. on July 1, 1995 will benefit, and since Germany already has a term of life +70 years, many works which have been in the public domain in the U.K. since as far back as 1975 will fall back into copyright. Moreover, anyone who at any time lawfully publishes a hitherto unpublished literary or artistic work whose copyright has expired will now get a new 25-year period of protection. At the same time, non-E.U. works may have their terms forcibly cut down to what is provided in their "home" country. The Directive leaves it entirely to Member States to determine the ownership of the resurrected rights (except for the new "publisher's term" of 25 years), and also what protection should be afforded (some is required to be) to persons who have changed their position in reliance on copyright having expired or being about to expire.

3.081   It will be appreciated that these provisions will greatly increase the burdens on those who want to operate lawfully. They will need to investigate the copyright laws of other E.U. Member States to see not only the term of copyright but also whether the particular work is regarded in those member states as meriting copyright. Just because a flying-duck wall-plaque is regarded in the U.K. as an artistic work, and just because Germany protects artistic works for life + 70 years, does not automatically mean the work will fall back into copyright. It seems it will be necessary to find out whether German law would regard a flying-duck wall-plaque (or indeed this particular flying-duck wall-plaque) as an artistic work. Since German law demands rather more by way of artistry than U.K. law (in practice it seems to be what the judging classes feel is "artistic"—or expert evidence may be required), the difficulties are not inconsiderable. Moreover, if the flying-duck turns out to be of U.S. or Japanese origin, the lengthened or revived term will not apply at all—though that may depend on how the U.S. or Japanese former copyright owner came by the design. If he was an assignee and the original author turns out to be a Luxembourgeois who died in 1930 from the effects of wounds received on the Somme, then the revived term will after all apply (subject to artistry), either for the benefit of the assigneee or for the benefit of the author's heirs.

3.082   Which it will be (and what safeguards a lawful exploiter between 1980 and 1995 will enjoy) will depend on how the U.K. chooses to allocate the revived rights. No implementing statutory instrument has yet been published, although by the time this book appears it is to be presumed there will be one, since the new law is required to be in place by July 1, 1995.[72] In the meantime,

---

[71] Adopted October 29, 1993 [1993] O.J. L290/9.

[72] It now seems likely that a statutory instrument will not come into effect until October 1, 1995.

all that can be said is that for E.U.-originated post-August 1, 1989 literary and artistic works the term should now be considered as life + 70, and that pre-August 1, 1989 works whose copyright expired within the last 20 years should be treated with caution. Photographs taken before June 1, 1957 are likely to enjoy a longer term than before, but typographical arrangement copyright will be unchanged. Computer-generated works where the maker of the necessary arrangements was a human being may have to adopt the life + 70 years term.

The Directive expressly states that it does not apply to moral rights. These are by Article 6 *bis* of the Berne Convention tied to copyright at least for the author's life, but the Article does in certain circumstances permit member countries not to apply some of the rights after his death.   **3.083**

The basic U.K. copyright rules, whatever they may now become, are substantially modified by the devices adopted to limit the enforceability of copyright where artistic works have formed the basis of industrial designs. Whatever happens to the underlying copyright term in the artistic work, it seems the Directive has nothing to say about any limitations which national laws may choose to impose on the enforcement of this copyright. In the remainder of this section, therefore, where copyright is said to continue unimpaired or to remain enforceable, the term should be regarded as life + 70, but where its enforceability has been affected by the other provisions considered, it can be treated as if the Directive did not exist.   **3.084**

"Old" designs made before June 1, 1957

An "old" design in this discussion is any design made before August 1, 1989 where copyright subsisted in an artistic work on which the design was based. These can be divided into those works made before and those made after June 1, 1957 when the Copyright Act 1956 came into effect.   **3.085**

If the work was made before June 1, 1957, the first question is whether it was at the time it was made used or intended to be used as a model or pattern to be multiplied by any industrial process.[73] If it was not, then any actual industrial exploitation which took place before August 1, 1989 will not affect the copyright, even if the design as industrially-exploited would have been registrable under either the 1949 Act or any of its predecessors.[74] If the work is industrially-exploited after August 1, 1989 by more than 50 copies being made and at least one marketed, then the abridged 25-year term for all industrial exploitations under section 52 will kick in,[75] provided the articles industrially-exploited are not "excluded articles" within the Copyright (Industrial Process and Excluded Articles) (No. 2) Order 1989[76]—"limited   **3.086**

---

[73] Copyright Act 1911, s.22.
[74] *King Features Syndicate Inc. v. O. & M. Kleeman Ltd* [1941] A.C. 417 (Popeye case) and 1956 Act, Sched. 7, para. 8(1).
[75] See 1988 Act, Sched 1, para. 20(2).
[76] S.I. 1989 No. 1070. See Chap. 2 above.

edition" (50 or fewer) sculptures, wall-plaques, medals, medallions and printed matter primarily of a literary or artistic character. If the copyright expires naturally before the 25 years are up, then that is that anyway. In principle, the work would after July 31, 1999 have to pass the section 51 test, if that were raised as a defence, before falling into section 52, but it is thought this is unlikely to cut out such a work in practice, either because it is or depicts an artistic work or because it will never have been a "design document or model", not being a design "for" anything—it was never used or intended to be used for industrial purposes. An example of this kind of artistic work is (as in the Popeye case) a regular newspaper strip cartoon.

3.087   If the work *was* used or initially intended to be used for industrial purposes, the next question is whether it was registrable under the Registered Designs Act 1949 or earlier Designs Acts. If it was, then whether or not it was actually registered, it did not have copyright under the 1911 Act, nor did it get it under the 1956 Act (Schedule 7, paragraph 8(2)), nor does it get it under the 1988 Act (Schedule 1, paragraph 6). An example would be an ornamental scent bottle.

3.088   If the artistic work depicted a design that was not registrable under any of the Designs Acts but was used or initially intended to be used for industrial purposes, it was likely not to have *artistic* copyright under the 1911 Act anyway, either because it was a prototype for some mechanical device like a hinge and therefore not an artistic work under section 35 (not a sculpture or work of artistic craftsmanship or a model for the artistic parts of a building) or because it was a drawing of such a device and hence classed as a "plan" and therefore as a literary work. If it was the former, it did no better under the 1956 Act, nor does it under the 1988 Act so far as copyright is concerned. But if it was the latter, then it seems that the 1956 Act converted it into an artistic work,[77] and entitled it to be sued on for unlicensed three-dimensional reproduction. It is not affected by any industrial exploitation since June 1, 1957, because by Schedule 7, paragraph 8(1) of the 1956 Act, section 10 of that Act never applied to it,[78] and even if it had, it would not have bitten because the design was not registrable. Its copyright therefore survives, and it is in the same position as the post-June 1, 1957 unregistrable designs discussed later.

3.089   Of course, a pre-June 1, 1957 artistic work might have been unregistrable under all the ruling Designs Acts throughout its life not because it was purely functional but because it was a design for a "rule 26" article like a seaside postcard—these being in practice not accepted for registration under the pre-1949 Designs Acts as a matter of the Registrar's discretion, despite

---

[77] Schedule 7, paragraph 45(1) applied the provisions of the Act to "things existing at the commencement of those provisions as they apply in relation to things coming into existence thereafter".
[78] Even though that paragraph refers to "artistic" works made before June 1, 1957, and it was not an artistic but a literary work when it was made, Schedule 7, paragraph 45(1), as mentioned in the previous note, retrospectively converted it into one.

industrial exploitation. Again, these works are considered below along with post-June 1, 1957 designs.

"Old" designs registrable under section 10 of the 1956 Act

If a copyright artistic work was made on or after June 1, 1957 and before **3.090** August 1, 1989, it is necessary to decide whether or not section 10 of the 1956 Act ever applied to it, to see whether it still has any enforceable copyright, and if so, for how long this lasts under the transitional provisions in Schedule 1, paragraphs 19 and 20 of the 1988 Act.[79] In its original form, section 10 applied where a design "corresponding" to a copyright artistic work was registered under the 1949 Act, or was applied industrially by or with the consent of the copyright owner to more than 50 articles (at least one of which was marketed), or to goods manufactured by the length or piece, such as textiles or wallpaper and other surface covering, so long as these were not hand-made.[80] A "corresponding" design (section 10(7)) was one which, when applied to an article, resulted in the article being a reproduction of the copyright artistic work. Once the design was registered or applied, copyright could no longer ever be invoked to restain manufacture or sale of any articles which either were, or would if a design had been registered have been, within the ambit of that design. Unregistrable designs (those which did not fall within the section 1(3) definition of "design", "rule 26" designs and designs for parts of articles not made and sold separately) thus did not lose their copyright, but the implications of this seem not to have been immediately recognised.

Dorling v. Honnor,[81] however, clearly confirmed that the section 10 **3.091** limitation of enforceable copyright in designs which had been industrially-applied without being registered caught only designs which could have been registered—those with some aesthetic appeal. Purely functional designs were not affected by it, and continued to enjoy the full term of copyright protection against unlicensed manufacture and sale. Articles which were not made and sold separately were also unregistrable and therefore not caught by the exclusion, so copyright could still be used to prevent copying of particular components or features not sold separately (provided they were the subject to separate drawings or formed a substantial part of drawings of the article as a whole), even if the article as a whole would have been registrable. Copying of part and assembly drawings by reproduction in two dimensions (*e.g.* taking photographs of infringing parts which themselves reproduced the drawings) could also be restrained, because the drawings could not have been registered under rule 26.

---

[79] These matters have already been dealt with in outline in Chapter 2; this account merely fills in the details.
[80] Copyright (Industrial Designs) Rules 1957, S.I. 1957 No. 867.
[81] [1963] R.P.C. 205; [1964] R.P.C. 160—sale of self-assembly kit of parts with plans and photographs for building your own sailing dinghy.

Copyright becomes available to registrable industrial designs

3.092 As a quite separate matter, with the increase in counterfeiting, complaints began to be made that registered design protection only was inadequate. It was too costly to register all designs, and in any case by the time the design was granted and could be sued on it was often too late to be of much use. The Design Copyright Act 1968 therefore amended section 10 by excluding reference to registered designs and effectively giving 15 years' copyright (dating from first marketing anywhere in the world) to "corresponding" designs which had been applied industrially, whether or not they had also been registered. Dual protection by both a registered design and copyright therefore became possible, registration no longer operating as a defence to copyright infringement. An example of this sort of design would be a women's high-heeled boot with leaf-shaped holes cut out of the uppers.

3.093 It was later argued in *British Leyland v. Armstrong*[82] that (as had been held in another case at first instance[83]) the amended wording of section 10 and the exclusion of references to registered designs now meant that it applied to unregistrable as well as registrable designs, and reduced the term of copyright in *all* industrially-applied designs to 15 years from first marketing. The Court of Appeal rejected this interpretation, and the argument was not pursued in the House of Lords. The *British Leyland* exhaust pipe was the classic example of an unregistrable design, its shape and configuration being dictated solely by function. A non-spare part example might be a ring-pull petfood can.

3.094 Of course, not all copyright artistic works made on or after June 1, 1957 and before August 1, 1989 which would have been registrable as designs for articles have been either registered or industrially-exploited, and section 10 never affected these.

3.095 On August 1, 1989, section 10 was repealed and replaced by the approximately (but not exactly, since it is not linked to registrability) equivalent section 52, with its 25-year rather than 15-year abridged period of enforceable copyright in artistic works where these become industrially-exploited.

The transitional provisions

3.096 When the 1988 Act came into effect, it was left with a heterogeneous collection of existing industrial-design-related artistic works to be fitted smoothly into the new system—some purely artistic, some purely functional, some industrially-exploited, some not, some registrable, some not. Two different periods of copyright, one life + 50, one 15 years only, could be

---

[82] [1986] R.P.C. 279.
[83] *Hoover plc v. George Hulme (Sto) Ltd* [1982] F.S.R. 565.

currently running, which would have given rise to differing expectations and quite possibly differing investment decisions. The old test of registrability, which had strongly influenced the incidence of copyright, had been dropped in the new system. There was the *British Leyland* decision to accommodate.

Because of vested rights and accrued expectations, and because *British Leyland* had taken care of the immediate spare parts problem, it was decided to postpone the application of the draconian section 51 to existing works until July 31, 1999, but subject to licences of right during the last five years and subject to the continuation of the *British Leyland* and any other defences available under the law at large, such as Euro-defences. This was achieved by Schedule 1, paragraph 19. Existing designs may therefore be sued on in copyright, but the imposition of any injunction or order for delivery up of infringing goods may be resisted by an undertaking to take a licence of right. This is now available in all "old" copyright actions, since they entered their final potential five years on August 1, 1994—"potential" because if copyright expires through natural causes in the meantime, it is not of course artificially prolonged by paragraph 19. The final five years means the final five years of the 10-year extension, not of the copyright term, whatever that might be, so that if copyright was due to run out in 1997 the licence of right period would not have begun in 1992, but on August 1, 1994 with all the rest. A licence of right will cover only those activities which would be exonerated from infringement under section 51, those relating to the making of articles to the design—it will not cover copying drawings or catalogues.[84] **3.097**

It should be noted that paragraph 19 adopts the wording of section 51 and speaks of works recorded or embodied in design documents and models before August 1, 1989. The effect of this seems to be that in determining the works to which the 10-year "hangover" applies, the artistic work in question must be subjected to the section 51 test as if it had been brought into being on or after that date. (This is so even though paragraph 19(1) expressly says section 51 "does not apply" for 10 years, because unless it is applied, it is impossible to decide whether a design is now subject to a licence of right.) If it is not a design document at all (like the cartoon strip mentioned above), then the 10-year term does not bite and the copyright continues unimpaired unless and until its owner decides to exploit it industrially and thus brings it within section 52. The seaside postcard, although probably a "design document", since it will have been industrially-exploited, again survives section 51 because it is not a three-dimensional article of the type which would have to be satisfied with unregistered design right. It will not be subject to the 10-year term. The exhaust-pipe, the hinge and the petfood can *will* all fail the section 51 test, whether stemming from drawings or prototypes, because they are designs for the respective articles, none of which is an artistic work. The hinge and the can will be subject to the 10-year term, the exhaust pipe will not survive at all because of the *British Leyland* exception preserved (though not **3.098**

---

[84] See *Baltimore Aircoil Co. Inc. v. Evapco (U.K.) Ltd*, SRIS/C/38/94.

by name, only as "any rule of law preventing or restricting the enforcement of copyright in relation to a design") in paragraph 19(9).

3.099   If it is right that the section 51 test must be projected backwards,[85] the boot would also fail it, except in so far as the cut-out leaves could be classified as "surface decoration". It is not an artistic work, and its design drawing is a design for a three-dimensional article, and the fact that it is a registrable design and thus may have a 15-year copyright term running under section 10 does not, it seems, matter. Paragraph 19 says nothing about registrability, and certainly has nothing to do with it when applied to new designs. But there are arguments to the contrary. As will be seen, paragraph 20 specifically eases the transition from section 10 to section 52, two sections which have a lot in common except for the length of their cut-down periods. It is not unreasonable to suppose that subsisting 15-year terms of enforceable copyright in registrable designs might have been allowed to live out their declining years without molestation—particularly from licences of right, which will be of no practical use to a copyright defendant where there happens to be an actual registered design in place during the copyright licence of right period. There are supporting indications in the wording in paragraph 19 itself: One is the reference in sub-paragraph (3) imposing licences of right to "so much of that last five years during which copyright subsists". Now as frequently observed, neither section 10 nor section 51 or section 52 affects the *subsistence* of copyright, merely its enforceability. The reference to subsistence in the context of sub-paragraph (3) seems apt to cover only expiry of copyright through natural causes, not the termination of an artificial "window of enforceability" by expiry of an existing 15-year period. Another indication is sub-paragraph (9). "Nothing in [paragraph 19] affects the operation of any rule of law preventing or restricting the enforcement of copyright" would cover a 15-year period already in place. The third is the overall policy of paragraphs 19 and 20 in giving some protection to vested rights and expectations; if hinge-makers can get 10 years, why should bootmakers not get the full 15 on which they may have relied in refraining from seeking a registration?

3.100   Before parting with paragraph 19, mention may be made of a "European" point raised against its continuation of copyright in purely functional designs for a further 10 years. This was argued to operate as a barrier to free trade by restraining the importing and marketing, from at least some other Member States where there is no equivalent protection, of articles depicted in engineering drawings, and this restriction is not justified for protecting the "specific subject-matter" of the copyright in such drawings, its "essential function", which is to protect the artistic and pictorial content of the

---

[85] And some back projection was done by His Honour Judge Ford in the Patents County Court (see Chap. 5) in *PSM International plc v. Specialised Fastener Products (Southern) Ltd* [1993] F.S.R. 113 when he held he had jurisdiction in an "old" copyright action because the document in question was a "design document" under section 51 and Schedule 1, paragraph 19 even though made before August 1, 1989.

draughtsman's work, not the manufacturing information. The Court of Appeal in *British Leyland*[86] admittedly rejected these arguments, but its authority was undermined by the House of Lords, which castigated the law as "absurd", "bizarre" and "contrary to the intention of Parliament".[87] E.U. law should operate as "a rule of law preventing or restricting the enforcement" of this copyright under paragraph 19(9), or there should at least be a reference to the European Court of Justice before paragraph 19 is used against a defendant.

This argument has not, however, persuaded the first instance judges before whom it has been urged, who have taken the view that the Court of Appeal's view in *British Leyland* is still binding.[88] The Court of Appeal itself has been able to avoid considering it. **3.101**

Paragraph 20 of the transitional provisions sets out to cope with the changeover from section 10 to section 52. This was necessary because section 10 was repealed along with the whole of the 1956 Act,[89] and arrangements had to be made for designs with subsisting 15-year periods granted by section 10 to be "taken over" by section 52. Paragraph 20(1) provides that where section 10 has applied to a work at any time before August 1, 1989 (because it has been registered or industrially-applied and marketed), section 52 "gives" only 15 rather than 25 years. Paragraph 20(2) says that except where section 10 applied before August 1, 1989, section 52 and its 25-year period applies "only" where marketing takes place after August 1, 1989. There is no provision for licences of right. **3.102**

Sub-paragraph (1) seems to provide a perfectly logical changeover whereby existing 15-year periods running for the benefit of "old" registrable designs are preserved but not given the benefit of the extension to 25 years which "new" industrial exploitations will enjoy. It protects vested rights while not giving any windfall. But as suggested above, if section 51 is to be applied before section 52, old registrable designs which fail the section 51 test, will have their 15-year periods cut down *and* subjected to licences of right, and it is only designs which would survive section 51 whose 15-year periods can, under sub-paragraph (1), run on unhindered until they expire, at latest, on July 31, 2004. Now that licences of right have become available for designs caught by section 51, some ruling on the meaning and co-operation of the transitional provisions may be expected. **3.103**

Paragraph 20(2) says that except where section 10 has applied to a work, section 52 applies only where articles are marketed after August 1, 1989. The sensible interpretation of this, in line with the suggested policy of preserving vested 15-year rights while not granting any windfalls, is that only where an **3.104**

---

[86] [1986] R.P.C. 279.
[87] [1986] A.C. 577.
[88] *Entec (Pollution Control) Ltd v. Abacus Mouldings* [1992] F.S.R. 332; *C. & H. Engineering v. F. Klucznik & Son Ltd* [1992] F.S.R. 421.
[89] 1988 Act, Sched. 8.

artistic work is *first* industrially-exploited after August 1, 1989, by actual marketing (even if the making of articles began before that date) should the section 52 25-year period apply. However, the sub-paragraph does not say "first marketed", it simply says "marketed", which suggests that continuation of marketing already begun would suffice. This has led to the ingenious argument that the wording could catch "old" unregistrable, as well as registrable, designs so as to deprive them of the 10-year protection left to them by paragraph 19, or some of it. Paragraph 20(2) applies section 52 to designs *other* than those covered by section 10, provided they are marketed (not "first" marketed) on or after August 1, 1989. Since section 52, unlike section 10, is not limited to registrable designs, its 25-year cut-down period could apply to deprive "old" unregistrable designs of copyright *before* July 31, 1999, provided they were first marketed early enough and continue to be marketed after commencement. Again, this depends on whether or not section 51 is to be applied before section 52, and also whether section 52's 25-year period can be back-projected to start on a date earlier than August 1, 1989, which would be unorthodox. But it is true that section 52 is not confined to registrable designs; there may be some purely functional designs covered by it which are not caught by section 51 (for example if "surface decoration" is not limited to purely "decorative" features) and it is certainly true that Parliament could have, but did not, put the matter beyond doubt by referring in paragraph 20(2) to "first marketing" rather than simply "marketing".

3.105   This seems pretty improbable, and no doubt the reason why the draftsman said "marketed" rather than "first marketed" is to take account of copyright owners who made and sold fewer than 50 articles before August 1, 1989, so never became subject to section 10, but continue to make and sell after that date. A maker of bespoke handmade coffins who had made and sold only 30 before August 1, 1989 but has since made and sold another 30 would escape section 52 if it only operated where his *first* marketing took place after that date.

Semiconductor topographies

3.106   Semiconductor topographies made before November 7, 1987 when the first Regulations[90] were introduced, enjoyed artistic copyright because their manufacture by photo-etching techniques made them "photographs". This copyright (which would otherwise fall within section 51) is extended by Schedule 1, paragraph 19 of the 1988 Act until July 31, 1999, but paragraph 10(3) of the 1989 Semiconductor Topographies Regulations[91] disapplies the licensing of right provision during the second five years of the term, so that such licences will not be available. Topographies created between November

[90] S.I. 1987 No. 1497.
[91] S.I. 1989 No. 1100.

7, 1987 and July 31, 1989, on the other hand, are deprived by paragraph 10(2) of the Schedule 1, paragraph 19 10-year exemption from section 51, so they ceased to be entitled to copyright as from August 1, 1989. The 1989 Regulations repealed the 1987 Regulations as from the same date, so for the remainder of their term topographies created under the 1987 Regulations will, it seems, be subject to the 1989 Regulations.

Typefaces

Under section 55 of the 1988 Act there is imposed a special abbreviated period of copyright enforceability for an artistic work consisting of the design of a typeface where articles specifically designed or adapted for producing material in that typeface have been marketed (by selling, hiring or offering or exposing for sale or hire, in the U.K. or elsewhere) by or with the licence of the copyright owner. After 25 years from the end of the calendar year in which the first such articles are marketed, the artistic work may, without infringement, be copied by making and dealing in such articles, or doing anything for the purpose of making them. This is very similar to section 52, except that there is no need for the copyright owner to have made or marketed a specified number of articles before the provision can apply.   **3.107**

"New" designs

Where copyright does continue to be applicable in the industrial design area to works made on or after August 1, 1989, they will enjoy the new full term of the author's life + 70 years if they are literary or artistic works, subject to the section 52 cut-down period for industrially-exploited artistic works. The statutory instrument giving effect to the E.U. harmonisation Directive will have to be consulted for details.[92]   **3.108**

REGISTERED DESIGNS

SUBSISTENCE

Whether a registered design subsists or not is an easy question: it subsists if it is registered at the Designs Registry, a subdivision of the Patent Office. If it is cancelled, or proved to be invalidly registered, this will in some cases have the effect of revoking it *ab initio*[93]; but in general, so long as it is on the Register, it subsists, and by section 17(8) the Register is prima facie evidence of anything required or authorised to be entered in it. The territorial ambit of a U.K. registered design is Great Britain, Northern Ireland, the Isle of Man, U.K.   **3.109**

[92] See 3.082 above.
[93] See 3.120 and 3.121 below.

territorial waters and structures and vessels exploiting natural resources on the U.K. continental shelf (sections 45–47A).

Application

3.110   This section does not purport to give more than an outline of the application procedure, which is mainly governed by section 3 of the 1949 Act (as amended by the 1988 Act) and by the detailed requirements of the Designs Rules.[94] Registration can only take place on formal application and payment of a fee. As explained in Chapter 2, registration is of the design as applied to an article, and a separate registration must be sought for each article to which it is intended to apply the design, except where several articles form a "set", when by section 44(2) any reference to an "article" is to be construed as a reference to any article of that set. Thus where the applicant wants to apply the same pattern, such as a cartoon figure, to a variety of articles not forming part of a set, he must make as many applications as there are articles.

3.111   It is possible under section 4 of the Act to make later applications for the same design as applied to different articles, but the later designs, which must be "associated" with the earlier ones, will last only as long as the earliest. However, the section is useful. If an applicant for a design finds his way blocked on novelty grounds by an earlier registration for the same or a substantially similar design in respect of another article, he may under section 4(2), if the earlier registered proprietor is willing, take an assignment of the earlier design and "associate" his current application with it, so as to overcome the novelty objection. It is probably not possible to use the section to catch a later competitor selling something which the earlier design could have, but did not, cover—for example where the registered proprietor of a design for a propelling pencil finds a competitor using the design, or part of it, for a fountain pen. This could have been covered by applying for the earlier design for "a writing instrument", and but for the competitor's intervention, an associated design could still be sought for a fountain pen, but since the competitor's pen does not infringe the earlier design, it will now destroy the novelty of a later application.

3.112   The application must include representations of the article in respect of which registration is sought; these will normally be drawings or photographs, although actual specimens are acceptable if they can be easily mounted on paper and stored without damaging other documents. Where the design consists of a repeating pattern, the representation must show the complete pattern and a "sufficient portion of the repeat in length and width". Where words, letters or numerals appear in the design (for example a design for a digital watch or other indicating means), the Registrar may require a disclaimer of their exclusive use, and this is normally shown by striking them

---

[94] Currently the 1989 version, S.I. 1989 No. 1105.

through on the representations. If a design features a portrait of one of the Royal Family, the name or portrait of a living or recently dead person, or the armorial bearings, flag or other insignia of a place, organisation or person, the Registrar may require appropriate consents to such use. Except in the case of wallpaper, textile or lace patterns, the applicant, as explained in Chapter 2, must furnish a statement of the features of the design for which novelty is claimed; this may be the design as a whole, or only certain elements of it. Care should be given to the drafting of the statement, because it will be taken into account in considering infringement. It may be desirable to register more than one design for the same article or set of articles, if there are elements of both shape and pattern which require protection; otherwise an infringer may be able to escape liability by taking only one element of the combined design.

A design is of course not registrable unless it is novel, as explained in   **3.113** Chapter 2; but the Act only permits, and does not require, the Registar to make searches in order to decide this (section 3(3)). Earlier registered designs are usually searched (using an informal classification system since designs are not filed in prescribed classes), but not applications which never proceeded to registration, as these do not affect novelty unless by some other means such as publication. Otherwise the extent of the search appears to be a matter of chance, manpower and the availability of materials. Designs are also checked for inherent registrability, and this is the point at which "must-match", "dictated solely by function", "who-cares-what-it-looks-like?" and the other registrability objections discussed in Chapter 2 are raised.

Much correspondence frequently takes place between the applicant and   **3.114** the Registry at the prosecution stage, and there may be oral hearings of greater or less formality. Written evidence may be filed, normally given by statutory declaration, but oral evidence on oath, with cross-examination, may also be taken at the Registrar's discretion. The Registrar has power to call for particular documents, information and evidence. There is no provision for third party pre-grant opposition, and the internal dealings between applicant and Registry are not publicly available for inspection after grant, except in the case of the "who-cares-what-it-looks-like?" exclusion, where the applicant must provide evidence that someone would care what the article looked like if his design were applied to it, and this evidence will be left on file for competitors or challengers to consider.

The Registrar has a discretion whether or not to register a design, and in   **3.115** what form to register it, but this must be exercised judicially and not arbitrarily, and before the discretion is exercised adversely the applicant must be given the opportunity of a hearing. Normally if there is a doubt about registrability, the applicant will be given the benefit of it, and in practice designs which differ very little from earlier registrations are often accepted. A later registered design does not, however, provide an automatic defence to an action for infringement based on an earlier design, a fact which often comes as an unpleasant surprise to the later proprietor. He will still have to disprove infringement and/or try to invalidate the earlier design.

3.116   One discretionary ground on which the Registrar may withhold registration is what may be called "public morality".[95] A recent example of this
was *Re Masterman's Design*.[96] The application was for a soft toy in the form
of a "Scotsman" (actually a vaguely humanoid, shaggy artefact) wearing a
kilt. One of the representations was a front view of the artefact with its kilt
raised to show rudimentary genitalia, thus satisfying the perennial, prurient
curiosity of English persons as to what Scotsmen wear beneath their kilts. The
Registrar, in deference to the offence he feared this might give to a
not-inconsiderable proportion of the public, refused to register that particular representation. He appreciated that his refusal would not prevent the toy
being sold, but felt that it should not be dignified with a legal monopoly.
Aldous J., sitting as the Registered Designs Appeal Tribunal, took a more
robust view and allowed registration. Offence given to some members of the
public was only one factor to be taken into account; other members of the
public would not be offended, there was no legislation under which sales of
the toy could be banned, and the designer was entitled to protection for her
skill and labour. Registration does not indicate that the Registrar approves of
a design, only that it is registrable.

3.117   It has recently been held that another ground on which the Registrar may,
in the exercise of his discretion, refuse to register a design is where the
applicant is not the proprietor.[97] This is dealt with further under 3.020 above.
Also under the 1988 amendments he may not (and this is not discretionary)
entertain an application for registration of a design in which unregistered
design right subsists unless it is made by the person claiming to be the
unregistered design right owner (section 3(2)).

3.118   Design registration is a Paris Convention right, so applications can be
based on an earlier application in a Convention country if made within six
months of that application (section 24). There are special rules dealing with
Convention applications, and difficulties sometimes arise where the overseas
rules governing what can be registered differ from the U.K. rules. In *Deyhle's
Design Applications*,[98] the Convention application was made in Germany,
where multiple applications can be made for registration of a single design (in
this case a cartoon figure) for application to a variety of articles. Thus it did
not specify the particular article for which U.K. registration was sought. It
was held that so long as the scope of the Convention application was wide
enough to permit registration in Germany of the design as applied to the
specific article for which U.K. registration was sought (which it was), this
would suffice.

3.119   Registry procedures are subject to time-limits, most of which can be
extended by the Registrar whether before or after they expire, but he may

---

[95] See s.43(1)—the Registrar is not authorised or required to register a design the use of which
would, in his opinion, be contrary to law or morality.
[96] [1991] R.P.C. 24.
[97] *Leara Trading Co. Ltd's Design* [1991] R.P.C. 609.
[98] [1982] R.P.C. 526.

require convincing evidence, whether from the applicant or his agent, to explain any delay and show who was responsible for it. If the default is that of the agent, the applicant should not necessarily be held responsible for it.[99]

Registration and Inspection

When a design is accepted, its registration certificate shows the date of registration as the date of application (or Convention priority date), although the Registrar does have power for purposes of determining novelty to specify a different date, for example where an application is divided-out from an earlier one because the earlier one was deemed to contain more than one design. In such a case the Registrar may permit the later application to benefit from the earlier filing date.[1] No proceedings may, however, be taken for infringement prior to actual registration (section 7(5)). The rationale for this is presumably that, unlike a patent, a design is not published until then. The Register contains details of the proprietor and any dealings with the design, and a representation may be inspected, except where a design is used for purposes of national defence (section 5(1)) or is one for wallpaper or for textiles or lace, which may enjoy two and three years' secrecy respectively (section 22(2)). This is quite adequate where a competitor is warned of a specific design, because he can readily check it. It is not, however, possible for the public or its advisers to make a general search for designs which may conflict with manufacturing plans, as representations of designs are not published. All that can be done is to ask the Registry staff to search, specifying as closely as possible the article concerned. As a design for one article may have its novelty destroyed by an earlier design for a quite different article, there being no formal classification system, this is unsatisfactory and, together with the haphazard system of examination into the prior art apart from earlier registered designs, casts some doubt on the assertion that with a registration system everyone knows where they are and what they may or may not do.

3.120

Cancellation and Rectification

Under section 11, the proprietor himself may request the Registrar to cancel a registered design, and any "person interested" may ask him to cancel it because it was invalidly registered (for want of novelty or any other ground on which registration could have been refused) or because it is based on an artistic work in which the copyright has expired. "Person interested" would presumably mean someone having a commercial interest in the subject-matter without necessarily being threatened with infringement proceedings or having his own application blocked because of a prior registration. Where

3.121

---

[99] *Tomy Kogyo Co. Inc's Design Application* [1983] R.P.C. 207.
[1] See *Amper S.A.'s Design Application* [1993] R.P.C. 453.

the proprietor requests cancellation, it takes effect on the date of cancellation, and where it is because an underlying copyright has expired, the effective date is the date of such expiry. Where the design was invalidly registered, cancellation takes effect as of the original registration date.

3.122   Rectification may be ordered by the court under section 20, and may cover not only removing a design from the Register but making an entry or varying an existing one. The applicant must be a person who is "aggrieved", not merely "interested", and will normally be a counterclaiming defendant in an infringement action, or someone who claims to be the true proprietor of a design. A new entry has effect from the date on which it should have been made, a varied one as if it had originally been made in its varied form, and a deleted entry "shall be deemed never to have had effect". The successful counterclaiming defendant will therefore not be liable for what would have been infringement had the design been valid. In the case of both cancellation and rectification *ab initio*, an earlier infringer who did not challenge the design will not be able to get his damages or costs back, or any money paid by way of settlement, because the money will have been paid under a mistake of law—that the design was validly registered. However, a person subject to a continuing injunction not to do certain specified acts which would hitherto have constituted infringement would be entitled to apply for discharge of that injunction; and an injunction which merely forbids infringement of the design in general terms will cease to have effect once the design is no longer there to be infringed.

Proprietorship

3.123   For designs registered under the 1949 Act before its amendment by the 1988 Act, section 2 provided that the "proprietor" of a design, and hence the person who could properly seek registration, was the author. This term was not defined, but by analogy with copyright would normally be the person who put pen to paper to produce the design. There was an exception where the design was made by the author for another person for good consideration, when that other person was to be treated as proprietor. This was not expressed to be subject to any contrary agreement, and the result in most cases was that not only the commissioner of a design from a freelance designer but also, where the designer was an employee, his employer, would be entitled to be proprietor, since if the designer was employed to design, his wage or salary would be "good consideration" for making the design.

3.124   Before the Copyright Act 1956 came into effect on June 1, 1957, there was no copyright in registrable industrial designs which were always intended for mass exploitation. This was because section 22 of the Copyright Act 1911 disapplied that Act to such designs unless they were not used or intended to be used as models or patterns "to be multiplied by any industrial process". Hence no problems as to design proprietorship because of the artistic copyright remaining with the designer would normally arise. Matters changed with the 1956 Act, which used the different machinery of giving copyright to the artistic works on which industrial designs were usually based but making it unenforceable either where a design was registered or where a registrable design was industrially-exploited with the copyright owner's consent. Because the rules on first ownership of copyright are different, this meant that where a design was commissioned, the title to the design and to the copyright in the underlying artistic work could be in different hands, and if no consent had been given to the registration or the industrial exploitation, problems could arise. Schedule 1 to the 1956 Act covered the case where a design had been registered without the knowledge of the copyright owner, who could sue the proprietor (but not his bona fide assignee or licensee without notice of any challenge to the registration) for copyright infringement. However, this did not really take into account the case where the design had been commissioned, so that the right to apply for registration properly belonged to the commissioner and not the author. In *Ornamin (U.K.) Ltd v. Bacsa Ltd*,[2] the defendant had commissioned the plaintiff to produce designs for transfers to be used on babyware, and had paid 12 guineas for them. The defendant then, without the knowledge of the plaintiff, registered the designs and began to reproduce them. The plaintiff sued for copright infringement and false registration of designs under Schedule 1, on the basis that the 12 guineas had bought only the transfers themselves. An interlocutory injunction was refused, the court finding that the plaintiff had not at that stage discharged the burden of invalidating the registration for incorrect proprietorship, and suggesting that the 12 guineas might be proved at trial, depending on the evidence, to have bought the copyright as well as the transfers themselves.

The problem was exacerbated after the Design Copyright Act 1968 gave 15 years' enforceable copyright to registrable but unregistered designs which had been industrially exploited, because in the absence of a registration the commissioner would have no rights in the design, the legal title to the copyright, at least, remaining in the designer.   **3.125**

Where the design had passed by assignment, transmission or operation of law (*e.g.* death or bankruptcy or a manufacturing licence) to another person, that person was to be treated as the design proprietor. But it had been held in *Guitermann's Registered Designs*[3] under earlier legislation that a mere importer, with no right to reproduce the design, could not register it, even with the proprietor's express consent; and in a recent Registry decision, *Leara Trading Co. Ltd's Designs*,[4] the hearing officer held that an assignment could not be spelt out merely from a suggestion in a telex of exclusive U.K. distribution rights for the registered proprietor, particularly since the suggestion was made by a company which itself did not own the design. An   **3.126**

[2] [1964] R.P.C. 293.
[3] (1886) 55 L.J.Ch. 309.
[4] [1991] R.P.C. 609.

application for cancellation of the registration under section 11(2) by another importer wishing to distribute identical products was therefore successful, on the ground that the Registrar could have refused, in the exercise of his discretion, to register the design because the applicant could not properly have claimed to be the proprietor.

3.127   The 1988 amendments to the 1949 Act spell matters out more clearly for designs applied for after July 31, 1989. The "author" is still primarily entitled to register, and he is now defined as the person who creates the design, except in the case of computer-generated designs, when it is again the person who makes the arrangements necessary for the creation of the design (section 2(3) and (4)). In an echo of the unregistered design right provisions, the original proprietor is by section 2(1A) the person who commissions a design for money or money's worth, and by section 2(1B) the employer of a designer who creates a design in the course of his employment. This is underlined by section 3(2), which precludes registration of a design in which unregistered design right subsists by anyone other than the person claiming to own that design right. There is no provision gathering in the copyright where the underlying artistic work is a design "for" an artistic work within section 51 of the 1988 Act. Where a design has actually been registered, section 53 of the 1988 Act, like Schedule 1 to the 1956 Act, protects a *bona fide* assignee or licensee of that design from attack by the copyright owner; but this does not resolve the position as between copyright owner and applicant for registration, and the latter will do well to make sure he gets an assignement of the copyright in the underlying artistic work from a freelance designer, who will keep his copyright even where he designs under commission. The design of tableware provides an example: if A commissions B for money to design both the shape and the surface pattern of a dinner service, A will be the "original proprietor" entitled to apply for registered designs for both shape and pattern (section 2(1A)), and will be first owner of unregistered design right in the shapes (section 215(2)); but B will retain the copyright in the pattern under section 213(3)(c) because it is "surface decoration" in which unregistered design right does not subsist.[5] This may not avail him as against A once the design is duly registered,[6] but if A should want to sue an infringer on copyright as well as the registered design, he will need to get in the legal title from B if he has not already done so.

DURATION

3.128   Under the 1949 Act before amendment, a registered design lasted for an initial period of five years from the date of application. It could be extended for two further periods of five years subject to timely application and payment of a prescribed fee, making a total of 15 years. There were two exceptions: where an existing registered design had been registered in respect

[5] See s.213 of the 1988 Act.
[6] *Ornamin (U.K.) Ltd v. Bacsa Ltd* [1964] R.P.C. 293.

of a further article or articles ("associated designs") when the later designs would expire at the same time as the earliest (section 4); and where a design was based on an existing copyright work not previously industrially-exploited (and so not destructive of novelty), when it would expire at the same time as the underlying copyright where that expired earlier than the normal registered design term: sections 6(4) and 8(3) (since the 1988 amendments section 8(5)) introduced into the 1949 Act by section 44 of the 1956 Copyright Act.

For designs registered pursuant to applications made on or after August 1, **3.129** 1989, but not for existing designs or those applied for before that date (section 269(2)), there may be four five-year extensions, making a total period of 25 years. The same exceptions as to later registrations of the same design and earlier expiry of copyright in the underlying artistic work apply (section 4 and section 8(4)). Applications for extension may be made up to six months after expiry of the previous period, and there is a new provision in section 8A for later restoration of a lapsed design where the proprietor can show he took reasonable care to arrange for extension but was, *e.g.* let down by his agent. The Registrar may in these cases make restoration subject to conditions; and section 8B contains provisions to safeguard the rights of anyone who began in good faith to "infringe" the design after lapse but before publication of notice of application for restoration, or made "effective and serious" preparations to do so. Such a person may not only continue to do these acts himself (though not to license third parties to do them) but, unlike the original parallel provision in section 64 of the Patents Act 1977 (now amended to the same effect by Schedule 5, paragraph 17 of the 1988 Act), this "personal" permission becomes an asset of the business in which he is engaged and may be exercised by partners or assigned with that part of the business to successors in title.

"Transitional" designs

Special arrangements govern certain designs applied for after January 12, **3.130** 1988 and before August 1, 1989. These are designs which, under the new Act "must-match" and "who-cares-what-it-looks-like?" exceptions, would no longer qualify for registration if applied for on or after August 1, 1989. Under transitional provisions in section 266 they were entitled to registration (if otherwise qualified), but they will expire at latest on July 31, 1999, and they are subject to licences of right from August 1, 1989. The significance of January 12, 1988 is that this was the date when the new restrictions on registration of these designs were first introduced in the House of Lords, thus giving covetous would-be design proprietors the chance to apply quickly for registrations which the government had already decided they would, under the new régime, no longer get. It is understood that only two applications for licences of right under such designs have so far been made, and these were withdrawn after the designs were held invalid in litigation.

173

4. Dealings

UNREGISTERED DESIGN RIGHT

ASSIGNMENTS AND OTHER TRANSMISIONS

4.001 Assigning unregistered design rights (including semiconductor topography rights) *inter vivos* is superficially easy: section 222 provides that it must be done in writing, and the document be signed by or on behalf of the assignor. The document need not be in any special form, so long as it identifies the right concerned: in particular, it need not be a deed under seal, although section 261 provides that the affixing of a body corporate's seal to an assignment will satisfy the "writing" requirement. Partnerships, companies and corporations can assign under the simple signature of a partner, director or other competent officer, unless some particular formality is demanded by their articles or governing documents. Design right can be disposed of by will, subject to the usual requirements governing wills; and it can pass by operation of law, as to administrators on intestacy or trustees or liquidators on insolvency, in accordance with the law governing these situations. It is treated as personal or moveable property.[1]

4.002   A disposition may be of the whole of the right, or of only one or some of the right owner's exclusive rights; it may be for the whole of the protection period or only part of it. The right owner's successors in title take subject to any licences previously granted, unless there has at some point been a *bona fide* purchaser for valuable consideration who took the right, or the relevant part of it, without notice (actual or constructive) of the licence. A person has constructive notice if he is aware of circumstances (for example the receipt of regular but fluctuating payments which might be royalties) from which he might infer the existence of a licence, even if he does not bother to check, or chooses not to do so.

4.003   However, there are pitfalls. A person signing an assignment on behalf of another must have that other's authority, so it may be necessary to check that this is the case where a signature other than that of the owner is tendered. And a common problem with intellectual property rights, of which accountants and company lawyers often seem unaware, is the failure of a company properly to assign these rights on a sale or group reorganisation, or on a name swap between companies within a group, or on the incorporation of what

[1] For covenants as to title implied by law on such dispositions, see Law of Property Act 1925, s.76 and now the major changes effected by the Law of Property (Miscellaneous Provisions) Act 1994. See note by Simon Stokes, [1995] 5 E.I.P.R. D–138.

was previously a partnership. All too often, there proves on investigation to be nothing but a document purporting to transfer things like stock and machinery, or mentioning some rights such as patents and registered designs, but not others such as copyright. Or there may be minutes of resolutions to sell or purchase, but no actual assignment. In the first case, some help can be obtained from section 224 where there is an assignment of a registered design which is the same as (or, probably, similar to) an unregistered design and the proprietors are the same: here, an assignment of the registered design will be deemed to carry with it the unregistered design right unless a contrary intention appears. Otherwise, and certainly in the case of a minute, it will be necessary to argue that the evidence indicates an agreement to assign, which can be perfected by a valid assignment, but this can be embarrassing if the assignor has in the meantime passed into different hands or been wound up.

Any assignment of an existing design right should be expressed to include **4.004** all accrued rights of action for infringement. If it does not, the assignor will have to be joined in any proceedings for pre-assignment infringement, or will have to execute a separate assignment of the rights.

Under section 223, there can be a prospective assignment (in whole or in **4.005** part) of design right in a design or class of designs which has yet to come into being. This is subject to the same formalities as an assignment of an existing design right under section 222, and will in the same way be subject to licences also granted prospectively. The section echoes the similar provisions in relation to copyright under section 91, but is less likely to be used because of the commissioning rules governing first ownership of design right.

A binding agreement, whether oral or written, to assign a design right **4.006** (existing or prospective) will normally be capable of enforcement by an action for specific performance; the court will order the owner to execute a formal assignment or, if necessary, appoint someone else to do so.

Tax (income, corporation, inheritance and capital) and stamp duty **4.007** implications should always be borne in mind on a disposal of intellectual property of any kind, whether total or partial, by assignment or licence, and specialist advice should be sought. The taxman's view of what constitutes a capital payment and what an income payment, for example, does not always accord with the layman's view. Overseas disposals may be subject to different régimes, so that the place and currency of payment may usefully be arranged accordingly. Schedule 7, paragraphs 13, 26 and 36 of the 1988 Act insert certain new provisions specific to design right into, respectively, the Taxes Management Act 1970, the Capital Gains Tax Act 1979 and the Income and Corporation Taxes Act 1988. Further, most U.K. disposals are assessable to stamp duty, even if none is actually payable, so even informal documents may have to be adjudicated (ruled upon) by the stamp duty authorities. Non-payment of stamp duty, as well as laying the non-payer open to penalties, renders a stampable document inadmissible in evidence in legal proceedings without the leave of the court.

4.008   The incidence of VAT must also be remembered. For a VATable entity, an assignment of intangible property (whether in writing or not), or the obligation to refrain from an act or to tolerate an act or situation (as where an intellectual property owner licenses what would otherwise be an infringement), in either case for a consideration such as a lump sum or a royalty, can constitute a supply of services, and hence attract VAT.[2] This can also apply to sums received as part of the settlement of legal proceedings.[3]

4.009   Where different persons are entitled to different "aspects" of design right in a work, for example following a partial assignment, or because different parts of the same piece of equipment have been designed or commissioned by different people, section 258(1) provides that each such owner can deal independently with his own "aspect". But where a design right or any aspect of it is owned by more than one person jointly, section 258(2) says that references in the Act to the design right owner are to all the owners "so that, in particular, any requirement of the licence of the design right owner requires the licence of all of them". Presumably, therefore, an assignment of jointly-owned design right would have to be by all the joint owners. If they have died or become insolvent, who can grant a licence (or execute an assignment) will depend on whether the rights were held jointly or by the owners as tenants in common. The latter is the more normal interpretation in commercial situations, and devolution on death is to the deceased joint owner's personal representatives rather than to the remaining joint owners by survivorship.

VOLUNTARY LICENCES

4.010   There is no obligation for licences of unregistered design right (except, arguably, exclusive licences) to be in writing. As with other intellectual property rights, licences may amount simply to permission to do some or all of the things which would otherwise be infringements if done without permission; but more commonly they will be embodied in relatively formal documents governing the relationship between the parties and containing the terms as to payment, warranties and the like with which the parties must comply. Exploitation licences are usually sole (whereby the licensor agrees that he will grant no other licences, although he does not give up the right to exploit himself, for example by parallel importing) or exclusive (whereby the licensor binds himself not only not to grant other licences, but not to exploit the design himself).[4] "Exclusive licence" is defined in section 225 as a licence in writing. This is not quite the same as saying (as with an assignment) that no exclusive licence is effective unless it is in writing, but since in the absence of

---

[2] Value Added Tax Act 1983, s.3(2) and Sixth Council Directive of European Communities, Arts 6(1) and 11.A.1.
[3] *Cooper Chasney Ltd v. Commissioners of Customs & Excise* [1992] F.S.R. 298.
[4] Joint owners therefore cannot grant exclusive licences without the concurrence of their fellows, as they cannot validly bind them not to exploit the rights on their own account.

writing an exclusive licensee will not be able to sue for infringement on his own account under section 234 (subject to formal joinder of the licensor as co-plaintiff or defendant), nor benefit from certain provisions relating to Crown use, the difference in wording may not have much practical significance.

Naturally the terms of any particular licence depend on agreement between the parties, and reference should be made to specialist works on the subject. But close regard must always be paid to the competition and free trade aspects of such arrangements, both under U.K. domestic law such as the Restrictive Trade Practices Act 1976 (see also Schedule 7, paragraph 18 of the 1988 Act) and under E.U. law. Not surprisingly, there is no block exemption for design right under Article 85 of the Treaty of Rome, so that any agreement which might fall foul of Article 85(1) will need to be notified to the Commission for exemption or negative clearance if it is capable of affecting trade between Member States. Nonetheless, useful guidance as to what is or is not likely to be acceptable can be gained from the "white" and "black" lists to be found in the block exemption covering patent licensing,[5] as well as from E.U. case law. The ability of design right to confer or contribute to the establishment of a dominant position must also not be overlooked.[6] **4.011**

LICENCES OF RIGHT

Outline

There are no provisions for compulsory licensing of design right on the ground that the proprietor is failing to exploit the design. What the Act decrees are two situations in which licences of right will become available, one exceptional and one universal. The Secretary of State for Trade and Industry (now known once more as the President of the Board of Trade) may under the Fair Trading Act 1973 and the Competition Act 1980 refer various possibly anti-competitive practices to the Monopolies and Mergers Commission for investigation. Under section 238 of the 1988 Act, where the Commission reports that (a) conditions in licences granted by a design right owner which restrict the use of the design by the licensee, or the right of the owner to grant other licences, or (b) the design right owner's refusal to grant licences on reasonable terms, operate, have operated or may be expected to operate against the public interest, the Secretary of State has power to cancel or modify the offending conditions and, instead or in addition, to provide that licences to use the design shall be available as of right on terms to be **4.012**

---

[5] Block Exemption for Patent Licensing, E.C. Regulation 2349/84.
[6] See, *e.g.* (T-51/89) *Tetra Pak Rausing S.A. v. E.C. Commission* [1991] 4 C.M.L.R. 334. For E.U. institutions' readiness to criticise or qualify national intellectual property rights (and to override the Berne Convention), see *ITP v. E.C. Commission (Magill TV Guide intervening)* [1991] 4 C.M.L.R. 745.

settled by the Comptroller-General of Patents, Designs and Trade Marks in default of agreement between the parties, This power, which may be exercised during the earlier years of design right before licences of right become generally available, is doubtless intended as a warning rather than as a power to be widely invoked. The procedure is cumbersome, lengthy and expensive and is only suitable for widespread abuse such as that found to have been committed by Ford in refusing to license the making of replacement body panels[7] (about which it was believed nothing could be done under the then law). If "must-fit" and "must-match" have their intended scope in relation to spare parts, the occasions for use of the section 238 power will be even rarer.

4.013 The real "anti-monopoly" provision is section 237, which decrees that "any person is entitled as of right to a licence to do in the last five years of the design right term anything which would otherwise infringe the design right".[8] This is not to be a royalty-free licence; a royalty, and any other terms are for agreement by the parties, but in default of agreement, the Comptroller will have the power to settle them. He can do this (section 247) upon an application made to him by the prospective licensee (not, apparently, the prospective licensor); this may be made up to one year before the earliest date on which the licence would take effect. In the case of such early applications, the licence will take effect from the earliest date on which it could do so—five years from the end of the calendar year in which there occurred the first marketing of articles made to the design which is to be licensed[9]; otherwise it will take effect from the date of application. Appeals from the Comptroller will lie (section 249), not to the High Court, but to the Registered Designs Appeal Tribunal. The Tribunal's decisions can be further challenged only by judicial review; there is no appeal in the ordinary sense.[10]

Need for licences of right?

4.014 This is the outline and it raises not a few questions and problems. First, why is it necessary to have licences of right at all? The original White Paper proposals[11] contained no "must-fit" or "must-match" exclusions. Spare parts were to be treated just like other designs. There was to be no *British Leyland* exception, and designers were to have five years to recoup their design costs,

---

[7] See MMC, A Report on the policy and practice of the Ford Motor Company Limited in not granting licences to manufacture or sell in the United Kingdom certain replacement body panels for Ford vehicles, Cmnd. 9437.

[8] As with copyright, dates run from the ends of calendar years. Under section 215, design right terms are reckoned from the end of the calendar year in which the design was first recorded or first marketing took place. The first design right licences of right will therefore have become available from January 1, 1995, and licences could have been applied for from January 1, 1994, (s.247(2)). It is understood that very few have been—single figures only.

[9] See n. 8 above.

[10] This is the same route as was taken in the *Ford/Fiat* "must-match" case discussed in Chap. 2, since appeals against refusal to register designs is also to the RDAT.

[11] Cmnd. 9712, paras. 3.26–3.27.

unless they abused their monopoly during that period, when there could be a reference to the Monopolies and Mergers Commission, as under section 238. Thereafter, competition would be ensured by licences of right, and it was pointed out that the spare parts aftermarket does not develop for some time after first marketing, so the possible monopoly protection period would in fact be less than five years.

But between the White Paper and the Bill, the government changed its mind **4.015** and introduced "must-fit" and "must-match", so that many spare parts never get design right at all. The main justification for licences of right thus disappeared, and yet the provisions, with their obvious capacity for provoking expensive litigation, were maintained in full. There are difficulties of principle internationally with compulsory licensing of aesthetic industrial designs (which plenty of unregistered designs will be), at least where there is no failure to work by the registered proprietor. These difficulties are greater where the design is for an article which is a "work of applied art" under the Berne Convention, and we have already considered in Chapter 2 whether the new U.K. régime makes adequate provision for these.[12] The 1988 Act has had to include, in section 237(3), a power to exclude certain designs from licences of right in order to comply with international obligations or ensure reciprocal protection for U.K. designs. (Semiconductor topographies are already excluded.[13]) To have compulsory licensing of aesthetic features which there is no technical need to copy amounts to introducing a doctrine of "aesthetic functionality" like that once in vogue in the USA under the Lanham Act,[14] whereby if a purely aesthetic feature is what "sells" a product, competitors must be allowed to copy it.

Again, licences of right are suitable where what a competitor intends is a **4.016** deliberate copy of someone else's design—as is necessarily the case with "must-fit", and also with "must-match", where the replacement car body panel must look the same as the original or the customer will not want it. But many U.K. industrial copyright cases have concerned products which were not identical copies but "our versions" of an existing product. The unsuccessful defendant did not set out to copy exactly, only to produce something for the same market, and could therefore argue that he had merely been "inspired" by the plaintiff's product, or had taken the idea but not the embodiment. Whether or not this defence was successful depended on the court's view of the defendant's behaviour overall and its interpretation of what constituted a "substantial part" of the plaintiff's design. Competitors

[12] Paris Convention, Art. 5B. *cf.* Art. 5A permitting compulsory licensing of patents in certain circumstances. The Registered Designs Act, section 10, in fact permits compulsory licensing, but only for failure to work to a reasonable extent. If there is a co-existing registered design, the unregistered design right licence of right will be of no practical use to a competitor, unless he is prepared to apply for a compulsory licence. Under the Berne Convention, see Art. 9(2).
[13] S.I. 1989 No. 1100, para. 9.
[14] See, *e.g. Pagliero v. Wallace China Co.* 198 F.2d 339 (9th Circuit, 1952). Such designs are admittedly now expressly prevented from being trade marks under section 5(2)(c) of the Trade Marks Act 1994.

like these will not care to be taken to admit, by applying for a licence of right, that they are planning to copy, or to engage to pay royalties for what they argue are features which should form part of the "common pool of experience"[15] in a particular field.

4.017   If, as a matter of caution, a competitor does take a licence rather than risk litigation, innovation may be stifled rather than encouraged. If an existing successful design can be copied for a modest royalty (as to the likely size of royalties, see below), why should a competitor bother to employ designers to try and improve the design? Or, from the point of view of the prospective licensor, why should he bother to create an improved design if someone else can copy it after five years? Why should a manufacturer agree to develop and exploit someone else's new design if he can only be given exclusivity for five years—licences of right naturally spelling an end to exclusivity?

E.U. Law

4.018   What will be the position with E.U. law? *Pharmon v. Hoechst*[16] decided that marketing within the E.U. by a compulsory licensee did not exhaust the licensor's rights, so that he could still use his national patent to prevent parallel imports of the licensee's goods. Presumably the same reasoning will apply with design licences of right—whose non-voluntary nature is under-lined by section 254, which forbids a licensee, on pain of an action for breach of statutory duty, to use any trade description indicating that he *is* a licensee of the design right owner without the latter's consent. This odd provision, adopting definitions contained in the Trade Descriptions Act 1968, may allow an unco-operative design right owner to prevent his licensee telling the public (even orally in response to inquiries) that his product is a lawful substitute for the original. What is obviously aimed at is that licensees should not be able to claim that their products are approved by the licensor, and it may be that the section can be circumvented by a statement in advertising literature that the product is compulsorily licensed, and therefore lawful, but not approved. It would be sensible for any licence, whether settled by the parites or by the Comptroller, to contain a term authorising acceptable wording.

---

[15] An expression used in the July 1981 Green Paper Reform of the Law relating to Copyright, Designs and Performers' Protection, Cmnd. 8302, para. 13, which propounded the government's then view that protecting purely functional industrial designs would lead to "a threat of stagnation of industrial development or at best of a substantial waste of time and money in changing perfectly satisfactory designs for no other reason than to avoid legal consequences".

[16] [1985] 3 C.M.L.R. 775.

Practical Complications: The Comptroller: Jurisdiction

Apart from philosophical difficulties, there are numerous practical ones with   **4.019**
the new legislation. Since there is no register which can be checked, and no
obligation to mark design right-protected products, competitors will often
not know when licences are due to become available. Again, the system is
better suited to the deliberate and systematic copier, or to the spare parts
manufacturer, both of whom will be watching the market. The competitor
who seeks the licence as a precaution may have only a vague idea when an
earlier product became available. All he knows is the presumption in section
228(4), of which his advisers will no doubt stridently remind him, that if
design right has at any time subsisted in an article, any possibly infringing
article is presumed, in the absence of contrary proof, to have been made
during subsistence of the design right. He will simply have to contact the
manufacturer and, if the latter is unco-operative, take the matter to the
Comptroller for a preliminary ruling under section 246—in this case, unlike
an order settling the terms of a licence, appealable to the High Court and
upwards in the usual way; and the Comptroller has power to refer section 246
disputes to the High Court himself (section 251).

What about designs as to which there is a genuine doubt whether design   **4.020**
right subsists? Those which may be too "commonplace" to be original, or
arguably "must-fit" or "must-match" or embody a method or principle of
construction? Or may be of unprotected foreign origin, although now made
or sold in the U.K.? Again, the Comptroller will have to decide in the absence
of agreement, and the prospective licensor will have to be involved in the
reference.

This highlights the problem which will be experienced where the identity of   **4.021**
the design right owner, and therefore prospective licensor, is unknown. The
Act (section 248) kindly provides for settlement of terms where the owner's
identity cannot on reasonable inquiry be discovered—a royalty-free licence
may be ordered; if the right owner turns up he can apply to vary the
terms—but the necessity for a licence cannot be determined under section 246
because there is, in the absence of the owner, no "dispute" to trigger the
Comptroller's jurisdiction. The Act does provide that if the owner later
emerges from the woodwork and demonstrates that for some reason a licence
was not available, the "licensee" will not be liable for damages or an account
for any period before he became aware of the owner's claim; but this is no
substitute for an advance ruling, at least on design-protectability in principle,
if not on term or first ownership. Additionally, it seems rather harsh (and as
commercially unrealistic for an established business as the law unfortunately
sometimes is) that the "licensee's" liability in damages should date from the
licensor's claim, rather than from a ruling as to the non-availability of the
licence. He will, after all, have had to pay the costs of a wasted application to
the Comptroller for settlement of the original terms, including those of
making "reasonable" inquiries as to the right owner's identity.

4.022   Rules[17] have been made under section 250 governing all these applications to the Comptroller. They include prescribed forms and fees. They require the filing of full statements by the applicant in each case, including the mention of all relevant documents, and the timetable for counterstatements and statements in reply is decidedly brisk compared with other proceedings before the Comptroller—28 and 21 days respectively in section 246 disputes, 6 and 4 weeks for settlement of terms—although they can be extended. The Comptroller then gives directions. Evidence will normally be by statutory declaration or affidavit, but cross-examination will normally be allowed. The Comptroller has in England and Wales the powers of a High Court judge to enforce the attendance of witnesses and to order discovery of documents, though he cannot punish summarily for contempt. He can decide without a hearing, if neither party wants one; and he can appoint an adviser if he wants to. He has power to award costs, and can order security against a party from outside the U.K. and E.U. Third parties having a "substantial interest" in any section 246 dispute may apply for leave to be made parties.

4.023   What no rules prescribe is any factors to which the Comptroller is to have regard in settling the terms (especially as to royalties), of licences of right. It was intended that a statutory instrument under section 247(4) should prescribe such factors, and what they might be was discussed during the Parliamentary debates. When the articles with which he will be dealing can range (particularly under extended old-style copyright) from simple bits of metal-bashing to state-of-the-art machinery for nuclear power stations, the Comptroller might be thought to have welcomed some indication of the extent to which he should, for example, take into account the R & D (if any) which went into the design, and its cost. The White Paper (paragraph 3.21) contained an indication that to achieve protection at all the original manufacturer should at least have "spent money on design"; this is not a requirement for protection under the Act, but might be a factor for the Comptroller to take into account. Lord Beaverbrook and John Butcher for the government anticipated during debate on the Bill[18] that he might be directed to have regard to design costs and to investment both in design and in establishing a market. The Notes on Clauses[19] say the same thing, and stress the desirability of prescribing the relevant factors by subordinate legislation to allow them to be changed from time to time.

4.024   Mr Butcher also conceded that the Comptroller might have power to lay down quality compliance standards binding on the licensee. If this were to be so, it must beg the question whether the licensor could be obliged to hand over know-how to ensure that the article complies with such standards, where simple reverse engineering will not secure such a good result. This was

---

[17] Design Right (Proceedings before Comptroller) Rules 1989, S.I. 1989 No. 1130, now amended by S.I. 1992 No. 615.
[18] *Hansard*, Vol. 491, col. 1139; Commons Standing Committee E, June 12, 1988, col. 599, 611.
[19] Explanatory notes provided to Committee members and some other interested parties by the sponsoring Department.

not the case under the old "implied licence" to infringe copyright where necessary to repair one's own car (or power station equipment), where the copyright owner was entitled to restrain use of his know-how.[20] The idea does not sit well with section 254 preventing the licensee from claiming kinship with the original design without his licensor's consent.

However, it appears that no rules for the Comptroller's guidance are to be made, and that he feels able to undertake his task without them, using the experience gained from his licences of right jurisdiction under the patent term extension introduced by the Patents Act 1977. This seems rather unfortunate. That jurisdiction, which has produced numerous appeals and several references to the European Court of Justice, and a stupefying body of case law, is not an edifying example. This is not only because of the complexities involved,[21] but also because the judicial authorities seem largely to have adopted a patentee-oriented approach and ordered high royalties. That may have been justified in a patent (usually a pharmaceutical patent) context, but could be an unfortunate precedent in many design cases, where the licensor's investment may have been negligible, and the public interest in ready availability of competitive products may be greater than any theroretical incentive to research and innovation.[22]   **4.025**

Since what is being licensed is only that which contributes to the shape or configuration of an article (or part of an article), it is only investment in that "appearance" aspect that can be taken into acount. But this will surely be very difficult in practice. There are unlikely, at least initially, to be any comparables. With a pharmaceutical patent the entire product, and its market, can be looked at; but how can any meaningful allocation of design costs be made in respect, perhaps, of one small part of a whole product? The originator may well not have separate or separable figures on which a royalty based on reimbursement of cost coupled with return on capital, or available profits,[23] might be based. If it is a spare part case, the licensee probably will have such figures, but as pointed out by the Court of Appeal in the *Cimetidine* case, this is not really the right test. It is the licensor's reasonable remuneration which should form the basis of a royalty, not the licensee's. Developments are awaited with interest.   **4.026**

One particular grey area will concern those elements of spare parts where a competitor has "design freedom", the "must-fit" exception covering only those elements which interface directly. In theory, a competitor will have to   **4.027**

---

[20] *Weir Pumps Ltd v. CML Pumps Ltd* [1984] F.S.R. 33.

[21] With design right these might in practice be rather less, since appeal is to the Registered Designs Appeal Tribunal and not to the Patents Court, and there is no further appeal, only judicial review, the grounds for which are narrower.

[22] Unduly favouring the licensor is not at all what the government had in mind. Lord Beaverbrook told dissenters that the proper way to look at the five-year licence of right term was as a fortunate extension to what was basically a right meant to last only five years: *Hansard*, Vol. 491, col. 1139.

[23] Two possible bases adopted in patent licensing cases, see, *e.g. Smith, Kline & French Ltd's (Cimetidine) Patents* [1990] R.P.C. 203.

wait until licences of right become available before he can start making exact copies. In practice, this will only be significant where the aftermarket does not develop until several years after the original article goes on sale: if it develops earlier, the competitor will have to fight any battles about the permissible extent of copying at an earlier stage, and will either have won them or redesigned where necessary, so that he will not need to bother with licensing. It will be interesting to see whether the Comptroller's section 246 jurisdiction plays a part in such matters. By section 246(2), in the absence of "infringement or other proceedings in which the issue arises incidentally" the Comptroller has exclusive originating jurisdiction in questions relating to the subsistence, term or first ownership of design right provided there is a "dispute" in existence. So it would seem that any competitor who wants a ruling about the ambit of "must-fit" (or the other exclusions) before he invests in a design must pick a fight with the original equipment manufacturer and go to the Comptroller, rather than seek from the court—whether High Court or Patents County Court—a declaration that no design right subsists. It may be that this will encourage aftermarket competitors to demand from the original equipment manufacturer a list of all components or parts thereof in which he claims design right, so that rulings can be obtained. If so, the Comptroller is going to be very busy.

4.028   With such a cumbersome system, once licences of right in a design have become available, competitors may choose to make use of section 239. This permits a defendant who is sued for design right infringement (or old-style copyright infringement until July 31, 1999) to escape an injunction by undertaking to take a licence of right on terms to be agreed or settled by the Comptroller, knowing that any financial compensation for infringement will be limited to twice the royalty ultimately settled. Such an undertaking can be given at any time before a final order in the action without being construed as an admission of liability (section 239(2)). This, according to the Notes on Clauses, is to allow the defendant to continue defending the case while limiting his ultimate liability if he loses. It does, however, presuppose that he will take the case to trial. A defendant who can stand the cost of interlocutory injunction proceedings might prefer to risk them in the hope of persuading the judge his opponent has no arguable case on design right, or at least obtaining some judicial indication of the strength of the case, before giving his undertaking, in the hope that it will improve his royalty bargaining position. Judges may wish to prevent themselves being used in this way, and may pressure defendants into giving an undertaking at an early stage. At present, most industrial design cases settle before trial, because of the cost and inherent unpredictability of any judicial process. It will be interesting to see whether the statutory licensing provisions make full trials more or less usual.

4.029   Where a defendant is successfully sued for design right infringement before licences of right become available, he should ask that any injunction should expire on the day when licences become available and tender an undertaking, to come into effect on the same day, to take a licence on terms to be agreed or settled, with the usual double royalty compensation provision. That way, he could restart manufacture without having to try and get the injunction lifted in fresh court proceedings.[24]

CROWN USE

Unregistered designs are liable to use by the Crown for certain purposes, on terms to be settled between government and owner or by the court.[25] Under section 240, a government department, or a person authorised in writing by a government department (whether before or after the act is done), may without infringing do anything for the purpose of supplying articles for, or disposing of articles no longer required for, defence and health service purposes. Anyone dealing with such articles will not be liable to the design right owner for infringement. "Defence" includes both defence of the realm and defence of another country pursuant to international agreement or arrangement with that country, or U.N. resolution. Nice questions of public international law could arise from this definition—for example, could an improved aiming device for a mortar have been used in Northern Ireland, where the purpose of military operations was arguably counter-insurgency rather than defence of the realm?[26] "Health service purposes" relate to pharmaceutical services and to general medical or dental purposes. Will supply to a Trust hospital fall within this definition?

4.030

For the purpose of settling terms, the government department concerned must, under section 241, notify the design right owner that it is using his design and the extent of such use, unless it thinks this would be against the public interest, or the right owner is then unknown. Any terms agreed between the government department and the design right owner must be approved by the Treasury. The government may of course use the design right owner or his licensees to work the design on its behalf, but this will be under the Crown use provisions rather than a normal government contract, and section 243 provides for compensation to the right owner or his exclusive licensee for any loss of profit resulting from his not being awarded a normal government contract, to the extent that he could have fulfilled such a contract from his existing manufacturing capacity.

4.031

Section 242 has the explanatory side-note "Rights of third parties in case of Crown use". It says, as might be expected, that licences, assignments or agreements between third parties and the design right owner cannot prevent

4.032

---

[24] He may not succeed in this sensible course. In *Victaulic plc v. E. Peart & Co. Ltd* SRIS/C/26/93 the defendant in an "old" copyright action before licences of right became available was sent about his business with an injunction and told to come back to court in due course if he wanted it discharged in order to apply for a licence of right.

[25] Crown use for unregistered designs was rudely termed "licensed burglary" during Parliamentary debate.

[26] Overseas humanitarian aid may be covered by the "special provisions for Crown use during emergency" section 244(1)(g).

Crown use, and it provides for the sharing of payments for Crown use between the right owner and such third parties. Where the third party is an exclusive licensee, his consent is required to the terms of any agreement for Crown use under section 241, and provisions differ depending on whether or not the exclusive licence was granted for a royalty. The section also permits the government department to copy and issue to the public copies of any model or document relating to the design used without infringing copyright in it. This permission, though necessary, is oddly placed in a section supposedly dealing only with the rights of third parties. It surely cannot be meant to apply only where there are third parties involved. Subsection (2) provides that the overriding of terms in agreements with third parties in the interests of Crown use does not authorise the disclosure of models, documents or information to the Crown in breach of such agreements. It is not made clear anywhere whether the design right owner can be compelled to make such disclosure, *e.g.* of manufacturing know-how, or whether the government must just reverse engineer as best it can. This might be one of the terms to be settled under section 241.

4.033   During periods of emergency (declared as such by Order in Council) the Crown use provisions are extended by section 244 to cover a range of additional purposes such as redressing the balance of trade, fostering the productivity of industry, commerce and agriculture, prosecuting wars efficiently, securing the welfare of the community and supplying humanitarian aid overseas where the need arises as the result of war.

4.034   Disputes about the settlement of terms for Crown use, rights of third parties and compensation for loss of profit may be referred by any party to the High Court or Patents County Court under section 252. One or more joint owners of design right may refer without the concurrence of the others, but the others must be joined as parties (without liability for costs unless they participate actively). Where a party seeks payment from a government department, the court is directed to have regard to any sums received by that party or his predecessor in title, directly or indirectly, from any government department in respect of the design. It must also have regard to whether he or his predecessor in title has, in the court's opinion, "without reasonable cause failed to comply with a request of the department for the use of the design on reasonable terms". (This must undercut the fiction normally adopted in compulsory licensing cases, and in assessing damages by reference to a reasonable royalty, that the parties are to be regarded as willing licensor and licensee bargaining at arms' length.) In the case of an exclusive licensee seeking a share in payment for Crown use, the court must take into account any financial contribution he has made to the development of the design or to the design right owner, other than royalties. The court also has power to order, where the identity of a design right owner is initially unknown, that no royalty or other sum shall be payable for Crown use until the owner appears and agrees terms or refers them to the court for determination (section 241(3)).

The Crown use provisions for unregistered designs received a good deal of **4.035** criticism in Parliament, and their extension to copyright works ancillary to designs (also provided for in the patents and registered designs legislation) contrasts with the position relating, *e.g.* to a privately-made map of remote territory which might be vital for military operations but for which the copyright owner could name his own price.

The Secretary of State has a general power under section 245, where it **4.036** appears to him to be necessary to comply with an international obligation or to secure or maintain reciprocal protection for U.K. designs, to make other rules providing that acts of specified descriptions do not infringe design right. An order under this section may make different provision for different descriptions of design or article.

COPYRIGHT

ASSIGNMENTS AND OTHER TRANSMISSIONS

The provisions governing dealings with copyright are similar to those **4.037** governing dealings with the unregistered design right, and the observations and warnings in 4.001–4.008 above are similarly applicable. It is section 90 of the 1988 Act which sets out the requirements for a valid assignment of the legal title to copyright, and section 91 which deals with assignments of copyright in works yet to be made, and section 176(1) permits a body corporate to assign (and to grant an exclusive licence) by affixing its seal, but these things may also be done merely by the signature of a duly authorised person. Transitional provisions covering pre-August 1, 1989 works and dealings therein before that date are to be found in Schedule 1, paragraphs 25–29. Particular care must be taken with works made and dealings effected before June 1, 1957, because of the "reversionary interest" under section 5(2) of the 1911 Act, which prevented a copyright owner depriving his heirs of their rights for more than 25 years after his death, and there was no provision for assignment of future copyrights before this was introduced by section 37 of the 1956 Act. Schedule 7 to the 1988 Act should be consulted for tax matters.

Again, the importance of ensuring that copyrights have been properly **4.038** assigned on the sale or takeover of a business needs to be emphasised, as do the points made elsewhere on getting in the legal title (or at least ensuring that it can be easily obtained) before litigation is begun.[27] Assignments of the legal title should include accrued rights of action, and notice of assignment of these rights should normally be given to a prospective defendant before an action is begun, if time permits. Clear agreements should always be made with outside designers and draughtsmen, advertising agencies, PR firms involved in the

---

[27] See Chap. 3.

design of catalogues, logos, letterheading, brochures and the like about who is to have the legal title, and where this is retained by the originators, the agreements should provide for them to join in any litigation, whether as non-participating parties or at the active plaintiff's expense. It should also be recalled that, although an equitable interest in a copyright may arise by operation of law (*e.g.* where a work is made for valuable consideration or the circumstances surrounding its making otherwise support the inference[28]), any assignment of such an equitable interest must be in writing.

4.039–
4.040 As section 90(2) permits partial assignment, and there are other circumstances in which different persons may be entitled to different "aspects" of copyright in a single work (for example, where the parts list in a catalogue had been compiled in-house but the layout, text and drawings were originated by an outside firm, or where a designer has assigned the right to reproduce the copyright work only for particular products), section 173 provides that the "copyright owner" is the person entitled to the relevant aspect in issue. And where copyright, or any aspect thereof, is owned by more than one person jointly, references in the Act to the copyright owner are to all the owners. This is particularly important in connection with licensing, where any otherwise infringing act needs the consent of the owners.

4.041 A provision relating only to copyright appears in section 93: where a will leaves someone an original document or other material thing recording or embodying a literary, dramatic, musical or artistic work, a sound recording or a film, unpublished at the testator's death, that bequest is to be taken as including the copyright in the work, unless a contrary intention is expressed elsewhere in the will or in a codicil to it. So someone who leaves all his unpublished manuscripts (whether in hard copy or on disk)—or indeed his holiday snaps or videos—to his sister, though with no expresss mention of copyright, but the residue of his estate to his son, will be taken to intend his sister to get the copyrights. But if he expressly includes all his copyrights in the residuary bequest to his son, this will override the inference otherwise to be drawn from the specific bequest of the manuscripts to his sister (and incidentally create friction between aunt and nephew). Transitional provisions for pre-Act works and bequests are to be found in Schedule 1, paragraph 30.

Moral rights

4.042 Moral rights cannot be assigned *inter vivos* (section 94). They can, however, under section 87, be waived. This may be done by instrument in writing signed by the person giving up the right, which may relate to a specific work or works of a specified description or to works generally, may relate to

---

[28] For an interesting summary of how far the law has recently gone in depriving originators of their copyrights in the interests of exploiters, and the suggestion that it has gone too far, see Gary Lea, "Expropriation or Business Necessity?" [1994] 10 E.I.P.R. 452.

existing or future works, and may be conditional or unconditional and may be expressed to be subject to revocation. If such a waiver is made in favour of the owner or prospective owner of the copyright in the works, it is presumed to extend to his licensees and successors in title unless a contrary intention is expressed. It will be appreciated that a moral right owner of small bargaining power will readily be prevailed upon to give up these so-called "inalienable" rights. As if this were not enough, section 87(4) provides that the general law of contract or estoppel shall continue to apply in relation to an "informal" waiver or other transaction. Moreover by section 95(4) any waiver or consent, formal or informal, binds the author's heirs. All this was heavily criticised by interested parties during passage of the Bill, because it means that careless or inexperienced people may be held to have given up their potentially very valuable moral rights through sheer inadvertence. It will bear particularly hardly on freelance designers; employed designers have no moral rights worth speaking of anyway. It should also be remembered that the right of paternity does not apply in relation to any act which would not infringe copyright in the artistic work underlying an industrial design by virtue of section 51 or 52.[29]

A few words should be said about the need to assert the section 77 right of paternity (right to be identified as author) before it can be enforced. Under section 78, this assertion may be made generally or in relation to any specified act or description of acts (a) on an assignment of copyright in the work, by including a statement of the assertion (when both the assignee and anyone claiming through him will be bound, with or without notice), or (b) by an instrument in writing signed by the author (when only a person "to whose notice the assertion is brought" will be bound). The author can also "assert" in relation to public exhibition of an artistic work under section 78(3), which was probably not intended to relate to industrial designs except in so far as they merited exhibition as such, but might do so since "exhibition" is not defined and might be stretched to cover exposure for sale. The author must either (a) secure that when he (or the first owner if a different person) parts with possession of the original or of a copy made by him or under his direction or control, he is identified on the original or copy or on a frame, mount or other thing to which it is attached (when anyone into whose hands that original or copy comes is bound, whether or not the identification is still present or visible—we are not told how the author is to prove that it is the original or that specific copy), or (b) include in any licence by which he or the first owner authorises the making of copies a signed statement by the licensor that he asserts his right to be identified in the event of public exhibition of a copy made under the licence (when the licensee and anyone else into whose hands a licensed copy comes, with or without notice, will be bound). This need for formalities seems contrary to the spirit of the Berne Convention, which covers moral rights under Article 6 *bis* but without the specific prohibition of formalities that appears in relation to economic rights under

4.043

---

[29] See sections 79(4)(f) and (g).

Article 5(2). It certainly creates an extra loophole through which an author may fall or be pushed.

4.044   Moral rights in works of joint authorship are regulated by section 88. Each joint author must make his own assertion under section 78; each may consent to derogatory treatment, but only on his own behalf; and a waiver by one does not affect the rights of any of the others.

4.045   On death, moral rights pass in accordance with any specific bequest. In the absence of such bequest, they pass to the person who inherits the corresponding copyright or, if that has been disposed of, to the personal representatives. If a corresponding copyright is split between various persons (*e.g.* as to term or type of right), and the moral right is not specifically disposed of, then it will be split in the same way. The exercise of moral rights which have become exercisable by more than one person is governed by section 95(3).

4.046   Transitional provisions in Schedule 1, paragraphs 22–24 apply moral rights to acts done, on or after August 1, 1989, to existing as well as new works except where the author had died before that date, but paragraph 23 contains exceptions where the author had assigned or licensed the copyright before that date or where copyright first vested in someone other than the author.

VOLUNTARY LICENCES

4.047   As with unregistered design right, there is no obligation for a copyright licence to be in writing, except where an exclusive licensee wishes to be able to sue infringers in his own name (section 102) or to restrain parallel import of his licensor's goods from anywhere outside the E.U. (section 27). Such an exclusive licence must, under section 92, be in writing and signed by or on behalf of the copyright owner. It must also authorise the licensee to exercise a right which would otherwise be exercisable only by the copyright owner. This means that a mere exclusive U.K. distributor of non-infringing copies, who does not need a copyright licence, because distribution of lawful copies is not a right exercisable only by the copyright owner[30] (whatever the contractual position may be), cannot sue infringers in his own name.[31] Under section 90(4), a copyright licence is binding on the licensor's successors in title except a *bona fide* purchaser for value without notice (actual or constructive) and his successors in title.

4.048   Any serious and long-term exploitation of a copyright work is likely to be by written licence, but the observations as to anti-competitive and Euro-offensive terms made in 4.011 above are applicable to copyright licences, whether or not in writing.[32]

---

[30] Except where he is putting *those* copies into circulation for the first time (section 18(1))–see Chap. 5.
[31] Unless he can sue for interference with his business by unlawful means, see Chap. 5.
[32] See *ITP v. E.C. Commission (Magill TV Guide intervening)* [1991] 4 C.M.L.R. 745.

Licences of right

Copyright is not subject to licences of right except in two cases: where it is being exercised in an abusive fashion, and during the last five years of the shortened 10-year copyright term allowed to unregistrable pre-August 1, 1989 designs.

4.049

The copyright equivalent of section 238 for unregistered designs and section 11A of the Registered Designs Act 1949 as amended (it is not exactly the same as either of them) is section 144. Following an adverse report by the Monopolies and Mergers Commission, the appropriate Minister has power to cancel or modify licence conditions restricting the licensee's use of the licensed work or the grant of other licences, or to order that licences of right be available where licences on reasonable terms are being refused. He is not supposed to do this unless he is "satisfied" that it does not contravene any international copyright convention. Article 9(2) of the Berne Convention prohibits national legislation for compulsory licensing which would conflict with a normal exploitation of the work and unreasonably prejudice the legitimate interests of the author. Words like "normal", "unreasonably" and "legitimate" would seem to offer the Minister a fairly free hand, though since the terms of any licence of right, including royalties, are to be settled by the Copyright Tribunal (subject to appeal to the High Court only on a point of law), it is difficult to see how he can judge their reasonableness at the time he exercises his powers. Copyright owners might wish to argue that legislation which indirectly permits their copyright to be expropriated for inadequate reward must contravene Article 9(2). But they are unlikely to succeed on judicial review, since the Minister has only to be "satisified"—a subjective test normally failed only where no reasonable Minister could possibly be satisfied in the circumstances—and it is difficult to see where else they could go, unless the European Court of Human Rights could assist.[33]

4.050

One of the objects of the 1988 Act was greatly to extend the scope of blanket licensing schemes covering a large number of works, and to encourage the establishment of right owners' organisations to administer these, under the supervision of the Copyright Tribunal. A list of the types of licence covered by the Act can be found in section 124; it includes licences to copy works, as well as the more traditional licences to perform works in public, and artistic works are covered. At present it is unlikely that such schemes would have much relevance to industrial design, but it is worth noting that schemes may be, or may have been, set up relating to the copying of abstracts of scientific or technical articles and the rental of computer software, both of which may be of significance for industrial concerns.

4.051

The other area where copyright licences of right are of importance, albeit short-lived, is in relation to "non-artistic" industrial designs made before

4.052

[33] There must be some doubt about the Berne Convention propriety of licences of right under the 1988 Act.

August 1, 1989, whose exclusion from copyright under section 51 is deferred for ten years from that date, subject to licences of right during the last five years of that term, or for such part of these five years during which copyright subsists. This means that licences of right have been available for such "old" designs since August 1, 1994, and if the copyright is anyway due to expire before July 31, 1999, it will do so and the licence of right period will be correspondingly less than five years. These transitional provisions are in Schedule 1, paragraph 19, which applies the unregistered design right sections 237–239, and also 247 and 248 (settlement of licence terms by Comptroller) and 249 and 250 (appeals and rules relating to Comptroller) to these copyrights.

4.053 The holder of any pre-August 1, 1989 copyright licence subsisting at August 1, 1994 may apply to the Comptroller to have its terms adjusted. He will of course lose any exclusivity and the benefits this gives him. He might ask that the adjusted terms continue to exclude the copyright owner himself from competition, since the latter cannot grant a licence of right to himself, but this might be thought not to fit in with the anti-monopolistic policy of the Act.

4.054 These copyright licences of right will relate only to acts which would be permitted by section 51 if the copyright work had been a design document or model made on or after August 1, 1989—making an article to the design or copying an article so made. They will not, for instance, allow the direct photocopying or tracing of production drawings, only reverse engineering of the article depicted.

4.055 Since paragraph 19(9) of Schedule 1 preserves the effect of any "rule of law preventing or restricting the enforcement of copyright in relation to a design" during the 10-year extension, licences of right will not be needed where the *British Leyland* spare parts exclusion would apply. No specific provision has been made about who is to decide this: the Comptroller has been given no jurisdiction similar to section 246 to enable him to decide disputes about enforceablility of copyright. Presumably a would-be competitor will have to take a gamble and wait to be sued, and if the court decides the exclusion does not apply, he can undertake to take a licence of right, under section 239 and avoid an injunction.

Crown use

4.056 Although, except as mentioned in connection with Crown use of unregistered and registered designs, there is no provision permitting the expropriation of copyright works for the purposes of the Crown, sections 45–50 of the 1988 Act specify certain "permitted uses" of copyright works for purposes of public administration.

4.057 Copyright is not infringed by anything done for the purposes of Parliamentary or judicial proceedings or the proceedings of a Royal Commission or statutory inquiry, or the reporting of any of these. Thus copies of engineering drawings or prototypes, or of catalogues or advertising matter, may be supplied for use in court or Parliamentary committee, or may be published as part of a law report or the report of a Royal Commission, without the copyright owner's consent. This would not necessarily affect the law of confidentiality, though it must be remembered that documents referred to in open court are likely to lose this protection.

Public records, and material open to public inspection pursuant to a **4.058** statutory requirement (such as matter on public registers, planning applications and related drawings, documents required to be filed at Companies House) may be copied for the purpose of facilitating such inspection or disseminating information about matters of general scientific, technical, commercial or economic interest, in each case by or with the authority of "the appropriate person"—the person maintaining the register or whose responsibility it is to make the material available to the public. These provisions may also by statutory instrument be extended to material made open to public inspection by specified international organisations and the like. Material communicated to the Crown with the copyright owner's consent in the course of public business may also be copied and published for any purpose which could reasonably have been anticipated by the copyright owner, provided it had not otherwise been published when communicated to the Crown. Finally, where the doing of any act is specifically authorised by Act of Parliament, whenever passed, then unless the Act provides otherwise, the doing of that act will not infringe.

CHARGES ON INTELLECTUAL PROPERTY BELONGING TO COMPANIES

A cautionary note: charges over intellectual property (including copyright **4.059** and registered and unregistered designs and any licence under or in respect of such rights) which forms part of the property of a company must, like other charges, be registered against the company by delivering particulars to the Registrar of Companies within 21 days of their creation, otherwise the security may be lost. Delivery of particulars is primarily the duty of the company, but it may be done by any person interested and the cost recouped from the company. Details may be found in sections 92–95 of the Companies Act 1989, inserting amended section into the Companies Act 1985.

REGISTERED DESIGNS

ASSIGNMENTS AND OTHER TRANSMISSIONS

Registered designs are personal property, and will pass as such on death or **4.060** insolvency. Under section 19(4) of the Registered Designs Act 1949, the person registered as proprietor has power to assign, grant licences under or otherwise deal with the design, subject to any conflicting rights (*e.g.* of mortgagees) noted on the Register. Although no method of assigning a registered design or rights therein is prescribed in the 1949 Act, either before or after the 1988 amendments, the provisions in the Act and Rules for recording dealings, and more general evidential considerations, make it manifestly sensible for assignments to be in writing and signed by or on behalf of the person to be bound. Where they contain terms binding the assignee, they should be signed by him as well. Agreements to assign will generally be specifically enforceable by order for execution of a formal assignment, but this can be troublesome and expensive, so all loose ends should be tied up and, as with unregistered designs, care should be taken that all joint proprietors have joined in an assignment and that it has been properly authorised. It will always be prudent when dealing with registered designs to search the Register to see who actually owns them: it is not unknown, for example, for an individual to be the registered proprietor even where the design is being exploited by a company,[34] so that an assignment by the company would be of no use—or at best, if the company had some equitable interest in the design, would pass only that interest, leaving the Register to be rectified. As usual, tax implications must not be overlooked.

Registration

4.061   Registration of assignments and other dealings is governed by section 19 of the 1949 Act and by rules 42–45 of the Registered Designs Rules 1989. Under section 19(1), any person becoming entitled by assignment, transmission or operation of law to a registered design or a share in a registered design, or becoming entitled as mortgagee, licensee or otherwise to any interest in a registered design, should apply to be registered as proprietor or co-proprietor or for entry of notice of his interest. He will be well advised to do so, since although there is no fine or other penalty for failure to register, in the absence of registration no document affecting title will be admitted in evidence in court proceedings, *e.g.* for infringement, without the leave of the court. An assignee of a registered design who has not registered his assignment will therefore run into difficulties in suing for infringement, since it is only the "registered proprietor" who is entitled to do this.[35] Further, without registration third parties will not have notice of his interest, and *bona fide* purchasers for value without notice will take free of it. Even purchasers with notice, or donees of an interest, who register their interests ahead of him will be able to embroil him in litigation before he can assert his rights.

[34] *Coffey's Registered Designs* [1982] F.S.R. 227.
[35] There is no provision in the 1949 Act parallel to sections 101 and 234 of the 1988 Act which expressly permit an exclusive licensee to sue for infringement without the concurrence of the right-owner. Exclusive licensees under registered designs should ensure that their licences require the registered proprietor to sue, at the licensee's expense if necessary; the licensee may join himself as a party.

Under section 19(2), application for registration of the transferee's interest **4.062** may also be made by the assignor, mortgagor, licensor, etc. Whoever does it, Designs rule 42 requires application to be made on Designs Form 12A (part of the Rules), providing details of the "transaction, event or document" conferring an interest. By rule 43, a certified copy of any document referred to must be filed with the form; for purposes of confidentiality it may be desirable to use a separate short form of assignment, etc., rather than submitting a document containing all the other terms of the transaction. A mortgagee or licensee ceasing to have an interest may apply on the same form for a note to be made that he no longer claims such an interest. If the Registrar is satisfied that title has been demonstrated (he will also require proof that any necessary stamp duty has been paid), he must make the appropriate Register entry.

The Registrar has a general dispensing power under Designs rule 49, **4.063** subject to the production of such evidence and the imposition of such terms as he thinks fit, to excuse a person from doing any act or thing or producing any document or evidence required under the Rules if he is satisfied that that person in unable to do so from any reasonable cause.

Although the benefit of an application to register may be assigned, **4.064** mortgaged and so on, no entry will be made until after registration has been granted, and since the certificate will issue in the name of the applicant, an assignee of the application must make sure that his interest is duly recorded afterwards. Any assignment of an application should therefore be expressed to cover the design itself, if and when registered, as well as the application.

Relationship with unregistered design right and copyright

Two new subsections were added to section 19 by the 1988 Act. By section **4.065** 19(3A), where design right subsists in a registered design (where an article which is the subject of the registration is depicted in a design document or model made on or after August 1, 1989), the Registrar is not to register a transaction relating to or interest in the design unless he is satisfied that the person entitled to that interest is also entitled to a corresponding interest in the design right. This may be inconvenient. Where the design has been commissioned, or has been made by an employee in the course of his employment, and the commissioner or employer is the design proprietor who is creating or assigning an interest, there should not often be a problem: section 224 of the 1988 Act presumes that an assignment of rights in the registered design also operates as an assignment of the unregistered right, where they are in the same hands, unless a contrary intention appears—if it does, the Registrar will be unable to proceed. But if a freelance designer chooses to retain (or omits to divest himself of) the unregistered right, while granting to a manufacturer the right to apply for registration of the design to an article (as he can under section 2(2) of the 1949 Act), so that the rights are not in the same hands, difficulties may arise. Section 224 refers only to an assignment of an existing registered design, not of an application. It is not clear how the Registrar is supposed to find out what has actually happened. Moreover, section 224 refers only to assignments, not other types of transaction.

4.066 Section 19(3B) provides that where unregistered design right subsists in a registered design and the proprietor of the registered design is also the unregistered design right owner, an assignment of the unregistered design right is to be taken to be also an assignment of the right in the registered design unless the contrary appears—the converse of section 224.

4.067 On the other hand, although copyright in any underlying drawing or work of artistic craftsmanship from which an article which is the subject of a registered design is made is not presumed to pass with an assignment of the registered design, by section 53 of the 1988 Act it is not infringed by anything done in good faith in reliance on an assignment or licence by the registered proprietor, even if he was improperly registered.[36] And by section 2(2) of the 1949 Act an assignment of copyright in a drawing or work of artistic craftsmanship would pass to the assignee the right to be treated as proprietor of a corresponding design for the article depicted or embodied therein.

4.068 The pottery scenario is gruesomely instructive. A foolish manufacturer buys for a new coffee service from separate freelance designers a flower pattern to be painted on the pieces (surface decoration, therefore copyright) and a moulded dragon design to form handles and spouts (since integral to the article's identity and utility, probably shape/configuration despite its decorativeness, and therefore unregistered design right), in each case obtaining only letters of consent to the registration of the designs as applied to the coffee service. He then sells the registrations to someone else. That person will be able to register his interest in the flowers because the Registrar is not required to trouble himself about the ownership of the copyright. But he will not be able to register his interest in the dragons because his assignor does not own the unregistered design right, having neglected to get it in.

LICENCES

Voluntary licences

4.069 Voluntary licences, whether bare, sole or exclusive, can readily be granted (section 19(4)). Exclusive licences are not defined, except in relation to Crown use in Schedule 1, paragraph 2(5), where the definition is similar to that for unregistered designs and copyright, but without the requirement of writing. There is no provision allowing an exclusive licensee to sue for infringement in his own right. Licences can and should be registered, for the

---

[36] See also Sched. 1 to the Copyright Act 1956.

reasons set out above. Their terms are subject to the same considerations as to compliance with U.K. and E.U. competition and free trade law as are mentioned in 4.011 above.

Compulsory licences

Compulsory licences are available, though very seldom sought, under section **4.070** 10 (and procedural provisions in the Designs Rules 1989). At any time after registration, any peson "interested" (presumably this means anyone who can show a genuine intention to work the design, not merely a busybody) may apply to the Registrar for a compulsory licence on showing that the design is not being industrially applied in the U.K. to an extent which is "reasonable" in the circumstances of the case. The Registrar "may" (subject to appeal to the Appeal Tribunal) make such order on the application as he thinks fit, and his order takes effect as if it were a deed executed by the registered proprietor and all other necessary parties.

The sole ground of application is non-application of the design in the U.K., **4.071** which could leave the way open for an application where the U.K. market is being supplied by importation, *inter alia*, from another E.U. Member State, a disgracefully non-communautaire state of affairs. However, section 10(3) decrees that the Registrar shall not make an order which would be at variance with any treaty, convention, arrangement or engagement applying to the U.K. and any convention (Paris Convention) country, which would seem to preclude any licence offensive under the Treaty of Rome.

Licences of right

Licences of right are not available under registered designs (apart from **4.072** Crown use) except in two instances. The new section 11A introduced provisions for countering the same abuses of the registered design monopoly as are caught by section 238 for unregistered designs (and section 144 for copyright). Where the Monopolies and Mergers Commission has reported to a Minister on a monopoly, merger or competition reference that certain situations, practices or courses of conduct involving registered designs or their licensing are against the public interest, the Minister may, having given public notice of the proposed application and considered any representations made to him by interested persons within 30 days, apply to the Registrar for relief. If the Registrar shares the Commission's view (he is not obliged to) that conditions in registered design licences restricting the licensee's use of the design or the proprietor's right to grant other licences, or a refusal by the proprietor to grant licences on reasonable terms, operate or may be expected to operate against the public interest, he may by order cancel or modify the conditions and/or make an entry in the Register signifying that licences of right are to be available. The terms of such licences are to be settled by him in default of agreement (with no fetters on his discretion), and are to be effective from the date of the application to him, which must be made by the prospective licensee. The Designs Rules 1989 contain procedural regulations for applications and evidence. Appeals from the Registrar's decisions under this section lie to the Registered Designs Appeal Tribunal.

4.073 Because of the longer term of registered designs and their monopoly nature, these powers may be more widely used than those relating to unregistered designs are likely to be. An obvious example would have been Ford's refusal to grant licences to spare parts manufacturers under their copyright and registered designs for body panels. Although new registrations of precisely this kind would now be precluded by the "must-match" exception, section 11A would apply to "old" designs. The power could also be invoked where, for example, an exclusive licence in circumstances where a product's appearance is all-important means that new suppliers cannot enter the market, because the proprietor is precluded from granting other licences (and must not work the design himself). There is, however, the additional hurdle of an application to the Registrar: the Minister cannot tamper with the Register or its contents himself.

4.074 The other licence of right situation arises under section 266 and affects only designs applied for after January 12, 1988 and before August 1, 1989 which would, if applied for after the latter date, have been rejected under the new "must-match" and "who-cares-what-it-looks-like?" exceptions. Such designs, as well as expiring no later than July 31, 1999, became subject to licences of right from August 1, 1989, *i.e.* in many cases from the moment of grant, with the usual provisions for settlement of terms by the Registrar in default of agreement and having regard to factors prescribed by the Secretary of State. Holders of existing licences may apply to the Registrar to have their terms adjusted.

4.075 With both types of licence of right, a defendant to an infringement suit may in accordance with section 11B escape an injunction and limit his damages by undertaking to take a licence of right.

CROWN USE

4.076 The Crown use provisions for registered designs are, under section 12 of the 1949 Act, to be found in the First Schedule to that Act, as now amended by section 271 of the 1988 Act in relation to any Crown use on or after August 1, 1989, even if terms for such use had been settled before that date (section 271(3)). It should be noted that under section 5 of the 1949 Act, the Registrar has every design application checked on behalf of the Ministry of Defence to see if it could be relevant for "defence purposes", and if it may be he can give directions restricting the publication or communication of information about it and by Designs Rule 68 the representations of it and any evidence of its aesthetic appeal will be excluded from public inspection. (What happens if the applicant puts his design on the market as soon as he has filed his application?) It is an offence under section 5(4) for a U.K. resident to file an overseas application for such a design without either getting written permission from the Registrar or making a U.K. application and waiting for six weeks to see if the Registrar invokes the secrecy procedure—although it is understood that this procedure is no longer applied in practice.

The scope of Crown use is not fully defined, but Schedule 1, paragraph 1(6)   **4.077** specifically includes the supply to the government of another country, pursuant to treaty obligations or other arrangements, of articles required for the defence of that country or of any other country whose government is party to treaty obligations or arrangements with the U.K. government for defence matters. It also includes the supply to the United Nations or its Member States of articles required by any armed forces for the implementation of U.N. resolutions. Defence of the U.K. or any of its overseas dependencies would obviously be a relevant purpose, and by analogy with the Patents Act (and now the provisions relating to Crown use of unregistered designs), health service purposes would doubtless also be included.

Government departments or those authorised by them (including existing   **4.078** licensees) may make use of designs without infringement, and dispose of surplus articles without rendering the purchasers liable for infringement. Compensation (normally a royalty) is payable to the proprietor once the design is registered. Presumably if it is rejected, the unregistered design provisions will apply. He will be notified of the use unless security otherwise requires. If and for so long as it does, he will lack the details to make a claim.

The rights of third parties are safeguarded in a way similar to that set out in   **4.079** section 242 for unregistered designs, and again the reproduction or publication of any model or document is not to be deemed an infringement of copyright or design right.

The new paragraph 2A gives compensation for loss of profit to a registered   **4.080** proprietor or exclusive licensee who, because of the Crown use appropriation, does not secure a normal government contract. This is subject to the same conditions as the corresponding section 243 for unregistered designs. Disputes relating to such compensation, and also to the settlement of terms and third party rights, may under paragraph 3 be referred by either party to the Patents Court (or Patents County Court), which may at any time refer the proceedings, or any question or issue of fact, to a special or official referee or arbitrator. The government department may put the validity of the design in issue and, if the registered proprietor is a party to the reference, apply for its cancellation. As under section 252, the court must take into acount any benefit or compensation in relation to a design which a party or his predecessor in title may be entitled to receive, directly or indirectly, from any government department. Unlike section 252, there is no provision for penalising a disobliging right owner who had refused a reasonable request for use of the design, perhaps because the Crown gets its hands on registered designs under section 5 without having to ask nicely for them.

4.081   Paragraph 4, like section 244, contains a list of additional purposes to which a registered design may be put by the Crown during periods of emergency.

5. Infringement and Remedies

UNREGISTERED DESIGN RIGHT

As with copyright, but not registered designs and other monopoly rights, **5.001** there are two types of design right infringement, "primary" and "secondary". Primary infringement is making infringing articles, or authorising others to make them, without the design right owner's consent. Secondary infringement is importing, selling and all the other "dealing" activities in relation to infringing articles which by the Act are prohibited without the design right owner's consent. The distinction is very important for prospective plaintiffs, because while for primary infringement the plaintiff need only prove that the act was done,[1] for secondary infringement he must prove that the prospective defendant knew or had reason to believe when doing the act that he was dealing with infringing articles. The rationale behind the primary/secondary infringement distinction is no doubt that while people may not know that what they have bought from someone else has been copied, they do know when they themselves have copied. This is often a fairy tale. Quite apart from the position of a sub-contract manufacturer who may be asked to make something he has no reason to suppose has been copied but who will still be a primary infringer, many past industrial copyright infringers who thought they were following the habits of a lifetime and improving on a known design have been startled to find themselves condemned for something they associated only with covert peerings at a schoolmate's exercise book. Nonetheless, the distinction is well-entrenched.

Because of the plaintiff's need to prove a secondary infringer knew or had **5.002** reason to believe his wares were infringing copies (if the plaintiff fails to prove this, he will lose his case[2]), care must be taken in suing traders. If your prospective defendant is selling from his market stall power tools with handles of a shape made famous by a multinational company (and in its familiar colours), but bearing strange pictogram markings and offered at £5 each, you are probably safe in assuming he has reason to believe they are not genuine, and can sue him[3] without qualms. But if a reputable High Street store is selling garments which appear in many respects identical to one of

---

[1] Subject to a very limited defence of innocence, to be proved by the defendant.
[2] *Arrowin Ltd v. Trimguard (U.K.) Ltd* [1984] R.P.C. 581; *Infabrics Ltd v. Jaytex Shirt Co. Ltd* [1982] A.C. 1. But see as to obtaining a permanent injunction as opposed to damages for past infringements *Linpac Mouldings Ltd v. Eagleton Direct Export Ltd* [1994] F.S.R. 545.
[3] And do other disagreeable things to him, see 5.052 below.

your designs, you might be wiser to write them a carefully-worded[4] letter notifying them that you claim design right and supplying them with a copy or photograph of your design document or prototype garment and details of the date and designer, and then allow a reasonable interval (perhaps 14 days) to elapse while they investigate your claim before you issue a writ. You will then have provided them with "reason to believe" they are dealing in infringing articles, even if they did not know it before.[5]

PRIMARY INFRINGEMENT

5.003   Under section 226(1) the design right owner has the exclusive right "to reproduce the design for commercial purposes by making articles to that design or by making a design document recording the design for the purpose of enabling such articles to be made". By subsection (3), the right is infringed by a person who without the licence of the design right owner does, or authorises another to do, anything which falls within that exclusive right. Making the article would cover making a manufacturing prototype. A design document, according to section 263(1) which is in the same terms as 51(3), is "any record of a design, whether in the form of a drawing, a written description, a photograph, data stored in a computer or otherwise". There seems no reason why "otherwise" should not include a recording of a spoken description or a film or video showing the product,[6] both of which may record the design for the purpose of "enabling" infringing articles to be made. It does not seem that taking a photograph or making a sketch of the protected article (or indeed of an infringing article copied from it) merely for the purpose of including it in a catalogue or other advertising material would constitute infringement under this section, since this would enable the infringing article to be sold, rather than made—unless the broad economic view is taken that the prospect of selling an article "enables" it to be made in that if it could not be sold there would be no point in making it.[7]

5.004   Several other points in section 226 call for comment. The exclusive right relates only to reproduction for commercial purposes. By section 263(3) acts done in relation to an article for commercial purposes are those done with a view to the article being sold or hired in the course of a business. So copying a monkey wrench to adorn one's wall at home would not be infringement nor, more importantly, would copying it for *use* in one's business, provided one did not sell or hire it.

---

[4] Additional care is needed because of the possibility of a "threats" action, see 5.071 below.
[5] Note, however, that section 230 gives a plaintiff an action for delivery up of infringing articles against an entirely innocent possessor, see 5.051 and 5.060 below.
[6] See Chap. 3 above.
[7] Oddly, because of section 51(1), it seems this would not be an infringement of copyright either, because it would be "copying an article made to the design", even though it involves indirectly reproducing the work, *e.g.* engineering drawing, in which copyright subsists.

It is important to note that design right is also infringed by doing or   **5.005**
authorising the doing of either of the acts of primary infringement set out in
section 226(1) in relation to a kit of parts for something like a car or a boat
intended for assembly by someone else into the protected article. A home
enthusiast buying a kit for home assembly would not infringe unless his
purposes were commercial, but the maker of the kit certainly would. This
provision is hidden far away in section 260, which also makes clear that it
does not affect the question whether design right subsists in the design of the
kit components as opposed to that of the assembled article. Provided the
components do not fall foul of any of the exceptions in section 213 and are
not commonplace, they too can enjoy design right.

Reproduction

"Reproduction" of a design by making an article or a design document is said   **5.006**
by section 226(2) to mean *copying* the design "so as to produce articles
exactly or substantially to that design". The express reference to copying
serves to underline that there can be no design right infringement where the
design has been independently created. No doubt, as with copyright, a
plaintiff will have to show, in addition to product similarity, that the
defendant had a chance, consciously or unconsciously, to copy[8]—because the
product is on the market, or was shown at an exhibition, or might have been
seen at a customer's, or the plaintiff has published drawings of it in a
catalogue, or the defendant is a former employee. It will then be for the
defendant to prove independent creation, or that he was merely "inspired" by
the design but did not actually copy it. Recent industrial copyright cases[9] have
demonstrated a more realistic approach to questions like these, accepting that
designers are likely to look closely at competitors' products, and may even
adopt similar features or solve the same problem in similar ways, provided
there are sound reasons for doing so. The courts are apparently now more
ready to distinguish a genuine design exercise which has in the end, after
independent thought and, perhaps, experimentation with unsuccessful
alternatives, come up with something similar, from a straight rip-off. What is
often a giveaway and will help a plaintiff prove copying is the reproduction of
an *unimportant* part which the defendant has not bothered to change.

However, design right, unlike copyright, has its far-reaching built-in   **5.007**
exclusions—must-fit, must-match, method or principle of construction—as
well as a higher ("not commonplace") standard of originality, and there will
probably be little room for arguments based on general "design constraints"
to counter allegations of copying where a design has survived all these tests.

---

[8] The two facts necessary to get a copyright infringement action off the ground and shift the
burden of disproving copying on to the defendant: *L. B. (Plastics) Ltd v. Swish Products Ltd*
[1979] R.P.C. 551.
[9] See, *e.g. Billhöfer Maschinenfabrik v. Dixon & Co. Ltd* [1990] F.S.R. 105; *Johnstone Safety
Ltd v. Peter Cook (International) plc* [1990] F.S.R. 161.

5.008   Copying a design "so as to produce articles exactly or substantially to the design" is an infringement test which differs in its phraseology both from the copyright test (copying the whole or a substantial part of the copyright work) and the registered design test (the application of a design the same as or not substantially different from the registered design). "Substantial" in copyright has always been applied as a test of quality as much as quantity, so that the taking of small but significant features[10] may infringe. In this respect, U.K. practice appears to differ from some of its European counterparts, where courts seem more impressed with catalogues of differences between one design and another, and to demand a close correspondence of most features before infringement will be found. The design right definition, "exactly or substantially" the same, suggests a rather more quantitative test.

5.009   However, both copyright and registered designs (unless in the case of the latter the statement of novelty[11] is limited to particular features) are concerned with the appearance of an article as a whole, even if it is in itself only a part of something else. Design right can, under section 213(2), subsist in "any aspect of the shape or configuration ... of the whole or part of an article", so it will be open to the courts to look at only a part of an article with which they are presented and find that the whole of that part has been reproduced even if the rest of the article has not been, or is not protected because it comes within one of the exclusions, or is "commonplace" and so not original. Competitors will need to be very careful in determining which parts of a design they are free to copy and which must be redesigned. Equally they will not want to make the mistake of deciding that because each individual part may be incapable of attracting design right, the arrangement as a whole cannot have it.

5.010   On January 23, 1992 the first, and so far the only, design right infringement case known to have come to trial, *C. & H. Engineering v. F. Klucznik & Son Ltd*,[12] was decided by Aldous J. As may be recalled, it concerned a pig fender, a moveable pen placed outside a pig-sty which is low enough to allow a sow to step over it but high enough to keep piglets inside. The counterclaiming defendant claimed design right in a drawing of a fender, for which the basic measurements had been provided by the customer. Pig fenders, in both metal and wood, were well-known at the date of the drawing, but the defendant's version had a 2″ metal pipe along the top to act as a roll-bar and prevent the sow catching her teats as she stepped over. The plaintiff was found to have copied this feature from the defendant, at the insistence of its customer, but its fender differed in other respects, notably in having flared sides to allow for stacking.

5.011   Aldous J. held that "original" in section 213(1) meant the same as in copyright law, *i.e.* that the drawing had to be the independent work of the

[10] Like Lord Beaverbrook's fins on the end of aircraft wings, see 2.243 above.
[11] See 2.112 above.
[12] [1992] F.S.R. 421. See now *Hourahine v. Everdell* 1995 L.P.D. 18.50 and *Volumatic Ltd v Myriad Technologies Ltd* 1995 I.P.D. 18.79.

designer, not copied from anything else. He held that section 213(4), providing that a design is not original if it is already commonplace in the design field in question, introduced "a consideration akin to novelty". Since pig fenders, in the sense of devices with three sides about 16″ high with means to connect them to the pig-sty, were already known, he found that the essence of the defendant's design was the incorporation of the 2″ pipe into a commonplace pig fender. Although superficially this might seem to conflict with Parliament's intention[13] that it is the design, not the article, whose commonplaceness must be judged, as a practical test it must be the right one where the part of an article concerned is such a simple item as a 2″ pipe. It would be ludicrous to suggest that since 2″ pipes as such are commonplace their incorporation into some other article can never give rise to design right. The "design" here clearly consisted of the fender with the pipe incorporated, and was therefore really a design of an article rather than the design of part of that article—although apparently it was not argued, for reasons connected with the facts of the case, that the roll-bar could be a "part" of the fender with its own design right.

On infringement, Aldous J. held that the design right test was different **5.012** from the copyright test. Copyright infringement requires that the work, or a substantial part of the work, be copied. Under section 226, "there will only be infringement if the design is copied so as to produce articles exactly or substantially to the design". Copying once having been established, the test of similarity is an objective one and must be judged "through the eyes of the person to whom the design is directed", in this case a pig farmer who, the judge had "no doubt" would buy pig fenders "taking into account price and design". It is through this person's eyes that the differences and similarities between the article as depicted in the design document and the allegedly infringing copy must be gauged. Applying this test, Aldous J. found that the plaintiff's design was not substantially the same as the defendant's. Metal pig fenders, he said, have an overall similarity due to the function they have to perform, but an interested buyer would appreciate that although the designs had the metal roll bar in common, there were eye-catching and functionally significant differences in other respects, particularly the flare which made the plaintiff's fenders stackable; "the interested man looking at the Plaintiff's and the Defendant's pig fenders would consider the two designs to be different, but with a similar design feature—namely, the bar around the top".

This decision makes clear that, at least in the view of Aldous J., **5.013** unregistered design right has more in common with registered designs than with copyright. It inclines towards the registered design test of infringement in adopting the customer's eye test—indeed it goes farther than the usual (though not invariable) registered design paractice in insisting that it is the design document, rather than the design right owner's product, with which the allegedly infringing copy must be compared, even though in most cases it

---

[13] See 2.257 above.

will be the product rather than the design document that has been copied. It impliedly disregards those features of a design that are dictated by function, though this may have been justified in the present case by the finding that these were "commonplace". It makes passing reference to eye-appeal. In particular, it may impliedly discard the copyright infringement "quality" test of what constitutes a "substantial part" of a design, in this case the copied metal roll-bar, although this had been the one feature on which the copier's customer had insisted. But as already mentioned, it was not argued that the roll-bar could constitute a part of an article (or aspect of a design) in which a separate right could subsist under section 213(2), so the judgment deals throughout with the pig fender as a whole, again as if it were a registered design. Had the point been argued, the outcome as to substantiality might have been different.

5.014   In its concentration on the eye of the target customer, the decision does lend support to the suggestion made earlier that in identifying "the design field in question" to assess commonplaceness the likely marketplace for the article will be taken into account. Indeed, as a matter of common sense it is difficult to see how it could be otherwise.

5.015   Reproduction of an unregistered design may be direct or indirect, and it is immaterial whether any intervening acts themselves infringe the design right (section 226(4)). This would cover, for example, cases where a written description becomes an industry standard, complying with which involves copying of the original design,[14] or where a sub-contractor previously licensed to make articles from drawings with which he was supplied fails to return the drawings on termination of his licence and uses them to make unlicensed copies.

5.016   What would be the position if a manufacturer obligingly printed a copy of his design drawing or written specification in an instruction manual, so that it could be copied directly? Copying it for the purpose of making the article would not be an infringement of copyright, because of section 51. It would, however, be an infringement of design right unless it could be argued that the manufacturer had, by printing the design, licensed others to reproduce it. This would depend on the purpose for which it was printed. This might be to facilitate repair or maintenance, in which case it is unlikely any licence would be implied other than for this limited purpose. Part drawings and assembly drawings issued with a kit of parts would probably be taken only as allowing the buyer of such a kit to assemble it himself, not to make other kits for sale. In *Roberts v. Candiware*,[15] it was doubted (on application for an interlocutory injunction) that the sale of knitting patterns would be held at trial to license their use in making garments for sale on a commercial scale.

---

[14] *Plix Products v. Frank M. Winstone (Merchants) Ltd* [1986] F.S.R. 608.
[15] [1980] F.S.R. 352.

The concept of "authorising" another to infringe is also taken from **5.017** copyright, where it has caused problems of interpretation.[16] In the design field, questions of authorisation most commonly arise where a defendant does not himself manufacture the articles in suit but sub-contracts their manufacture (and often the making of detailed production drawings— "design documents") to others. He is not then himself a primary infringer by manufacturing, but it is well settled that he has thereby authorised another to infringe.[17] Someone who orally describes a design to another, with a view to that person making articles to the design, is also authorising—and if he permits his oral description to be recorded or written down, he has no doubt authorised the making of a design document too.

Semiconductor Topographies

A rather different régime applies to semiconductor topographies. The Design **5.018** Right (Semiconductor Topographies) Regulations 1989,[18] paragraph 8 substitutes its own version of section 226(1), removing the reference to "commercial purposes" but adding subsection (1A) under which subsection (1) does not apply to "the reproduction of a design privately for non-commercial aims" (presumably, therefore, reproducing a topography for use in one's own business would not be exempt, as it seems to be for other unregistered designs), nor to reproduction "for the purpose of analysing or evaluating the design or analysing, evaluating or teaching the concepts, processes, systems or techniques embodied in it".

SECONDARY INFRINGEMENT

Infringing articles

Secondary infringement consists of doing a variety of acts (set out in section **5.019** 227) in relation to "infringing articles" where the defendant knows or has reason to believe that the articles are infringing articles. These are defined in section 228. An article is an infringing article "if its making to that design was an infringement of design right in the design". Under subsection (3) it is also an infringing article if it has been or is proposed to be imported into the U.K.

---

[16] *CBS v. Ames* [1981] 2 W.L.R. 973 (no authorisation of infringement where record shop proprietor operated record loan service and also sold blank tapes on to which borrowed records could be unlawfully copied); *CBS v. Amstrad* [1986] R.P.C. 567 (no authorisation where Amstrad sold to retailers fast tape-to-tape copying equipment, coupled with TV advertising suggesting this could be used to copy your favourite cassettes). In neither case was the connection between defendant and infringing member of public close enough, and infringement by the latter was in any case not *bound* to occur—the equipment could be used lawfully.

[17] *e.g. Standen Engineering v. A. Spalding & Sons* [1984] F.S.R. 554.

[18] S.I. 1989 No. 1100.

and its making to that design in the U.K. would have infringed design right or would have been a breach of an exclusive licence relating to the design. This reference to an exclusive licence will permit a U.K. exclusive licensee of a foreign design right owner (other than one from within the E.U.) to prevent parallel imports of his licensor's own legitimate goods by use of design right rather than only by an action for breach of contract. In *CBS United Kingdom Ltd v. Charmdale Record Distributors Ltd*,[19] the local subsidiary of CBS Inc. was held unable to rely on his exclusive copyright licence from the parent company to press records in the U.K. against a parallel importer of CBS Inc.'s records. The reasoning was that these would not have infringed copyright if made here, since they were in fact made by the copyright owner, the local company's exclusive licence being merely a matter of contract between it and its parent.

5.020   The government made clear that it intended to remove the effect of this decision, for both copyright and design right, in so far as it was free to do so. It had no such freedom in relation to goods of E.U. origin. The European Court of Justice's doctrines of free movement of goods and exhaustion of rights[20] prevent an intellectual property owner from exercising his national rights to restrain parallel import from another Member State of goods already marketed there or elsewhere in the E.U. by him or with his consent, and this state of affairs is recognised in section 228(5).

5.021   It is not clear what is meant to be covered by the reference to an article "proposed to be imported" as well as to one actually imported. Does the mere making, by prospective importer or supplier, of a proposal to import turn a non-actionable article into an infringing one? If so, what is the point? As will be seen, no infringement occurs until actual import (with the requisite knowledge or belief) takes place. Is it to facilitate seizure by H.M. Customs? If so, where?—unless actual "import" only takes place once goods are landed rather than when they enter territorial waters or airspace, and the wording is intended to permit seizure before landing. *Quia timet* proceedings for an injunction, based on apprehension of, rather than an actual, infringing act, would be available without specific provision.

5.022   There is a rebuttable presumption in section 228(4) that where an article is made to a design in which design right subsists or has subsisted at any time, the article was made during the time the right subsisted; it is for the alleged infringer to prove it did not.

5.023   Finally, under subsection (6) (except for semiconductor topographies[21]) "infringing article" does not include a design document, even though its making may have infringed design right under section 226(1)(b) and section

---

[19] [1980] F.S.R. 279.
[20] See, *e.g. Centrafarm v. Sterling Drug Inc* [1974] 2 C.M.L.R. 480; *Centrafarm v. Winthrop* [1974] 2 C.M.L.R. 480; *Deutsche Grammophon v. Metro SB Grossmarkte* [1971] C.M.L.R. 631. See below for related provisions for semiconductor topographies.
[21] S.I. 1989 No. 1100, para. 8(3).

226(3) because it was made for the purpose of enabling an infringing article to be made. Since, as appears below, secondary infringement can only take place in relation to infringing articles, it seems to follow that there can be no secondary infringement of design right in design documents. It would not be actionable to import production drawings made elsewhere, even though they would have been primary infringements if made in the U.K., nor to sell or hire them out. This exclusion might have been motivated by the fact that an unauthorised copy of a design document would normally infringe copyright in the original document, even if copied only indirectly by copying the article made from it,[22] and would therefore be actionable as such without the need for making design documents "infringing articles" under design right. But section 51(1) prevents this, because it provides that it is not an infringement of copyright in a design document (other than one "for" an artistic work) to copy an article made to the design recorded in it: as long as the competitor's design document was copied from the original product and not directly from the design document, there will be no infringement of copyright. Only in the relatively rare cases where the competitor's design document was copied directly from the original (by an ex-employee or ex-subcontractor, for example, or by someone hacking into the design right owner's computer) will the competitor's document be an "infringing copy" under the section 27 copyright definition.

Acts of secondary infringement

Several different acts are capable of constituting secondary infringement under section 227: import or possession for commercial purposes; and selling, letting for hire and offering or exposing for sale or hire, all in the course of a business. The "commercial purposes" qualification, as with primary infringement, means that both import and possession must be with a view to the articles being sold or hired in the course of a business so, unlike secondary infringement of copyright under section 22 and section 23(a) (and the original White Paper proposals[23]), there is no design right infringement if an infringing article is imported or possessed simply for use in one's own business. Again unlike copyright, mere exhibition or disribution of infringing articles is not secondary infringement: there must be sale or hire or offer or exposure for these purposes. Presumably the delightfully old-fashioned term "exposes for sale" is meant to cover inclusion in a catalogue or advertisement, as well as setting out one's stall or dressing one's windows, since none of these activities is in classic contract law an offer for sale or hire but only an "invitation to treat".

5.024

Like primary infringement, secondary infringement can also take place in relation to a kit of parts intended for assembly into an infringing article,

5.025

[22] s.17.
[23] Cmnd. 9712, para. 3.31.

provided there is the requisite knowledge or reason for belief on the part of the secondary infringer that he is dealing in infringing articles (section 260).

Semiconductor Topographies

5.026　Again there are different provisions for semiconductor topographies. Paragraph 8(2) of the 1989 Regulations disapplies the whole of section 227 if the article in question has previously been sold or hired within the U.K. by or with the licence of the owner of design right in its topography, or in the territory of any other E.U. Member State, or Gibraltar, by or with the consent of the person for the time being entitled to import it into or sell or hire it within that territory.

"Knows or has reason to believe"

5.027　As already pointed out, none of the activities set out in section 227 will amount to secondary infringement as such unless the alleged infringer knows or has reason to believe that he is dealing with an infringing article, and it is the plaintiff who must prove this. (There is an odd exception, introduced by section 230, whereby a plaintiff can obtain delivery up of infringing articles against an entirely innocent possessor,[24] but this is not secondary infringement.) Secondary infringement of copyright under the 1956 Act required the defendant to "know" that he was dealing with infringing copies.[25] The standard of proof has deliberately been lowered, both for copyright and design right; it will suffice for the plaintiff to show that the defendant was in possession of knowledge which would have led a reasonable person in his position to realise that he was dealing with an infringing article, without having to enter into that particular defendant's state of mind. In fact there is unlikely to be much difference in practice, since plaintiffs have usually only been able to prove facts as to defendants' sources of knowledge[26] from which they have asked the court to infer that the requisite knowledge existed; and courts have been quite ready to do so. But the lower standard would be useful in the odd case where a credible but credulous defendant might otherwise convince the court that whatever grounds he might objectively have had for being in possession of the necessary knowledge, it had in fact not penetrated his consciousness.

5.028　Dealings with non-infringing articles which have been legitimately put on the market, however tiresome or damaging to the design right owner such dealings may be, do not infringe. Examples would be the circulation of legitimate goods outside a regular distribution network, sales of second-hand goods, and repeated hiring-out of goods such as heavy-duty lawnmowers and

---

[24] See 5.051 and 5.060 below.
[25] See, *e.g. Hoover plc v. George Hulme (Sto) Ltd* [1982] F.S.R. 565.
[26] See 5.002 above for an example.

strimmers. There is no equivalent to the "rental right" newly introduced to ensure that owners of copyright in records, videos and software get a share of the profits derived from hiring-out.[27]

DEFENCES

Chapter III of Part III of the Act is headed "Exceptions to Rights of Design Owners". Most of its sections cover matters dealt with elsewhere,[28] and under section 245 the Secretary of State has power, by regulation approved by both Houses of Parliament, to prescribe other exceptions to design right infringement, which may make different provision for different descriptions of design or article, if such exceptions are needed to comply with any international obligation or to secure or maintain reciprocal protection for British designs in other countries. As yet he has not felt moved to exercise this power.

5.029

The relationship with copyright: section 236

An exception that requires to be dealt with here is section 236, which maintains the scheme for separating design right from copyright and is the obverse of section 51, though much less significant in practice, since it will only operate where a plaintiff, believing he has no copyright to bless himself with, is suing for design right infringement. It provides that "where copyright subsists in a work which consists of or includes a design in which design right subsists, it is not an infringement of design right in the design to do anything which is an infringement of copyright in that work". The major effect is that when one of those artistic (or literary) works which record or embody "a design for anything other than an artistic work or a typeface" (section 51) is copied in any way other than by making or copying the articles it records or embodies, it is not design right but copyright that must be relied on. Any attempt to sue for design right infringement where a defendant has made his design document by tracing or photocopying the plaintiff's engineering drawing (graphic artistic work) or taking illicit copies of his pipe-bending program, can be met by a defence based on section 236.

5.030

The section thus seems to override sections 226(1)(b) and 226(3) where what would otherwise be a design right-infringing design document (recording the infringing design for the purpose of enabling infringing articles to be made) has come into being by direct copying of the plaintiff's copyright work rather than by reverse engineering from his product. It is not always going to be easy for a plaintiff to know which has actually happened, so he will be wise to plead both in the alternative. This is not particularly

5.031

---

[27] s.18(2). Distribution outside a network or selling second-hand goods as new may of course amount to passing off.
[28] See Chap. 4 and 5.036 below.

convenient, especially where the copyright in the artistic work may be outstanding in someone other than the design right owner. It makes sense not to complicate things by involving design right where a drawing is, for example, copied for inclusion in a textbook, or for sale as a print to hang on the wall. And since design right lasts at the most for 15 years, the drawing may have a long life during which design right would be irrelevant anyway. But likewise it would make sense to try and keep copyright out of things where the drawing is copied, even directly, purely as a stage in the manufacture of infringing *articles* (when it is functioning as a "design document" which is copied to make the infringer's design document), which is what section 226(1)(b) is clearly aimed at. But why then not allow it to be sued on in design right for as long as design right subsists in the article for which it records or embodies the design? It could be exceedingly tiresome for a design right owner who does not own the copyright in his design document, perhaps because it was made by a commissioned outside designer, to find himself partially defeated because the defendant happens to have copied the design document directly so that design right cannot be relied on for this aspect of the case.

5.032   It is difficult to imagine when a plaintiff who does have copyright (because his product is at least arguably an artistic work or his artistic work is not a design document but a painting[29]) would want to sue in design right. It is also not clear why a defendant sued in design right would rush to invoke section 236 as a defence, given that in terms of infringement, duration and licensing, design right is easier on defendants than copyright. It could be used to ambush a plaintiff who has pleaded carelessly, for example by forgetting about surface decoration being a matter for copyright rather than design right, or who is embarrassed by the absence of a necessary party because the copyright has not been gathered in.[30] This might be enjoyable, but the defect will usually be remediable by amendment or joinder of extra parties, and the ambush is unlikely to gain judicial sympathy if left until a late stage. The section is more likely to be productive of time- and cost-consuming strike-out applications where a plaintiff has asserted design right in garden gnomes and a defendant argues that these are sculptures and therefore not caught by section 51 and therefore there is an enforceable copyright which must be sued on. Or where there is doubt about whether surface features in relief are "decoration".[31] Or a motor manufacturer might sue for design right infringement a defendant who has copied a clay model for a car body (a "sculpture" in its own right even though a "model" for a motor car which is not itself an artistic work), not by making cars but by making quarter-size plaster models of the sculpture for sale as garden ornaments. There could then be delightful interlocutory arguments about whether the defendant had "made an article to the design" or had "reproduced the artistic work".

---

[29] In which case he would probably not have design right at all, because there would be no "design"—see 2.191 above.
[30] See Chap. 3 above.
[31] If they are, there will be no design right anyway: s.213(3)(c).

Since drawings or photographs of infringing articles (or of the original   **5.033**
articles) for use in catalogues and other advertising material are probably not
"design documents" within section 226(1)(b) because they do not "enable"
infringing articles to be made, no question of design infringement will arise.
But if an attempt is made to sue on them, section 236 could not be invoked,
provided the illustrations are taken from the articles themselves and not from
the design right owner's catalogue, etc., because they would not infringe
copyright either—under section 51(1) they will be copies of articles made to
the design. An otherwise successful design right plaintiff will not therefore be
able to complain about the defendant's publicity material as well as his
products, unless there has been direct copying from the plaintiff's own
material. Where the precise facts are unknown, both causes of action should
initially be pleaded.

Semiconductor topographies and reverse engineering

Semiconductor topographies have their own special defence to infringement.   **5.034**
Under paragraph 8(4) of the Regulations, it is not an infringement of design
right in a topography to:

(a) create another original semiconductor topography as a result of an
    analysis or evaluation of the first topography or of the concepts,
    processes, systems or techniques embodied in it, or
(b) to reproduce that other topography.

This is intended, in line with E.U. Directive 87/54 which itself echoes the U.S.
Semiconductor Chip Protection Act 1984, to permit reverse engineering, in
the sense of a close study of a competitor's product and, perhaps, its use as the
basis for an improved product. It appears not yet to have been tested in court,
although the provision has been part of U.K. law since 1987, when the first
Semiconductor Products (Protection of Topography) Regulations[32] were
introduced. The second topography must be "original" (in the design right
sense of "not commonplace" in the field of topography), and it would be
interesting to see whether this provision in practice produced results much
different from those recently reached in some industrial copyright cases,
where close study of a competitor's product did not lead to a finding of
copying where an independent design effort was shown to have been made.

Implied licence?

Under copyright, as under patent law, the owner of an article protected by   **5.035**
copyright is entitled to infringe by repairing it, or having it repaired, with
identical parts, so long as the "repair" does not amount to the making of an

---

[32] S.I. 1987 No. 1497.

entire new article.[33] This is the "implied licence" which the copyright owner is deemed to have given the original purchaser (and any sub-purchaser) in the absence of any express reservation on the sale of the article. Its justification is said to be "business efficacy", the inconvenience of having to have an article repaired only by the manufacturer. Before *British Leyland*,[34] attempts were made, without success, to extend the doctrine to cover the manufacture of parts ahead of need, so that when the owner legitimately required a repair, the parts would be waiting for him. The implied licence lost a lot of its significance following the *British Leyland* decision, because the "spare parts exception" covered many of the circumstances in which it would otherwise have been invoked. But it seems reasonable to suppose that it would apply as a defence to design right infringement in relation to the overall design of an article. More problematic is the case where design right is claimed in only a part of an article, as is permitted by section 213(2), and the whole of that part needs replacement. It is likely to be worth pleading as a defence, until there are decisions to the contrary, where its absence would lead to the consumer inconvenience and potential monopoly problems which prevailed with the House of Lords in *British Leyland*. For reasons discussed earlier,[35] it is not thought that the *British Leyland* defence itself is likely to apply to design right.

"*Catnic* defence"?

5.036   A variation on the theme of implied licence in copyright cases was (or is) the argument that a copyright owner "abandons" his copyright in design drawings by applying for a patent incorporating those drawings or schematic versions of them.[36] The feeling was that it was wrong to allow the patent monopoly to be prolonged for the full copyright period, the essence of a patent being the dedication of the invention to the public once the monopoly expired. In the patent and copyright case of *Catnic Components Ltd v. Hill & Smith Ltd*[37] counsel conceded that this could be so, and Whitford J., *obiter*, favoured the view. It was thought to be mistaken, because *Werner Motors Ltd v. A. W. Gamage Ltd*[38] had confirmed that a plaintiff could enjoy more than one intellectual property right at the same time (patent and registered design), but it was still raised from time to time, by Whitford J. most recently in *Rose Plastics GmbH v. Beckett*.[39] As originally drafted, the 1988 Act contained a "*Catnic*" defence, but it was deleted on the ground that it might

---

[33] See 2.268 above. See also *Gardner & Sons Ltd v. Paul Sykes Organisation Ltd* [1981] F.S.R. 281 (whole diesel engines reconditioned—implied licence arguable defence).
[34] [1986] A.C. 577.
[35] See 2.267 above.
[36] This argument could not be raised in relation to a registered design because of the express permitting of dual protection by the Design Copyright Act 1968.
[37] [1978] F.S.R. 405.
[38] (1904) 21 R.P.C. 621.
[39] [1989] F.S.R. 13.

discourage small inventors from patenting.[40] But since a patent specification ("written description"), as well as any related drawing, falls within the definition of design document, it is unlikely the doctrine, even if it has any remaining life in relation to copyright infringement, would be applicable to design right.

E.C. law

Attempts will certainly be made to plead breaches of E.C. competition law by the plaintiff as a defence in design right infringement actions, either during the first five years (as an alternative to using the cumbersome Monopolies and Mergers Commission route), or to avoid the need for taking a licence of right. Article 85 of the Treaty of Rome (prohibiting agreements between undertakings, decisions by associations of undertakings and concerted practices which may affect trade between Member States and have as their object or effect the prevention, restriction or distortion of competition) and Article 86 (prohibiting abuse of a dominant position), have regularly, but on the whole with little success (including before the European Court of Justice), been invoked by intellectual property defendants.[41] The difficulty is usually to demonstrate a nexus between the alleged breaches of competition law and the infringement. A plaintiff does not disqualify himself from relief for infringement of his statutory rights merely by being a shabby fellow in unrelated ways. However, in *Pitney Bowes Inc. v. Francotyp-Postalia GmbH*[42] Hoffmann J. refused to strike out certain allegations made by way of defence and counterclaim that the plaintiff, having a dominant position, was abusing it by charging unfairly high prices, discriminating against smaller customers by charging them higher prices without objective justification, and discriminating against the home market by exporting at lower prices. More recently in *Chiron Corporation v. Murex Diagnostics Ltd (No. 2)*[43] Aldous J. stuck out some Euro-allegations based on Article 86 because of the lack of effect on trade between Member States. His decision was upheld by the Court of Appeal, Staughton L.J. making some sour observations about the tiresomeness of Euro-defences in intellectual property actions and the desirability of complaining to the Commission instead.

5.037

---

[40] *Hansard*, Vol. 494, col. 133.
[41] *e.g. ICI Ltd v. Berk Pharmaceuticals Ltd* [1981] F.S.R. 1; *British Leyland v. Armstrong Patents Co. Ltd* [1986] R.P.C. 279 (C.A.); *Volvo AB v. Erik Veng (U.K.) Ltd* [1989] 4 C.M.L.R. 122; *Ransburg-Gema AG v. Electrostatic Plant Systems Ltd* [1990] F.S.R. 287.
[42] [1990] 3 C.M.L.R. 466.
[43] [1992] 3 C.M.L.R. 813, [1994] F.S.R. 187 (C.A.).

Territorial questions

5.038   It is likely, but not incontrovertible, that only design right infringements committed in the U.K., which under section 257 includes territorial waters and structures or vessels on the U.K. sector of the continental shelf such as oil rigs and support ships, are actionable here (other than on a *quia timet* basis as apprehended infringements). This appears to be the position in relation to infringements of copyright, but whereas section 16 of the Act, in listing the "restricted acts" which only a copyright owner or his licensee may do, speaks of the exclusive right to do these acts "in the U.K.", section 226 contains no such territorial limitation. However, intellectual property rights are generally regarded as territorially limited to the state which confers them,[44] and under section 255, the design right sections of the Act extend only to England and Wales, Scotland and Northern Ireland, with provision for extension by statutory instrument to the Channel Islands, the Isle of Man and any colony.

5.039   Nonetheless, it is possible for an overseas defendant to be found to have performed infringing acts in this country. In *Wilden Pump v. Fusfeld*[45] Whitford J. held, *obiter*, that a letter sent from Germany amounting to an authorisation of a copyright infringement to be carried out in the U.K. could be actionable as an authorisation committed here. This decision was based on the rules determining the place where a contract entered into by post is made. It was also influenced by *Diamond v. Bank of London & Montreal Ltd*,[46] which held that a misrepresentation takes effect in the place where it is received and acted on. In *Morton-Norwich Products Inc. v. Intercen Ltd*[47] the defendant was found to have infringed a U.K. patent by importation because it had consigned the infringing goods from the Netherlands on c.i.f. terms, which meant that the property passed here on receipt of the bills of lading. The 1968 Brussels Convention on Jurisdiction, incorporated into U.K. law by the Civil Jurisdiction and Judgments Act 1982 and binding all E.U. Member States, also provides that actions in "tort, delict and quasi-delict" may be brought against foreign nationals in the state where the damage occurred as well as in the states of the defendant's domicile or where the tortious act was committed. This topic is too complex to pursue here, but the possibilities of litigating in the U.K. (if desired) even where there are strong foreign elements should not be overlooked.

[44] See, *e.g. Tyburn Productions Ltd v. Doyle* [1990] R.P.C. 185.
[45] (1985–87) 8 I.P.R. 250.
[46] [1979] 1 Q.B. 333.
[47] [1978] R.P.C. 501.

REMEDIES

Parties

Under section 229(1) a design right infringement is actionable by the design 5.040 right owner (designer, commissioner, employer, person who arranged for the creation of the design in the case of a computer-generated work, first marketer or assignee of any of these). Where a design is owned jointly (section 259), it is probably permissible, as it is with copyright, for one owner to take proceedings without the presence or concurrence of the others, though he may be able to recover only the damage suffered by himself. If he elects to take an account of the defendant's profits, he would presumably either get only his own share, or he would have to account to his co-owners for their shares. Where there is a subsisting exclusive licence (under section 225(1) a licence in writing signed by or on behalf of the design right owner authorising the licensee, to the exclusion of everyone else, including the design right owner, to exercise what would otherwise be the design owner's exclusive right to make articles according to the design or a design document for making such articles), the design right owner must before trial (unless the court otherwise orders) join the exclusive licensee, either as co-plaintiff, or as a nominal defendant who will not be liable for any costs unless he takes part in the proceedings (section 235).

An exclusive licensee may start proceedings (and obtain interlocutory 5.041 relief) in his own name (section 234), but must likewise before trial join the design right owner either as co-plaintiff or as nominal defendant. It is important to note that this provision applies only to exclusive licensees as defined in section 225: neither oral exclusive licensees nor sole licensees (those whose licences exclude everyone except the design right owner) can take advantage of it. Nor can mere distributors, who do not manufacture, but only market legitimate articles, and need no licence from the design right owner to do this. (This of course does not refer to "first marketers"[48] who have their own design right.)

Exclusive distributors might, however, be able to take advantage of the tort 5.042 of interference with their business by unlawful means, resurrected by the Court of Appeal in *Lonrho plc v. Fayed*.[49] That case was part of the saga of Lonrho's attempts to upset the Fayed brothers' successful bid for Harrods. Lonrho complained that the Fayeds, by fraudulently misrepresenting their commercial standing and worth to the Department of Trade and Industry, had been permitted to bid for the store, while Lonhro was still prevented from doing so by an earlier undertaking it had given. Lonrho's case was that this fraud perpetrated on the DTI constituted unlawful means by which Lonhro's

---

[48] See 3.039 above.
[49] [1989] 2 All E.R. 65.

business had been interfered with. The Fayeds argued that for the cause of action to succeed, Lonhro would have to prove that the Fayeds' predominant purpose in misleading the DTI was to damage Lonhro, and sought to strike out the action. The Court of Appeal refused to do so, saying that it would be enough for Lonrho to show that the Fayeds' actions were "directed against" or "intended to harm" it. There was an appeal to the House of Lords on a different aspect of the case, but their Lordships did not dissent from the Court of Appeal's view on wrongful interference.

5.043   The Court of Appeal stressed that in refusing to strike out they were not finding Lonrho's allegations proved, only that they were arguable. But similar reasoning could, where the facts warrant it, support an action by an exclusive distributor against an infringer. The infringement as against the design right owner constitutes the "lawful means", and provided the distributor can show that the infringer knew of him and his position (*e.g.* because his exclusive distributorship is made plain from publicity material) he may persuade the court that the infringer's activities were "directed against" or "intended to harm" him. He may not. The court may decide that even though damaging the distributor need not be the infringer's predominant purpose, something more than foreseeability of, or recklessness as to, such damage would be needed. But the possibility of an action along these lines would be a useful weapon for distributors, who may suffer serious loss from infringement. In at least one case since *Lonrho*,[50] a Deputy Judge declined to strike out a claim for wrongful interference by the U.K. exclusive distributor of a Swedish industrial design copyright owner—though different considerations might have applied if the right owner had been an E.U. company.

5.044   It is quite common in industrial design cases, mainly where the defendant is a small private company, to join individual directors or others closely concerned in the management of the company as defendants in their own right, on the basis that they have themselves "personally directed and procured" (or some similar formulation) the infringing acts.[51] Proper particulars of such allegations must be given, and the persons sued must have been sufficiently involved in what has been done to be liable individually even if the company had not existed. It is not enough simply to point to the fact that these people are directors or major shareholders. Joining individuals can be useful as not only does this increase the pressure on the defence, but the individuals will often have more than the company in the way of realisable assets out of which any judgment can be satisfied. Parent or associated companies may also be joined if their involvement is close enough to make them joint tortfeasors. Where action pursuant to a common design can be alleged, there may also be a cause of action in conspiracy.[52]

[50] *EKS v. Hanson*, July 20, 1989, T. Blanco White Q.C. See for a recent affirmation of the *Lonrho* doctrine, again in the context of a refusal to strike out a statement of claim, *Millar v. Bassey* [1994] E.M.L.R. 44.
[51] For recent statements of the principles governing such joinder see *C. Evans v. Spritebrand Ltd* [1985] F.S.R. 267; *PLG Research Ltd v. Ardon International Ltd* [1992] F.S.R. 59.
[52] *Lonrho plc v. Fayed* [1992] 1 A.C. 448.

Forum

High Court actions should be brought in the Chancery Division, or District   5.045
Registries for areas enjoying the services of a Chancery judge; but the Patents
County Court in London has jurisdiction over unregistered as well as
registered designs,[53] and has a procedure which may be more expeditious.
Time-limits are less readily extended. Discovery of documents is not
automatic, and will only be allowed in suitable cases. Particulars of pleadings
are not normally ordered, the idea being to encourage parties to state their
case in full at the earliest possible moment rather than having it prised out of
them bit by bit, with consequent delay and expense. Much emphasis is placed
on the "preliminary consideration", a pre-trial review where the parties are
encouraged (and coerced if necessary) to crystallise all the issues of fact and
law which will have to be decided at trial. The High Court summons for
directions is supposed to serve a similar purpose, but rarely does. Cases
brought in one forum may be transferred to the other at the discretion of the
transferring court, and there have been decisions in patent cases which have
laid down judicial guidelines for the exercise of this discretion.[54] These
include the willingness or otherwise of the parties to dispense with counsel
and/or solicitors in the Patents County Court where patent agents and
solicitors have rights of audience; the size and financial position of the parties
and the comparative costs of proceeding in one forum or the other, the PCC
being designed with small and medium sized enterprises particularly in mind;
the comparative speeds with which the matter might come to trial; the likely
need for extensive discovery, and other procedural advantages and disadvan-
tages; and the stage the proceedings have already reached and the consequent
risk of duplicating pleadings and steps already taken.

Disputes about the subsistence or term of design right, or the identity of the   5.046
first owner, may be referred to the Comptroller-General under section 246
for a binding decision, subject to appeal to the court. The Comptroller, if he
wishes, may refer a matter to the court himself. He has jurisdiction to decide
any incidental question of fact or law arising in the course of a reference, but it
is unlikely this would include any serious questions relating to infringement.
No doubt with a view to encouraging parties to make use of this jurisdiction,
section 246(2) provides that no other court or tribunal may decide any of the
three matters concerned except on a reference or appeal from the Comptroller, or as incidental issues in infringement or other proceedings, or in
proceedings brought with the agreement of the parties or the Comptroller's
leave. Given this last possibility, and the existence of a right of appeal, it does
not seem likely that many litigants will want to use this jurisdiction to add a
further layer of litigation.

---

[53] Established by section 287(1) of the 1988 Act and the Patents County Court (Designation and
Jurisdiction) Order 1990, S.I. 1990 No. 1496. See also County Court Rules 1981, Order 48A.
[54] See, *e.g. Memminger-IRO GmbH v. Trip-Lite Ltd* [1992] R.P.C. 210; *Mannesmann Kienzle
GmbH v. Microsystem Design Ltd* [1992] R.P.C. 569; *Composite Gutters Ltd v. Pre-Formed
Components Ltd* [1993] F.S.R. 305.

Injunctions

5.047   The remedies available in both High Court and Patents County Court are an injunction (interlocutory or final), damages or an account of profits (both with interest), orders for delivery up or disposal of infringing articles, and costs. Declarations of infringement or non-infringement may also be sought. Interlocutory (interim) injunctions may be granted *ex parte* (without notice to the other party) as an emergency measure, if circumstances warrant it—for example if infringing articles are being displayed or offered for sale at an exhibition, or to restrain the imminent launch of a new product. Applications with no notice at all to the other side are now rather frowned on unless the emergency is dire or the defendant likely to destroy evidence; the practice now usually adopted is the "opposed *ex parte*" where the defendant is warned of the application shortly before it is made to enable him to instruct counsel to attend and argue against the grant or form of an injunction on the materials available.

5.048   Except where a defendant gives in, the matter is then usually stood over for an *inter partes* hearing, with a timetable laid down for the service of the affidavit evidence on which injunction applications are heard. The same occurs if the application is launched giving the usual two clear days' notice; a temporary injunction may be granted pending the hearing, if this is shown to be necessary. Injunctions are granted or refused on the usual principles—the plaintiff must show an arguable case and persuade the court that the "balance of convenience" (or "balance of risk of doing an injustice") favours grant rather than refusal of an injunction pending trial.[55] Relative damage to the parties if an injunction is granted or refused, ability to pay damages (or an offer to pay a proportion of turnover into a joint account pending trial), elements of unquantifiable damage which cannot be compensated by money, preservation of the status quo and, as a last resort, the relative strengths of the parties' cases as they appear from items of uncontested evidence are all taken into account. Orders may also be made at this stage for disclosure of the names of the defendant's suppliers and customers, interim preservation of property or evidence, inspection of manufacturing processes or of particular documents and the like.

5.049   Instead of the court granting an injunction, the defendant may give undertakings to the court. These are often regarded by litigants as being face-saving, but they are enforceable in the same way as injunctions (with minor differences as to service of the court order), namely by a motion for contempt of court in the event of breach. This is a disagreeable procedure which may result in imprisonment for the disobedient party, or sequestration of assets, but is more commonly in intellectual property cases punished by a fine. Proof of the breaches must be to the criminal standard of "beyond

---

[55] See *American Cyanamid Co. v. Ethicon Ltd* [1975] A.C. 396; *Cayne v. Global Natural Resources Ltd* [1984] 1 All E.R. 225.

reasonable doubt", rather than the civil standard of balance of probabilities, but the rules of evidence are less rigorous than in criminal proceedings.[56]

It is a condition of obtaining all orders for interlocutory relief where defendants who ultimately win the action may suffer financial loss, perhaps as a result of being kept out of the market pending trial, that plaintiffs give a "cross-undertaking in damages" to the court, making them liable, if they fail to substantiate their case at trial, to compensate the defendant. These cross-undertakings may (though this is not common) have to be fortified by the provision of security in the form of a payment into court or a bond.   **5.050**

Where licences of right are available, section 239 provides that no injunction may be granted if the defendant undertakes to take a licence on such terms as may be agreed or, in default of agreement, settled by the Comptroller-General of Patents, Designs and Trade Marks. Such an under-taking may be given at any stage of the proceedings before a final order is made, and there is no need to admit liability. Further, no injunction can be granted in cases of "innocent" secondary infringement, as discussed in 5.058 below.   **5.051**

As an alternative to granting an injunction the court may order a speedy trial, with acceleration under strict time-limits of all the normal interlocutory procedures—exchange of pleadings, mutual disclosure and inspection of *all* relevant documents (not merely those which favour each party's case), exchange of experts' reports and, nowadays, written statements of all witnesses. If the plaintiff considers the defendant to have no viable defence, he may apply for summary judgment,[57] when it will be for the defendant to show that he has an arguable defence and should have leave to bring it forward. And by section 230, it seems that plaintiffs would now be able to start proceedings limited to delivery up of infringing articles against possessors of these (such as retailers) who may not know or believe that they are infringing articles, and therefore are not themselves infringers, and may obtain *ex parte* interim orders for delivery up of the (allegedly) infringing articles pending trial.[58]   **5.052**

More drastic *Anton Piller* and *Mareva* injunctions, providing respectively for search of the defendant's premises and seizure of infringing articles and related documents, and for freezing of the defendant's assets, may also be granted if justified[59]—normally this will be done on *ex parte* application in camera at the beginning of the action, if there is a likelihood that the defendant will destroy or remove evidence to try to conceal his assets. The *Anton Piller* order is *not* a form of civil search warrant: there is no power to enter premises if the defendant refuses to admit the searchers. It is, however, a   **5.053**

---

[56] See Rules of the Supreme Court, Order 52.
[57] See Rules of the Supreme Court, Order 14 and 14A.
[58] This was the interpretation given to the almost identically-worded s.99 in the copyright case of *Lagenes Ltd v. It's At (U.K.) Ltd* [1992] F.S.R. 492.
[59] See Rules of the Supreme Court, Ord. 29, r. 1.

221

contempt of court for the defendant to do this, once he has been given a chance to take legal advice within a reasonable time. There is a risk in these emergency procedures where the defendants are secondary infringers and have not been formally put on notice, but normally if the evidence is strong enough to justify seeking this sort of relief, the risk that the defendant will turn out not to have had the requisite knowledge or reasons for belief will not be great.

5.054   The costs of *Anton Piller* orders have recently been greatly increased by new guidelines laid down in *Universal Thermosensors Ltd v. Hibben*[60] and latter incorporated in a Practice Direction laying down detailed rules and revised forms of order.[61] Following a number of cases in which plaintiff's solicitors had been heavy-handed in the exercise of search and seize powers[62] (unlike many European jurisdictions, these orders are executed by the plaintiff's advisers, not by a court official), plaintiffs must now have these orders served by an independent "supervising solicitor", who must present to the court a report of what took place. There are strict procedures for dealing with evidence or documents found in the course of a search. This is highly laudable for the protection of defendants, but will bear very hard on small and medium-sized plaintiffs. It will normally be necessary for the plaintiff's usual solicitors to attend as well, since they will be familiar with the evidence and documents to be searched for and the supervising solicitor will not. This will double the costs, and plaintiffs for whom expense is a major consideration will have to think very carefully before embarking on such a course, and may have to be content simply with an order for interim delivery up (familiarly known as a "doorstep" order) without the means of checking whether the defendant actually complies with it.

5.055   Final injunctions will normally be granted at trial to successful plaintiffs, but the remedy is discretionary, and where the right is near the end of its life or in other special circumstances, it may be refused, or an award made of damages in lieu. Final injunctions are enforceable by contempt proceedings in the same way as interlocutory injunctions.

Damages

5.056   Damages, once ordered, are normally dealt with in separate proceedings known as an "inquiry" which must be pursued after the trial on liability. This is standard Chancery procedure, but is time-consuming and costly, and inquiries frequently settle rather than fight. The measure of damages is usually the plaintiff's loss of profit on infringing sales where the parties are direct competitors, or they may be calculated on a notional royalty basis. A

---

[60] [1992] F.S.R. 361.
[61] July 28, 1994; [1994] R.P.C. 617.
[62] e.g. *CBS v. Robinson* [1986] F.S.R. 387; *Manor Electronics Ltd v. Dickson* [1988] R.P.C. 618; *VDU Installations Ltd v. Integrated Computer Systems and Cybernetics Ltd* [1989] F.S.R. 378.

mixture of the two is possible. Where design right is successfully asserted in only part of an article, it is to be assumed that some apportionment will be made. In addition, "having regard to all the circumstances and in particular to the flagrancy of the infringement and any benefit accruing to the defendant by reason of the infringement" the court may award "such additional damages as the justice of the case may require" (section 229(3)). This is nice but vague. Awards under similar provisions in copyright law have tended not to be particularly high.[63] Exemplary damages at common law may also theoretically be available,[64] but are unlikely to be awarded given the express provision for additional damages.

"Innocence"

Where a defendant can show that at the time of a primary infringement he did   **5.057**
not know and had no reason to believe that design right subsisted in the design in suit, he will escape liability for damages (but only for damages). There may be some scope for this defence in the early years of design right, when there may be uncertainty as to the date of the design in suit, and also perhaps in the second five years, if there are numerous manufacturers operating under licences of right so that a defendant might reasonably suppose that the design was in the public domain. He will, however, have to rebut the presumption in section 228(4) that, if design right has subsisted at any time, the infringing article was made at a time when it did subsist. And mere uncertainty, however genuine, as to whether a design was original, or whether one of the exceptions such as "must-fit" applied, may not amount to having "no reason" to believe that design right subsisted. A defendant who is in doubt about any of these matters may, once challenged (but not before, because the jurisdiction can only be invoked by a party to a "dispute") refer the matter to the comptroller for a ruling under section 246.

Where a defendant to a claim for secondary infringement proves that he or   **5.058**
his predecessor in title[65] acquired the infringing article not knowing and having no reason to believe that it was an infringing article, "the only remedy available against him in respect of the infringement is damages not exceeding a reasonable royalty in respect of the acts complained of" (section 233(2)). The scope of this section is not clear. It can only have any meaning once the defendant has been fixed with or shown to have had knowledge or reason to believe that he has been dealing with infringing articles, because until then he is not an infringer at all. Does it apply only to stocks already in the defendant's possession when he becomes an infringer, so that he can safely

---

[63] *e.g. Ravenscroft v. Herbert* [1980] R.P.C. 193; *Nichols Advanced Vehicle Services v. Rees* [1988] R.P.C. 71.

[64] See *Rookes v. Barnard* [1964] A.C. 1129; *Broome v. Cassell* [1972] A.C. 1027.

[65] Presumably this cannot be taken literally: would a defendant who at all times himself knew the articles infringed escape liability simply by showing that his supplier acquired them innocently?

sell these off knowing he will only have to pay a reasonable royalty, but would be liable in the ordinary way for any further consignments he ordered? (This is presumably what is intended.) Or, since his supplier's state of mind is expressly brought in, will he be entitled to continue buying infringing goods from that supplier, so long as the latter retains his innocence (or any innocently-acquired stocks), if it is still worth his while to sell them even after paying a royalty? The section does not define either "the infringement" or "the acts complained of". Will applications for interlocutory injunctions be successfully fought off where the defendant says he is going to prove "innocence" under this subsection in relation to his original stocks, provided he can satisfy the court he will be able to pay the royalty on sales pending trial? This section may not be welcome to plaintiffs in *e.g.* the garment trade, who will be unable, at least in regard to a defendant's existing stocks, to deploy balance of convenience arguments about the damage to their exclusivity. In practice, no doubt, a defendant proposing to rely on this defence will be ordered immediately to disclose details of his supplier so that the latter's innocence can be shattered, and also to provide information about the amounts and dates of acquisition of his stocks.

Account of profits

5.059   As an alternative to damages, a plaintiff may opt at the end of the trial for an account of profits. Here the defendant, again in separate proceedings taking place after the trial on liability, and usually even more expensive and time-consuming, is ordered to identify and hand over to the plaintiff all the profits he has made by virtue of the infringement, rather than all the profits the plaintiff has lost. This alternative may be chosen where, for example, the defendant has beaten the plaintiff on to the market, or is known to have had a higher mark-up because his manufacturing or selling costs have been less as a result of pirating the plaintiff's R & D or taking advantage of his established market.[66]

Exclusive licence in force

5.060   Where there is a subsisting exclusive licence of the design right, so that the owner and the licensee have concurrent rights of action, section 235 requires the court in assessing damages to take into account the terms of the licence (*e.g.* providing for any agreed apportionment of damages recovered) and any pecuniary remedy already awarded or available to either party in respect of the infringement. Thus the owner may recover the royalties he has lost

---

[66] For recent cases on accounts of profits, see *Potton Ltd v. Yorkclose Ltd* [1990] F.S.R. 11 (an architectural copyright case); *Dart Industries Inc. v. Decor Corporation Pty Ltd* [1994] F.S.R. 567 (an Australian patent case). To help in electing which remedy to use, a plaintiff may obtain an order that the defendant furnish an audited schedule of sales and stock: *Island Recods Ltd v. Tring International plc, The Times*, April 28, 1995, a copyright case.

through the licensee's lost sales, but the licensee will then recover his loss exclusive of the element of royalty, to prevent double recovery against the defendant. No account of profits may be ordered if an award of damages, or an acount of profits, has already been ordered against the other party to the licence, and if an account is ordered, the court must apportion the profits between owner and licensee as it considers just, subject to any agreement between them.

Delivery up

Delivery up of infringing articles may be sought (except where licences of right are available and the defendant undertakes to take one), and not only against the infringing defendant; anyone having infringing articles in his possession custody or control for commercial purposes (sale or hire in the course of a business, so warehousemen or carriers would be excluded) may be ordered to deliver them up, whether or not he knows they are infringing articles (section 230(1)(a)). The equivalent provision where copyright infringement is concerned (section 99) has been held[67] to confer a separate cause of action against the possessor of such goods even where, because he does not have the requisite knowledge or belief, he is not an infringer. This represents a change from the position under the 1956 Act, where a plaintiff could not get delivery up against the defendant's customers unless he went through the procedure of putting them on notice and making them secondary infringers in their own right.   **5.061**

Section 230 further provides that "anything specifically designed or adapted for making articles to a particular design" may be ordered to be delivered up, where the person having such a thing in his possession, custody or control knows or has reason to believe that it has been or is to be used for making an infringing article. This is aimed at moulds, dies, plates, special tooling and the like.   **5.062**

No delivery up order may be made more than six years from the date the article or thing was made, unless the design owner was during all or part of that time under a disability (*e.g.* of unsound mind) or prevented by fraud or concealment from discovering the facts entitling him to an order (section 230(3) and (4)). Nor may an order be made unless the court makes, or it appears to it there are grounds for making, an order for forfeiture or destruction under section 231 (section 230(2)). The person to whom delivery up is made (the plaintiff or such other person as the court may direct, commonly one of the parties' solicitors) must, where no forfeiture or destruction order is made at the time, as with interim delivery up, retain the articles pending such an order. Under section 235 there are provisions governing delivery up orders where there is an exclusive licence of the design right in force.   **5.063**

[67] *Lagenes Ltd v. It's At (U.K.) Ltd* [1992] F.S.R. 492.

Order for disposal

5.064   Section 231 empowers the court to make, or decline to make, a final order for disposal of infringing articles or things for making them, which have been delivered up under section 230 (or, presumably, given the reference to "seizure" in subsection (5), seized under an *Anton Piller* order). It may order that the items be forfeited to the design right owner, or be destroyed or otherwise dealt with as it thinks fit; or it may decide to make no order at all, in which case the person in whose possession, custody or control the item was before it was delivered up or seized will get it back. The court must in every case consider whether financial compensation or an injunction would not provide adequate security for the plaintiff, so as to obviate the need for depriving the defendant of the goods altogether, for example if he could dismantle them and use the components for something else which would not infringe. It is to be hoped that the courts will pay due regard to the interests of innocent parties whose goods have been seized under the new provision in section 230. There are requirements for giving notice to any other persons having an interest in the goods (including anyone having rights in relation to copyright and counterfeit goods), who may appear in the proceedings (whether served with notice or not) or appeal against any order made (whether or not he appeared in the proceedings). Where there is more than one person interested, the court is to adjudicate between them in such manner as it thinks just, and may direct that the goods be sold or otherwise dealt with and the proceeds divided between the interested parties.

5.065   Under section 232, an ordinary County Court may deal with applications for delivery up (including those by an exclusive licensee under section 235(5)) and disposal, where the value of the items in question does not exceed the County Court financial limit.

COSTS

5.066   The winning party will almost invariably be awarded his costs, since although costs are in the court's discretion, this is exercised on well-established principles. There is authority in copyright and trade mark cases[68] that an intellectual property plaintiff is entitled to an injunction in open court recognising the infringement of his right, and to the costs of getting this, even where a defendant offered undertakings and all other relief sought before the writ was issued. Costs of interlocutory applications are normally dealt with at the time they are made, and may be awarded to one or other party depending on the merits of the application and irrespective of the outcome of the trial itself, although in most cases they will not be payable until the end of the action. If the parties cannot agree on a costs figure, the winning party's costs

---

[68] *Savory (E. W.) v. World of Golf Ltd* [1914] 2 Ch. 566; *Colgate Palmolive Ltd v. Markwell Finance Ltd* [1990] R.P.C. 197.

will be "taxed" by a court official who scrutinises them (both parties having the chance to attend and argue) and decides whether any should be disallowed for various reasons. How much is actually recovered depends on the basis on which taxation is ordered by the judge: normally the "standard" basis which gives the winning party about two-thirds of his costs, but in certain cases, such as successful contempt of court motions, it will be the "indemnity" basis, under which he recovers most of what he has to pay his lawyers.

It is also possible for an award of costs to be made against a non-party to the action in suitable circumstances.[69]   **5.067**

Despite the authorities mentioned in the previous paragraph,[70] the bulk of   **5.068** intellectual property actions settle before trial, and with a view to encouraging this there is a growing use of what are loosely termed Calderbank letters,[71] now recognised in the Rules of the Supreme Court.[72] There has long been a device in actions for purely money claims called "payment into court", whereby a defendant pays into court a sum calculated to cover the damages a plaintiff is likely to get, plus interest. If the plaintiff accepts the sum, he is entitled to his costs against the defendant to the date of payment in and the action is at an end. However, if he gambles on getting more by taking the case to trial, but recovers only the same amount or less (the fact of payment in is not made known to the trial judge), he will have to pay the defendant's costs from the date of payment in. This salutary procedure is not suitable in intellectual property cases (except inquiries as to damages or accounts, or taxation of costs) because injunctive and other relief is normally sought. But a Calderbank letter marked "without prejudice save as to costs" can be written at any stage, setting out the defendant's settlement proposals, and if the plaintiff refuses these, goes to trail, but gets less than was proposed (*e.g.* if a narrower injunction than that sought is granted, or no order for disposal is made), then the trial judge will be made aware of the offer and will take it into account in deciding who is to pay the costs. Care must be taken in drafting a Calderbank offer, and it must be said that so far defendants have not been particularly successful with them in intellectual property cases[73]; but the possibility should always be borne in mind.

The incidence of VAT on money received in settlement of intellectual   **5.069** property proceedings was mentioned in 4.008 above, and should also be borne in mind when negotiating.

Defendants who are warned of a possible action for infringement but   **5.070** believe they may be able to attack the subsistence of design right may take the

---

[69] See R.S.C., Ord. 62 and *Symphony Group plc v. Hodgson* [1994] Q.B. 179.
[70] See n. 68 above.
[71] Named after the family law case in which the practice was recognised.
[72] R.S.C., Ord. 22, r. 14.
[73] *McDonald's Hamburgers Ltd v. Burgerking (U.K.) Ltd* [1987] F.S.R. 112; *Colgate Palmolive Ltd v. Markwell Finance Ltd* [1990] R.P.C. 197; *C. & H. Engineering v. F. Klucznik & Sons Ltd* [1992] F.S.R. 667.

initiative by applying to the Comptroller for a ruling under section 246. The applicant will have the benefit of opening, and the costs may be lower. The decision may be appealed, but in a borderline case where the alleged right owner is not too certain of his ground or is short of funds, a quick burst before the Comptroller might discourage him from further skirmishing.

THREATS

5.071 Both the Patents Act 1977 (section 70) and the Registered Designs Act 1949 (section 26) contain sections intended to safeguard other traders against unjustified allegations of infringement. These may be written or oral, and they may be made to rival traders themselves or to their customers. The latter can be particularly damaging. Customers are understandably unwilling to be "mixed up" in infringement proceedings, even if only as witnesses, and they may cease dealing with the aggrieved trader for fear of supplies of goods, or maintenance services for their own customers, drying up as the result of an injunction. Where such allegations are completely groundless and made simply with intent to injure a rival, there may be an action for "trade libel" or injurious falsehood. But this cause of action requires the aggrieved trader to prove malice, and this will usually be difficult where the threatener holds a patent or registered design granted by a public authority and prima facie valid. The "threats" provisions allow the aggrieved trader to force his persecutor to put his monopoly where his mouth is and justify his threats in court (though it is not necessary that a threatener should actually have any right himself—he may be a solicitor, a patent agent or just a busybody).

5.072 It was recognised by the framers of the 1988 Act that assertions of design right infringement could have similarly damaging effects, even though the right is not a monopoly, and the result was section 253. This provides that where a person threatens another with proceedings for infringement, a person aggrieved may bring proceedings claiming a declaration that the threats are unjustifiable, an injunction against their continuance, and damages for any loss sustained because of them. The plaintiff need only prove that the threats have been made; it is then for the defendant to show that the plaintiff's acts did constitute (or, if done, would have constitued) infringement. Interlocutory injunctions against repetition of the threats pending trial have quite frequently been granted in patent and registered design cases.

5.073 It is permissible under section 253(3) to make a threat where the alleged infringement consists of "making or importing anything". You may threaten the manufacturer or importer direct (the subsection says nothing about someone who merely authorises another to manufacture, even if he is the prime mover in the alleged infringement). But as soon as you address yourself to his customers, or prospective customers, you are on uncertain ground. Even though you may intend to imply only that you are contemplating suing the manufacturer, so that the continuity of the customer's supplies may be at risk, he may get the wrong idea and think that he himself is being threatened. Moreover it was recently accepted in a patent case that a threat to a customer to sue a manufacturing supplier in respect of the supplier's *sales* of infringing articles *already* made or imported might be actionable, since the defence is specifically limited to infringement by making or importing.[74]

It behoves design right owners to bear these risks well in mind. Threats may be written or oral, veiled or implicit as well as explicit. The over-zealous salesman is deservedly part of intellectual property demonology, with his unspecific but menacing references to infringement, and competitors, and "vigorous enforcement of our rights". What is actually said often matters less than the impression that is left. If the customer believes that either he or his supplier is being threatened, the damage is done. A design right owner, replete with outraged virtue and shaping up to sue for infringement, can then find himself in receipt of a writ and a motion for an interlocutory injunction. If he has a good case, it need not matter much; but he will have lost the initiative and the moral commanding heights.   **5.074**

Because a right is of limited use if you cannot safely tell people about it, section 253(4) provides that "mere notification that a design is protected by design right does not constitute a threat of proceedings". The patents and registered designs threats sections contain a similar proviso.[75] You are therefore entitled to write to all types of infringer drawing their attention to your claimed right and asking for their comments. You may probably also put a time-limit on the receipt of these comments. If you want to do any more, such as suggest terms of settlement you would be prepared to accept in lieu of fighting an action, you may be wise issue your writ first; you will not then be "threatening". But there is a problem with secondary infringers of unregistered design right which does not affect the monopoly rights: you have to make sure they know they are infringing before you can safely sue them. With copyright, this problem does not exist. There is no "threats" section, and when you write to a secondary infringer putting him on notice and providing him with the means to assess your claim (copy and details of the work relied on, identification of the article complained of), you are free to threaten him that all the types of redress which the law affords will be visited on him without further notice unless he gives you comprehensive undertakings against future infringement, promises to pay you damages and costs, and reveals his suppliers, customers, sales to date, and the name of his grandmother's cat. But with designs you cannot. All you can do within section 253(4) is notify him and provide the details to fix him with knowledge. Moreover, you must take care not to say anything which might be construed as threatening his supplier. Where there is any risk or uncertainty, and particularly until there has been some case law, it might be   **5.075**

---

[74] *Bowden Controls v. Acco Cable Controls* [1990] R.P.C. 427.

[75] But their task is easy, because they can simply identify their patent or design by its number and leave it to the defendant to check. The design right owner must given considerably more detail in order for his letter to make sense.

wise to issue a writ before writing the letter, and then if necessary issue another once the secondary infringer is securely fixed with knowledge and proceed on the second one. If this seems excessively cautious, his advisers should at least warn the design right owner of the risks of "threats".

COPYRIGHT

5.076 Despite the overall policy of the 1988 Act, copyright has not been wholly banished from the field of industrial designs. It still remains relevant in a number of situations, including the following:

— until July 31, 1999 (or such earlier date as the copyright expires), those artistic works forming the basis of unregistrable designs which came into being before August 1, 1989 and whose continued protection is secured by the transitional provisions in Schedule 1, paragraph 19[76]—subject to licences of right during the last five years of their life. This extension of "old" copyright also applies to semiconductor topographies created before November 7, 1987 (which were entitled to copyright before the specially-tailored right became available under the 1987 Regulations[77] by virtue of coming within the 1956 Act definition of "photograph" or being based on a drawing), but there will be no licences of right during the last five years except if an order has been made following a finding of abusive conduct by the Monopolies and Mergers Commission[78]

— until July 31, 1999 or July 31, 2004, those artistic works forming the basis of registrable designs which under section 10 of the 1956 Act as amended by the Design Copyright Act 1968 enjoyed only 15 years' copyright, for the remainder of any term already running on August 1, 1989, whether for a 10-year term subject to licences of right under Schedule 1, paragraph 19 or the 15-year term under Schedule 1, paragraph 20[79]

— "surface decoration", excluded from design right by section 213(3)(c)[80]

— artistic works which are designs "for" other artistic works not excluded from copyright under section 51(1),[81] or those artistic works themselves

— artistic works exploited industrially during their shorter term of copyright under section 52[82]

— those articles which by Designs rule 26[83] are not registrable as designs and which are also excluded from the shorter term of copyright

---

[76] See 3.096 above.
[77] S.I. 1987 No. 1497.
[78] s.144.
[79] See 3.101 above.
[80] See 2.251 above.
[81] See 2.189 above.
[82] See 2.210 above.
[83] See 2.079 above.

ordained by section 52, notwithstanding their industrial exploitation, by paragraph 3(1) of the Copyright (Industrial Process and Excluded Articles) (No. 2) Order 1989[84]—works of sculpture, other than casts or models used or intended to be used as models or patterns to be multiplied by an industrial process; wall plaques, medals and medallions; and printed matter primarily of a literary or artistic character, including book jackets, calendars, certificates, coupons, dress-making patterns, greetings cards, labels, leaflets, maps, plans, playing cards, postcards, stamps, trade advertisements, trade forms and cards, transfers and similar articles. Among these would be included promotional and marketing materials such as catalogues, product information and instructions for use (leaflets, trade advertisements), and assembly diagrams (plans)

— literary works whose literary content is reproduced as a step in the making of an article[85]
— photographs, videos and sound recordings (including video soundtracks) used for promotional purposes or which constitute design documents.

It must be remembered that under section 236[86] such of the above as are design documents or models for articles in which unregistered design right subsists must still be sued on in copyright when the alleged infringement is anything other than making an article to the design or copying an article made to the design.

Infringement of works continuing to enjoy "old" copyright under the transitional provisions is governed by the 1988 Act, except where the infringing acts took place before August 1, 1989.[87] But subsistence of copyright will continue to be governed by the 1956 Act, where the work came into being on or after June 1, 1957 and before August 1, 1989, or by the 1911 Act. This will make little difference in practice, but pleadings should use the correct terminology and refer to the appropriate Act; and there are also some differences in relation to first ownership, notably in relation to photographs and engravings.[88]   5.077

Like design right, copyright is a right infringed by *copying*,[89] not a monopoly right, and is subject to the primary/secondary infringement distinction.[90] Care must similarly be taken to fix secondary infringers with notice, except where the circumstantial evidence is so strong and the risks of alerting the infringer so great as to make it in all probability safe, and certainly desirable, to sue before writing a warning letter.   5.078

---

[84] See 2.214 above.
[85] See *Anacon Corporation Ltd v. Environmental Research Technology Ltd* [1994] F.S.R. 359, discussed at 2.172 above.
[86] See 5.030 and 5.033 above.
[87] Sched. 1, para. 14(1).
[88] See 3.060 above.
[89] And certain other specific acts mentioned below.
[90] See 5.001 above.

PRIMARY INFRINGEMENT

5.079   The "restricted acts"[91] the doing or authorising of which by anyone other than the copyright owner or with his consent (section 16(2)) constitutes primary infringement are listed in section 16(1) of the 1988 Act, and further amplified in sections 17–21. They are the copying of the work, the issue of copies to the public, the performance, showing or playing of the work in public, the broadcasting of the work or its inclusion in a cable programme service, and the making of an adaptation of the work (but adaptation is not an infringing act in relation to artistic works). Copying (section 17) and the issue of copies to the public (section 18) are the significant restricted acts in relation to industrial design, but it is worth remembering that various promotional activities such as the showing of demonstration videos to prospective customers and the adaptation and updating of catalogues and instructional literature can amount to infringement[92] if the copyright does not belong to the company concerned and the copyright owner's permission has not been obtained. Particular care needs to be taken with software, which is usually subject to strict controls imposed by the supplier by means of conditions in the licence under which it is sold (or hired). Infringement may occur by doing any of the restricted acts in relation to any substantial part of a work as well as to the whole of it (section 16(3)(a)), and by doing them indirectly as well as directly, and regardless of whether, in the case of indirect infringement, any intervening acts themselves infringe copyright (section 16(3)(b)). The most obvious case of this, in the field of industrial design, is where the defendant copies the plaintiff's product (itself a non-infringing copy), and thereby infringes the copyright in the work (usually a drawing) from which the product is derived.

Copying

5.080   Copying a literary or artistic work means reproducing it in any material form (section 17(1)). For an artistic work, this includes making a three-dimensional copy of a two-dimensional work and vice versa: making a vase from a drawing of it, taking a photograph of a sculpture (section 17(3)). For both literary and artistic works, copying also includes storing the work in any medium by electronic means, so that inputting the instructions for using or assembling a product, or a table of dimensions, into a computer will infringe the literary copyright in the instructions or the table, and scanning a drawing or photograph will infringe the artistic copyright in these. Needless to say, making unauthorised copies of software is an infringing act. Copying also includes making copies which are "transient or incidental to some other use of the work", so that rough drafts subsequently torn up, or erased from computer memory, are still infringing copies.

[91] As s.2 terms them.
[92] By showing the work in public (section 19(3)) and adaptation (section 21) respectively.

A plaintiff sets about proving copying by pointing to similarities between   **5.081**
the work and the allegedly infringing copies and demonstrating that the
defendant had a chance to copy.[93] The burden then shifts to the defendant to
prove that he did not copy but evolved his design independently. It is easy
enough to raise an initial case of copying if the plaintiff's product is on the
market, or has been shown at an exhibition. It may have appeared in a
catalogue, or been regularly shown in a TV commercial so that the defendant
might have taken a photograph of it off the screen, though this is unlikely to
be sufficient unless what has been copied is something simple like a logo.
Products made in the Middle or Far East are often copied at the manufacturing end. Copying does not have to have been slavish or deliberate—a
defendant may genuinely believe he has "designed round" or only been
"inspired by" another product on the market; the court may take a different
view. It is even possible to copy "subconsciously". This possibility was
expressly recognised in *EMI Music Publishing Ltd v. Papathanassiou*[94] where
the defendant Vangelis was accused of copying part of the *Chariots of Fire*
theme from a melody recorded on a demo tape given or sent to him several
years before. The court was not satisfied there was sufficient similarity
between the two passages, or as to the circumstances in which the tape was
allegedly supplied, so the plaintiff did not succeed, but Whitford J. accepted
that if copying had taken place it could have happened without Vangelis
having been aware of it.

Indirect copying

Indirect copying can take place not only by copying a product made from a   **5.082**
drawing but by following the instructions in a description of that product or
of the drawing.[95] In *Solar Thomson Engineering Co. v. Barton*[96] the
defendant made a spare part for a pulley-wheel at least partly from a
description of the original. A case distressing to the honest competitor was
Plix Products Ltd v. Frank M. Winstone (Merchants).[97] The products were
trays for storing and transporting kiwi fruit. The plaintiff's design had been
adopted as an industry standard and incorporated in detailed written
specifications produced by the New Zealand Kiwifruit Authority. The
defendants wished to break into the kiwi fruit tray market, of which the
plaintiff had until then enjoyed a *de facto* monopoly, but they wanted to
make sure they did so lawfully, so acting on legal advice[98] they employed a
designer unacquainted with kiwi fruit trays, forbade him to talk to anyone

---

[93] See, *e.g. L. B. (Plastics) Ltd v. Swish Products Ltd* [1979] R.P.C. 551 and the discussion at
5.006 above.
[94] [1993] E.M.L.R. 306.
[95] *Anacon* (see n. 85 above) might perhaps have been decided on this basis, since there was an
original artistic work in the form of the plaintiff's circuit diagram, which was "described" in
the defendant's "net list" of the components. The difference is that in the cases about to be
discussed, the description was not itself an infringing copy.
[96] [1977] R.P.C. 537.
[97] [1986] F.S.R. 63.
[98] The case must have been equally distressing to the feelings of the defendants' lawyers.

who knew anything about them, supplied him with a copy of the specifications and a handful of kiwi fruit and told him to get on with it. What he
produced in strict accordance with these instructions unfortunately infringed
the plaintiff's copyright, because the specifications embodied the information
contained in its drawings, and by following them the designer necessarily
reproduced the features of the drawings. Primary infringement of copyright
can occur despite the best intentions.

5.083   However, it is necessary for the plaintiff to show that he has, or at least had,
an original artistic work which has been reproduced. If his product has been
copied, but all he can produce is a drawing made "for the record" but not
actually used in his manufacturing process, he will have failed to show an
adequate causal connection between that drawing and the defendant's
product. In *Duriron Co. Inc. v. Hugh Jennings & Co. Ltd*,[99] the defendant
may have copied the plaintiff's product (an anode), but the plaintiff failed to
satisfy the judge or the Court of Appeal that it actually used the drawing
relied on in making the anodes that were copied. It merely checked them after
they were made against a table of dimensions (a literary work, of course)
which also appeared on the drawing. There was thus no causal connection
between the artistic part of the drawing and the defendant's product.[1] This is
not to say that a plaintiff who did initially make his product from a drawing
but has since lost it will fail. So long as he can establish by other evidence what
the drawing was like,[2] and show the requisite causal connection, he can still
succeed if there has been copying.

Copying a substantial part

5.084   It is rare, except in cases of straight counterfeiting, for the whole of a work to
be copied, and most cases, once copying has been established, involve judging
whether what has been copied is a substantial part of the copyright work.
Quality counts as much as, if not more than, quantity.[3] As Aldous J. remarked
in *C. & H. Engineering v. F. Klucznik & Son Ltd*,[4]

> "Whether a part copied is a substantial part of a work depends upon the
> importance of the part that has been copied, not on analysis of the parts
> that have not been copied. Thus a close analysis of the differences is
> seldom useful. The correct approach is to look at the similarities between
> the drawing and the alleged infringement, decide whether they were
> taken from the plaintiff's drawing and thereafter decide whether the part
> taken is a substantial part of the drawing. In considering whether it is a

[99] [1984] F.S.R. 1.
[1] See also observations by Nicholls L.J. in *Entec (Pollution Control) Ltd v. Abacus Mouldings*
[1992] F.S.R. 332 at 348 about non-scale sketches of septic tanks.
[2] See, *e.g. Alan Nuttall Ltd v. Equipashop Ltd*, SRIS/C/105/91.
[3] What is taken need not constitute the whole of the defendant's work either. In *Ravenscroft v.
Herbert* [1980] R.P.C. 193 the infringing part of the defendant's book was no more than 4 per
cent by volume (though 15 per cent by "value").
[4] [1992] F.S.R. 421.

substantial part, the Court must have regard to the nature of the drawing and the importance of the part taken as envisaged by the person to whom the drawing is addressed."

Recent industrial design cases have resiled somewhat from the courts' earlier position that the reproduction of anything which was "significant" to the *functioning* of the plaintiff's product would constitute the taking of a substantial part. It was remembered that industrial design copyright was based on the copying of an artistic work, so that what was taken had to be artistically significant; functional importance was not enough. By the same token, a "new" drawing which substantially reproduced an earlier one with only minor amendments to its appearance might be insufficiently original to attract copyright. *Interlego v. Tyco*[5] was an early example of the new approach. The important technical changes made to the Lego bricks over the years occasioned only "minute differences" in appearance on the new drawings. These differences in the artistic elements of the drawings were "visually insignificant", and the drawings were therefore not original and could not attract a fresh copyright. **5.085**

Their Lordships in *Interlego* referred with approval to the decision of Whitford J. in *Rose Plastics GmbH v. Wm Beckett & Co. (Plastics) Ltd.*[6] This concerned telescopic plastic containers, the plaintiff's drawings depicting a ratchet and notch arrangement with the ratchets mounted on opposed round corners. The defendant's earliest drawings had in fact copied the plaintiff's product, but this design had never been produced. What was produced was a container which utilised the functionally-significant ratchet and notch principle but which, because the corners were chamfered rather than radiused, and the base had been changed, so differed from the plaintiff's drawings in overall appearance that it did not infringe. The defendant had not "taken a substantial part of what can properly be considered as being the artistic work". **5.086**

Billhöfer Maschinenfabrik GmbH v. Dixon & Co. Ltd[7] was about sheet-fed film laminating machines. The defendant's designer was fully conversant with the plaintiff's product, and had adopted certain of the plaintiff's dimensions and spatial relationships between components in designing the defendant's drum dryer; but it was held that these elements in the context of the whole of the Billhöfer drawing would not have been of sufficient visual significance to an engineer to amount to reproduction of a substantial part. The judge was satisifed that the defendant had made its own genuine design effort, and observed that a more effective test of copying than the adoption of a functionally important but indispensable part would be the taking of inessential elements, particularly if these did not work very well. **5.087**

[5] [1988] R.P.C. 343, see Chap. 2 above, *passim*.
[6] [1989] F.S.R. 113.
[7] [1990] F.S.R. 105.

5.088   The Court of Appeal in *Johnstone Safety Ltd v. Peter Cook (International) plc*[8] adopted a similar approach. Here the defendant's designer of traffic cones had previously been a director of the plaintiff, and was found, contrary to his assertions, to have knowingly adopted from the plaintiff's successful cone the functionally important features of a collar and a skirt with step. The latter looked very like the plaintiff's. However, both these features were known in the industry, and the court held that the stepped skirt was not enough to be, visually, a substantial part of the plaintiff's drawing. The judge had erred in placing too much stress on its functional significance. The court also recognised that any designer of traffic cones would work under functional constraints, imposed by government regulations, industry standards and customer requirements, which would be likely to lead to strong similarities between various manufacturers' products.

5.089   At least in the three latter cases the defendants could demonstrate that they had invested their own skill, labour, time and money in producing their designs, even though in each case they had studied and taken some inspiration from the plaintiffs' products. It should not be assumed that the courts will not still be astute to catch those who are merely hitching a free ride, but it is refreshing to see, in the dying days of old-style industrial copyright, this new approach which takes far more account of commercial and engineering reality than was customary during the previous 15 years.

5.090   It must not be forgotten that products of the kind considered in these cases will only be the subject of copyright actions for a few more years, and that they are now subject to licences of right, so that the "visual significance" of functional features will no longer be of much practical concern. But even with artistic works which survive section 51 the "substantial part" test can be perplexing and involve fine judgments of what is visually striking enough in the features or attitude of, say, a mass-produced garden statue of the undraped human form to be a substantial part of it. Rationally, the courts need to bear in mind what it is that gives the plaintiff's product a competitive edge over others of its kind, and if this had been taken, infringement can be found.

5.091   Where the copyright work is something like a catalogue, copying of a single illustration on a single page is quite capable of being a substantial part.

5.092   As with design right, it is a primary infringement to authorise someone else to do a restricted act, and reference should be made to the discussion of this at 5.017 and of the international aspects of authorisation at 5.039 above. This is of increasing importance where design and manufacture of infringing, as well as lawfully-made, products may take place in different countries.

[8] [1990] F.S.R. 161.

Issuing copies to the public

This is a new type of primary infringement introduced by section 18 of the   **5.093**
1988 Act. The 1956 Act had included "publishing" a work as one of the acts
of primary infringement, but this was interpreted in *Infabrics Ltd v. Jaytex
Shirt Co. Ltd*[9] as meaning only first publication, so that a defendant who
imported shirts made of an infringing fabric which had already been put on
the market in Hong Kong did not commit the primary infringement of
publication but only (and only once he had been put on notice) the secondary
infringement of importing infringing copies knowing them to be so. Concern
was felt by book publishers, because the decision appeared to mean that a
rival who had an unlicensed paperback edition of a book printed abroad (so
that he would not be liable for copying or authorising copying[10]), imported
the whole edition in bulk and distributed it before he could be put on notice,
might escape liability. The book as such would already have been "published" by the publication of the hardback edition.

So section 18, which makes issuing copies of a work to the public a   **5.094**
restricted act, goes on to provide that issue to the public of copies of a work
means "the act of putting into circulation copies not previously put into
circulation, in the U.K. or elsewhere", though not to any subsequent
distribution, sale, hiring or loan of those copies nor to their subsequent
importation into the U.K. It appears to cover a numbr of situations, the first,
like "publication" in the 1956 Act, being where an unlicensed person
publishes a book or industrial design for the first time anywhere—perhaps
where he illicitly obtains a manuscript or a prototype of a new gatepost lion
and rushes copies into the bookshops or garden centres ahead of the planned
launch by the legitimate publisher or manufacturer.

It will also catch the unlicensed paperback publisher or person who   **5.095**
deliberately commissions the making of copy widgets abroad in order to
avoid allegations of primary infringement by copying, and imports them for
U.K. distribution, because in both cases the first putting into circulation of
those copies will take place here, even though the hardback book and the
original widgets will already have been "published" here. In both these cases
the defendant would also be a secondary infringer (because the copies are
infringing copies) provided the plaintiff could prove that he knew or had
reason to believe he was dealing with infringing copies; but section 18 saves
the plaintiff having to do this and allows him to recover damages even if he
has missed his chance of an injunction in relation to the first consignment. For
this interpretation to work, it must be assumed that "putting into circulation" means "making available to the public at large", not "inserting into
the channels of distribution", because otherwise the sale by the overseas
manufacturer to the defendant would put the copies into circulation and the

---

[9] [1981] F.S.R. 261 (H.L.).
[10] But see section 24(2) dealt with under secondary infringement below.

defendant would be saved from primary infringement by section 18(2) which explicitly provides that any "subsequent" importation of them into the U.K. or distribution of them here would not be a primary infringement.

5.096   But if this is so, the section may be wider than was intended,[11] because it could also catch the innocent importer who is offered samples abroad, unaware that they are infringing copies, and places an order for further copies which he then imports. *Those copies* will likewise not previously have been put into circulation. The innocent importer is thus deprived of the protection presumably intended to be given to him by the secondary infringement rules (and section 18(2)) which require him to be put on notice before he becomes liable for dealing in infringing copies. Only where the goods he imports had alrady been made and at least offered for sale to any interested buyers will their putting into circulation already have taken place. A way round this may be to argue that an offer of samples on the open market to anyone interested in placing orders is equivalent to putting into circulation all copies of those samples which may thereafter be made in response to individual orders.

5.097   The section might in certain circumstances also be apt to catch dealings in copies which are *not* infringing copies, so that there could be no secondary infringement. Normally, there is no restraint on subsequent dealings with lawful copies, as section 18(2) recognises, unless there is some breach of a condition successfully annexed to the copies on first sale and "running" with them; and breach of such a condition is a breach of contract, or an interference with a contract, rather than a breach of copyright. But under section 18 it seems that the selling off of old stock by a former licensee after termination of his licence might infringe. So long as the copies were made while the licence subsisted, they are not infringing copies, but their sale can be tiresome if it competes with the activities of a new licensee. The old licensee may deliberately have made more than he could sell before the licence terminated, with a view to continuing to cash in, but he could now fall foul of section 18 because he will be putting into circulation *particular copies* not previously circulated, and this is now something for which he will need consent because it is a restricted act.

SECONDARY INFRINGEMENT

Infringing copies

5.098   Secondary infringement is the doing of a variety of acts set out in sections 22–26 in relation to what the defendant knows or has reason to believe are "infringing copies". These are defined in section 27, which is in very similar terms to the definition of "infringing article" in section 227 in relation to design right. Once again (section 27(2), (3) and (5)), an article is an infringing

---

[11] *Hansard*, Vol. 501, col. 214.

copy if its making constituted an infringement of copyright or, if it has been or is proposed to be imported into the U.K., its making in the U.K. would have constituted an infringement or a breach of an exclusive licence agreement (but parallel imports from other E.U. Member States may not be treated as infringing copies). Reference may be made to the discussion of these points at 5.019–5.021 above. By Schedule 1, paagraph 14(3), the infringing nature of copies made under earlier Acts is to be judged by the law in force when they were made.

There is a rebuttable presumption that where an article is shown to be a **5.099** copy of a work, then where copyright subsists or has at any time subsisted in the work, the article was made during such subsistence. The defendant is taken to be the person best able to show when the article actually was made.

Several sections of the Act permit the making of what would otherwise be **5.100** infringing copies for certain specified purposes, among them being copies made for educational and archive purposes and back-up copies or adaptations of proprietary software, provided those copies are not thereafter used for commercial purposes (or in the case of software retained after transfer of the original software to another person). If the permitted copies are so used or retained, section 27(6) provides that they thereupon become infringing copies, and can therefore become the subject of secondary infringements.

Acts of secondary infringement

The three sections 22, 23 and 24 set out a number of acts which, if done **5.101** without the licence of the copyright owner and in relation to what the defendant knows or has reason to believe are infringing copies, amount to secondary infringement. Under section 22, importing, other than for private or domestic purposes, and under section 23 possessing in the course of a business, selling or letting for hire or offering or exposing for sale or hire, exhibiting in public or distributing in the course of a business, and distributing otherwise than in the course of a business but to such an extent as prejudicially to affect the copyright owner, are all capable of being acts of secondary infringement. It will be observed that, except for prejudicial distribution other than in the course of a business (which might cover, say, running off dozens of copies of a computer game as Christmas presents for all one's friends' children), all these acts have to have been done for some commercial purpose.

Most of these acts are self-explanatory, but "possessing in the course of a **5.102** business" is not quite as clear as might be wished. It covers having goods in stock for the purposes of a business in those goods, but would be unlikely to catch a solicitor in possession of goods merely on behalf of a client in the course of litigation.[12] It is not clear whether it would catch a warehouseman,

[12] *L. A. Gear Inc. v. Hi-Tec Sports plc* [1992] F.S.R. 121.

carrier or other bailee who carries on the business of storing or transporting goods on behalf of others, if he is duly put on notice that the goods he is storing or carrying are infringing copies. Common sense suggests that it should not: he is hardly in a position himself to investigate allegations of copying, other than by going to his bailor, which would be exceedingly inconvenient for him, and risk his being sued in the meantime if the plaintiff lost patience. In any event, the plaintiff can, in cases of emergency, presumably obtain an interim order for delivery up under section 99[13] against such a person, which would also safeguard the latter from claims by his bailor. Would "possessing" cover an infringing article which is *used* in the course of a business, such as an infringing machine or software? Historically, use of an infringing copy has not constituted infringement, unlike the case with patents, where use of a patented article is explicitly an infringing act. If use was to become an infringing act in copyright, the change might have been expected to be widely-heralded. However, Parliament has specifically provided by section 54(1) that use of a typeface in the normal course of a printer's business, as opposed to dealings in articles (nowadays frequently disks embodying software) for producing material in a particular typeface, does not infringe, which suggests that in the absence of that defence it would. On the other hand, "possession" is an odd expression to use of part of a business's assets, as opposed to its stock, unless it is meant to cover equipment which is leased rather than owned. Again, it would be possible to seek an order under section 99 in cases of real necessity.

5.103   Under section 24, copyright is infringed if an unlicensed person makes, imports, possesses in the course of a business or sells or lets for hire or offers or exposes for sale or hire an article specifically designed or adapted for making copies of the work, knowing or having reason to believe that it is to be used to make infringing copies. This is aimed at printing plates, moulds, tools, master recordings, templates, photographic negatives or anything else which is only going to be used ("specifically designed or adapted") for making infringing copies. It does not cover recording or disc-pressing equipment, photocopiers and the like which are capable of perfectly legitimate uses,[14] even if the use to which they are put by a particular defendant is wholly unlawful. There is an interesting addition to the law in section 24(2), which provides that copyright is infringed by an unlicensed person who transmits a copyright work by means of a telcommunications system[15] knowing or having reason to believe that infringing copies of the work will be made by means of the reception of the transmission in the U.K. *or elsewhere.* Anyone

---

[13] See below. The equivalent section 230 for design right would not allow this course, because the possession, custody or control for "commercial purposes" which it contemplates the respondent to such an application as enjoying is limited by the definition in section 263 to purposes of sale or hire.

[14] See, *e.g. Hansard*, Vol. 493, col. 1134. This was the position under the old law, which used the wider wording "used or intended to be used" (s.18). It is also in line with the authorisation cases discussed at 5.017, note 16 above on supply of blank tapes and fast tape-copying equipment.

[15] Other than by broadcasting or inclusion in a cable programme service.

who hopes, by having infringing copies made abroad, to avoid primary infringement had better send his instructions and patterns by post rather than down a data line.

As observed in connection with secondary infringement of design right,[16] **5.104** the previous requirement that a secondary infringer "know" that he is dealing with infringing copies has been relaxed so as to make having reason to believe sufficient. A recent formulation of what the test means (knowledge of facts from which a reasonable man would arrive at the relevant belief, given a reasonable period for investigation of the claim) was given by Morritt J. and approved by the Court of Appeal in *L. A. Gear v. Hi-Tec*,[17] where it was also held that even if the relevant knowledge or reason for belief did not exist at the date of the writ, so that there could be no award of damages or order for delivery up, if they were proved by the date of trial or hearing an interlocutory or final injunction against future infringements could be granted.

TERRITORIAL CONSIDERATIONS

It is clear from section 16(1) that the exclusive right given to a copyright **5.105** owner to do the restricted acts is limited to the U.K. and therefore the primary infringements which are committed where anyone else does these acts without the copyright owner's consent may also be limited to those committed in the U.K., though section 16(2), which prohibits the doing of the restricted acts without consent by anyone else, does not specifically say so; nor are secondary infringements, apart from importation, expressly limited to the U.K. This is a change from the 1956 Act, which at every point limited infringement to acts done in the U.K.[18] The normal U.K. rule is that intellectual property rights can only be enforced in the country which grants them,[19] and in *Def Lepp Music v. Stuart-Brown*[20] Browne-Wilkinson V.C. set aside service outside the jurisdiction of a writ alleging copyright infringement by some of the defendants in the Netherlands, albeit on the basis of the stricter wording in the 1956 Act. The Civil Jurisdiction and Judgments Act 1982[21] permits[22] an action to be brought in "tort, delict or quasi-delict" in the place where damage is suffered as well as the place where the tort is committed, which might be the place where the plaintiff suffers financial loss, so that a U.K. plaintiff could sue in the U.K. a foreign defendant who had infringed elsewhere in the E.U. However, the Vice-Chancellor in *Def Lepp* also ruled

[16] See 5.027 above.
[17] [1992] F.S.R. 121.
[18] See sections 1(1) and (2) and 5(2) and (3).
[19] See *Tyburn Productions Ltd v. Doyle* [1990] R.P.C. 185, where Vinelott J. refused to grant a declaration in the U.K. that the defendant's U.S. copyright in the Sherlock Holmes stories would not be infringed by the film the plaintiff proposed to make.
[20] [1986] R.P.C. 273.
[21] Which was not yet in force at the date of *Def Lepp*.
[22] Via Article 5(3) of the Brussels Convention scheduled to it, as interpreted by the E.C.J. in *Bier BV v. Mines de Potasse d'Alsace S.A.* [1976] E.C.R. 1735; [1978] Q.B. 708.

that infringement of copyright is not a tort[23] at all but purely a creature of statute. In this he was probably wrong.[24] In any event the Convention expression "tort, delict or quasi-delict" is to be interpreted in a uniform sense so as to cover all civil wrongs other than breaches of contract.[25] All that can finally be said is that the law is still unclear, although it may be possible on the facts in some cases to sue a foreign defendant in the U.K. for having authorised an infringement here.[26]

DEFENCES

5.106   Apart from challenging the subsistence or the plaintiff's ownership of the copyright, the basic defence to copyright infringement is that the defendant did not copy—that his work was independently created. As already mentioned, once similarity and the chance to copy have been shown, the burden of proving independent design in effect shifts to the defendant. It will not be fatal to such a defence that the defendant has seen or even studied the plaintiff's work,[27] if he can convince the court that his product is the result of a genuine independent design effort. It would be ludicrous if an industrial designer were precluded from investigating competing products and studying the market by the fear of an infringement action. Difficulties do of course arise where a designer moves to a rival company or sets up in business on his own account to design the same type of product, particularly if it is largely functional. Plaintiffs will often be over-ready to assume that he has copied his own earlier design (in which they as his former employer will of course have the copyright) rather than simply used his acquired skill to solve known problems. Designers in their turn may be over-ready to assume they are free to use particular features or solutions which they themselves devised while in the plaintiff's service. Cases like this of necessity often turn on whether the judge thinks the designer is a credible witness who has genuinely tried to address the design problem afresh, even if he has come up with the same solution. This is all much less of a problem where the design is an aesthetic one, so within a few years the lot of the copyright judge will become easier—though the problem persists with design right.

---

[23] And therefore could not benefit from the "double actionability" conflict of laws rule which allows acts committed abroad to be sued on here if they are actionable as torts here and "not justifiable" in the place where they are committed.

[24] Although it is a breach of statutory duty rather than a common law tort, copyright infringement is usually treated as a tort, *e.g.* for purposes of calculating limitation periods and (probably) conferring jurisdiction on the County Court quite apart from the special jurisdiction of the Patents County Court.

[25] *Kalfelis v. Schroder, Munchmeyer, Hengst & Co., The Times*, October 5, 1988.

[26] See 5.039 above. See "Can an English Court Restrain Infringement of a Foreign Patent?" by Christopher Floyd & Iain Purvis, [1995] 3 E.I.P.R. 110

[27] See the cases discussed at 5.086–5.089 above.

Miscellaneous defences

There is a limited defence of "innocence", which is considered below in **5.107** relation to remedies, as it affects only the plaintiff's right to damages; and the "implied licence", "*Catnic*" and "*Euro*" defences have already been dealt with at 5.035–5.037 above. Defences based on the free movement of goods provisions of the Treaty of Rome will no doubt be less widely-canvassed now that U.K. copyright is no longer so out of step with other European systems. The *British Leyland* defence and its subsequent application is described at 2.181–2.187 above, and the incidence and effect of licences of right for "hangover" copyright is governed by Schedule, 1, paragraph 19, which applies the corresponding design right provisions.

In what must by now be a very limited number of cases, where articles **5.108** made before August 1, 1989 are still being disposed of, the old "non-expert" or "lay recognition" defence under section 9(8) of the 1956 Act may still be relied on, for what it is worth. This applied where a three-dimensional allegedly infringing copy "would not appear, to persons who are not experts in relation to objects of that description, to be a reproduction" of a two-dimensional drawing. The idea was that while anyone would recognise that a Popeye brooch was a three-dimensional reproduction of the cartoon character, owing most of its appeal to the artistic skill which went into the drawing, the average person unused to reading blueprints would not readily recognise the vacuum cleaner component (or printed circuit board) he held in his hand as the thing depicted in the drawing. But the subsection had the lack of effect its woolliness perhaps deserved. Judges declined to entertain parades of non-experts called by each side to swear to their entire ignorance of the subject-matter in question and, respectively, the consummate ease or total bewilderment with which they compared the object and the drawing. Judges constituted themselves lay recognisers, and after several days becoming fully familiarised with the articles in suit (the defence was a last-ditch one, the test never being made until copying had been found to have occurred) almost without exception[28] duly recognised. The defence was not re-enacted in the 1988 Act, but if it could be made to apply to articles made before August 1, 1989, it would still be available to counter an allegation of section 18 or secondary infringement.

Statutory defences

There are numerous defences to copyright infringement, contained in **5.109** sections 29–76 of the 1988 Act under the heading "Acts permitted in relation to copyright works". These include making copies for research and private study, or for educational, archival, judicial and public administration

---

[28] See, *e.g. Guilford Kapwood Ltd v. Embsay Fabrics Ltd* [1983] F.S.R. 567, *Merlet v. Mothercare plc* [1984] F.S.R. 358.

purposes. Only those with significance for industrial designs will here be considered.

5.110   Of these, the most important are sections 51, 52 and 53, which have already been dealt with elsewhere.[29] For completeness, it should be noted that under section 51(2) it is not an infringement to issue to the public or include in a film, broadcast or cable programme service any articles or copies of articles which are made to a design recorded or embodied in an artistic work which is a design document or model for anything other than an artisitic work or a typeface. Schedule 1, paragraph 14(4) "back-projects" this defence to articles made before August 1, 1989 which *were* infringing copies when they were made (although if made since that date section 51(1) would ensure that they were not), and thus can still be sued on until July 31, 1999.

5.111   It is not under section 54(1) an infringement of copyright in an artistic work consisting of the design of a typeface to use the typeface in the ordinary course of typing, composing text, typesetting or printing, or to possess an article for the purpose of such use, or to do anything in relation to material produced by such use. This subsection is intended to[30] and does allow use of a typeface in the ordinary course of a printing business, even if it turns out to be an infringing copy. The copyright owner would then have to sue the supplier rather than the user. However, it is not permissible under section 54(2) to make, import or deal with articles specifically designed or adapted for producing material in a particular typeface, or to possess such articles for the purpose of dealing with them, without the copyright owner's consent; and this would also catch a printer importing an infringing typeface even for his own use, though presumably only if he can be proved to have had the necessary knowledge or belief as to its infringing nature at the time he imported it. Importing is only a secondary infringement, unless there is some further distribution of copies within section 18.

5.112   Under section 62, it is not an infringement of copyright in a building, or in a sculpture, model for a building or work of artistic craftsmanship which is permanently situated in a public place or in premises open to the public, *inter alia* to make a graphic work, photograph or film representing it, or to issue copies of any of these to the public. So the sculptor of a statue in a public park, or the maker of a piece of jewellery permanently on show in a museum or an altar-cloth in a cathedral cannot derive any financial benefit from its exploitation on postcards or greetings cards or as a calendar illustration. It is not clear whether the premises concerned must be open to the public at all times or only by the whim of the proprietor so that limitations may be imposed as conditions of entry.

5.113   It is not an infringement in relation to an artistic work to copy it, or issue copies to the public, for the purpose of advertising the sale of the work, but if

---

[29] See Chap. 2 above.
[30] See, *e.g. Hansard*, Vol. 495, col. 646. For further information on typeface copyright, see "Protection of Software Fonts in UK Law", Watts & Blakemore, [1995] 3 E.I.P.R. 133.

such copies (for example auction catalogues or posters or point-of-sale displays) are subsequently dealt in commercially for their own sake, they become infringing copies (section 63). Would this transformation apply where the original copy of the work, for example the photograph of the new range of garden gnomes forming the basis of the surplus posters being sold off by the garden centre proprietor, did not need to take advantage of section 63 because it was made by the copyright owner or with his consent?

Where the author of an artistic work is not the copyright owner (because he **5.114** has parted with the copyright or made the work in the course of his employment), it is not an infringement of copyright for him to copy the work in making another artistic work, provided he does not repeat or imitate the main design of the earlier work (section 64). There was a similar provision in section 9(9) of the 1956 Act, but limited to the situation where the artist in making the later work used a sketch, plan, study, model, cast, or mould made for the earlier work. Lord Beaverbrook said[31] that the exception was meant to allow Monet to paint Rouen Cathedral more than once or an architect to re-use details or motifs of, say, doorways or window surrounds. The section might be applied to help resolve the problems of the designer who changes his job[32] and starts designing the same type of product for someone else, but it is bound to lead to argument about what constitutes "the main design".

Anything done for the purposes of reconstructing a building does not **5.115** infringe any copyright in the building or the drawings or plans for it (section 65). Reconstruction does not mean extension.[33]

Finally, section 31 provides that copyright in an artistic (or any other) work **5.116** is not infringed by its "incidental inclusion" in an artistic work, sound recording, film, broadcast or cable programme. The predecessor of this section, section 9(5) of the 1956 Act, only applied to inclusion of an artistic work in a film or TV broadcast "by way of background" or otherwise incidentally. The ambit of the defence is not clear; it would certainly cover a painting on the wall behind, or artefacts on the desk of, a person being interviewed or (probably) having his portrait painted, since the broadcaster or artist is not normally responsible for or in a position to quarrel with what the subject chooses to surround himself with. But it is suggested that where a set is carefully dressed for a film or an advertisement with props all deliberately chosen, there is room to argue that the items are not "incidentally" included, unless they are very much in the background. An advertising photograph of a lamp having a shade made from fabric in which the plaintiff owns the copyright, or a TV commercial for a rough-hewn lager showing the picture of the green-faced Oriental lady as an instant aid to cultural and class identification should both give rise to a royalty.

[31] *Hansard*, Vol. 491, col. 191.
[32] See 5.106 above.
[33] See 2.160 above.

Moral Rights

5.117   The content of these was described at 3.072–3.077. The right of paternity, provided it has been duly asserted and not waived or consented to under section 87, is infringed *inter alia* by failure to identify the author on each copy of a work as commercially published[34] or exhibited, or if this is not appropriate, in some other manner likely to bring his identity to the notice of a person acquiring a copy or seeing the exhibition. An architect is entitled to be identified on his building by appropriate means visible to persons entering or approaching the building. This is already standard practice, and in some fields of industry, such as clothing, it has always been common. The writer has not observed any increased incidence of labelling on industrial artefacts, labels, packaging and the like since the moral rights provisions were introduced. The right does not in any case apply to anything done by or with the authority of the copyright owner where the designer was an employee, nor where an act would not infringe copyright by virtue of sections 51 or 52.[35]

5.118   The right to object to derogatory treatment is infringed, *inter alia*, by commercial publication or exhibition of a work which has been so treated or of copies of a graphic work or photograph representing a sculpture, model for a building or work of artistic craftsmanship which has been so treated (section 90). There can also be secondary infringement in relation to works or copies of works which have been so treated (section 83). This is a right which could give rise to interesting questions—for example in relation to advertisements which deliberately refer to other advertisements, or to parodies—but it can only be assumed that as a matter of commercial convenience consents or waivers will normally be obtained, or care will be taken not to identify the author or to issue a sufficient disclaimer (section 82).

5.119   Where there has been false attribution of a work under section 84, it is an infringement to issue copies of or display material relating to or exhibit a work containing a false attribution. There is also secondary infringement where copies of a work are dealt with when the dealer knows or has reason to believe there is an attribution and that it is false or, in the case of an artistic work which has been altered since the author parted with possession of it, where the dealer knows or has reason to believe that this is so but still deals with it as the author's unaltered work.

---

[34] Where copies are issued to the public at a time when copies made in advance of the receipt of orders are generally available to the public, or where the work is made available to the public by means of an electronic retrieval system: s.175(2).

[35] See s.79.

REMEDIES

Parties

By section 97(1), an infringement of copyright is actionable by the current 5.120 copyright owner. Title should be carefully checked. If, as will often be the case with industrial designs, the prospective plaintiff is not the author of the design, and can produce no written assignment whether of subsisting copyright under section 90 or of future copyright under section 91[36] the circumstances in which the design was made must be investigated to see whether the designer was then an employee, or whether an equitable title can be made out[37] to support a demand for a confirmatory assignment. An action can be begun and an interlocutory injunction obtained on the basis of an equitable title alone, the legal title being got in afterwards or the legal owner being joined as a co-plaintiff or non-participating defendant, but it is much better to get matters sorted out in advance of proceedings if time permits. Documents should be scrutinised to ensure that they do amount to assignments[38] and are not merely company resolutions or assignments of goodwill or stock-in-trade or something else inadequate. Where the prospective plaintiff is a company it is always wise to make a company search to ensure that the right company will be suing: companies which are members of groups have a tiresome habit of swapping names or reorganising themselves for tax reasons. Documents should also be checked to see that they are properly stamped or have been adjudicated as not liable for stamping, since unstamped documents may not be relied on without the leave of the court.

Membership of one or other of the Berne or Universal Copyright 5.121 Conventions is now so widespread that non-subsistence of copyright because the author was not a qualifying person or the work was not first published in a Convention country is very unusual; but if there is any doubt, this will have to be checked. Where there may be traps is where the copyright may vest in different people in different countries. U.S. law, for example, has a wide concept of a "work made for hire" which may place the U.S. copyright in the hirer when by U.K. law it belongs to the author. Pre-June 1, 1957 films, for example, were not protected as such in U.K. law, so the copyright would not necessarily vest in the studio as it did under U.S. law. They were either dramatic works, the author of which might be the director, or a series of photographs, where the copyright probably would belong to the studio, but the term of these copyrights was significantly different.

There are rebuttable presumptions as to title in section 104 which are 5.122 helpful in launching an action in cases of doubt. Where in the case of, *inter alia*, literary and artistic works, a name purporting to be that of the author

---

[36] Sections 36 and 37 respectively of the 1956 Act for pre-August 1, 1989 assignments.
[37] See Chaps. 3 and 4 above.
[38] And are assignments of the whole or of the relevant part of the copyright.

appeared on copies of the work as published or on the work when it was made, he is to be presumed until the contrary is proved to be the author of the work and to have made it in circumstances where the copyright vested in him—not, for example, in the course of employment. Where the work is alleged to be one of joint authorship, the presumption applies to each person alleged to be one of the authors. Where no author's name appeared but the work qualifies by virtue of the country of first publication and a name purporting to be that of the publisher appeared on copies of the work as first published, then he is presumed to have owned the copyright at the time of publication. If the author is dead or his identity cannot be ascertained by reasonable inquiry, the presumption is that the work is original and that the plaintiff's allegations as to what was the first publication of the work and as to the country of first publication are correct.

5.123   Joint owners of copyright may sue without joining their co-owners, and may indeed sue their co-owners to restrain infringement.[39]

5.124   As with design right, an exclusive licensee whose licence is in writing may sue in his own name. His position is dealt with in sections 101 and 102 which are in almost identical terms to sections 234 and 235, and reference should be made to the account of these sections in 5.040–5.041—and also to subsequent paragraphs for a discussion of actions for unlawful interference with trade or business, joinder of individual directors as defendants and joint tortfeasors.

5.125   Where a particular infringement comprehends the works of a multiplicity of copyright owners (such as an illustrated commentary on the work of numerous different designers), it can be convenient for a trade association or professional organisation to act on behalf of all of them, as is provided for in many overseas jurisdictions. The position of such organisations in English law is not satisfactory. Some "collecting societies" which administer blanket licensing schemes on behalf of their members, such as the Performing Right Society (PRS) whose members are composers and music publishers, take outright assignments of the appropriate part of their members' copyright, which then allows the society to sue in its own name to enforce these rights. Others such as the Mechanical-Copyright Protection Society which administers the right to reproduce musical works in the form of sound recordings, include in their membership arrangements an authority to sue as each member's agent. But others, such as the Design and Artists' Copyright Society (DACS) do not, and their position as litigants is then very weak, unless they take individual *ad hoc* assignments of their members' rights of action or authority to sue as agents, a procedure not free from difficulty. In *Thames & Hudson Ltd v. DACS*,[40] it was observed in the High Court that DACS had no standing to litigate on behalf of its members, which means that each aggrieved member must be joined as a party, or use the mechanism of a

---

[39] *Cescinsky v. George Routledge & Sons Ltd* [1916] 2 K.B. 325.
[40] [1995] F.S.R. 153.

representative action (one or a few members suing in their own right and on behalf of a class having identical interests), which is suitable for obtaining injunctions or declarations but not for recovering damages. Matters are easier before the Copyright Tribunal which regulates licensing schemes (section 116), and also in criminal law, where organisations can undertake private prosecutions, as will appear below, but with the rapid spread of databases incorporating the work of numerous different contributors and the enormous cost of litigation, it would be convenient if some more suitable arrangements could be devised.

Where there is doubt about the identity of a defendant, a plaintiff (and this applies to all intellectual property rights) may bring an action for discovery alone against anyone who, albeit innocently, has become mixed up with the defendant's wrongdoing and can identify him. The leading case was *Norwich Pharmacal Co. v. Commissioners of Customs & Excise*,[41] where the Commissioners were ordered to disclose the identity of importers of goods which infringed the plaintiff's patent. This is now a well-established jurisdiction and is used to support orders, for example, to disclose the identity of the renter of a box number, or placers of classified advertisements, and generally where even a willing discloser owes some duty of confidentiality and wants to have the protection of having acted under a court order. The applicants for such orders must pay the respondent's costs, but these can be recovered as a head of damages in the main action.[42]

5.126

Forum

Copyright actions are assigned to the Chancery Division of the High Court or District Registry, and industrial design copyright may also be litigated within the special jurisdiction of the Patents County Court, at least if it is ancillary to other matters within that jurisdiction, as it was in *McDonald v. Graham*.[43] In that case the Court of Appeal approved Judge Ford's purposive construction of his powers, in the interests of avoiding multiplicity of proceedings. Judge Ford also held in *PSM International plc v. Specialised Fastener Products (Southern) Ltd*[44] that he had power under his special jurisdiction to hear an action based on "old" pre-August 1, 1989 copyright because the drawings in question were "design documents" within the meaning of Schedule 1, paragraph 19(1) which temporarily disapplies section 51 to them while still treating them as such. County Courts in any event have a tort jurisdiction which includes copyright,[45] and the sensible course for a plaintiff wanting to use the Patents County Court would be to sue in the Central London County

5.127

[41] [1974] A.C. 133.
[42] *Morton-Norwich v. Intercen (No. 2)* [1981] F.S.R. 337.
[43] [1994] R.P.C. 407.
[44] [1993] F.S.R. 113.
[45] As impliedly held *obiter* by the Court of Appeal in *McDonald v. Graham*, see also *Baumann v. Fussell* [1978] R.P.C. 485 and *pace* the Vice-Chancellor in *Def Lepp Music v. Stuart-Brown* [1986] R.P.C. 273.

Court and try to ensure the case is dealt with by the Patents County Court judge. This is not an ideal solution, because the usual County Court rule as to venue is that the appropriate court is the defendant's local court (though the irregularity could be waived), and also an ordinary County Court judge has no power to grant *Anton Piller* or *Mareva* injunctions even if he happens also to be the Patents County Court judge who would have the power in that capacity.[46] It is a pity that Parliament did not make the matter clearer.

Injunctions

5.128   The principles governing the grant or withholding of interlocutory and final injunctions, including *Anton Piller* and *Mareva*[47] orders, have been considered at 5.047–5.055. As with design right, where licences of right are available, no injunction or delivery up order may be made against a defendant who undertakes to take a licence. This procedure is governed for "hangover" copyright by Schedule 1, paragraph 19, which refers to the corresponding design right provisions, and where licences of right are available by virtue of an order made under section 144 pursuant to a report by the Monopolies and Mergers Commission,[48] section 98 contains a similar provision.

5.129   Much of the *Anton Piller* jurisdiction has been developed in relation to copyright actions, and a point that must be stressed is the necessity, on any type of *ex parte* application but particularly with *Anton Piller* and *Mareva* orders, that the plaintiff make full disclosure of all relevant matters, including those which tell against him, such as his weak financial position[49] which may devalue his cross-undertaking. He should disclose any communications that have taken place between him and the defendant, make any indicated inquiries even if their result may not be to his liking, and in every way provide the court with the full picture. In a copyright or design right action, this will obviously include the availability of licences of right, which could significantly affect the court's exercise of its discretion in deciding whether or not to grant an order. If in doubt, disclosure should always be made, because the penalty for failing to disclose what turn out to be material facts which the plaintiff knew or could on inquiry have learnt may be discharge of the injunction and an order to hand back everything found on its execution.[50]

5.130   Infringements of moral rights are actionable as breaches of statutory duty, and injunctions, as well as other remedies, are available. It would seem that in

---

[46] See *McDonald v. Graham*.
[47] In *CBS v. Lambert* [1983] Ch. 37 the court imposed a freeze on specific items of property which it was persuaded had most likely been bought with the ill-gotten gains of large-scale copyright infringement. In this case, the defendants were living on social security benefits, so it was reasonable to assume their cars, etc., had come from their only other known source of income. The facts would have to be strong to support such an order.
[48] See 4.409–4.052 above.
[49] *Manor Electronics Ltd v. Dickson* [1988] R.P.C. 618.
[50] See *Brinks Mat Ltd v. Elcombe* [1988] 1 W.L.R. 1350 (C.A.).

the rare cases where moral rights have not been waived but licences of right are available under the copyright, the court will have to effect some reconciliation of the right to copy, if the defendant pleases, with some modifications, with the right to object to derogatory treatment. The court may, under section 103(2), grant an injunction on terms prohibiting the doing of any act unless a suitable disclaimer is made dissociating the author from the treatment. The right of paternity will not be a problem, since the plaintiff will doubtless not wish his name to appear on anything over whose quality he has no control; he will more likely want to invoke the right to prevent false attribution.

The court has power to grant declarations of both infringement and non-infringement (a defendant who fears proceedings may make a pre-emptive strike by applying for such a declaration, and will secure the right to open and reply), but because they determine rights it will not normally grant them on an interlocutory basis or without full argument. However, in *Patten v. Burke Publishing Co. Ltd*[51] it granted a final declaration in default of defence where the defendant publishers, with whom the plaintiff had a publishing agreement under which they were given exclusive rights, were in receivership and he needed to know that he was free to offer his book elsewhere.   **5.131**

Damages/Account of profits

Again, these topics have been dealt with under design right. "Additional" damages in cases of flagrant copyright infringement can be claimed under section 97(2).[52] "Conversion" damages based on the fiction that each infringing copy made belonged to the plaintiff, allowing him to claim the whole of the defendant's turnover less only the costs of promotion and distribution, were abolished by the 1988 Act except in relation to proceedings already begun before August 1, 1989, and can be awarded only down to that date.[53]   **5.132**

There is a limited defence of innocence in section 97(1) but only to a claim for damages: other remedies, including an account of profits, remain fully available. The defence is made out where the defendant shows that at the time of the infringement he did not know, and had no reason to believe, that copyright subsisted in the work. Ignorance of the law of copyright is of course no excuse; people are presumed to know the law, however arcane. They are also expected to make any reasonable inquiries and not simply shut their eyes to possibilities. Although the section appears to require proof of two   **5.133**

---

[51] [1991] F.S.R. 483.
[52] For a recent example, see *Noah v. Shuba* [1991] F.S.R. 14.
[53] Sched. 1, para. 31(2) and see *Ransburg-Gema AG v. Electrostatic Plant Systems Ltd* [1991] F.S.R. 508 and *Banks v. CBS Songs Ltd* [1992] F.S.R. 278.

negatives, a defendant will probably need to put forward a positive and credible case that because, say, of the age of the work copied or its apparently obscure foreign origin, or close resemblance to something very well-known like an Ionic column, he supposed, on careful consideration, that it would be out of copyright, or would never have had it, or was not original. Possibly someone who copied the Piltdown skull would have a reasonable defence under section 97(1) to an action for infringement by the forger.

5.134   Where there is an exclusive licence in force, the court must under section 102 take into account the same factors as to the award of pecuniary remedies as are mentioned in 5.060 above.

Delivery up/disposal

5.135   Under the 1956 Act, a successful copyright plaintiff had an automatic right to delivery up of infringing copies because of the fiction that they belonged to him. Now the court has a wider range of options, and delivery up as a final order, or forfeiture, is at the court's discretion under sections 99 and 114 (an ordinary County Court also has this jurisdiction under section 115) which it should only exercise after considering whether pecuniary compensation and a final injunction might not be adequate to protect the plaintiff's interests. The position of other persons having an interest in the goods must also be taken into account, and the court has power to order a sale and divide the proceeds. It can also order that the goods be destroyed. If the goods are not delivered up, destroyed or sold, they are to be given back to the person who originally had them.

5.136   In the recent case of *Victaulic plc v. E. Peart & Co. Ltd*[54] a final order for delivery up of allegedly infringing cast-iron pipe couplings and moulds was resisted by the defendant on the ground that it would prevent it scrapping them and re-using the metal. The plaintiff argued that it wanted to hold the goods as security for damages pending the inquiry, and that the court had power to order delivery up for this purpose. In the event, the court made an order for destruction.

5.137   Section 99[55] was held in *Lagenes Ltd v. It's At (U.K.) Ltd*[56] to extend to granting an interlocutory as well as a final order for delivery up, including against a third party who is wholly innocent, and without the copies ordered to be delivered up having been proved to infringe. This appears to have been wrong, since the court is not supposed to grant an order unless it makes, or it appears to it that there are grounds for making, an order for disposal under section 114. The true position seems to be that section 99, although available against persons innocently holding infringing copies, only permits the

[54] SRIS/C/26/93.
[55] *cf.* s.230.
[56] [1991] F.S.R. 492.

making of final orders, after infringement has been proved (although interlocutory orders may be made under the court's inherent jurisdiction to order delivery up in an appropriate case). The section also allows for delivery up of articles specifically designed or adapted for making copies of a particular copyright work, but in this case only where the party sued knows or has reason to believe that they have been or are to be used for making infringing copies. As observed earlier, the party sued must have the infringing copies in his possession, custody or control in the course of a business, but this is not, as with design right, limited to a business involving the sale or hire of the goods in question, so the section can apparently be used against warehousemen and carriers.

Seizure

There is another delightful remedy available to copyright owners but not to design right owners or registered design proprietors, and that is what is known as the "do-it-yourself *Anton Piller* order". Under section 100, an infringing copy of a work which is found exposed or otherwise immediately available for sale or hire, and in respect of which the copyright owner would be entitled to apply for an order under section 99, may be seized and detained by him or by a person authorised by him. A person may, in order to exercise this right, enter any premises[57] to which the public have access, but may not seize anything in the possession, custody or control of a person at a regular or permanent place of business of his, and may not use any force. Before anything is seized, notice of the time and place of the proposed seizure must be given to a local police station; and when anything is seized, a notice must be left containing prescribed particulars of the person by whom or on whose authority the seizure is made and the grounds on which it has been made.

5.138

This provision (which by Schedule 1, paragraph 19(8) does not apply to "hangover" copyright except where it would survive the section 51 test) is meant to catch itinerant traders who hawk infringing copies at football matches, rock concerts and festivals, tube stations and the like. Market traders with regular pitches are not within its ambit, but car-boot sales would be, although the requirement to give notice at a local police station may be inconvenient where the sale is taking place in a field in the middle of the country. It can be a useful power, but clients should be discouraged from too enthusiastic use of it. It will be noted that there is no obligation on the seizor to follow up the seizure by taking proceedings, nor is there any express requirement in the section that he hold the goods pending further order. However, section 114 refers to goods seized *and detained* under section 100, and a seizor would be ill-advised to dispose of the goods without an order. It is always open to the aggrieved seizee to apply to the court under section 114.

5.139

---

[57] "Premises" includes land, buildings, moveable structures, vehicles, vessels, aircraft and hovercraft.

Threats

5.140   There is no "threats" action in copyright as there is for registered and unregistered designs, and prospective plaintiffs and their advisers can (and do) threaten proceedings as floridly as they please. It was suggested by Whitford J. in *Jaybeam Ltd v. Abru Aluminium Ltd*[58] that some sort of control might be exercised by the law of malicious falsehood or unlawful interference with business, but this was only at the interlocutory stage and the case never went to trial. In *Granby Marketing Services Ltd v. Interlego AG*[59] the plaintiff complained that the defendant had interfered with its business as a marketing consultant by unlawful threats of copyright infringement proceedings against its client, Kelloggs. A marketing promotion devised for Kelloggs by Granby featured LEGO-like bricks. The defendant menaced Kelloggs, who scrapped the promotion and declined to pay Granby. Vinelott J. struck out Granby's action. In the absence of abuse of process or a specific prohibition of threats (or malice), a person is perfectly entitled to threaten proceedings if he believes he has a cause of action, even if it may be a weak one.

CRIMINAL LIABILITY FOR COPYRIGHT INFRINGEMENT

5.141   Unlike both registered and unregistered designs, breaches of copyright can give rise to criminal liability. Historically this was not much used, but with the increase in commercial counterfeiting and piracy, upgraded and extended criminal sanctions have been made available and are becoming widely-used.

5.142   The 1988 Act by section 107 makes a number of activities done without the copyright owner's licence criminal offences. These are making for sale or hire; importing into the U.K. other than for private and domestic use; possessing in the course of a business with a view to committing an infringing act; selling, letting for hire, offering or exposing for sale or hire; exhibiting or distributing in the course of a business; or distributing in the course of a business to such an extent as prejudicially to affect the copyright owner, articles which in every case the accused knows or has reason to believe are infringing copies. It is also an offence to make or have in one's possession an article specifically designed or adapted for making copies of a particular copyright work, knowing or having reason to believe that it is to be used to make infringing copies for sale or hire or for use in the course of a business. Penalties are a fine and/or up to six months' imprisonment on summary conviction, and a fine and/or up to two years' imprisonment on indictment. Orders for delivery up can be made under section 108, the goods delivered up being later dealt with under section 114. The police have power to obtain search and seizure warrants (section 109), and may be accompanied on the execution of these by

[58] [1976] R.P.C. 308.
[59] [1984] R.P.C. 209.

authorised representatives of the complainants. Warrants are of course obtained without notice to the accused, and are valid for 28 days.

Directors or other officers of companies found guilty of an offence who have connived at or consented to the offences can be separately prosecuted (section 110).   **5.143**

Large-scale operators may also be prosecuted for conspiracy to commit these offences, with correspondingly greater penalties. If a person agrees with another or others to pursue a course of conduct which will necessarily involve the commission of a statutory offence by one or more of them if the agreement is carried out, he is guilty of conspiring to commit the offence, even if he does not himself commit it. A cinema projectionist was prosecuted for conspiracy to commit an offence under section 21 of the 1956 Act when he temporarily removed prints of films from his place of work to lend to others who made master videotapes of them for multiple counterfeiting.[60]   **5.144**

Use of the criminal law is in some respects less satisfactory than civil proceedings, because the standard of proof is the criminal standard of "beyond reasonable doubt" rather than the civil standard of "balance of probabilities"; the rules of evidence are much more stringent; there is no provision for financial compensation; and costs awards are often rather low.   **5.145**

On the other hand, prosecutions can be and often are brought by trade associations such as FACT (Federation Against Copyright Theft), FAST (Federation Against Software Theft) and the Business Software Alliance, and the whole process is much cheaper. Now that *Anton Piller* orders, due to the additional safeguards introduced, are well beyond the pockets of any but the very rich or the legally-aided very poor, a private prosecution, with accompanying odium, can be an effective way of proceeding. And since magistrates are unlikely to know much about copyright law, a complainant may obtain most gratifying and quite startling results, as in *Manners v. The Reject Shop plc.*[61]   **5.146**

INVOLVEMENT OF HM CUSTOMS & EXCISE

At present, the ability of a copyright owner under section 111 of the 1988 Act to request the Customs to seize infringing goods does not extend to artistic works. But there is to be an E.U. Council Regulation[62] which will supersede the current Regulation 3842/86 extending only to trade marks, and will provide copyright and industrial design owners with powers to request the Customs to detain infringing goods, whether imported, exported or in transit, and also tools, moulds and packaging, other than those for private use   **5.147**

---

[60] *R. v. Lloyd* [1985] 2 All E.R. 661. He was not guilty of theft, because he did not intend permanently to deprive his employers of the prints, and there is no offence of theft of the *content* of a document, etc.
[61] See Case Comment at [1995] 1 E.I.P.R. 46 and 2.155 above.
[62] For draft, see [1994] F.S.R. 325.

only. The copyright or design owner will have 10 days to inspect the goods and start legal proceedings so that the court can decide whether they infringe. If they do, they must be confiscated and disposed of outside normal commercial channels.

5.148   It is a requirement of the GATT TRIPs Agreement that procedures of this type be provided by member countries.

REGISTERED DESIGNS

Infringement

What acts constitute infringement

5.149   Unlike copyright, where transitional provisions ensure that in most cases infringements occurring on or after August 1, 1989 are judged by the test set out in the 1988 Act, with registered designs different tests of infringement apply depending on the date on which the allegedly infringing design was applied for. This is the effect of section 268 of the 1988 Act, which amends section 7 of the Registered Designs Act 1949 but only (section 268(2)) in relation to designs registered pursuant to applications made on or after August 1, 1989.

5.150   The unamended section 7 gave to the registered proprietor the exclusive right in the U.K. and the Isle of Man to make or import for sale or for use for the purposes of any trade or business, or to sell, hire or offer for sale or hire, any article in respect of which the design was registered, being an article to which the design or a design not substantially different from it had been applied, and to make anything for enabling any such article to be made, whether in the U.K. or the Isle of Man or elsewhere. So anyone who did anything which fell within this exclusive right, without the consent of the registered proprietor, would be an infringer, provided the design was valid.

5.151   The 1988 amendment slightly recasts the section, with some alterations, and also adds other matters. The new section 7(1) now brings within the proprietor's exclusive right making or importing for hire, and exposing for sale or hire—the latter no doubt to get round the technical difficulty of contract law that including an article in a catalogue or setting it out on a shelf in a shop does not constitute an offer for sale but only an invitation to potential customers to make an offer to buy. Subsection (2) makes explicit what was formerly implicit, that is that a person who without the proprietor's licence does any of the acts falling within the exclusive right infringes the design. Subsection (4) introduces infringement by doing any of the acts within the exclusive right in relation to a "kit", meaning a complete or substantially complete set of components intended to be assembled into an article. "Set of components" does not mean the same as "set of articles", which is confined by section 44(1) to a collection of articles all effectively conforming to the registered design.[63]

Subsection (5) also contains the prohibition, previously to be found in section 3(5), against taking proceedings for any infringement occurring before the date on which the certificate of registration is granted, even though the registration then dates back to the date of application. There is no provision such as there is in the Patents Act 1977 allowing a patentee to sue, once his patent is granted, for infringements occurring between publication and grant. This drawback was one of the main reasons for allowing an enforceable copyright to registrable designs under the Design Copyright Act 1968: if a proprietor had to wait for grant before he could sue, and could never catch infringements committed pre-grant, he would often be without an effective remedy against opportunists who copied as soon as his designs went on the market and thus hit what might be his peak trading season. Nowadays an expectant proprietor will during the gestation of his registration be able to sue on his unregistered design right (or copyright if any).   **5.152**

The ambit of the exclusive right under both the old and the new section 7(1) is clear: making or importing for private use does not fall within it, but, *e.g.* importing a tool covered by a registration for use in one's own business does, unlike the position with unregistered design right. Simple possession of an infringing article is not an infringing act, but if, *e.g.* a plaintiff can show that a defendant who has made or imported it is storing it in his warehouse along with other goods he plans to sell or hire, it would probably in practice be for the defendant to show that, notwithstanding appearances, he has not made or imported it for sale or hire. Since a registered design confers a monopoly right, there is no division into primary and secondary infringement. All the plaintiff need do is demonstrate infringement, and it will be for the defendant, if he can, to make out the limited defence of innocence, which is available under section 9.   **5.153**

Where infringement takes place

The old section expressly limits the exclusive right to the U.K. and the Isle of Man, which the new section 7 does not. The Act as a whole extends to Scotland, Northern Ireland and the Isle of Man (sections 45, 46 and 47), and by section 47A, introduced by the 1988 Act, now extends also to U.K. territorial waters and things done in the U.K. sector of the continental shelf on a structure or vessel which is there for exploration of the seabed or subsoil or the exploitation of their natural resources. It is not clear why the old section 7 limitation to the U.K. was removed, but since national design registrations have only national effect, it is unlikely to make any difference.   **5.154**

A rather longer arm is however provided both by the old section 7(1) and the new section 7(3) to catch infringers who seek to escape by having their   **5.155**

---

[63] See 2.014 above.

products assembled overseas: it is an infringing act to make anything for enabling an infringing article to be made, in the U.K. or elsewhere. In *Haddon v. Bannerman*,[64] a defendant who had in England made matrices for production of the typeface protected by the plaintiff's registration, but planned to ship them to India where production of the type would take place, was nonetheless found (under earlier but similar legislation) to have infringed in the U.K.

5.156   However, in *Haddon* what had been made in the U.K. was what would in copyright law have been termed a "plate" or "mould" which enabled an entire infringing article (or in this case set of articles) to be made. Merely supplying components which, when assembled with others, may result in an infringement may not amount to making something "for enabling" an infringing article to be made. In *Aberdale Cycle Co. Ltd v. Charles Twigg & Co. Ltd*,[65] the registered design was for a toy tricycle with a container ("boot") mounted between the back wheels. The defendant sold tricycles without this container, but made and sold it separately with instructions for fitting it to the tricycles. The judge refused to find that this supply of a single component, which might or might not be used for the recommended purpose, amounted to making something for enabling the protected article to be made. In his view, only something like a printing roller engraved or embossed to enable it to print (and only to print) a registered textile design would fall within the prohibition. Similarly, in *Dorling v. Honnor*,[66] Harman L.J. declined to regard the individual parts in the kit of parts for a self-assembled sailing dinghy as things for enabling the completed boat to be made. He too believed the Act to refer to things like tools or moulds, and not to parts of the article itself. So although the making in the U.K. of a complete paper pattern for a dress to be cut out and made up elsewhere might infringe a registered design for the completed dress, the making and export merely of trimmings for such a dress, such as ribbons and lace, would not.

5.157   "New" designs will benefit from the "kit" provision, which also covers making anything for enabling a kit to be assembled, in the U.K. or elsewhere, if the resulting article would infringe the registered design. Under this provision, not only would supply of the kit (as in *Dorling*) now infringe a registered design for the completed article, but it might be enough to supply one or two components of the kit only, because without them the boat could not be completely assembled. It could also, if malevolently interpreted, perhaps even cover the manufacture of glue, screws or solder specifically for such a kit, even though it was the risk of catching such items as these which encouraged Harman L.J. to give a limited interpretation to the old provision. It might even catch the printing ("making") of instruction leaflets to be used with the kit.

---

[64] (1912) 29 R.P.C. 611.
[65] (1952) 69 R.P.C. 137.
[66] [1964] R.P.C. 160.

Test of infringement

Case law has articulated how the test of whether the registered design or a **5.158** design not substantially different from it has been applied to the allegedly infringing article is to be carried out. None of the reported cases to date deals with section 7 as amended, but since the general principles are the same and the effects of the *Interlego v. Tyco* heresy[67] were put right by the new section 7(6) before they could do much harm, the earlier authorities will be equally applicable to "new" designs. It is the eye of the court which is to be the judge of similarities and differences, but not its naked eye: regard must be had to intended purchasers of the article all along the line of distribution. If the article is bought by the general public as is, then the judge's eye will be as good as the next man's, although the Court of Appeal in *Sommer Allibert (U.K.) Ltd v. Flair Plastics Ltd*[68] pointed out that he should adopt the state of mind of a customer interested in buying one of the articles concerned, not merely a casual window-shopper. But if the article is one which is incorporated in another one before it reaches the public, the eye of an intermediate purchaser must also be peered through. In *Kevi A/S v. Suspa-Verein U.K. Ltd*,[69] the article was a furniture castor used mainly in office furniture, and Falconer J. held that he had to assess the design's eye-appeal through the eyes both of trade customers (office furniture manufacturers and retailers stocking the office furniture) and of the ultimate office-furniture-buying customer— though he doubted there would be much difference in that particular case.

In some cases trade customers might notice features which would not be **5.159** apparent to the consumer, but care should be taken to omit features which in truth appeal to the trade customer for functional reasons such as ease of fitting rather than because he believes they will enhance the article's visual appeal to ultimate consumers. What matters at each stage, according to Lord Reid in *Amp v. Utilux*,[70] is "the commercial value resulting from customers preferring the appearance of articles which have the design to that of those which do not have it". Expert evidence, perhaps from designers, advertising consultants, and traders (and probably market researchers, though these do not seem to have penetrated the design field so far) is admissible,[71] so long as the judge makes up his own mind.

The test of infringement is one of fact. While the Court of Appeal will pay **5.160** due deference to the experience of the specialist judge who will have heard the case at first instance, it is both entitled and bound to substitute its own view if it disagrees with him.[72]

---

[67] [1988] R.P.C. 343, and see 2.045 above. The heresy was that purely functional features might be taken into account in assessing infringement.
[68] [1987] R.P.C. 599.
[69] [1982] R.P.C. 173.
[70] [1972] R.P.C. 103.
[71] See, for example, *Prince Manufacturing Inc. v. Dunlop Slazenger International Ltd*, SRIS/CC/29/94.
[72] *Benchairs Ltd v. Chair Centre Ltd* [1974] R.P.C. 429.

5.161 Although the scope of the monopoly is established by the representations accompanying the registration (and the statement of novelty required by the Rules though not by the Act), it is well-established that the court can look at the plaintiff's article as actually sold.[73] This is realistic but, arguably, pernicious. The article as sold has nothing to do with, and may indeed differ from, the monopoly as claimed, but it could influence the court against a defendant who may have copied the article without infringing the design. Aldous J. in *Gaskell & Chambers Ltd v. Measure Master Ltd*[74] looked only at the representations, and expressly refused to be swayed by arguments that the defendant had copied.

Construing the design

5.162 Before the court can commence its delicate stereoscopic task it must sort out what it may and what it may not take into account. First of all, an article will only infringe a registered design if it is an article in respect of which the design is registered. The application, and the certificate of registration, have to state what article the registration covers, and the allegedly infringing article must be capable of being brought within the same description. In *Bourjois Ltd v. British Home Stores Ltd*,[75] the registration was for "a container for a perfume bottle" and showed a bucket with a lid moulded to look like ice with the neck of a champagne bottle sticking out of it. The actual perfume bottle, in the article as sold, was concealed in the bucket. The defendant's article was a lidless bucket containing simulated ice and the actual perfume bottle, got up to look like a champagne bottle, which poked out of it. It was held, admittedly not after a full trial, that while the plaintiff's article was a container for a perfume bottle, the defendant's was not, because the get-up featured the bottle itself. This was perhaps a rather hard decision, but shows the importance of care in drafting applications to register.

5.163 Secondly, the court must construe the design and see what it actually does cover. It must have regard to the statement of novelty, which determines the scope of the monopoly; and it must look for, and discount, any features which are mere methods or principles of construction, or which are dictated solely by function, or, for post-July 31, 1989 designs, which "must-match". Indeed, for post-July 31, 1989 designs, the new section 7(6) expressly spells out that a design is not infringed by reproduction of a "dictated solely by function" or

---

[73] *Dunlop Rubber Co. Ltd v. Golf Ball Developments Ltd* (1931) 48 R.P.C. 268 (where the embodiments were made specifically for the proceedings, the design never having been exploited by the proprietor); *Lusty (W.) & Sons Ltd v. Morris Wilkinson & Co. (Nottingham) Ltd* (1954) 71 R.P.C. 174 (what the plaintiff had made was conceded to be an embodiment, and it could be looked at to save the mental effort of visualising a 3D article from the 2D representation); *Benchairs Ltd v. Chair Centre Ltd* above (provided evidence was given that there was no variation between the representation and the embodiment).
[74] 1992 I.P.D. 15144.
[75] (1951) 68 R.P.C. 280.

"must-match" feature which is left out of account in assessing registrability. This subsection was inserted to restore what had been believed to be the position until the Privy Council's decision in *Interlego*.[76] The court must also consider whether there are any features which are not novel or, with pre-August 1, 1989 designs, original.

Statements of novelty are seldom very informative, consisting in most cases **5.164** of standard claims like "Novelty resides in the shape or configuration of the article as shown in the representations". This form means that the claimed monopoly covers the three-dimensional appearance of the whole article as illustrated, no special features being relied on. Statements of novelty which do claim a special feature give hostages to fortune, because a defendant will escape infringement if his design, though otherwise similar, lacks that feature—as in *Portable Concrete Buildings Ltd v. Bathcrete Ltd*,[77] where the statement of novelty for a portable garage claimed a particular feature at both ends and the defendant had it only at one end.

A shape and configuration claim does not cover any pattern or ornament **5.165** applied to the article, so the defendant will not escape infringement by pointing to a different pattern or ornament applied to his article, which otherwise resembles the registered design. But in *Sommer Allibert v. Flair*,[78] the plaintiff was unsuccessful in arguing that shallow vertical grooves on the back and seat of its moulded plastic chair were mere pattern or ornament, so that the somewhat different appearance of the defendant's horizontal grooves should be disregarded in assessing infringement of a shape and configuration design. Both Whitford J. and the Court of Appeal held that, having regard to the way in which moulded plastic articles are made, the grooves were part of the configuration of the chair, and it did not matter that they might have been conceived for the purpose of ornament. Both courts quoted from the decision in *Cow (P. B.) & Co. Ltd v. Cannon Rubber Manufacturers Ltd*,[79] a case where the parallel ribs on the surface of a rubber hot water bottle were held to be features of configuration. Lloyd-Jacob J. in that case gave the further example of a pat of butter in the shape of a roll with a corrugated surface: the tubular form of the roll would be "shape", the corrugations "configuration".

Pattern or ornament designs are therefore to be taken as substantially **5.166** two-dimensional, as indeed was said by Luxmoore J. in *Kestos Ltd v. Kempat Ltd*,[80] who observed that "An article can exist without any pattern or ornament upon it, whereas it can have no existence at all apart from its shape or configuration". A registered design for something like pottery may of course claim both shape/configuration and pattern/ornament, but it is wiser to have two separate registrations because otherwise a copier who takes the

[76] [1988] R.P.C. 343. See Lord Young of Graffham, *Hansard*, Vol. 501, col. 329.
[77] [1962] R.P.C. 49.
[78] [1987] R.P.C. 599.
[79] [1959] R.P.C. 240, 347.
[80] (1936) 53 R.P.C. 139.

shape but not the pattern or vice versa will be able to show that his design is substantially different.

5.167   The next stage is for the judge to discount features which embody methods or principles of construction,[81] features dictated solely by function (in shape and configuration designs), in "old" pattern or ornament designs features not "judged solely" by the eye,[82] and in "new" designs, "must-match" features. He must bear in mind that "dictated solely by" function means, according to the House of Lords in *Amp*,[83] "attributable to or caused or prompted by" function; a shape (or configuration) "not there to appeal to the eye but solely to make the article work". Using these criteria, Falconer J. in the *Kevi* castor case found on the evidence that a metal plate acting as a locking device was, but a hood which had the function of hiding worn wheels but was also there to improve the look of the product was not, solely dictated by function. The plate was to be disregarded in assessing infringement, but not the hood. In *Sommer Allibert v. Flair*,[84] the Court of Appeal took a broad view of functionality: Slade L.J. said[85]:

> "The function which the [plaintiff's] and the [defendant's] chairs have to perform is that of a stacking garden armchair. All armchairs will have certain features in common, in particular a back, a seat, arms and legs. Furthermore, the overall proportions of both chairs were dictated by the function of providing a comfortable chair on which to sit, the parties in their design following recognised ergonomic standards in the industry. As a start, in considering infringement, we must ignore the fact that the [plaintiff's] and the [defendant's] chair possess these common characteristics. However, as [the plaintiff's designer] accepted in cross-examination, the particular method of stacking both these chairs imposes certain further constraints on the design of chairs of this sort. The spacing of the rear legs must be narrower than the spacing of the front legs. The arms must lie outside the spacing or width of the rear legs. There must be a gap between the sides of the seat and the insides of the arms, to serve as a space for the rear legs. All these constraints are dictated solely by the function of rendering possible stacking by this particular method. All of them render it inevitable that armchairs which are designed to perform these functions must possess many common features, whether or not they also possess many dissimilar features; and all must be disregarded for present purposes."

Slade L.J. also reminds us of two further features that must be disregarded as forming no part of a registered design: colour (except in very limited

---

[81] See 2.030 above.
[82] *Lamson Industries Ltd's Design Application* [1978] R.P.C. 1 (computer printout paper with alternate "staves" of orange and green lines—decorative but also facilitated reading of matter printed out, so not judged "solely" by eye; *cf.* treatment of partly functional but nonetheless registrable feature in *Kevi v. Suspa-Verein* [1982] R.P.C. 173.
[83] [1972] R.P.C. 103.
[84] [1987] R.P.C. 599.
[85] At p. 622.

circumstances) and material. The obvious similarity engendered by the fact that both parties' chairs were made of white plastic could not be taken into account. Nor, as the above citation makes clear, must the court allow itself to be influenced by similarities arising from the fact that both parties' products perform identical functions. Both the plaintiff's and the defendant's chairs were stackable, but there was nothing offensive about this. What the report does not make clear, and would have been interesting to know, is whether they were inter-stackable, so that a large-scale user who did not care about the difference in grooving might have been tempted to replace broken chairs made by the plaintiff with new ones made by the defendant.

Finally, the judge must rule out from comparison features which lack **5.168** novelty or, in "old" designs, originality, over the prior art as at the date of the application to register. Either party may produce prior art, whether earlier registered designs, or products, or photographs or possibly descriptions of products: the defendant to show similarities, the plaintiff to show differences. In practice, the judge will not, except in clear cases, perform this test solely by comparing the registered design with the prior art: he is likely to be addressing a "squeeze" argument that if the registered design is novel over the prior art, then the defendant's article does not infringe because it differs just as much from the registered design as the latter does from the prior art—the test of novelty and the test of infringement being substantially the same. Small differences over the prior art make for a registration of limited scope.[86] The judge will take into account the Registrar's view that the plaintiff's design merited registration, but he is in no way bound by this. The Registrar's practice is, after all, to give the applicant the benefit of any doubt there may be, and leave it to the court to sort out. In the same way the judge will take into account the fact that the defendant's design may itself have been registered over the plaintiff's (which sometimes happens); but he must always form his own view.

Making the comparison

Except in the rare case where the defendant's design is identical to the **5.169** plaintiff's (such cases are unlikely to come to full trial, since a counterfeiter will usually have been seen off at a much earlier stage), the defendant will try to persuade the court that his design shows substantial differences from the plaintiff's. He will normally do this by a feature-by-feature comparison, trying to show that as many as possible of the embarrassingly similar features are solely dictated by function or not novel, and that the rest are noticeably different. The plaintiff's interest, on the other hand, will often be to persuade

---

[86] See, *e.g. Valor Heating Co. Ltd v. Main Gas Appliances Ltd* [1973] R.P.C. 871 (it is instructive to look at the pictures published with the report and see if you agree with the learned judge); *Walker & Co. Ltd v. Scott & Co. Ltd* (1892) 9 R.P.C. 482 (only difference between registered design for oilcan and prior art was rounded edges; defendant's can lacked these features so did not infringe).

the court to take an overall view, and he is at an advantage in opening the case because he may be able to impress the judge with apparently sinister similarities before the defendant gets a chance to destroy these by analysis. He will argue that even though certain, or even all, the individual features may not be novel, his overall arrangement of them, which the defendant has reproduced, creates a novel impression.

5.170   The plaintiff will also rely on the doctrine of "imperfect recollection", an import from trade mark law. Although the competing designs must be considered side by side, it is also legitimate to envisage a purchaser shopping around, looking at one design in one shop, others elsewhere, and then being faced with what might be either the plaintiff's or the defendant's, and being in a quandary as to which it might be, detailed differences having become blurred by the passage of time. This practice was endorsed in *Sommer Allibert v. Flair*, subject to the proviso that the purchaser must be assumed to care about the appearance of what he is buying and not, for example, be motivated by considerations of price alone. A distinction should perhaps be drawn here between trade and consumer purchasers. A trader will have a more experienced eye, and also a more leisurely and careful one, since he may be contemplating substantial investment in components for his own product. An ordinary member of the public, trudging round the furniture stores or garden centres on a Saturday afternoon, may be readier, under pressure from bored partners and squawking children, to take horizontally rather than vertically grooved garden chairs, grooving of some kind having been the feature that stuck in his or her mind.

5.171   Although it is not necessary in assessing design infringement to show that the products are confusingly similar, evidence of how they are marketed seems relevant in so far as "imperfect recollection" is relied on as a pointer to infringement. If products are clearly and emphatically labelled, or are sold through radically-different outlets, or catalogues are provided so that selection can be made at leisure, there should be less room for the application of the doctrine. Similarly, how the goods are displayed at point of sale may have a bearing on what features are particularly likely to be noticed.

5.172   Where the plaintiff's design has a particular striking feature which catches the eye, whether specifically claimed or not, the comparison between the products is simpler: either the defendant's product possesses it or it does not. In *Dunlop Rubber Co. Ltd v. Golf Ball Developments Ltd*,[87] the judge found that a star was the most striking feature of the plaintiff's design; since the defendant's ball did not possess a star, it was found not to infringe. But opinions may differ as to what is a striking feature: in *Benchairs Ltd v. Chair Centre Ltd*,[88] Graham J. at first instance found the particular arrangement of the back and legs of the chair to be a striking feature also possessed by the defendant's chair and granted an interlocutory injunction accordingly. The

---

[87] (1931) 48 R.P.C. 268.
[88] [1974] R.P.C. 429.

Court of Appeal discharged it, saying that they did not think these features striking at all in either the plaintiff's or the defendant's chair.

"Squeeze" arguments based on comparisons between the prior art, the **5.173** plaintiff's design and the defendant's article have already been considered. Aldous J. considered their application in the recent case of *Gaskell & Chambers Ltd v. Measure Master Ltd*[89] in the context of what a purchaser would notice about a design. Where a registered design differs from the prior art only in small details, the customer's eye might be more readily drawn to these, whereas if the registered design (as in that case) was very different, he would be more likely to concentrate on, and remember, the general form of the new design rather than the details. One way of combating squeeze arguments is if the plaintiff can demonstrate that his design has enjoyed commercial success despite the earlier existence of the prior art. If he can persuade the court that this success is due to the appearance of his design (and not, for example, to improved functional qualities, lower price, or heavy promotion) it may find that apparently small visual differences did in fact count for a good deal.

In the end, though, what counts is what the judge thinks on the day, which **5.174** makes registered design infringement cases difficult to advise on, particularly if the judge, like Aldous J. in *Gaskell & Chambers*, declines to be influenced by suggestions of deliberate copying. (This refusal is of course entirely proper: the test is whether the defendant's design is the same as or not substantially different from the plaintiff's, not whether it has been copied; but aggrieved plaintiffs are not always pleased to be told this.) The cases abound with judicial impressions that one design is "more massive", "plumper", "squarer and more upright", "more rounded" than another, and these impressions are very subjective.[90] In matters of aesthetics, this is probably inevitable. Defences

DEFENCES

Functionality of a design, "must-match", "who-cares-what-it-looks-like?", **5.175** method or principle of construction and want of novelty (and want of originality for "old" designs), and also attacks on the plaintiff's title to be registered proprietor of the design if he is not the original creator or commissioner, are all defences to an action for registered design infringement, and they also put the validity of the registration in question. It is usual, but not obligatory, for a defendant raising all or any of these defences to counterclaim for rectification of the Register. What is not a defence, since this is a monopoly right, is independent creation of the defendant's article, *i.e.*

---

[89] 1992 I.P.D. 15144.
[90] The Court of Appeal in *Benchairs* spoke of one party's chair giving the impression of "a terrier with a good stance". This is a particularly instructive case in demonstrating the different conclusions which can be reached by different people.

that he did not copy it, except perhaps in the limited instances where innocence is a defence to a claim for damages, as described below.

5.176   Nor is it a defence that the registration is for something which is flexible, so that the defendant's design, though infringing the design representations in some postures, can be manipulated so that it is substantially different in others.[91]

5.177   The "implied licence" defence[92] applies to design-registered articles, which may be repaired by their owners with what would otherwise be infringing parts, provided what is done does not amount to complete replacement. The *British Leyland* defence does not apply.[93]

5.178   E.C. law can also be invoked as a defence if there is a nexus between the plaintiff's Euro-offensive acts and what the defendant has done, as discussed in 5.037 above. However, recent domestic and European Court cases involving registered body panel designs owned by Ford, Volvo and other major car manufacturers, and spare parts made by independent fabricators,[94] as well as the older *Nancy Kean* case,[95] show the courts, in the absence of any E.U.-wide harmonisation of registered design law, unwilling to interfere with the existence or the exercise of national rights. The *content* of national registered designs laws, including the U.K.'s will have to change with the coming into effect of the proposed Community Design Harmonisation Directive[96] (expected in the relatively near but not immediate future); but recital 19 of its Preamble expresses this to be without prejudice to Articles 85 and 86.

Remedies

Parties

5.179   The Registered Designs Act 1949, even as amended, contains no provision allowing an exclusive licensee to sue on his own account. He must therefore, like other licensees (and, presumably, chargees), try to secure a term in his licence obliging the registered proprietor to sue at his request, and probably at his expense, and making provision for the sharing of any financial compensation awarded. If the proprietor sues, the licensee, whether exclusive or not, might as well join himself as co-plaintiff and leave it to the defendant to try and strike him out. In *Trico Products Corp. v. Romac Motor Accessories*[97] a

---

[91] *Schmittzehe v. Roberts* (1955) 72 R.P.C. 122 (doll with moveable head, arms and legs).
[92] See 5.034 above.
[93] [1986] A.C. 577.
[94] See, *e.g. Volvo AB v. Erik Veng (U.K.) Ltd* [1989] 4 C.M.L.R. 122; *Consorzio Italiano della Componentistica di Ricambio per Autoveicoli & Maxicar v. Régie Nationale des Usines Renault* [1990] 4 C.M.L.R. 265.
[95] *Keurkoop BV v. Nancy Kean Gifts* [1983] 2 C.M.L.R. 47.
[96] 93/C 345/09 COM(93) 344 *final*—COD 464.
[97] (1934) 51 R.P.C. 90.

defendant failed to strike out a sole licensee joined as co-plaintiff; and the *Lonrho v. Fayed* tort of unlawful interference with trade discussed at 5.042 above might also be relied on. It is perfectly proper, and desirable, to join all potential defendants in the same action, even though one may be a manufacturing and one a selling infringer.

Forum

Actions for registered design infringement may be brought in either the High **5.180** Court or the Patents County Court.[98] In the High Court they are assigned to the Chancery Division, where they will be heard by a specialist judge of the Patents Court. Order 104 of the Rules of the Supreme Court contains special procedural provisions for registered design cases. Counterclaims for rectification on the grounds of invalidity may be brought in both courts, and rules require that they contain or be accompanied by Particulars of Objections to validity, citing any prior art relied on. Since the state of the Register is being called into question, copies of the counterclaim and Particulars of Objections must be served on the Registrar, *i.e.* the Comptroller-General. If a prospective defendant wants to pre-empt infringement proceedings, he may apply to the Registrar under section 11(2), or by originating motion direct to the court under section 20, for cancellation/rectification.

Injunctions

Injunctions, both interlocutory and final, are available in both courts on the **5.181** same basis as for unregistered design right, except that there is no need to worry about "selling" defendants not having been put on notice. An undertaking can be offered instead of an injunction. In the very limited circumstances where licences of right are available under registered designs (see section 11A, section 266 of the 1988 Act and 4.072–4.074 above), section 11B provides that no injunction shall be granted in an infringement action if the defendant, at any time before final judgment and without the need for any admission of liability, undertakes to take a licence on such terms as may be agreed or settled by the Registrar in default of agreement. Financial compensation is also limited to twice the amount payable under the licence if it had been granted before the earliest infringement.

An injunction, being originally an equitable remedy, is technically **5.182** discretionary, and it is sometimes argued that one should not be granted if the

---

[98] See discussion at 5.044 above. There have been several registered design cases dealt with by the PCC, among them *Parmenter v. Malt House Joinery* 1992 I.P.D. 15025, *Sony KK v. Win-Technic Electronics Pty Ltd* SRIS/CC/84/92 and *Prince Manufacturing Inc. v. Dunlop Slazenger International Ltd* SRIS/CC/29/94.

plaintiff's own conduct has not been unimpeachable—if he has neglected to observe the old maxim that "he who comes to equity must come with clean hands". Such arguments rarely succeed nowadays, but one piece of grubbiness that might be raised (it scarcely adds to the costs and might just stick) would be if the plaintiff had falsely claimed that his design was registered when it was not—either because the application had not yet been granted, or because the design had expired through lapse of time or failure to renew or restore. This is also a criminal offence under section 35, and under section 35A any officer of a body corporate (or person holding himself out as such) who has connived in or consented to such an offence may be also be prosecuted. Damages in lieu of an injunction may be awarded. If the design is about to expire an injunction may not be granted, or will be limited to expire at the same time as the design, unless perhaps the defendant can be shown to have won by his infringement an illicit springboard which will allow him to compete more effectively once the design expires.

Damages/account of profits

5.183 As with unregistered design right, these are alternative remedies, both dealt with in separate proceedings after the trial on liability. The grant of an inquiry or account might be refused if the defendant could persuade the court that his sales have been minimal. However, courts are reluctant to shut successful plaintiffs out of compensation by refusing an inquiry,[99] and if the defendant can prove his sales really are minimal, he might be well-advised to disclose his documents evidencing them along with his discovery on liability (which he need not normally do), and tender a witness at the main trial for cross-examination. Damages are calculated by reference to the plaintiff's loss of profit where he can show that the defendant has taken sales from him because of his use of the infringing design. Alternatively they may be on a royalty basis, particularly if the plaintiff has been licensing the design to others. Defendants may argue that part of their success was due to their superior marketing efforts or expertise.[1] Plaintiffs in turn may argue that their loss goes beyond loss of sales, for example because their market credibility has been spoilt[2]—this might not be uncommon with short-lived designs. They may also look for interest on money borrowed to maintain cashflow. A recent case canvassing some of these points on the inquiry in a patent action is *Catnic Components Ltd v. Hill & Smith Ltd.*[3] There is no provision in the 1949 Act for "additional" damages in cases of flagrancy. Interest on damages or the sums found due on an account must be specifically claimed, but will normally be awarded from the date of infringement took place (the same applies to unregistered design right and copyright). It can be quite substantial,

[99] *Carlis Ware v. E. Radford* [1959] R.P.C. 38.
[1] *Cow (P. B.) Ltd v. Cannon Rubber Manufacturers Ltd* [1961] R.P.C. 236.
[2] *Khawan & Co. v. Chellaram & Sons (Nigeria) Ltd* [1964] R.P.C. 337 (Privy Council, dealing with Nigerian Design Ordinance).
[3] [1983] F.S.R. 512.

the current rate of interest on judgments often being adopted. For a good many years this was 15 per cent per year, but it has now dropped to 8 per cent.

"Innocence"

There is a limited provision in section 9 of the Registered Designs Act   **5.184**
whereby an infringer can escape liability for damages (but only for damages—an injunction continues to be available) if he can prove that at the date of the infringement (by which is probably meant each separate act of infringement) he was not aware, and had no reasonable ground for supposing, that the decision was registered. The burden of proof is on the defendant, but section 9(1) also provides that he shall not be deemed to have been aware or to have had reasonable grounds by reason *only* that an article had been marked with the word "registered" or some abbreviation thereof or any word or words expressing or implying registration, unless the design number also appeared with the word or words. Obviously common sense must be used in applying this section. A defendant who deliberately shuts his eyes to clear indications, or is boundlessly stupid on any objective test, or who has actually copied the plaintiff's goods,[4] is unlikely to succeed; nor, it is thought, would one who has shown his patent agent an article marked "registered" and the agent has failed to check the Register—though the defendant may sue the agent. On the other hand, a plaintiff who launches fully-marked goods on to the market only after the defendant has infringed on a large scale will not be able to claim damages.

It seems, however, that he would still be able to claim an account of profits.   **5.185**
This was not mentioned as a remedy under the 1949 Act as originally drafted, but it was always accepted that an account would be available; and the remedy is now expressly mentioned in section 11B, which limits the amounts recoverable by way of damages "or on an account of profits" to double the royalty fixed under a licence of right.

DELIVERY UP/COSTS

The 1949 Act does not specifically provide for these forms of relief, but they   **5.186**
are routinely granted in the High Court, and also in the Patents County Court under the general rather than the special County Court jurisdiction. Destruction of infringing articles by the defendant is an alternative to delivery up; it seems the defendant gets to choose, but he must certify on oath that destruction has taken place, and will be in serious trouble if it has not. The principles as to costs, settlements and Calderbank offers discussed in 5.066–5.068 above are equally applicable to registered design cases.

---

[4] See *Lancer Boss Ltd v. Henley Forklift Co. Ltd* [1975] R.P.C. 307, a patent case on a section with similar wording.

CERTIFICATE OF CONTESTED VALIDITY

5.187 A registered proprietor the validity of whose design has been unsuccessfully challenged before the court (not the Registrar) may ask for a certificate of contested validity under section 25, provided the matter has actually been fought out—it is not enough that the challenge has been made in proceedings that were settled. The grant of a certificate is discretionary, but it will normally be given. Armed with such a certificate, a proprietor whose design is again unsuccessfully challenged by another defendant in later proceedings will normally be entitled to his costs against that defendant on an indemnity basis (*i.e.* he recovers more of them). It is not clear what happens where the second unsuccessful challenge is on a ground not canvassed in the earlier proceedings, *e.g.* where a further piece of prior art has been uncovered in the meantime. Presumably the court's discretion as to costs, preserved in section 25(2), could come to the second unsuccessful defendant's rescue.

THREATS

5.188 The 1949 Act has its own "threats" section, section 26, and the reader is referred to the discussion at 5.071–5.075 above. The wording of section 26 is more specific than section 253: it is made clear that an actionable threat may be made by someone having no interest in the registered design or application; the threats may be made "by circulars, advertisements or otherwise"; and where the defendant says he will show that the acts in respect of which the threats were made did or would have infringed, the plaintiff may hit back (by counterclaim to counterclaim) by challenging the validity of the design. By a 1988 amendment, it is permissible to threaten manufacturers and importers, but the same caveats as with unregistered designs apply to threats made other than to such people directly, or to threats in relation to sales of goods already manufactured or imported.

5.189 Case law demonstrates that advertisements or circulars in general terms (such as those which regularly appear in trade journals) threatening proceedings for infringement of a registered design may be permissible, but that if they are aimed at an identifiable person or product, they will be actionable. Solicitors and patent agents who make threats in letters (or orally) may be sued personally.[5]

5.190 "Mere" notifications that a design is registered are not actionable, and it is safe to write a short letter identifying the design and the defendant's product, and (probably) urging a reply within a specified time. But anything more is risky, and *Jaybeam Ltd v. Abru Aluminium Ltd*[6] provides an awful warning. The prospective plaintiff, Abru, was relying on both registered design and copyright infringement. Its solicitors wrote the usual copyright letter before

[5] *Benmax v. Austin Motor Co. Ltd* (1953) 70 R.P.C. 284.
[6] [1976] R.P.C. 308.

action threatening proceedings. The final paragraph consisted of an entirely proper "mere" notification of the existence of a registered design. The letter was sent to Jaybeam, and also, which was particularly damaging, to IPC, one of whose publications was to carry Jaybeam's advertisements. Jaybeam secured a "threats" injunction; the judge held that the mere notification, however unexceptionable in itself, was tainted by its context. Anyone receiving such a letter would assume that proceedings for registered design as well as copyright infringement were being threatened. Now that copyright is of declining importance for industrial design, there is less likelihood that both causes of action will be being sued on. Where they are, it would be as well to send the design notification under separate cover, and perhaps even to arrive by a different post or document exchange delivery, and preferably before the copyright letter, so that the design notification can initially be evaluated in a stress-free environment.

As an indication of the type of damages recoverable in a successful threats **5.191** action, the plaintiffs in *J. R. Hosiery Co. Ltd v. B. R. S. Kumar Brothers Ltd and Oliver Wilner & Jones (a firm)*[7] were awarded a sum representing their loss of profits while their allegedly infringing garments were, on their solicitors' advice as a result of the threats, removed from display, and their air fare to Hong Kong to investigate the truth of the allegations—but not the whole of their hotel bills, because they had taken the opportunity of transacting other business while they were there.

---

[7] 1983 I.P.D. 6004.

6. E.U. Proposals For Design Protection

INTRODUCTION AND OUTLINE

6.001   The Proposal for a European Parliament and Council Regulation on Community Design[1] and the Proposal for a European Parliament and Council Directive on the Legal Protection of Design,[2] both dated December 3, 1993, are the culmination of the Commission's efforts to provide a Community-wide system to protect design and to bring about some harmonisation of national laws in this area. Most, but not all, Member States have national laws (the Benelux countries have a single unified system) for the protection of industrial design based on Paris Convention-style registration or deposit systems, and giving a monopoly right for a limited period to strictly-defined designs. But they do not all protect the same design to the same extent, nor for the benefit of the same owner. Except where the Hague Agreement international deposit system is used,[3] each national right must be the subject of a separate application for the same design. These national variations can raise artificial barriers to trade between Member States.

6.002   There are wider variations in the extent to which industrial designs may be protected by copyright. Opposite ends of the spectrum are represented by Italy, which protects very few industrial designs in this way, and France, which is liberal. Until recently the U.K. was probably the most liberal of all, but the Copyright, Designs and Patents Act 1988 changed all that with the introduction of unregistered design right and the banishment of copyright to two-dimensional designs except in limited circumstances.

6.003   The Commission published preliminary drafts in a Green Paper on the Legal Protection of Industrial Design in July 1991,[4] which contains a lengthy Explanatory Memorandum. Quite significant changes have since been made, and the spare parts problem continues to bedevil the negotiations. Conveniently, both the drafts, as well as having the usual preambles setting out their background and general goals, are equipped with commentaries on each Article, helpfully explaining what they are intended to mean.

---

[1] 94/C 29/02. COM(93) 342 *final*—COD 463.
[2] 93/C 345/09. COM(93) 344 *final*—COD 464.
[3] Allowing a single central deposit with the World Intellectual Property Organisation in Geneva which would give national rights in each of the states which are parties to the Agreement, unless within a year the national designs authority indicated a refusal to protect because of non-compliance with national law. The U.K. is not a party to this Agreement. Attempts are being made to revise it so as to make it more appealing to more countries.
[4] III/F/5131/91–EN.

The draft Regulation is intended to have direct effect in Member States and **6.004** to provide a Community-wide unitary design protection system to run in parallel with national systems. The draft harmonisation Directive would require Member States to reform their laws to whatever extent is necessary to secure compliance. These changes will mainly affect national registered designs laws (which will become compulsory as one of the methods for protecting industrial designs), but there will also be effects on copyright: it will be mandatory for all Member States, at least in principle, to accord copyright to designs which qualify as Community designs. This requirement, together with its possible effects on the new U.K. scheme of things, is considered in more detail later.

Outline of proposals

A **new** design, having **an individual character** in comparison with other **6.005** designs currently exploited in the market or other Community or national registered designs would enjoy:

— a limited period (**three years** from first marketing) of **automatic** protection against **copying** and dealings in copied products ("unregistered Community design"—UCD)
— followed, if desired, by up to **25 years** registered **monopoly** protection on application to a central Community Design Office (CDO) by the end of a one-year grace period to allow test marketing ("registered Community design"—RCD)
— both rights having a prescribed **scope**
— but there being certain **exclusions** to safeguard competition
— uniform rules as to **ownership** of and **dealings** with these rights being provided
— both rights being **enforceable** anywhere in the Community (subject to jurisdiction-allocating rules) by **nationally-designated courts** (Community design court—CDC) providing certain basic **remedies**, but with the facility of challenging validity alone before the CDO
— and being permitted to co-exist with national copyright/registered or unregistered design right/unfair competition/trade mark/patent/utility model rights.

The harmonisation Directive will require Member States to bring their **6.006** national registered design laws into conformity, as to scope, term, threshold of protection, grace period and validity, with an RCD (and to introduce such national laws where they do not yet have them). It will also require all nationally-registered design rights to be "eligible for protection" by national copyright law, although "the extent to which, and the conditions under which such a protection is conferred, including the level of originality required" shall be determined by each Member State.

273

THE DRAFT REGULATION—A COMMUNITY DESIGN

6.007 The Regulation is a substantial document with 128 Articles. Only those dealing with the basic proposals as outlined above are considered in this chapter.

DEFINITIONS

6.008 Definitions of "design" and "product" appear in Article 3.[5]

> " 'Design' means the appearance of the whole or a part of a product resulting from the specific features of the lines, contours, colours, shape and/or materials of the product and/or its ornamentation.

> 'Product' means any industrial or handicraft item, including parts intended to be assembled into a complex item, sets or compositions of items, packaging, get-ups, graphic symbols and typographic typefaces, but excluding a computer program or a semiconductor product."

6.009 As with U.K. designs, both registered and unregistered, what is being protected is the *appearance of a product*. As with U.K. registered, but not unregistered, designs, the definition comprehends features of pattern or ornament as well as shape and configuration; but there is no requirement of eye appeal, so functional as well as aesthetic designs would be covered. This is confirmed by the commentary, which also stresses that the design does not have to be "decisive" for an end user's choice of the product. This is unfortunately rather a vague formulation, and falls short of saying that the end-user's motivation does not matter at all. The commentary also observes that colour or material would not be protectable *per se*, but the effect of colour in combination with other design elements is to be taken into account, and a material might impart specific textural effects which would merit protection. This links in with the point also made in the commentary that the sense of touch as well as sight is to play a significant part in assessing a design, so that weight and flexibility may "in some cases" be design features.

6.010 Although a "design" is not bound as tightly to a particular article as in U.K. registered designs law, since by Article 40 multiple filings within one application are to be permitted, three-dimensional designs are of necessity linked closely to the products embodying them. For a multiple filing, all designs other than for ornamentation must belong to the same sub-class of the 1968 Locarno Agreement classification[6] or to the same set or composition

---

[5] Article 1 of the Directive, which however does *not* exclude semiconductor products because these may be protected by national registered designs legislation. They have been excluded from the Regulation because they are expressly provided for by Directive 87/54 on topography protection, referred to elsewhere.

[6] The adoption of this classification for Community designs does not appear to require its introduction to U.K. national designs law (nor the affording of facilities for multiple filings),

of items. The commentary to Article 40 suggests that "set" may mean much the same as in U.K. law, "composition" something rather wider. It is apparently intended that "interior decoration" resulting from a "unitary design idea" should be capable of protection by reference to a "composition of items".

Again as with U.K. law, a design may relate to only part of a product as well as the whole; and "product" includes parts intended to be assembled into a complex item. The definition does not say, but the commentary does, that such parts can have their own individual protection "provided they can be marketed separately" (and of course comply with the "new" and "individual" criteria). It is clear from other parts of the Regulation that spare parts are treated as capable of separate marketing, so the *Ford/Fiat* reasoning would not apply and the U.K. 1949 Act will have to be amended, or at least interpreted, accordingly. **6.011**

The inclusion of packaging and graphic symbols within the definition of "product" suggests that there will be no room for, or amendments will have to be made to, section 1(5) of the U.K. Act and Designs rule 26, excluding articles primarily of a literary or artistic character from registered protection. There would equally be no warrant for excluding wall-plaques, etc. The commentary spells out that VDU icons and menus are meant to be included among "graphic symbols". **6.012**

NOVELTY/INDIVIDUALITY

Article 4[7] sets out the general requirements that a Community design must be new and have an individual character, and that the design of a product which constitutes a part of a complex item must possess its *own* novelty and individuality. Thus a car bonnet having some unusual features, whether of a functional or styling nature, would qualify, but a basic rear door or windscreen might not. Provided the applications are filed at the same time, an RCD for a bonnet would not be anticipated by one for the car as a whole. There might be problems with a UCD where, as is normal, the car as a whole is marketed before any spares go on sale, since the novelty requirement applies equally to UCDs. For components which are visible from the external appearance of the car as marketed, the sensible interpretation would be that the design, *e.g.* of individual panels is adequately "made available to the public" (see below) by marketing of the whole car. This might not apply so readily to internal parts. Manufacturers would be well-advised to publish in their manuals drawings of all internal parts for which protection is likely to be claimed. **6.013**

since by Recital 7 of the Preamble to the draft harmonisation Directive, procedural provisions concerning registration (and invalidation) of national designs are not at present to be harmonised.
[7] Art. 3.2 and 3.3 of the Directive.

Novelty

6.014   Under Article 5[8] a design is "new" if no identical design has been "made available to the public" before the date of reference.[9] Designs are deemed to be "identical" if they differ only in "immaterial details". There is no time limitation, so very old designs may be invoked. The commentary adds that (unlike the U.K. test as it stands at present) novelty is world-wide. The criterion is objective: it makes no difference whether the creator of the Community design copied it from the prior art or devised it himself. This is a standard novelty test for *registered* designs, but it must be remembered that the Community design has a phase of unregistered protection which, like copyright and U.K. unregistered design right, comes into being automatically and is infringed only by copying. U.K. design right has the additional "not commonplace" test, but no novelty test like this one—which will in due course have to be introduced into the 1949, though not the 1988, Act.

6.015   "Made available to the public" means published following registration or otherwise, exhibited, used in trade or otherwise disclosed, but *not* where the disclosure has been made in breach of explicit or implicit obligations of confidence. So an earlier design which happens to have been improperly disclosed does *not* destroy the novelty of a Community design—a rather odd provision in this context, except where a Community design would otherwise be anticipated by its designer's own earlier design disclosed in breach of *his* confidence. How is anyone to set about proving it? In practice, establishing the existence of a novelty-destroying design, other than one which has been registered somewhere so that an international search (no doubt at vast expense) might find it, must be very much a matter of chance. It has been suggested, though the commentary does not mention it, that one of the aims of the world-wide novelty requirement is to stop Community designers taking ethnic (or indeed any) designs from overseas and claiming a Community-wide monopoly of them—not an unreasonable aim in the interests of free trade.

6.016   It should be mentioned here that although first making available to the public is also the start point for UCDs, RCDs will have a "grace period" under Article 8, in that an application to register need not be made until the end of the first year of availability, so that a designer or exploiter can test market without compromising his novelty.

Individuality

6.017   This is a wholly new test and underlines that a Community design, which is intended to be a strong right giving wide protection, is not to be lightly

[8] Art. 4 of the Directive.
[9] "Date of reference" is considered below.

granted. Article 6[10] provides that a design possesses an individual character "if the overall impression it produces on the informed user differs significantly from the overall impression produced on such a user" by an earlier relevant design, this being one which is *either* "commercialised in the marketplace whether in the Community or elsewhere" *or* has been published following registration as an RCD or as a design right of a Member State, provided that protection has not expired. It is therefore implicitly a time-limited test, in the sense that a new design will not be defeated by one that is more than 25 years old (assuming that the previous registered design has been renewed for its full term), or that is not still current. The commentary emphasises that individuality is not to be defeated by invoking an ancient design, the revival of which, so long as there are sufficient differences to avoid a straight novelty attack, may be meritorious. A textile design inspired by ancient Egyptian sources, or indeed a William Morris or Unicorn tapestry-inspired wallpaper, would not be ruled out on individuality grounds, at least in favour of the first reviver—though this writer doubts the propriety of permitting even a first reviver to monopolise parts of the common cultural heritage, even against another independently-"inspired" designer, for 25 years.

To help in assessing "overall dissimilarity" from existing designs, Article 6.3 directs that common features shall "as a matter of principle" be given more weight than differences, and that design freedom shall be taken into consideration. This guidance, expressly written into the text of the draft Regulation, again stresses the stringency of the individuality test: a catalogue of small differences will not be allowed to contradict an overall impression of "déjà vu", as the commentary puts it. To make the test workable, actual prior art will presumably have to be produced—it will not be enough for the informed user to say "I'm sure I've seen something like this before". In a crowded design field like cutlery or clothing, will smaller differences be acceptable, or will the test mean that fewer designs get protection? The direction to take design freedom into account may well mean that heavily functional designs, or those which are "fashion"-led can be distinguished by smaller differences of detail; but the protection will be correspondingly narrow, as will be seen when the scope of protection against infringement is considered. **6.018**

The "informed user" may join the man on the Clapham omnibus and (for connoisseurs of the 1956 Copyright Act[10A]) the lay recogniser as a fictional character endowed with certain standard characteristics whose spectacles an already heavily-bespectacled judge will have to assume when making comparisons. But the commentary suggests that at least in some cases he will have to be a flesh-and-blood person. He is *not* to be a "design expert", but "a certain level of knowledge or design awareness is presupposed depending on the character of the design". He may be the end-user, but not if this person **6.019**

[10] Art. 5 of the Directive.
[10A] ss.9(8).

277

would be unaware of what the product looks like. If the product is an internal part which is only seen in the course of a repair, then he will be the repairer. Will the judge's ability to act as an informed user (which a U.K. judge will always be tempted to do) then depend on his actual credentials as a habitual car or domestic appliance maintainer or a computer buff? Will judicial quips like "Who is Gazza?"[10B] mean that a trial must be stopped while solicitors go out and waylay a football supporter to give evidence about the individuality of a football shirt? Will motor mechanics be able to run profitable sidelines as "informed users"? This sort of requirement, though admirable in theory, may cause difficulties in practice, particularly on interlocutory injunction applications where preparation time is short. There will almost certainly, under the U.K. adversarial system, be battles of informed users paraded by both sides.

6.020   It would seem that the 1949 Act will have to be amended to introduce the individuality test, unless the "common trade variant" test can be stretched to cover it. It will also cause considerable difficulties for the Registry so long as a pre-grant examination system is maintained. It may be necessary to introduce a requirement for evidence, as is now provided for "who-cares-what-it-looks-like?" designs.

Date of reference

6.021   Article 7 defines the date at which novelty and individuality are to be assessed. For UCDs, it is the date on which the design is first made available to the public by the designer or his successor in title or by a third person as a result of information provided or action taken by the designer or his successor in title. Presumably "made available to the public" will have the same meaning as in the novelty test, discussed at 6.015 above. "Used in trade or otherwise disclosed" may be wide enough to catch a designer hawking his design around to potential exploiters, and he will therefore be well-advised to disclose it only under obligations of confidentiality. For an RCD, the date is the date of filing or, if a Paris Convention priority is claimed (which it can be), that priority date. But for RCDs there is a year's grace period under Article 8[11] during which disclosure by the designer or his successor in title, or as a result of information provided or action taken by them, or as a result of a breach of confidence, will not prejudice the novelty or individuality of the RCD. This will not apply if an "abusive" disclosure has resulted in the acquisition by the abuser of his own RCD, when the injured designer or exploiter will have to take "entitlement" proceedings under Article 16 within two years after publication to regain possession of his design—or of a national registration, whch will be invalid and will have to be challenged under national law, by proceedings for rectification or cancellation.

[10B] Paul Gascoigne, a footballer.
[11] Art. 6 of the Directive, limited to national registrations.

EXCLUSIONS

"Non-arbitrary technical designs and designs of interconnections"

This is the general heading of Article 9, which provides an equivalent of both 6.022
the "dictated solely by function" exclusion for U.K. registered designs and
"must-fit" for unregistered designs. Article 9.1 denies Community design
right "to the extent that the realisation of a technical function leaves no
freedom as regards arbitrary features of appearance". This is likely to be
construed in the "narrow" pre-*Amp v. Utilux*[12] sense customary in Continental jurisdictions[13] by asking whether there was any alternative appearance
which *could* have been imparted to the product while still allowing it to do its
job, rather than by asking whether the designer was *in fact* motivated only by
functional requirements when he made the design. This approach is not free
from problems, since it may be difficult to envisage a case where there could
be *no* alternative shape—even keys for particular locks does not work, since
skeleton keys exist—but it would certainly have led to a different result in
Amp, since alternatively-shaped electrical terminals were produced in
evidence, and the design in suit secured registration because it had a different
"look" about it. It must be rarely that there can be *no* design freedom at all.
The commentary observes that the exclusion may only apply to particular
features of a design, in which case the rest may still be protected.

The Article 9(1) exclusion will have, under Article 7 of the harmonisation 6.023
Directive, to apply in U.K. registered designs law, but it may not be necessary
to alter the present wording—merely, the courts should interpret it in a
different way, also taking into account the existence of a specific "must-fit"
exclusion which will have to be provided in accordance with Article 9.2.

Article 9.2 denies protection: 6.024

> "to the extent that [a design] must necessarily be reproduced in its exact
> form and dimensions in order to permit the product in which the design
> is incorporated or to which it is applied to be mechanically assembled or
> connected with another product."

This is clearly "must-fit"; there is no express reference to the need for
interconnection being so that either product may perform its function, as in
section 213(3)(b)(i) of the 1988 Act, but this must be implied. It may be
narrower than section 213(3)(b)(i) because exact reproduction must be
"necessary" to permit interconnection, not merely "enable" it. Like must-fit,
it applies only to the actual interconnections, copying of other parts of a
design not being permitted, and so it has not pleased the motor spares
industry and is still the subject of lobbying. Some feel that it should be limited

[12] [1972] R.P.C. 103.
[13] See 2.039 above.

even further by being expressly confined to a repair/replacement situation,[14] maybe even only for short-life parts for mass-produced consumer goods rather than high-cost low-volume machinery and the like. Others feel that there should be no such exception, any abusive behaviour resulting from a monopoly being left to competition law.

6.025   The limitation to mechanical assembly would seem to exclude other types of interfacing such as the need to make computer systems mutually compatible, in so far as this might lead to features of appearance, *e.g.* of printed circuit boards; though it would include features of a telephone handset or other control panels which have to interconnect with the underlying equipment.

6.026   The "interconnections" exclusion also provoked an outcry from the LEGO interests, so an exclusion-from-the-exclusion was introduced by Article 9.3 which provides that a Community design right may nonetheless subsist:

> "in a design serving the purpose of allowing simultaneous and infinite or multiple assembly or connection of identical or mutually interchangeable products within a modular system."

This clearly saves LEGO, but what else does it cover? Would it save principles like interstackability or internestability, which under U.K. law would be regarded as methods or principles of construction or dictated solely by function?[15] The answer, according to the commentary, is yes.

Designs contrary to public policy

6.027   Article 10[16] precludes design right in a design the exploitation or publication of which is contrary to public policy or to accepted principles of morality. This resembles section 43(1) of the Registered Designs Act, but unlike that section it is not a matter of discretion but is mandatory, and it does not refer to a design the exploitation or publication of which would be illegal (such as an "obscene publication") but to something rather vaguer. In an earlier draft, this exclusion was to operate Community-wide, so that if a design was unacceptable on this ground anywhere in the Community[17] it would have to be rejected everywhere. But now under Article 27.3(a) it is only invalid in any Member State or states where it is unacceptable.

---

[14] As with the limited "must-match" defence which becomes available after three years—see below.
[15] See, *e.g. Sommer Allibert (U.K.) Ltd v. Flair Plastics Ltd* [1987] R.P.C. 599.
[16] Article 8 of the Directive for national laws.
[17] Perhaps a design for a contraceptive device.

SUBSISTENCE AND OWNERSHIP

The right to a UCD arises automatically when the design is first made available to the public. An RCD comes into being when it it registered following application to the Community Design Office, or to a national office for forwarding to the CDO, in accordance with Titles IV and V of the Regulation. Examination by the CDO is only for compliance with formalities, although any design which is "obviously" not a "design" within Article 3 will be rejected. An RCD will be published on registration in a *Community Design Bulletin* to be established, and this will include a representation of the design as well as particulars of proprietorship and the date of filing, and of priority if any (Article 51). Publication of a representation may on request be deferred for up to 30 months, but any rightholder wishing to sue on the design within the period of deferred publication must give the prospective defendant details of the design before doing so (Article 52).

6.028

Under Article 14, the right to a Community design initially belongs to the designer, unless he is an employee and made it in the course of his employment, when it vests in the employer unless otherwise agreed. Presumably the question of whether or not someone is an employee will be governed by national law. There is no commissioning provision as there is for U.K. registered or unregistered designs, so litigants here will face additional problems of getting in title to the Community design rights. The frequent references in the Regulation to the designer's successor in title suggests, and the commentary confirms, that there may be early assignment of the designer's rights by agreement where someone else is to exploit the design, so if care is taken in a commissioning situation, the effect in practice may not be far different. There may be joint ownership of a Community design where it has been "jointly developed". Joint designs must be jointly exercised in the absence of contrary agreement.

6.029

There is an initial presumption that the person who files for an RCD is the person entitled in any proceedings before the CDO, but where a Community design is claimed by, or an RCD is registered in the name of, a person not entitled under Article 14, the true owner may under Article 16, without prejudice to any other remedy open to him, claim to have the Community design transferred to him. Such a claim would apparently be brought before a Community Design Court in a Member State, applying the law of the Regulation, which requires the claim, except where the holder of the RCD knew he was not entitled to it, to be brought within two years of the RCD's publication. The fact of institution of such proceedings, and their outcome, must be noted on the Register. Where the proceedings result in a complete change of ownership, any existing rights acquired through the "wrong" proprietor will lapse, but there is a provision for persons who have already *in good faith* exploited, or made serious and effective preparations to exploit, the design to continue doing so provided they seek a non-exclusive licence

6.030

from the new owner within a prescribed period. This licence must be for a reasonable period and upon reasonable terms. It is not spelt out who is to decide upon such reasonableness.

6.031   Under Article 19, the designer or designers have a right to be named as such on the Register.

Duration

6.032   Under Article 122, a UCD lasts for three years from the date on which the design is first made available to the public by the designer or his successor in title or by a third person as a result of information provided or action taken by either of these. It is not clear what is to happen if the design is copied as a result of industrial espionage before there has been any "making available". In the U.K. any period between the recording of a design and its first marketing is covered by unregistered design right (section 215), provided five years have not yet elapsed from the date the design was made. Presumably the Community designer would have to rely on copyright, if any, in the document or prototype his design is recorded or embodied in.

6.033   Under Article 13[18] an RCD once granted lasts initially for five years from the filing date (as defined in Article 41), and this period may be extended in further five-year periods up to a maximum of 25 years. The filing date is the date of filing at the CDO or at a national designs office for onward transmission to the CDO. If the initial filing is deficient in that it fails properly to identify the design or the applicant, but is later remedied, the filing date will under Article 49(2) be the date on which those deficiencies are remedied. If an RCD lapses for failure to renew in time, there is provision for restoration (Article 71), but without prejudice to rights acquired in the meantime.

Dealings in community designs

6.034   UCDs and RCDs (including applications) will be freely transferable (Articles 30 and 26). This will be another right to be borne in mind when transferring a business. The applicable law will be that of the Member State where the holder has his seat or domicile or an establishment on the relevant date (Article 29). They will normally have to be dealt with in their entirety and for the whole area of the Community, but they may be licensed for the whole or only part of the Community.

6.035   Licences may be exclusive or non-exclusive. The licence may allocate rights of action for infringement, but otherwise the licensee may sue only with the licensor's consent unless he is an exclusive licensee who has already, without success, called on the licensor to sue. Licensees may intervene in proceedings by their licensor to obtain financial compensation (Article 34).

---

[18] Art. 10 of the Directive.

Dealings with RCDs must be entered on the Register if they are to bind **6.036**
third parties without knowledge of the transaction (Article 35).

INVALIDITY

The grounds for invalidity in Article 27[19] are want of novelty or individuality, **6.037**
the effect of one of the Article 9 or 10 exclusions (the latter only in the
Member State or states which find the design offensive to public policy or
morality), and a Court finding of non-entitlement of the rightholder. This,
according to the commentary, is meant to cover the case where the true
proprietor has successfully brought "entitlement" proceedings under Article
16 but rather than securing a transfer of the design into his own name prefers
to destroy it altogether. It might also on its literal wording cover a case where
it is too late to bring Article 16 proceedings because the two-year limitation
period under that Article has run out, but an entitlement point has been raised
in other proceedings, *e.g.* by way of counterclaim in an infringement action.
But the commentary does not envisage this, and it may be that such a
counterclaim would be impossible if brought outside the Article 16 frame-
work—rather an odd situation from the U.K. standpoint, where the rules of
procedure are sufficiently liberal to allow any apparently relevant point to be
raised. There is a further ground in Article 27(2) where there is a conflicting
design made available to the public after the date of reference of the design in
question but stemming from an RCD or national registered design with a
filing or priority date earlier than the date of reference; but if this conflicting
design is only a national right, then the design in question will only be invalid
in the Member State where that right subsists. The commentary adds,
although the text does not seem to warrant this,[20] that such a right can be
invoked only by its owner and not by a third-party infringer.

Only a Community Design Court on a counterclaim in infringement **6.038**
proceedings, or additionally the Community Design Office in relation to an
RCD, may declare a Community design invalid. A declaration of invalidity
revokes the design *ab initio*. This does not affect any final decision on
infringement which has been enforced before the declaration,[21] nor any
contract so far as it has already been performed, but this is subject to any
national provisions which may permit recovery of compensation (*e.g.* for
abuse of process or unjust enrichment) in such circumstances. Article 28.2(b),
which deals with contracts, appears also to envisage some repayment to be

---

[19] Article 11 of the Directive, except that here the non-entitlement ground refers to non-
entitlement to a national registered design by the laws of the Member State, which are still to
govern matters of subsistence and ownership and dealings with registered designs.
[20] But see Art. 88.2.
[21] Presumably it must be possible to discharge any subsisting injunction, whether interlocutory
or final. If an interlocutory injunction has already been enforced by contempt proceedings,
then damages could be claimed under the cross-undertaking, at least to recover the amount of
any fine or sequestration. It is not clear what would happen if the contempt had been punished
by imprisonment, or if the injunction was a final one.

claimed *under the Regulation* "on grounds of equity". A declaration may therefore under Article 26(2)[22] be sought even after an RCD has lapsed or been surrendered (which may be done by writing to the CDO with notice to any licensee) because it may be in someone's interest to show that it was invalid *ab initio*.

INFRINGEMENT

Test of infringement

6.039 This is laid down in Article 11[23] under the heading "Scope of protection". It includes any design which "produces on the informed user a significantly similar overall impression" to the Community design, common features being given more weight than differences and design freedom being taken into consideration. It is thus the same test, to be performed by the same person, as is used in assessing the "individual character" of a design to qualify it for protection, as discussed in 6.017–6.019 above. The informed user is meant to be the person who is most directly involved in using products incorporating the design—*e.g.* the repairer rather than the user if it is a component which is being considered. He is supposed to have a certain level of knowledge and design awareness "depending on the character of the design". He is not intended to be an expert, but he may "find striking differences, which would totally escape the attention of an ordinary consumer". He is thus not the necessarily the same person as the ordinary consumer, or even perhaps the *Sommer Allibert* consumer who is meant to be interested in making a purchase and not just rubbernecking.

6.040 The commentary explains that the reason for requiring design freedom to be taken into account is to ensure that similarities attributable to functional constraints should not be given undue weight in assessing the significantly similar overall impression. The effect of this will probably be to exclude from design protection in practice many functional designs, or parts of them, despite the general principle that they are as entitled to benefit as are aesthetic designs.

Infringing acts

6.041 Infringement of a UCD (or of an RCD whose publication has been deferred[24]) will be by unlicensed *copying* of the design or by using a design resulting from such copying. This use includes "in particular, making, offering, putting on the market, or using a product in which the design has been incorporated or

---

[22] Art. 16 of the Directive.
[23] Art. 9 of the Directive.
[24] Art. 21.2.

to which it has been applied, and importing, exporting or stocking such a product for those purposes" (Article 20). There is no parallel to the U.K. concept of secondary infringement: a plaintiff need not prove that someone merely dealing in infringing products knew or had reason to believe that they did infringe. Nor is there any defence of "innocent acquisition". There is no express provision covering the making of tools, moulds, printing plates, machine-programming devices and the like for enabling infringing products to be made but these could all be caught under the general heading of "using" a copied design—as, presumably, could be authorising someone else to do any of the forbidden acts.

Because a UCD is infringed only by copying, independent design is always a **6.042** defence, if the defendant can prove it.

Under Article 21,[25] an RCD is infringed by the same acts, except that it is a **6.043** monopoly right so that the types of prohibited use need not result from copying. There is no defence of innocence like the limited defence to a claim for damages only in section 9 of the Registered Designs Act 1949. But there is a defence under Article 25 where before the filing or priority date the defendant has in good faith commenced, or made serious preparations to commence, exploitation within the Community of an independently-made design which would infringe the RCD. Such a person may continue to exploit the design for the needs of the undertaking in which the use was effected or anticipated, but the right cannot be transferred separately from the undertaking. Under E.U. competition law a single person can be an "undertaking", so a designer exploiting his own design would be covered, but not, it seems, one still seeking an industrial partner through whom to exploit it.

Other defences

Under Articles 22[26] and 24,[27] defences to both UCD and RCD infringement **6.044** are:

— acts done privately and for non-commercial purposes
— experimental use
— reproduction only for purposes of citation or teaching, provided such use is compatible with fair trade practice and does not unduly prejudice normal exploitation of the design (so that large-scale copying for educational resource centres and the like is not exempt), and provided also that mention is made of the source
— use of equipment on ships and aircraft registered in a third country when these temporarily enter Community territory, repair of such equipment, and the import of spare parts and accessories for the purpose of such repairs

---

[25] Art. 12 of the Directive.
[26] Art. 13 of the Directive.
[27] Art. 15 of the Directive.

— exhaustion of rights where the product incorporating the design has been placed on the market within the Community by or with consent of the rightholder.

6.045   The most contentious defence is that introduced by Article 23,[28] in the case only of an RCD: after three years from the first putting on the market of a product incorporating the design (*not* from first making available to the public, so that this defence can never kick in until after the UCD has expired) it is a defence that:

(a) what is being made, sold, etc., is a product which is part of a complex product upon whose appearance the protected design is dependent,
(b) the purpose of such use is to permit the repair of the complex product so as to restore its original appearance, and
(c) the public is not misled as to the origin of the product used for the repair.

Thus there arises after three years (which may be two years or less from the date of registration if the rightholder has taken full advantage of the grace period) a right to repair based on "must-match", although possibly wider than the U.K. exception in that the original wing-mirrors, wheels, etc., are not, according to *Ford/Fiat*, covered in the U.K., but do serve to restore the product to its original appearance in the same way as the actual body panels. It is "the public" who must not be misled, which suggests that independent spares manufacturers must educate repairers always to point out to the motorist (in practice this exception is most likely to benefit mainly motorists) whenever they propose to use non-original spares.

6.046   What changes will have to be made to the Registered Designs Act 1949 to accommodate these defences? There is at present no defence for a *bona fide* person who has begun to exploit the design, except in section 8B where a design is restored after having lapsed for non-renewal. There is a general limitation to acts done for sale or hire or for use for the purposes of a trade or business, so in effect there is already a private use, or at least non-commercial exception. But there are no specific exceptions for experimental or teaching use, nor for equipment on ships or aircraft and its repair. Exhaustion of rights applies by virtue of the direct application of Community law on free movement of goods; but "must-match" will need rewording and moving into the infringement sector of the Act.[29] Under the 1949 Act there are provisions for Crown user of designs. There is no equivalent in the draft Directive, but it seems likely that national provisions for use of designs for purposes of national security or whatever would be permitted. Compulsory licensing is presently allowed under the 1949 Act, but rarely if ever takes place, and there is limited provision for licences of right, *e.g.* where there has been an abuse of monopoly. There are no parallel provisions in the Regulations or Directive.

---

[28] Art. 14 of the Directive.
[29] Opponents of the U.K. "must-match" exception argued strongly in Parliament for a properly-drafted right to repair, but without success.

ENFORCEMENT

Jurisdiction

This is dealt with in Articles 83–99 of the draft Regulation. Article 84 requires **6.047** each Member State to designate, within three years, as limited a number as possible of national courts and tribunal of first and second instance as Community Design Courts (CDCs) and to notify these to the Commission, which will then communicate them to Member States. In the meantime, jurisdiction will lie with whatever court would normally have it by reason of territory and subject-matter. Our existing system of Patents Court/Patents County Court would appear adequate.

Article 85 gives to CDCs *exclusive* jurisdiction in infringement actions **6.048** (including counterclaims of invalidity), in *quia timet* infringement actions and actions for declarations of non-infringement (if permitted under that court's national law) and in actions for declarations of invalidity of UCDs.

Most Member States are members of the 1968 Brussels Convention on **6.049** Jurisdiction and Enforcement of Judgments in Civil and Commercial Matters (enacted into U.K. law by the Civil Jurisdiction and Judgments Act 1982). This Convention provides uniform rules for the allocation of jurisdiction, but only between parties domiciled in Member States. It does not provide for the case where a defendant is based outside Convention territory, which is left to be dealt with by the conflict of laws rules of individual Member States.

Article 83, while generally applying the Convention to Community Design **6.050** matters, disapplies it (including the exclusive jurisdiction provision in Article 16(4) for proceedings concerned with the registration or validity of designs) in relation to the exclusive jurisdiction of CDCs in favour of rules contained in Article 86 which provide a selection of bases for allocating jurisdiction to one or another national CDC. These are, in descending order:

— the Member State in which the defendant is domiciled or, if he is not so domiciled, the Member State in which he has "an establishment"
— if the defendant has neither domicile nor establishment in a Member State, then the Member State in which the plaintiff is domiciled or has an establishment
— if neither party has a Community domicile or establishment (Community design rights are not limited to persons of community origin), then the Member State where the Community Design Office is situated.

Parties may agree on which CDC is to have jurisdiction, and if the defendant enters an appearance before a CDC in which he is sued, even if it is the "wrong" one, then he submits to its jurisdiction and it is that CDC which has jurisdiction.

6.051   As an alternative, Article 86.5 allows an action to be brought in the CDC of the Member State where a particular act of infringement has been committed or threatened—but only an action for infringement and resulting counter-claim for invalidity, not for declarations of non-infringement or for invalidity of a UCD. And although under Article 87.1 a CDC will normally have jurisdiction over acts of infringement in all the other Member States, under Article 86.5 it will be limited to infringements committed or threatened within its own Member State.

6.052   Under Article 90.3, CDCs faced with counterclaims for invalidity of an *RCD* may, on application by the registered proprietor and after hearing the other parties, stay the proceedings and request the counterclaiming defendant to apply to the Community Design Office to determine the question, within a set time-limit. If this is not done, the counterclaim will be deemed withdrawn and the action will continue. Under Article 95 a CDC hearing an infringement action shall also, in the absence of special grounds for continuing the hearing, of its own motion after hearing the parties, or at the request of one of the parties and after hearing the others, stay the action if the validity of the design is already in issue before another CDC by counterclaim or, in the case of an RCD, before the CDO. The CDO should also stay an application for a declaration of invalidity where validity is already in issue in a CDC, unless that CDC is asked to stay its proceedings. Where it does so, Article 95.3 allows it to grant interim relief for the duration of the stay.

6.053   Article 94 allows the courts of a Member State (and not only CDCs) to grant "provisional" and "protective" measures in accordance with the law on national design rights, even where jurisdiction in the substantive action will belong elsewhere; and except where that state's court has jurisdiction only by virtue of Article 86.5, its orders may be enforced (under the Brussels Convention) in all other Member States. Invalidity may be argued by way of defence in an Article 94 application, even though it has not yet formally been raised by counterclaim, and the commentary suggests that the judge may find this "extremely useful"—U.K. judges may not find it so easy to apply the *American Cyanamid*[30] rule!

6.054   Under Article 99, where there are actions pending before two different courts, one on the basis of a Community design right and the other on the basis of a national design right, the court second seised must decline jurisdiction in favour of the court first seised (or stay its proceedings if the jurisdiction of the court first seised is contested). There is therefore considerable advantage, where circumstances permit, in asserting a national right in your home court quickly.

6.055   Article 96 provides that there shall be appeal from CDCs of first instance to CDCs of second instance, subject to national rules relating to appeals. Any further appeal shall also be subject to such rules.

[30] See 5.048 above.

Applicable law

Once the appropriate court has been identified, Article 92 provides that the   6.056
law to be applied will be the Regulation, but where that makes no specific
provision, it will be the national law of the Member State, including its
conflict of laws rules, and procedural rules unless otherwise prescribed.
Article 89 provides a presumption of validity unless the defendant puts this in
issue by counterclaim, except where he alleges invalidity by reference to a
national design right belonging to him (or in applications for provisional or
protective measures). Further, in an infringement action, where a plaintiff
adduces evidence of the individual character of his design, the court shall treat
the design as new unless the defendant proves otherwise.

Remedies

These will normally be a matter for the national law of the CDC, but Article   6.057
93 requires that where infringement is found, the court shall, in the absence of
special reasons, grant an injunction restraining it, and also order seizure of
infringing products and disclosure of the origin of the products and the
channels through which they are commercialised. None of these requirements will come as surprise to U.K. courts, which grant final injunctions as a
matter of course, unless there are very special reasons to the contrary, *e.g.* the
imminent expiry of a registered design, and will also normally order
disclosure of suppliers and customers (where this has not emerged on
discovery). The 1988 Act no longer requires orders for delivery up as a matter
of course (see sections 99 and 230), in copyright or unregistered design right
actions, but courts will no doubt continue to make them, and to make orders
for forfeiture under sections 114 and 231. There are no express provisions
covering these points in the 1949 Act, except that section 9 makes clear the
defence of innocence to a claim for damages does not affect the power to
grant an injunction. The innocence defence itself relates only to a financial
remedy, and this is a matter for each Member State, so there seems no reason
why it should not remain.

HARMONISATION AND COPYRIGHT

Article 100.1 of the draft Regulation and Article 17 of the draft Directive   6.058
expressly provide for cumulation of Community design protection with any
national rights based on patents, utility models, typeface rights, trade marks
or other distinctive signs, civil liability or unfair competition. Unregistered
design rights are also included in this list, thus setting the Commission's seal
of approval on the U.K.'s new creation, gracefully if rather narrowly
described in the commentary as "a different answer to the need for protection
of technical innovation not reaching the level required for patent protection".

6.059 The new U.K. copyright régime, however, earns a sour observation and forcible amendment under Article 18 of the Directive. The Commission takes great exception to the section 52 abridgement of the period of enforceable copyright to 25 years where an artistic work is industrially-exploited. Inexplicably, the commentary observes that this is "an arbitrary figure, which finds a historical explanation in the practice of the national industrial property office in the first years of this century" which "should no longer have a place in contemporary protection of works of applied art". With the greatest respect to the Commission, there is nothing remotely arbitrary about 25 years as a suitable copyright protection period for works of applied art, nor has it anything to do with the practice of industrial property offices. It is the minimum term of protection for works of applied art laid down by Article 7(4) of the Berne Covention—which does not even *require* such works to get copyright, since by Article 2(7) Member States may choose to protect them only by special industrial designs legislation. Notwithstanding this, it seems that the carefully-crafted provisions of section 52 will have to go,[31] in so far as they would affect any design which would qualify as a Community design (and any actual national registered design) and thus have to enjoy the cumulative protection by copyright which is enjoined by Article 100.2 of the draft Regulation and Article 18 of the draft Directive respectively.

6.060 Nothing is said directly about section 51 and its exclusion from copyright of anything which is not itself an artistic work or surface decoration. Informal discussions suggest that section 51 is not intended to be "got at", because it does not *deprive* any artistic works which are design documents or models, but not "for" artistic works, of copyright but merely makes their copyright unenforceable in relation to the three-dimensional articles which those works depict or embody. But nor does section 52 *deprive* industrially-exploited artistic works of copyright after 25 years; again it merely operates as a defence to actions for infringement. And the insistence that Community design right (and national registered designs harmonised into conformity with it) can protect functional designs means that the compulsory affording of copyright to eligible Community designs and all national registered designs may cut clean across section 51. Admittedly Article 18 of the draft Directive and Article 100.1 of the draft Regulation expressly leave to national law the extent and the conditions under which copyright is conferred, including the level of originality required (not that level of originality has anything to do with section 51). But if this is construed as exempting section 51 from interference, why not leave the much less draconian section 52 alone? This is all most unsatisfactory, and it is to be hoped that the question will be fully clarified before the new instruments come into effect.

6.061 This is, it is understood, not now expected to be before some time in 1997, even though the draft Directive speaks of harmonisation by October 31,

---

[31] Along with Italian law's refusal of copyright to industrial designs except where it is conceptually possible to separate ("scindère") the "artistic" elements of a design from its underlying product.

1996. The whole process is taking much longer than was originally expected, partly because of the never-ending arguments between the conflicting spare parts interests and partly because of some problems with the legal basis of the draft Regulation which, instead of being intended to be promulgated under Article 235 of the Treaty of Rome, is being put forward under the same Article 100a as the draft Directive.

To complete this brief discussion of copyright harmonisation, it should be noted that Article 18.2 of the draft Directive and Article 100.3 of the draft Regulation both require that each Member State extend copyright to a design registered in or for that state, or a Community design, even if, in the Member State which is the country of origin of the design, it does not fulfil the conditions for protection under copyright. This is aimed at removing the disagreeably nationalistic practice permitted by Article 2(7) of the Berne Convention under which some countries would only extend copyright to overseas designs if they were so protected in their country of origin. This was a derogation from the normal "national treatment" principle prohibiting less favourable treatment of overseas than of national works, and meant that France, for example, would refuse copyright to an Italian design because it did not have copyright in Italy, even though the same design would have been protected if it had originated in France. Although section 33 of the 1956 Act preserved the possibility of the U.K. doing this, as does section 160 of the 1988 Act, we have not done so in relation to industrial designs. Our courts have extended an effusive welcome to the overseas design seeking asylum beneath the capacious wings of copyright law. We have nothing to blush for here.

6.062

Index

Anton Piller order,
  copyright infringement, on, 5.128, 5.129
  costs, 5.054
  design right infringement, on, 5.053
Architectural works,
  artistic nature of, 2.161
  copyright in, 2.159–2.161
  meaning, 2.159
  parts of buildings, relating to, 2.160
Article,
  appearance, when irrelevant, 2.068–2.078
  dependency on another article, 2.055, 2.057
  design applied to, 2.011–2.013
  design right, in relation to, 2.223, 2.224
  function, features dictated by, 2.032–2.047
  industrial process, design applied by, 2.012
  integral part of other article, as, 2.050–2.067
  literary or artistic character, with,
    adornment content, 2.081
    catalogue of typefaces, 2.081
    copyright, protection under, 2.079–2.081
    functionality, 2.086
    mere carrier, as, 2.086
    packaging designs, 2.085
    printed matter, 2.087
    registration of designs, exclusion from, 2.079–2.087
    sculpture, works of, 2.079, 2.084
    textile designs, 2.087
    trade advertisement, 2.085
    transfers, 2.087
  manufacture, of, 2.012
  meaning, 2.012, 2.193
  part of, design of, 2.228–2.234
  parts made and sold separately, 2.017–2.021, 2.228
  sets of, 2.014–2.016
Artistic works. *See* **Copyright**

Berne Convention,
  artistic works, application of copyright to, 3.007
  national treatment requirements, 3.004, 3.005

Building,
  architectural works, copyright in, 2.159–2.161
  articles, not, 2.012
  parts of, 2.160
  reconstruction of, 5.115
  representations of, issuing copies of, 5.112

Character merchandising,
  protection of, 1.033
Charges,
  intellectual property, on, 4.059
Charts,
  artistic works, as, 1.016
Circuit diagrams,
  copyright in, 2.170, 2.172–2.174
  literary work, as, 2.173, 2.174
Collage,
  copyright in, 2.153
Colour,
  novelty, and, 2.108, 2.109
  registered designs, relevance for, 2.010
  sports garments, of, 2.109
Competition,
  spare parts, in, 1.006
Computer,
  data stored in as design document, 3.013
  designs generated by, creator of, 3.019, 3.020
  drawings produced by, 2.114
  works generated by, duration of copyright in, 3.078
Configuration,
  appearance of another article, dependent on, 2.055
  design, of, 2.193–2.195
  design right, in relation to, 2.225–2.227
  features dictated by function,
    emphasis, shift of, 2.045
    exclusion from definition of design, 2.032–2.047
  features of, 2.005–2.010
  novelty, 2.006
  ornamental surface, features of, 2.006
  relief surface decoration as aspect of, 2.194
  three-dimensional designs, 2.005–2.007
Construction,
  method or principle, exclusion from protection, 2.030, 2.031, 2.236

292

293